Business and Economics: Global Perspectives

Business and Economics: Global Perspectives

Edited by
Marshall Blair

Willford Press
www.willfordpress.com

Published by Willford Press,
118-35 Queens Blvd., Suite 400,
Forest Hills, NY 11375, USA

ISBN: 978-1-68285-679-6

Cataloging-in-Publication Data

Business and economics : global perspectives / edited by Marshall Blair.
p. cm.
Includes bibliographical references and index.
ISBN 978-1-68285-679-6
1. Business. 2. Economics. 3. Management. I. Blair, Marshall.
HF1008 .B87 2019
650--dc23

For information on all Willford Press publications
visit our website at www.willfordpress.com

Willford Press

Printed in China.

Contents

Preface

This book aims to highlight the current researches and provides a platform to further the scope of innovations in this area. This book is a product of the combined efforts of many researchers and scientists, after going through thorough studies and analysis from different parts of the world. The objective of this book is to provide the readers with the latest information of the field.

As a field of social science, economics deals with the study of production, consumption and distribution of various goods and services. It explores the workings of the economies around the world and studies the behavior and interaction of economic agents. Economics is broadly divided into two sub-fields: macroeconomics and microeconomics. The practice of earning money through selling, buying, or producing goods or services is termed as business. It can be classified into company, a cooperative, charter cooperation, partnership or sole proprietorship. Business is conducted in different sectors, such as agriculture, public services, real estate, entertainment, industrial manufacturing, transportation, etc. Economics plays a crucial role in the success of a business. This book is a valuable compilation of topics, ranging from the basic to the most complex research advancements in the fields of business and economics. Different approaches, evaluations, methodologies and advanced studies on these subjects have been included in it. Coherent flow of topics, student-friendly language and extensive use of examples make this book an invaluable source of knowledge.

I would like to express my sincere thanks to the authors for their dedicated efforts in the completion of this book. I acknowledge the efforts of the publisher for providing constant support. Lastly, I would like to thank my family for their support in all academic endeavors.

Editor

1

Characteristics of the Dual Model among the OECD Countries – An FOI Model Analysis

ZOLTÁN BARTHA, Ph.D.
ASSOCIATE PROFESSOR

e-mail: zolib@hu.inter.net

ANDREA S. GUBIK, Ph.D.
ASSOCIATE PROFESSOR

e-mail: getgubik@uni-miskolc.hu

SUMMARY

Deciding on the development path of the economy has been a delicate question in economic policy, not least because of the trade-off effects which immediately worsen certain economic indicators as steps are taken to improve on others. The paper offers help to decide on such policy dilemmas, based on an analysis conducted among OECD countries with the FOI model (focusing on the future, outside and inside potentials). Several development models can be deduced with this method, from which only the dual model is discussed in detail. The dual model implies a development strategy focused on the attraction of outside resources, the instruments of which are also presented. The findings presented in the paper are part of a large OTKA (Hungarian Scientific Research Fund) study, which develops step by the step the methodology of the FOI model and discusses all of the development models found among OECD countries.
Keywords: development models; FOI model; dual model

GROWTH AND DEVELOPMENT IN ECONOMICS

Growth and development are mentioned almost as synonyms in this paper, although the literature usually addresses them separately. The simplest approach is to say that growth is the narrower, and development is the more complex class, as growth is usually defined as an increase in certain quantitative variables, while development describes a process of moving from a lower level of quality to a higher one (Szentes 2011). As the measurement of the phenomena economics usually deals with is problematic anyway, the most popular, formalised growthmodels (e.g. Domar 1947, Harrod 1948, Solow 1956, Romer 1986, Lucas 1988) concentrate on the national income or on its per capita version. These models therefore map the problem of growth/development through the quantitative change of a single indicator, so they offer tools to analyse the problem of growth, the narrower category.

The GDP however – being an aggregate indicator – veils more profound processes that are crucial for development, such as the structure of the economic system, changes in employment, income distribution or the institutional framework, etc. For this reason, from now on, we will use the more complex approach to development whenever we touch upon issues of growth and/or development paths, factors of growth and/or development, meaning that we interpret development as a combination of two things: growth in the indicators of national income, and the modernising of the socioeconomic structures.

Theories of Development

The different schools of economics have had different views on the rules of the economy, and they do not agree on the basic assumptions either; hence, a wide variety of theories have been developed over the centuries. While most schools implicitly assume that the models used are universal, List (1841) was convinced that the classical theories may only apply to the most developed economies; the followers of new institutionalism (see Williamson 2000, for example) point out that the institutional structure of different countries can be very different. A similar confrontation can be observed regarding the development paths. It is widely accepted that development is unilinear, meaning that all countries have to go through the same development stages (with timing being the only difference among them). Veblen (1919) on the other hand argued against the teleological approach of economics, and suggested an evolutionary one instead.

It worth mentioning that mainstream theories do not consider the effects of national interests and bargaining power in their models; heterodox schools on the other hand cannot accept the independent development of countries (although there is no agreement among them considering the exact nature of the interdependencies). It may seem natural to choose the countries and national economies as the unit of analysis; Wallerstein (1974), however, when describing the economic history of medieval Europe, concludes that modernisation cannot be understood within the national economy framework. He chooses the worldsystem as the unit of analysis instead.

Some scholars have developed models with few explanatory factors; others have gone for more variables. The well-known growth theories pick one or two variables; Porter's diamond model (1990) combines four quite complex factors; the empirical study of Barro (1998) of 100 countries spanning over 30 years finds seven factors that are strongly connected to the growth rate of the real GDP.

The factors of development identified in the economics literature can be categorised along many principles, but the location of factors is probably the most important division line. One camp of economists traces back differences in economic development to reasons that can be found inside the country. They point to factors whose presence (e.g. physical or human capital) or lack (e.g. government failures) enables high growth rates. Another group of economists finds the causes of underdevelopment in outside factors. Usually these theories take the differences in the development level as given in the world economy, and they assume that these differences lead to asymmetric dependencies. The asymmetric dependencies on the other hand make it very difficult for underdeveloped countries to catch up with the rich world.The inside-outside distinction among the factors of development plays a crucial role in the model developed during our research.

The Inside Factors of Development

Adam Smith (1776) saw the division of labour as the main source of wealth. The countries that are able to extend the division of labour among their firms and citizens can become wealthier, as they are able to produce a higher quantity with the same labour input. The main finding of the Harrod–Domar model (1947, 1948) is that investments are the key to economic growth. Investments on the other hand are mainly dependent on the savings rate. Around a decade later Solow (1956) pointed out that investments and savings cannot contribute to growth in the long run. In his view, long-term economic growth is driven by technical change.

Keynes (1936) suggested crises are generated by limits in demand, and the latter may be strengthened by large income differences. The speculative demand for money of those who are well off can be especially high, which prevents a substantial part of the income from turning into effective market demand. Inequalities in income distribution thus can be a setback for balanced growth.

Schumpeter (1934) stressed that cyclical fluctuations should be regarded as a natural part of the economy, as entrepreneurs may only draw profits if they break the status quo of equilibrium. The way to break the status quo is through innovation, which therefore becomes the primary driver of the cyclical development. McClelland (1957) also emphasised the importance of the entrepreneurial class. In his view entrepreneurs are the pioneers of development, and their biggest motivator is not profit, but the achievement of some special goals (N-achievement).

When the big colonial empires collapsed, several academics explained the situation of the underdeveloped former colonies with a value system and social structure that was different from the Western one. In underdeveloped countries the rural characteristics of the society are dominant, meaning that labour is inefficient, immobile, the social structure is rigid, and the general attitude rejects individualism and risk taking (Meier 1964). When local values confront the Western values, the society is split into two groups, and a dual social structure is formed (Boeke 1953), which is completed with a dual economic structure as well (where the traditional and modern sectors are insulated from each other).

The role of human capital in growth and development is highlighted in various forms in the literature. Szentes (2011) quotes from A. Marshall: from a national perspective the capital invested in workers' children is just as productive as capital invested in horses or machinery. Newer theories unquestionably suggest that capital invested in children is far more productive than that invested in horses and machinery. Endogenous growth theories see increasing returns as a prime source of long- term growth, and they directly or indirectly explain increasing returns with human capital. Lucas (1988) treats human capital as a reproducible one, an element of capital that the society is able to broaden at a constant rate. The expansion of human capital, on the other hand, leads to a constant increase in the productivity of the physical capital. Romer (1986) also can be connected to human capital. In his model, investments made in research and development produce positive externalities that enable a constant increase in the productivity of physical capital.

Veblen (1919) points out that human behaviour is deeply affected by institutionalised rules of society. His views were taken over by new institutional economists (e.g. North 1993, Williamson 1998). According to them institutions affect the incentive system of an economy, while the incentive system on the other hand influences the behaviour, size and competition of firms, the level of investments and technological development, and so, ultimately the level of development of an economy. Underdevelopment thus is explained by institutional frameworks consisting of bad incentives, according to the new institutional school.

Partially connected to the institutional approach is the theory of government failures, which was mainly brought into the attention of development experts by Tullock (1993). It was back in the 1960es when Tullock suggested (1967) that the super profit that monopolistic structures offer can be an incentive for firms to lobby for government regulations granting monopolistic positions and monopoly profits. According to calculations made by Krueger (1974), the rent seeking behaviour of firms in the field of import licences caused a 7.3% GDP loss in India, and a 15% GDP loss In Turkey in 1964. The more corrupt a country is, the weaker the state is, the heavier the costs of rent seeking are, and so rent seeking can be one of the major obstacles of economic development.

Porter's (1990) national competitiveness theory adds some highly complex factors to the literature of economic development. A somewhat similar idea is suggested by Freeman (1987), who developed the theory of national innovation systems. These systems are centred around cooperation among businesses, the education system and the research infrastructure.

The Outside Factors of Development

The theory of comparative advantage developed by Ricardo (1817) had become one of the cornerstones of the laissez-faire approach of international relations. According to Ricardo the highest welfare level can only be ensured if trade is conducted along the lines of comparative advantages, and there is a free flow of goods. This free trade principle was questioned by many. List (1841) argued against laissez-faire. He defended protectionism, and suggested protective tariffs for newly established industries (the infant industry argument). His suggestions echoed those of Alexander Hamilton (1791) made in the newly formed USA.

After the Second World War the focus of development economics shifted towards the power relations of different countries. Prebisch (1964) and Myrdal (1957) point out that underdeveloped states are dependent on richer countries, and so the current system of international division of labour is not based on comparative advantages. The internal economic structures of most of the developing countries are directly influenced by the developed ones through the colonial system (Myrdal: forced bilateralism). Balogh (1963) argues that as a result of power inequalities among parties, the economic structure of the developing countries has to be adjusted time after time to the changes generated by technical progress made in the developed economies, and the adjustment process prevents them from achieving longterm growth. The dependency relations lead to one-track specialisation (Singer 1964). The majority of exports of the developing countries are primary products and commodities, which leads to a decrease in the terms of trade over the long run. Bhagwati in his 1958 paper titled "Immiserizing growth" showed that the decrease in terms of trade can result in a decrease in the national income even if there is dynamic growth in the production of the export sector. One lesson learned from the literature of interdependencies is that a diversified export structure can be an important development factor.

Emmanuel (1972) has gone as far as claiming that trade between developing and developed countries is an unequal exchange, which is a manifestation of the imperialism of trade. Unequal exchange was triggered by wage differences, and is sustained by the immobility of labour. Wallerstein (1974) also accepted the concept of unequal exchange, though he argued that it is a result of the different bargaining power of nations. The core-periphery relations and the geographical position basically predestine the fate of nations, according to Wallerstein.

Table 1
Inside and outside development factors

Inside factors	Outside factors
Division of labour (Smith)	Free trade – international division of labour (Ricardo)
Savings rate (Harrod-Domar) Abundance-scarcity of capital	Protectionism Defence of infant industries (List)
Equal-unequal income distribution (Keynes)	Equal or unequal trade partners (Balogh) Pressure to fit to modern patterns (Balogh)
Drive to innovate (Schumpeter)	Unilateral dependency - diversification (Myrdal)
Entrepreneurial behaviour (McClelland)	One-sided specialisation (Singer)
Rigid-flexible social structure (Meier) Imported or organically developed social structures (Boeke)	Immiserising growth – terms of trade (Bhagwati) Forced bilateralism (Myrdal)
Dual-homogeneous economic structures (Meier)	International wage division-mobility of labour (Emmanuel)
Investments into human capital (Marshall) Human capital, as a renewable resource (Lucas) Positive externalities of R&D (Romer)	Geographical position – core and periphery (Wallerstein)
Institutional incentives (North) Path-dependent development	Investment strategies of multinational companies (Furtado)
Government failure (Tullock) Rent-seeking (Krueger)	Demonstration effect
National diamond (Porter) Innovation systems (Freeman)	
Rule of law, democracy (Barro)	

As the role played by transnational companies in the international flow of goods and capital became more and more dominant, a great deal of attention was directed towards them. Furtado (1970) suggested that the most important development factor is not the interdependencies among countries any more, but the investment strategies of transnational companies. Transnational companies can bring capital to a country, creating jobs, but the newly formed subsidiaries may be isolated from the local economy (Singer 1964). The ability of a country to attract foreign capital, especially if the capital is invested in fields that can fit in well to the current economic structure of the economy, is another important development factor.

The demonstration effects of modern consumer societies are worth mentioning, too. Generally the consumers of the developing countries try to follow the consumption patterns of the developed nations. This usually has a cut-down effect on local growth, as the goods fitting to the most current consumption trends are generally produced overseas, so following the trends increases imports, and can contribute to the trade balance deficit.

The Role of Institutions in Development

According to the followers of the institutional school, institutions affect human behaviour, in other words they influence the decisions of economic agents. Veblen was the first to point that out (1919), and also added that it is an oversimplification to assume that market decisions can be analysed independently from any other outside factors, like family, culture, community, politics, etc. His views were neglected by mainstream economics, but the topic was brought into the forefront again by two new research agendas.

On the one hand it was proved by a series of psychological experiments that we are not capable of making such rational decisions as is assumed by economics. The notion of homo economicus was debunked by the theory of bounded rationality (Simon 1957). Agents with bounded rationality behave opportunistically. On the other hand Coase's pioneering article (Coase 1937) shed light on the fact that the transactions conducted among agents are not frictionless, and depending on the rate of frictions, very different market solutions may prove to be the most efficient ones. If we take a closer look at market transactions, it becomes clear that there are numerous social phenomena that are disregarded by mainstream economics, yet they influence the opportunistic behaviour of market agents and the rate of frictions during transactions. These social phenomena are collectively called institutions.

Hodgson defines institutions (2006) as systems of established and prevalent social rules that structure social interactions. According to the definition above, language, money, etiquette, the measurement system, and firms can all be regarded as institutions. Institutions make it easier to calculate and forecast the behaviour of agents, thus they contribute to the decrease of uncertainty and frictions during transactions. North (1993) offers a similar definition of institutions: institutions are the rules of the game in a society or, more formally, are the humanly devised constraints that shape human interaction.

Williamson (1998) suggested a hierarchy that proved very useful during our analysis. He separated social analysis into four levels (Figure 1). The different levels are ranked according to the time needed to change them, but they also show what influences what in the society. Higher levels directly influence the level just below them, meaning that no practices may be adopted on the lower levels that are not compatible with the superior levels.

Social embeddedness is on top of the hierarchy (L1). Williamson puts norms, customs, ethical principles, traditions, conventions and religion into this category. Some development factors found in the literature at least partly belong to this level (e.g. the dual structure of the society, entrepreneurial behaviour).

The institutional environment forms the second level (L2). While the informal rules were placed in Level 1, the rules of L2 are formal, codified ones (e.g. constitution, laws, property rights). Although the change of Level 2 rules is also partly evolutionary in nature, calculated interference is also possible on this level (unlike on L1). Such interferences are called first-order economising, which is about finding the ideal combination of formal rules. Many of the development factors belong to the institutional environment: the rule of law, democratic rights, market regulation and protectionism.

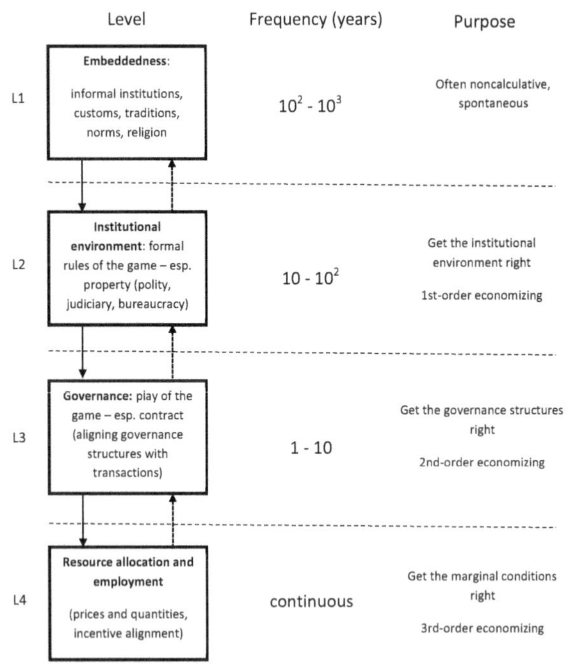

Figure 1. Economics of institutions (Williamson 1998, p. 26)

First-order economising, however, does not ensure the optimal economic structure. As agents behave opportunistically, they do not keep the formal rules of the economy all the time. Jurisdiction has also got its frictions, meaning that those who follow the rules are not able to enforce their rights against the opportunists instantly and without any costs. This is where the third level (L3) kicks in, called governance by Williamson. The unit of analysis in governance is the transactions made among economic agents, and the contracts mediating those transactions. Such development factors as the coordination of education and research, Porter's national diamond, government failures or rent seeking, can all be reckoned among L3 items.

The final level (L4) is concerned with the allocation of resources, an area which is traditionally addressed by neoclassical economics. The factors of the better-known growth theories (quantities of labour and capital, savings, investments, etc.) all belong to this level.

Williams thinks that new institutional economics addresses problems belonging mainly to Levels 2 and 3. North's and Hodgson's definitions cited above, however, suggest that all phenomena belonging to L1, L2 and L3 can be regarded as institutions. This paper therefore treats all factors as institutional factors that can be categorised in one of the top three levels of Williamson's hierarchy.

METHODOLOGY

Structure of the Model

To identify the crucial development factors of Hungary, and in order to sketch potential development paths for the country, we developed the FOI model. The model is primarily based on the factors collected from the literature, but these factors are structured in a unique way which allows us to draw up characteristic development paths that can be clearly separated from each other. We used the following assumptions when the FOI model was set up:

- National economies are the unit of our analysis; international interdependencies are mostly disregarded in the paper.
- The key to development is not a single factor, but rather a combination of many factors. According to our assumption there are several important motors of development; sometimes these factors do influence each other, and it is very difficult to determine what causes what, still they can be equally important, and they all have to be used to draw up a potential development path for Hungary.
- Among the many factors considered in the model, the so-called institutional factors play a primary role. Institutional factors are detected using the hierarchy put forward by Williamson (1998). In fact the model was developed with the aim of stressing the importance of institutional factors in development.
- Development can take more than one shape and form. There are several feasible development paths, and Hungary is not constrained to only one of them, but may choose from a (limited) number of such paths. To determine these development paths, the FOI model was used to test the OECD countries.

The FOI model offers a new typology of development factors, but it is also capable of structuring these factors along three clear directions of development. As shown previously, the inside-outside typology of development factors is a standard part of the literature.The FOI model, however, is based on a three-dimensional structure. These three dimensions are:

- F, i.e. the future potential of a country;
- O, i.e. the outside potential of a country;
- I, i.e. the inside potential of a country.

All three dimensions are complex, composed of a large scale of factors. Yet they can still be clearly distinguished from each other, which is useful because the clear distinction can help in the formulation of distinctive development strategies.

The future potential includes factors that are regarded to be crucial for the sustainability and future competitiveness of the Hungarian economy. As sustainability has become one of the main paradigms of all social sciences, we felt that the inclusion of it as a separate development dimension was essential. In our case sustainability translates to ensuring that the typical signs and indicators of a developed country characterisenot only the current state of the economy but also the relatively distant future.

The outside potential includes factors that are crucial to the current world market position of Hungary. This second dimension can be treated as an equivalent of the outside factors listed based on the literature. Some of the elements of the outside potential may not be influenced from the inside; others, like the conditions affecting the international flow of goods, services and factors of production, are a standard part of economic policy.

The inside potential is made up of factors that are regarded to be crucial to the current well-being and development of Hungary. Most of the inside factors listed in Table 1 fall into this potential. Countries that offer favourable conditions to local entrepreneurs, and provide a high level of quality of life to their inhabitants, can have remarkable inside potential.

It is not difficult to spot that certain trade-offs exist among the three potentials. Higher wage levels, for example, are absolutely favourable from the perspective of the inside potential, but they can be dangerous for the outside potential of the country. They can also be threatening to the future potential, if the result of a high wage level is overconsumption. If a country is well endowed with natural resources, this can boost its inside and outside potentials, but the abundance of resources usually leads to high proportions of waste, which again harms the future potential. The three potentials were drafted with these trade-offs in mind.

Formulating a Measurement Method

During a brainstorming session a list of 50 indicators was compiled with the help of experts. These 50 indicators were chosen to measure the relevant development factors, and they were all included in a questionnaire. Experts were asked to rank all 50 indicators on a 1-7 scale (1=not relevant at all; 7= of highest significance). Each indicator received three separate scores: one for future potential, one for outside potential and one for inside potential. The respondents had to give a high score to an indicator if they believed it greatly contributed to the sustainability and future competitiveness (F potential), current world market position (O potential) or current well-being (I potential) of Hungary. The questionnaire was completed by 28 experts. Most of them were active members of the Committee on Future Research of the Hungarian Academy of Sciences. Representing several academic fields (arts, engineering, medicine, natural and social sciences), they offered a wide perspective and a strong future-oriented attitude, values that are highly useful in this kind of research.

Table 2
The components of the future, outside and inside potentials

Future potential	Outside potential	Inside potential
Social responsibility (L1-3)	Trade to GDP ratio (L3-4)	Burden of government regulation (L2-3)
Industrial disputes (L1)	Country credit rating (L4)	Quality of life (L4)
Energy infrastructure (L3)	Exchange rate stability (L3)	Collected total tax revenues (L3)
Total public expenditure on education per capita (L3)	Financial institutions' transparency (L3)	Pension funding (L2-3)
Ageing of society (L1-2)	English proficiency (L4)	GDP (PPP) per capita (L4)
Renewable energies (L3)		Real GDP Growth (L4)
Healthy life expectancy (L3)		Ease of access to loans (L3)
Ecological footprint (L1-2)		Rigidity of employment (L3)
Total expenditure on R&D per capita (L3)		Labour force (L4)
Total R&D personnel nationwide per capita (L3)		Skilled labour (L3)
Educational assessment / Mathematics (L3)		

During the processing of the questionnaires every indicator was placed in the group (F, O or I potential) where it scored highest, meaning that an indicator could only be part of one of the potentials. In order to eliminate some of the less important factors (which received low scores in all three dimensions), we disregarded everything that had a score below average. The final transformation left us with 27 factors: 12 of them influence the future potential, 10 the inside and 5 the outside potential (Table 2).

The final version of the model was fine-tuned usingthe statistical data of the OECD countries.

THE FOI ANALYSIS OF THE OECD COUNTRIES

To quantify the future, outside and inside potentials, the FOI-indices were calculated. The value of the 27 components (listed in Table 2) were gathered for all 34 OECD members for the year 2010, and then all values were transformed to a 1-7 scale using the min-max method. By averaging the standardised values, we were able to calculate the F-, O- and I-indices of all 34 countries (Table 3).

Table 3
The F-, O- and I-indices of the OECD countries

	F	O	I
Australia	4.20	5.32	4.35
Austria	4.70	5.41	4.05
Belgium	3.90	5.56	3.47
Canada	3.90	5.41	4.50
Chile	3.80	5.03	4.13
Czech Republic	3.10	4.97	3.57
Denmark	4.80	5.77	4.30
Estonia	3.00	4.94	3.08
Finland	5.00	5.72	4.02
France	4.40	4.46	3.04
Germany	4.30	5.26	3.73
Greece	2.90	3.66	2.50
Hungary	2.90	4.56	2.55
Iceland	5.90	2.33	4.42
Ireland	3.90	4.17	3.91
Israel	3.60	4.89	4.13
Italy	3.50	3.82	2.66

	F	O	I
Japan	4.80	3.68	4.01
South Korea	4.00	4.26	3.33
Luxembourg	5.30	6.56	4.45
Mexico	2.70	3.98	2.85
Netherlands	4.40	5.54	3.83
New Zealand	4.20	4.52	4.00
Norway	5.20	5.70	4.13
Poland	2.90	4.42	3.07
Portugal	3.50	4.33	2.91
Slovakia	3.00	4.82	3.25
Slovenia	3.40	5.08	2.70
Spain	3.40	4.23	2.99
Sweden	5.10	5.22	4.13
Switzerland	5.40	5.37	4.89
Turkey	3.30	3.63	3.14
United Kingdom	3.90	4.35	3.60
USA	3.80	4.27	4.47

Factor Analysis

In order to better understand, what background factors drive the value of the different F-, O- and I-indices, a factor analysis was conducted with SPSS 19. Almost 150 variables were tested during the analysis. In the first step, we checked how closely related those variables are to the three index values in the OECD countries, and what the direction of the relationship is. As a second step, all variables were only considered in the factor analysis of the index they had the highest correlational relationship with.

We were able to establish three main groups of indicators that showed a significant correlation with the index of the future potential of the OECD countries. They were labelled Human capital, Accountable corporations and Quality of the education system. The Human capital factor is a combination of indicators measuring the education and health sectors, and the productivity. The Accountable corporations factor combines such factors as the ethical and social responsibility of organisations and the credibility of managers, and so it represents the social, ethical and environmental considerations of businesses. The third factor, Quality of education system, shows the returns on efforts made in the education system.

Two factors were found with the factor analysis of the O-index, namely National goodwill and Investment conditions. The main distinction between the two factors is the time frame within which their indicators may be influenced by the decision maker. The Investment conditions factor includes variables that can be influenced relatively easily, even over the short term; the National goodwill on the other hand may only be changed over the very long term.

Variables having a significant correlation with the I-index can be separated into three factors. These factors were labelled Business competitiveness, Government intervention and Availability of resources.The Business competitiveness factor measures the microeconomic position of all businesses (small and medium-sized enterprises and large corporations) along such dimensions as productivity, efficiency and R&D&I. The other two factors describe the macroeconomic environment of the businesses, where the Government interventions consists of the regulation part and the Availability of resources the allocation part.

Table 4
The factors of the F-, O- and I-index

F-index	O-index	I-index
F1 Human capital	O1 National goodwill	I1 Business competitiveness
Labour productivity (PPP) Overall productivity (PPP) Total health expenditure per capita Total public expenditure on education per capita Healthy life expectancy Total expenditure on R&D per capita	Parallel economy Investment risk Image abroad Country credit rating Brain drain Risk of political instability	Innovative capacity Productivity of companies Small and medium-size enterprises Information technology Large corporations
F2 Accountable corporations	O2 Investment conditions	I2 Government intervention
Ethical practices Social responsibility Credibility of managers	Foreign investors Exchange rate stability Capital markets Investment incentives State ownership of enterprises	Subsidies Finance and banking regulation Protectionism Legal and regulatory framework Ease of doing business Bureaucracy
F3 Quality of the education system		I3 Availability of resources
Educational assessment / Mathematics Educational assessment / Sciences Science in schools Educational system		Labour force Total primary energy supply per capita Burden of government regulation Employment rate Gross domestic savings

F-index: KMO=0.823, explained proportion 76.4%; O-index: KMO=0.803, explained proportion 73.7%; I-index: KMO=0.791, explained proportion 73.408%[1]

Forming Clusters

The FOI-indices and the factors determined during the factor analysis were used to identify typical clusters within the OECD countries. These artificial clusters were created based on the values of the F-, O- , and I-index, with the so-called half-scale method. As the indices canhave a value between 1 and 7, 4 is the mid-value. So all three indices were split into two groups: the values from 1 to 4 went into the group labelled as "low" (1), while the values above 4 were labelled as "high" (2).

[1] *The Kaiser-Meyer-Olkin (KMO) value helps in determining how suited our variables are to factor analysis. A KMO value above 0.8 means that the variables are highly suitable. Principal component analysis and Varimax rotation were used during the analysis.*

Theoretically all 8 clusters could represent feasible combinations, but most of the 34 OECD members fall into 4 groups (the distribution is shown in Table 5). Inour interpretation these four groups of countries represent the development models within the OECD.

The current paper focuses on Group 3, which is called the dual model. As half-scaling was used as a method of clustering, it is obvious that the countries of the dual model perform above average in their outside potential. A closer inspection of the factors shows, however, that these countries are especially strong in ensuring favourable Investment conditions, and their National goodwill (the other factor of the O-index) is below average. They are all characterised by liberalised capital flow regulations, exchange rate stability, accessible capital markets and incentive policies for investments. As far as the F-index is concerned, they perform poorly in the Quality of the education system and Human capital, while they are barely below average in the Accountable corporations factor. In the case of the I-index, the value of the Government intervention factor is slightly above average, although that cannot compensate for their weak performance in the other factors of Business competitiveness and Availability of resources.

Table 5
The clusters of OECD countries according to the half-scale method

Group & Code	Country
1 (111)	Greece, Italy, Mexico, Portugal, Turkey
3 (112)	Chile, Czech Republic, Estonia, Hungary, Israel, Poland, Slovakia, Slovenia, Spain
5 (211)	United Kingdom
6 (212)	Iceland
7 (221)	Belgium, France, Netherlands, Ireland, South Korea, New Zealand
8 (222)	Australia, Austria, Canada, Denmark, Finland, Germany, Japan, Luxembourg, Norway, Sweden, Switzerland, United States

The F-, O- and I-index values are indicated in brackets, where 1=countries with index values between 1 and 4; 2=above 4.
No countries fell into Groups 2 or 4.

It is not difficult to spot a strong focus on outside resources in the factor structure of the third cluster. These countries create a favourable environment for the world market-oriented companies, and they adopt policies that lead to a more liberalised government regulation. For this reason their economies may be characterised with the classical dual structure: a competitive, outside-oriented sector that relies substantially on outside resources, and a traditional sector applying local capital that is at least partially isolated from the other sector. The main characteristic of the dual model therefore is a strong focus on attracting outside resources, with the help of which the economy can be modernised and a higher growth rate might be achieved.

The Dual Model as a Development Strategy

The cluster and factor analysis based on the FOI-indices lead us to three promising development models (Clusters 3, 7 and 8). Here we discuss in detail the dual model, which implies a strategy that is focused on the attraction of outside resources. In other words we argue that if the goal is to move towards the dual model, the economic policy should concentrate on a strategy centred on the attraction of outside resources. If we draw a parallel between the development model (deducted from the clusters of countries) and the economic policy strategy, we can also tell which factors are most important for the outside-resources-oriented strategy. We have seen that the third cluster exceeds in one of the outside factors, called Investment conditions, and in one of the inside ones, called Government intervention. These two will be the areas that the economic policy needs to address when the strengthening of the dual model is the goal.

As a next step we checked which of the OECD members scored well in these two factors, and which of them has a comparable size to Hungary. In Investment conditions Ireland scores the highest, Austria is seventh, Finland and Denmark are eleventh and twelfth respectively; in Government intervention Finland is second, Denmark is fifth, Ireland is ninth and Austria is eleventh. Country studies were prepared of these four countries to detect those best practices that allowed them to excel in the areas measured by the two factors above. The country studies are fairly extensive and therefore cannot be included in the paper, but the lessons learned from them are featured in the final sections (the country studies are accessible in the Appendix of Bartha, Gubik and Tóthné Szita 2013). The final goal is to use the FOI analysis and the country studies to offer relevant policy recommendations for Hungary.

The Strategy Based on the Attraction of Outside Resources

In 2010 Hungary was part of the third cluster of the OECD countries, so it can be best characterised with the dual model. For this reason Hungary's adjustment strategy has been closest to the one based on the attraction of outside resources. This argument is further backed by the fact the best two scores of Hungary come in those two factors that are identified as the strongest of the dual model: the country is ninth in Investment conditions and eighteenth in Government intervention (this may not seem to be a good ranking, but they both can be considered as strengths compared to Hungary's twenty-fourth overall place). The outside-oriented strategy is not uncommon in the region either: all of the ex-communist OECD members (the Czech Republic,

Estonia, Poland, Slovakia and Slovenia) fall into the third group. But despite the fact that Hungary's two best scores come in Government intervention and Investment conditions, there is still plenty of room for improvement.

Table 6
Development areas for the strategy focused on the attraction of outside resources

Level	Component
L2	Advanced political culture Low level of corruption Stable and foreseeable socio-economic environment Stable public finances Exchange rate stability – Eurozone membership
L2-L3 transition	Social partnership in labour market affairs Collective agreement of employers and employees on national, sectorial and company level
L3	Transparent government, e-government solutions Regulatory impact assessment – measuring the effects of government interventions
L3-L4 transition	Persistently low corporate tax rate, with additional tax exemptions State of the art infrastructure Stable investment environment, coordinated tax and subsidy system Support for company-university-researcher cooperation
L4	Clearly defined development goals: research and development, information and communication technologies Substantial state subsidies on corporate innovation Substantial central help for start-ups and export expansion, involving subsidies, information and counselling services, and business support agencies Low level of corporate tax rates Flexible labour market

Our suggestions were put forward using Williamson's (1998) hierarchy (Table 6). As the lowest level (L4) summarises the current issues of resource allocation, the actions listed here theoretically can have an instant effect on the economy. Economic policy measures may belong to this level as well, if we assume that changes in regulations, taxes or subsidies have an instant effect on the market behaviour of firms and individuals. The longer-term effect of central intervention is that persistent measures change the structure of the market and the economy, and the relationships among firms. These belong to the governance part of the economy (L3). The strategy focusing on the attraction of outside resources requires a predictable government, and that on the other hand requires the stability of the political system. That is why Level 2 is also present in Table 6, but it has to be said that changes on this level may take decades, according to Williamson.

We shall start the presentation of our suggestions with those belonging to the highest level (L2). Because of the hierarchical system, the factors higher above are the prerequisites of anything below them. We have found that one of the pillars of best practice is the reliability of the economic policy. The corporate tax decrease policy in Ireland was started more than two decades ago, and it was consistently carried out; the many decades of minority governments has led to a special culture of political consensus seeking in Denmark that makes it possible to carefully plan and fine-tune long- term social policies; the state is committed to long-term development goals in Austria and Finland. Political stability is coupled with the transparency of the public sector and a very low level of corruption in all cases. The latter two further enforce the reliability of economic policy, as they decrease the chance of interest groups capturing the state, and destabilising the policy making.

Disciplined public finances are also an important part of the best practices. After the 2008 financial crisis it is clear that balanced budgets are important, but they seem to be an absolute must for a reliable investment environment. A stable budget position guarantees that the government does not have to take unexpected measures that affect company costs (e.g. tax raises or new taxes, withdrawing tax remedies, subsidies).

The reliability of monetary policy, more particularly the reliability of exchange rate policy, is equally as important as that of fiscal policy. It is well known that exchange rate stability is a central element of the economic policy measures of open economies. The euro partially ensures that stability, although the exchange rate against other major currencies can still be very volatile. Because at least two-thirds of the trade of the European countries is conducted within Europe, the euro is able to provide a relative stability on the continent, and lets the member countries get rid of the best part of their exchange rate risks.

The institutional framework that ensures the stability of the labour market was placed between Levels 2 and 3. Labour market issues are basically part of the allocation problem, so they should belong to Level 4. But it is also known that the pure market model is not an efficient one on the labour market, and usually there are dozens of institutional factors regulating it. This why the institutional framework of the labour market is higher up in Williamson's hierarchy. In Austria and Denmark the collective bargaining system is completely integrated into the institutions of the central government, and therefore it is linked to Level 2, but it also has an effect on the governance of companies (L3), which is why it was put as a transition between the two levels.

The dependency on the higher level structures is especially true of labour market institutions. More precisely, the Danish-Austrian type of social partnership and collective bargaining system can only be successful if the willingness to seek compromises and solidarity are an integral part of a country's culture (factors belonging to L1 and L2). Hungary had experimented with the system in the 1990es, but gave up on it after several failures, so the suggestions on L2-L3 are only for the sake of comparison. Immediate action cannot be taken based on them. What is worth remembering is that long-term labour market stability is key to the outside-resources-oriented strategy, and this can only be achieved if a well-functioning institutional framework is in place. Some areas require some sort of central regulation and planning: the smoothing of cyclical fluctuations (e.g. compensating for lost income in case of becoming unemployed); balancing structural weaknesses (e.g. the feedback of labour market needs to the education system). In other cases institutional guarantees may be needed to prevent the state from distorting the market (e.g. separating real wage changes from market powers).

The second-order economising called governance by Williamson (L3) represents the efficiency of the government regulations in case of an economic policy analysis. This is important for the attraction of outside resources, because the administrative burdens of the bureaucracy increase the transaction costs of everyone, including the owners of foreign resources. The extent of transaction costs caused by the state therefore is a prime indicator of both capital investors and immigrants. Denmark and Finland are front runners in e-government solutions. These solutions provide huge advantages: e.g. they make bureaucracy more transparent, increase the speed at which services can be provided by the state, make it easier to declare and pay taxes, and help in creating huge databases that make public policy decisions more reliable.

Ireland is a great example for regulatory impact analysis. Stating from 2000 they gradually adopted the principle that the market distortion effects of government regulations are assessed. Basically a systematic attempt was made to quantify the transaction costs and changes in market behaviour caused by the intervention of the state. Thanks to the regulatory impact analysis the instruments that have the strongest market distortion effect may be filtered out, and the costs of both the state and the business sector can be decreased. The introduction of this approach has the added bonus of showing a more rational image of the bureaucracy, and making it look more attractive for investors.

All of our other suggestions consist of economic policy measures that have a direct effect on the allocation of resources, and an instant impact on the economy, and so they belong to Level 4 (or to the transition between L3 and L4). The hierarchical structure still applies,of course; the lower-level suggestions can only work efficiently if they are compatible with the higher-level characteristics of the country.

Ireland, Denmark and Austria have each set up a tax system where the relatively high overall tax burden is achieved with a low corporate tax rate (although the orders of magnitude are different: Ireland has one the lowest corporate tax rates in the world, its effective value is below 10%; the Danish is somewhat higher than the Irish, while the Austrian corporate tax rate can only be considered low if we compare it to the average of the developed welfare states). As the tax rate is a pivotal point in the investment decisions of the transnational companies, a consistently low corporate tax can be a great attraction.

In all countries the state support for clusters is a main priority. Clusters usually involve the cooperation of companies, research institutes, universities, development agencies and risk capital firms, but they are also supported by the state. The practice of Denmark, Austria, Ireland or Finland shows that state support alone is not enough; the clusters may only be successful if they carry special knowledge that is competitive in the world market. Those industries are worth supporting that have traditionally performed well and whose main companies are well known on the world market (good examples for the Danish are food, pharmaceutics and wind energy, for the Finnish wood or information technology, for the Irish process innovation, and for the Austrians car manufacturing clusters).

The flexible labour market is another attraction for transnational companies. If the termination of employment does not require a lot of administrative tasks, and can be carried out with relatively low costs, companies are able to adjust to the fluctuations in the world market demand. Denmark also has a social safety net, and applies several active labour market instruments that ensure that the unemployed can find a new job relatively quickly.

The suggestions in Table 6 will not only strengthen the model based on the attraction of outside resources, but the FOI analysis showed that they primarily affect the factors that are the pillars of such an economic policy orientation. The economic policy should concentrate on these instruments, if the main priority is the attraction of outside resources.

CONCLUSION

The dual model detected with the FOI model can be characterised as a development strategy based on the attraction of outside resources. Countries choosing this as a priority try to create an internal business and regulation environment that will make them attractive to outside investors. The more attractive environment may encourage the inflow of outside resources, which are needed because the local capital and knowledge generation is not sufficient. Many historical examples confirm that such a development strategy can prove successful, but the global environment has its risks as well. On the one hand overreliance on outside resources can result in a dependent position, because the sudden withdrawal of resources may lead to the collapse of the economy. The dependent position on the other hand can push the country toward an institutional environment favouring outside agents to the local ones – a process that further strengthens the exposure of the country.

What steps are recommended to adopt a development strategy based on the attraction of outside resources?

- Long-term commitment to relevant policy incentives, such as:
  - decreasing and keeping corporate tax rates low;
  - exchange rate stability;
  - tax remedies and subsidies targeted towards large corporations;
  - infrastructure development;
  - or a combination of the above.
- Making the central bureaucracy and government decision-making process more transparent, introducing a wide variety of e-government solutions.
- Labour market mix: easing of the recruitment and layoff rules, increasing the flexibility on the one hand, maintaining stability on the other hand (minimal loss of working hours, modest wage increase).

The hierarchy presented in Figure 1 shows that careful consideration of instruments is needed before any steps are taken, because positive outcomes can only be expected from economic policy measures that are in harmony with the institutional framework of the country.

Acknowledgement

The paper was prepared within the framework of OTKA project No. K 76870/2009-13.

REFERENCES

BALOGH, T. (1963): Unequal Partners 1-2. Blackwell, Oxford.

BARRO, J.B. (1998): Determinants of Economic Growth: A Cross-Country Empirical Study. MIT Press Books, Cambridge, Massachusetts.

BARTHA, Z., GUBIK, S. A. &TÓTHNÉ SZITA, K. (2013): Intézményi megoldások, fejlődési modellek (Institutional solutions, development models). GNR Szolgáltató és Kereskedelmi Bt., Miskolc.

BHAGWATI, J. (1958): Immiserizing Growth: A Geometrical Note. The Review of Economic Studies, 25(3), pp 201-205.

BOEKE, J.H. (1953): Economics and Economic Policy of Dual Societies. Institute of Pacific Relations, New York.

COASE, R.H. (1937): The Nature of the Firm. Economica 4(16), pp 386-405.

DOMAR, E. (1947): Expansion and Employment. American Economic Review, 37(1), pp 343-355.

EMMANUEL, A. (1972): Unequal Exchange: A Study of the Imperialism of Trade. Monthly Review Press, New York.

FREEMAN, C. (1987): Technology Policy and Economic Performance: Lessons from Japan. Pinter Publishers, London.

FURTADO, C. (1970): Economic Development of Latin America. Cambridge University Press, London.

HAMILTON, A (1791): Report on Manufactures. Philadelphia.

HARROD, R.F. (1948): Towards a Dynamic Economics. MacMillan, London.

HODGSON, M.H. (2006): What Are Institutions? Journal of Economic Issues, 40(1), pp 1-25.

KEYNES, J.M. (1936): The General Theory of Employment, Interest and Money. MacMillan, London.

KRUEGER, A.O. (1974): The political economy of the rent seeking society. American

LIST, F (1841): Das Nationale System der Politischen Ökonomie. Cotta'schen Verlag, Stuttgart.

LUCAS, R.E. (1988): On the Mechanics of Economic Development. Journal of Monetary Economics, 22(1), pp 3-42.

MARSHALL, A. (1890): Principles of Economics (First Edition ed.). Macmillan, London.

MCCLELLAND, D.C. (1957): Community development and the nature of human motivation. Harvard University, Cambridge.

MEIER, G.M. (1964): Leading Issues in Economic Development. Oxford University Press, New York.

MYRDAL, G. (1957): Economic Theory and Underdeveloped Regions. Gerald Duckworth, London.

NORTH, D.C. (1993): Institutions, institutional change and economic performance. Cambridge University Press, Cambridge.

PORTER, M.E. (1990): The Competitive Advantage of Nations. Harvard Business Review, 68(2), pp 73-91.

PREBISCH, R. (1964): Towards a new trade policy for development. United Nations, New York.

RICARDO, D. (1817): On the Principles of Political Economy and Taxation. John Murray, London.

ROMER, P. (1986): Increasing Return and Long Run Growth. Journal of Political Economy, 94(5), pp 1002-1037.
SCHUMPETER, J.A. (1934): The Theory of Economic Development: An Inquiry Into Profits, Capital, Credit, Interest, and the Business Cycle. Harvard University Press, Cambridge.
SIMON, H.A. (1957): Models of Man. Wiley, New York.
SINGER, H.W. (1964): International Development: Growth and Change. McGraw-Hill, New York.
SMITH, A. (1776): Enquiry into the Nature and Causes of the Wealth of Nations. J. R. McCulloch, Edinburgh.
SOLOW, R. (1956): A Contribution to the Theory of Economic Growth. Quarterly Journal of Economics, 70(1), pp 65-94.
SZENTES T. (2011): Fejlődés-gazdaságtan (Development economics). Akadémiai Kiadó, Budapest.
TULLOCK, G. (1967): The Welfare Costs of Tariffs, Monopolies and Theft. Western Economic Journal, 5(3), pp 224-232.
TULLOCK, G. (1993): Rent Seeking. Edward Elgar Publishing, Brookfield.
VEBLEN, T. (1919): The Place of Science in Modern Civilization. B. W. Huensch, New York.
WALLERSTEIN, I. (1974): The Modern World System: Capitalist Agriculture and the Origins of the European World Economy in the Sixteenth Century. Academic Press, New York.
WILLIAMSON, O.E. (1998): Transaction Cost Economics: How It Works; Where It Is Headed. De Economist, 146(1), pp 23-58.
WILLIAMSON, O.E. (2000): The New Institutional Economics: Taking Stock, Looking Ahead. Journal of Economic Literature, 38(3), pp 595-613.

Quality Improvement in Accounting

GYULA FÜLÖP, Ph.D.
UNIVERSITY PROFESSOR

e-mail: vgtfulop@uni-miksolc.hu

BETTINA HÓDI HERNÁDI
ASSISTANT LECTURER

e-mail: vgtbetti@uni-miskolc.hu

SUMMARY

Over the last decade the expectations of quality have become involved in the product, service, production and business process. In the last few years, however, quality related expectations have been completed with sustainability (economic, social and ecological) considerations. Therefore the application of the appropriate management/business process and systems are needed to measure the fulfillment of the new quality expectations or company's performance. The aim of this paper is to introduce the new approaches for the appraisal of the company's performance, beginning with conventional accounting through environmental accounting to sustainability accounting. A case study demonstrates the successful implementation of the sustainability accounting system in a Hungarian company.
Keywords: quality; sustainability; sustainability accounting

INTRODUCTION

Sustainability: the new quality? Over the last decades the role and importance of quality was overestimated because quality is a device for obtaining a competitive advantage. According to its general (ISO) definition quality reflects the real and latent expectations of the customer with reference to the product, service and process. These quality-related expectations should not only be involved in the production processes but in the business process, too, more precisely in the course of the operation of an accounting system.

Although the notion of quality is related to the product, service (output) and process, it also could be connected with the customer. However, this does not mean that output can be only a tangible product or service, or the customer only could be interpreted as an external utilizer. The accounting information produced within the company also could be considered as a special output for which the principle of quality is valid as well. The internal organization units of the company too can be a receiver or utilizer of information, thus those expectations relating to quality cannot be less important than the expectations of an external customer. In the 21st century these expectations comprise the requirements – economic, social and ecological values – of sustainability, too as a new component of quality. All this can be provided by planning and operating a sustainability accounting information system.

From the changes of recent decades it is clear that traditional accounting does not offer sufficient relevant information for stakeholders about the creation of sustainability, and thus it must be reformulated and expanded. This had led to developments in accounting. In spite of the fact that there is now a relatively wide range of literature dealing with environmental accounting (Gray 1993, Debnath et al. 2012), and many have studied the subject from many perspectives, only a few articles have focused on sustainability accounting (Jasch & Lavicka 2006, Ngwakwe 2012).

The aim of this paper is to introduce the approaches for the appraisal of a company's performance. We shall begin with conventional accounting, discuss environmental accounting, and finally focus on sustainability accounting. A case study is discussed to demonstrate the contribution of sustainability accounting to obtaining a competitive advantage in a Hungarian company. The article brings new insights to the discussion on planning and operating sustainability accounting system; thus, it fills the gap between theory and practice.

FROM SUSTAINABILITY TO CORPORATE SUSTAINABILITY

A very rich literature is available on sustainability, so it is an important task to properly define the content of this concept as a starting point of further examination. After clarifying its content, the incorporation of the conceptual elements of corporate sustainability becomes possible.

The Dimensions of Sustainability

The philosophy of sustainability derives from the ideas laid down in the so-called Brundtland Report (1987). According to the report, 'sustainable development' is defined as follows:

"Humanity has the ability to make development sustainable to ensure that it meets the needs of the present without compromising the ability of future generations to meet their own needs (...) Sustainable development is not a fixed state of harmony, but rather a process of change in which

- the exploitation of resources,
- the direction of investments,
- the orientation of technological development, and
- institutional change

are made consistent with future as well as present needs." (Brundtland 1987, p. 16-17)

According to a wider interpretation of the above-mentioned definition, sustainable development means the harmonisation of economic, social and ecological values. The three "dimensions" of sustainability strongly interact with one another, including a variety of factors as shown in Figure 1.

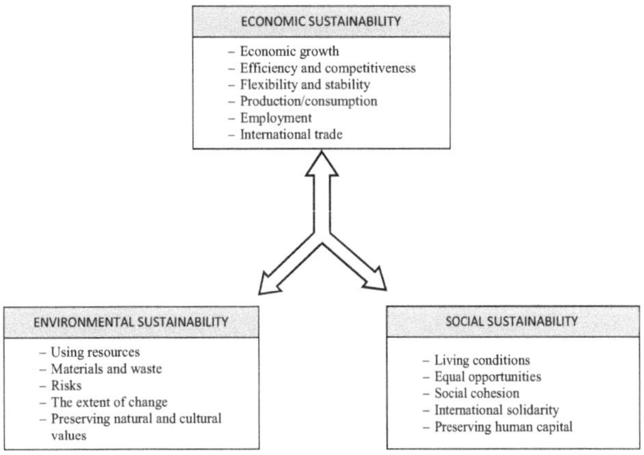

Source: own construction, 2013

Figure 1. Three dimensions of sustainability

There is no doubt that a complex, multifactorial system is needed for the management of the implementation of sustainability, making the measurement of the achieved results complicated. While improvement is experienced in one dimension, in some cases deterioration can be seen in another one. Usually, there is a debate over whether an overall improvement or deterioration has occurred. In addition, it also has to be taken into account that the results achieved at the global level do not necessarily mean efficiency at the level of each and every nation, region, company and individual. However, the established goal has to be the aim of improvement at every level, which, based on our current knowledge, is a major challenge to achieve (Szlávik 2007).

The issues of sustainability can be discussed at various levels, and therefore they require several different approaches. In this study the concept of sustainability is associated with companies and examined at the level of companies.

The Theoretical Foundations of Corporate Sustainability

In the majority of cases, corporate sustainability is seen as an alternative to the traditional growth and profit maximization model by the corporate executives. In reality, it is a new, emerging paradigm. While acknowledging the need for profitability, it differs from the traditional growth and profit maximization models. It expects companies to keep social and environmental goals in mind, particularly the goals related to sustainable development, such as the environment, social justice and equity, and economic growth.

The concept of corporate sustainability borrows elements from the following four well-established concepts:

- sustainable development,
- corporate social responsibility,
- stakeholder theory,
- corporate accountability.

The contribution of sustainable development to corporate sustainability is twofold. First, it helps set out the areas that companies should focus on: environmental, social, and economic performance. Second, it provides a common societal goal for corporations, governments, and civil society to work toward: ecological, social, and economic sustainability.

In the most general terms, corporate social responsibility deals with the role of business in society. Its basic premise is that corporate managers have an ethical obligation to consider and address the needs of society, not just to act solely in the interests of the shareholders or their own self-interest (Kerekes & Wetzker 2007).

Stakeholder theory defines a stakeholder as "any group or individual who can affect or is affected by the achievement of the organization's objectives." The basic premise of stakeholder theory is that the stronger your relationships are with other external parties, the easier it will be to meet your corporate business objectives; the worse your relationships, the harder it will be (Freeman 1984).

The concept of corporate accountability refers to the legal or ethical responsibility to provide an account or reckoning of the actions for which one is held responsible. Accountability differs from responsibility in that the latter refers to one's duty to act in a certain way, whereas accountability refers to one's duty to explain, justify, or report on his or her actions (Fama & Jensen, 1983). Clarify the reporting requirements to help determine the nature of the relationship between the company's managers and the rest of society.

Based on the above concepts Schaltegger et al. (2006) define the concept of corporate sustainability as follows: the economic, social and environmental dimensions of sustainability are integrated into corporate strategies and activities. Therefore it is necessary to secure the sustainable operation of the company from each of the three sides.

- In economic terms, a company can be considered to be sustainable if – beyond the reimbursement of fixed costs – it fulfills the owners' profitability requirements, with the potential of making some more profit and in addition it brings. The economic turning point comes when all costs are paid back and the profitability requirements of the company are also met (Illés 2002).
- In social terms, companies operating in a sustainable way make their contribution to social value creation through increasing individual human capital and supporting social goals. They manage social capital in such a way that stakeholders can understand its motivations and can broadly agree with the company's value system (Dyllick & Hockerts 2002).
- According to the ecological approach, sustainable companies are characterized by the rational exploitation of natural resources and the aim to minimize the damaging environmental impact of their production activities. All this is done to preserve the quality of natural resources as well as the economic opportunities offered by them (Institute for Development and Methodology, State Audit Office of Hungary, 2005).

Currently, not all companies operate in line with the principles of sustainability. However, some companies are publicly committed to the application of the appropriate sustainability management methods and tools.

Comparison of Traditional, Environmental and Sustainability Accounting Systems

Based on the above approach, companies need to build up and operate an accounting information system that meets the requirements of sustainability. The development stages of accounting towards this direction are described below.

Changes in Traditional Accounting

Traditional accounting systems are information systems supporting the daily operation of economic organizations, with the purpose of observing, collecting, recording, measuring, and classifying the economic events that have an influence of the company's assets, financial and earnings position, together with their impact. Therefore, the aim of accounting for stakeholders (owners, managers, creditors, inspection bodies, etc.) is to provide accurate information for making future decisions.

The modern approach to traditional accounting can be divided into two areas: financial accounting and management accounting. Financial accounting provides external stakeholders with information by financial reports through "the changes in the tools and resources required for the management as well as the accounts of the economic performance" (Musinszki 2012, p 35), and its practical implementation is regulated by the Act on Accounting. Whereas management accounting is "the complex of decision support methods and procedures, satisfying the information needs of the various management levels and internal users", its task is to identify, estimate, analyze, and provide cost and other internal information for the management (Musinszki 2012, p 35).

In the light of sustainability, however, the generally accepted accounting principles, the range of those demanding accounting information and the content of accounting information all have to be reinterpreted.

1. A new approach to the going concern principle:

One of the most fundamental principles in accounting is the going concern principle, which states that "in the course of book-keeping and preparing the accounts, it must be assumed that the enterprise will maintain its operation in the foreseeable future, will be able to carry on its activities, and a significant decrease or closing down its activities is not expected for any reason" (Act C on Accounting §15 (1), 2000). This wording suggests that only a stable external environment allows the company's activities on an unchanged continuation, and assumes what is also emphasized in Aras and Crowther's (2008) work, namely, observing the going concern principle results in keeping the company's operations maintainable. However, a company's external environment should include the business (economic) environment in which it operates, the local and regional social environment in which it is located, and the natural environment, which, in turn, gives natural limitations to the company's operations (Hódi Hernádi, 2012).

2. Reconsidering the content and the range of those demanding accounting information:

Since the information provided by accounting systems is suitable for preparing and establishing decisions, it is important to make the demanded information available. However, it would be reasonable to give an extended interpretation on the range of stakeholders. Therefore, according to Hódi Hernádi (2012), the population, meaning society itself, the natural environment, especially at local and regional levels, as well as future owners, employees, the next generations, and the future state of the natural environment all have to be taken into account. After all, the point of sustainability focuses on their needs in order to make all those decision-making opportunities accessible to them that are currently in place for present-day stakeholders.

The fundamental task of accounting is to provide reliable and real information on the operation of the company for market participants. However, different information is needed by different stakeholders. Therefore, an accounting information system should be established that is capable of collecting and organizing the social and environmental information necessary for making various decisions, and is capable of presenting and interpreting them to both internal and external users in a reliable and accurate way. In response to these changing requirements, traditional accounting systems have to change and improve accordingly. The next step of this improvement is the development and the implementation of environmental accounting systems.

The Characteristics of Environmental Accounting

The concept of environmental accounting and reporting appeared in the literature nearly a decade ago. According to Schaltegger and Burritt's (2000, p. 30) definition, "environmental accounting is a branch of accounting that deals with activities, methods and systems; recording, analysis and reporting; and environmentally induced financial impacts and ecological impacts of a defined economic system". Environmental accounting systems basically consist of two parts, one of which deals with the environment-induced financial impacts, i.e. environment-related expenditures and savings, while the other part is concerned with the environmental impacts of the company's business, that is, how the natural environment changes as a result of the company's operations (Almássy 2006). Environmental accounting systems present the above-mentioned effects both by measuring in natural units and expressing in terms of money, as – opposed to traditional accounting – non-monetary and qualitative factors are also strongly emphasized here.

Thus, basically there are four areas of environmental accounting (Csutora & Kerekes 2004): internal ecological accounting, environmental management accounting, external ecological accounting, and environmental financial accounting. "So environmental accounting facilitates establishing a connection between environmental and economic performance together with the presentation of the interaction between these two types of performances" (Pál 2011, p. 128).

By focusing on the company's financial and environmental dimensions, environmental accounting systems ignore the impact of corporate activities on society. However, there are approaches (Yakhou & Dorweiler, 2004) that interpret society as part of the natural environment and consider the sustainability of the natural environment to be the basis of man's well-being, therefore they should not be treated separately. However, according to the conclusion of the present paper, all three dimensions must be taken into account in the development of accounting systems, giving way to sustainability accounting systems.

The Theoretical Framework of Sustainability Accounting

Borrowing the notion made by Burritt and Schaltegger (2010) sustainability accounting is the peak of accounting. Sustainability accounting, reaching far beyond environmental accounting, examines business operations by putting all three – economic, social and environmental – dimensions into its focus, and most importantly, it emphasizes the interaction of these dimensions in accordance with corporate sustainability.

The most widely accepted definition was presented by Schaltegger and Burritt (2010, p. 377):

- "Sustainability accounting describes a subset of accounting that deals with activities, methods and systems to record, analyse and report:
- First, environmentally and socially induced financial impacts,
- Second, ecological and social impacts of a defined economic system, and
- Third, and perhaps most important, the interactions and linkages between social, environmental and economic issues constituting the three dimensions of sustainability."

It can be legitimately asked whether sustainability accounting systems should be treated as completely self-contained, new accounting systems or as simply part of or an extension of traditional accounting systems. According to Schaltegger et al. (2006), the former alternative would be desirable, as it gives opportunities for the actual mapping of the economic, social and environmental risks and benefits, and to the integration of these dimensions into the company's accounting system. Most authors, however, believe that the latter approach is closer to the actual practice, since the gradual modification and expansion of the existing accounting system causes a minor change in the company's strategic management process.

The development of a sustainability accounting system includes the following five elements: the aim of operating a sustainability accounting system; the principles and requirements of operating the system; methods and devices for data collection, data recording, measurement and analysis; sustainability accounts and reports; and the qualitative characteristics of the resulting information (Lamberton 2005). The components of a logical model of sustainability accounting systems as well as the relationships between them are shown in Figure 2.

1. The aim of sustainability accounting systems:

Sustainability accounting information systems are primarily designed to evaluate the performance of the economic organization in terms of sustainability, i.e. paying special attention to its economic, social and environmental aspects.

Similarly to traditional accounting, sustainability accounting can also be divided into two areas according to whether it provides external or internal users with the necessary information. The external stakeholders' need for information focuses on the accountability of the organization's operations both in social and environmental terms. In addition to this, sustainability accounting information systems provide internal stakeholders – the management – with information relevant to decision making, thus playing an important role in strengthening the internal management of the organization. As it is possible to determine the effects and consequences of the measures taken to achieve sustainability objectives in the course of performance evaluation, it gives a good basis for the preparation of a possible intervention, that is, for feedback.

2. The principles and requirements of operating a sustainability accounting system:

During the development of a sustainability accounting system, some important principles and requirements should be taken into consideration that specify the methods and devices applied in the course of data collection, measurement, and evaluation, as well as the content and the process of reporting.

The sustainability accounting system is elaborated at a corporate level, and because of this, it applies to economic organizations obliged to prepare reports and it is not relevant at the macro-level.

As already mentioned, with the reinterpretation of the going concern principle, existing accounting principles also gain new meanings both in social and environmental terms. Lamberton (2005) highlights one of those principles, namely the principles of sufficiency. According to his approach, it is not possible to record and analyze all impacts on society and the natural environment, thus, those impacts should be put forward that pose potential threats to mankind and the natural environment or that are essential for the company's decisions.

The following principle is the interpretation of sustainability at a corporate level. It is an important issue because it determines the framework of the whole system. The company's sustainability goals, the compound realization of economic, social and environmental sustainability raise the issue of their integrated measurement and performance evaluation. Due to the complexity of the company's sustainability performance evaluation, the boundaries of the sustainability accounting system have to be clearly marked in a way that the system can still be managed by the company. It has three levels. First, the essential inputs and resources that influence or incidentally limit the operation of the company have to be taken into consideration, then the direct effects of the company's activities on the society and the natural environment, that is the outputs. The supply of inputs, in other words, the environmental and social performance of suppliers, also has to be taken into account (Lamberton, 2005).

The following essential requirement is the selection of the proper period for accounting, evaluation and analysis, that is, the determination of the period in which the company is evaluated in terms of sustainability. It is advisable to choose a monthly, quarterly or annual period in accordance with the traditional accounting standard. However, the sustainability accounting system needs to be applied in a longer time frame since it has to take into account the social and environmental impacts of the company's products and services through their entire life-cycle.

The evaluation of the social and environmental impacts caused by corporate activities or the entire life cycle of a product requires the application of non-monetary, qualitative indicators beside the usual monetary indicators for measuring economic or financial performance.

3. Methods and devices for data collection, data record, measurement and analysis:

The sources used for collecting and recording data are wide-ranging and abundant, however, in the selection process some cost-benefit aspects should be enforced.

Based on the collected economic, social and environmental data, it becomes possible to measure the company's sustainability performance, and this requires a variety of benchmarks and evaluation methods. Some of these are the cost estimation of decision alternatives regarding sustainability (Bebbington & Gray, 2001), input-output analyses, life cycle analyses, and the mapping of social and environmental impacts. One of the most complete methods available for the management is the Sustainability Balanced Scorecard (SBSC), an integrated indicator system aimed at evaluating the company's performance (Fülöp and Hódi Hernádi, 2012), which is the basis for decision-making and monitoring the realization of objectives.

Considerable attention should be paid to the evaluation of environmental protection measures and the costs of social and environmental liabilities in order to make the company accountable in terms of sustainability.

4. Sustainability accounts and reports:

The fourth part of sustainability accounting focuses on distributing both quantitative and qualitative information to users. Here, there are two key questions to be answered. What is the appropriate form and content of a sustainability account? How often should these reports be prepared and published?

Sustainability accounting information are presented by the SBSC including a wide variety of performance indicators, and other sustainability reports based on the guidance of the Global Reporting Initiative (GRI).

Such reports should be made regularly through the entire lifetime of a product. It is reasonable to present and publish the company's accounting information related to sustainability on its website. The sustainability of the company's accounting information should be presented and published on the website, thus this continuously updated information on sustainability is made available promptly to the stakeholders.

5. The qualitative characteristics of information on sustainability:

The information provided by sustainability accounting systems has to meet a number of important requirements. These are based on the characteristics of traditional accounting information, as well as on the guidelines of GRI sustainability reports. The two highlighted features are transparency and controllability. Transparency demands the complete publication of processes, procedures and assumptions (GRI, 2002). Controllability requires that the recording, organizing, analysis and publication of the presented data and information should be done in a way that enables auditors to certify data reliability (GRI, 2002).

The further requirements concerning sustainability information are: completeness, credibility, neutrality, clarity, materiality, timeliness, comparability and readiness for interpretation in the context of sustainability.

It is reasonable for companies wishing to comply with the requirements of sustainability to design and operate sustainability accounting systems since it is a kind of financial language for decision-makers. According to SIGMA (2003), sustainability accounting is a bridge which leads the company to the bank of a sustainable operation and behavior. The main characteristics of the different accounting systems are summarized in Table 1.

Since traditional, environmental and sustainability accounting systems examine the company's sustainability performance through different dimensions, the content of the obtained information varies,, giving different tasks to the particular accounting systems. The modified range of tasks is noticeable in the areas and the applied methods of the accounting systems. Despite the fact that there are so far no compulsory standards for the operation of sustainability accounting systems, these requirements will certainly appear in the long term.

Table 1

Comparison of the characteristics of traditional, environmental and sustainability accounting systems

Aspects for comparison	Traditional accounting system	Environmental accounting system	Sustainability accounting system
Dimension	– Economic (financial) situation	– Relationship between economy (company) and environment	– Integrating economy (company), society and environment
Target	– Presenting general economic situation – Cost management	– Presenting environmental performance – Presenting environmental liabilities and costs	– Presenting sustainability performance (including economic, social and environmental performances)
Field of application	– Financial accounting – Management accounting	– Environmental financial accounting – External ecological accounting – Environmental management accounting – Internal ecological accounting	– Sustainability financial accounting – Sustainability management accounting
Method	– Evaluation processes – Cost accounting	– Evaluating environmental performance – Life-cycle analysis – Analyses on environmental costs and savings	– Evaluating sustainability performance by applying the methods of other disciplines (biology, sociology) – Sustainability Balanced Scorecard
Unit of measurement	– Money (inventories excluded)	– Money and natural units	– Money and natural units
Forms of accounts	– Financial and accounting reports – Internal reports	– Environmental reports and accounts	– Sustainability reports and accounts – Global Reporting Initiative
Regulation strictness	– Compulsory due to legal regulations (financial accounting) – Voluntary (management accounting)	– As part of the Act on Accounting, some reporting requirements on environmental performance	– Not regulated, voluntary

Source: Hódi Hernádi, 2012

The Illustration of the Operation of a Sustainability Accounting System

The following case study illustrates how a sustainability accounting system can be operated in one of Hungary's largest chemical companies.

Background Information on TVK

The Tiszai Vegyi Kombinát Public Limited Company (TVK) has 1,097 employees today and its annual sales revenue is about 374,584 million HUF. It is a production company which makes ethylene and propylene by processing naphtha and gasoline as raw materials that are further processed into small-, medium- and high-density polyethylene and polypropylene by applying state-of-the-art technologies. It supplies raw materials not only to the domestic market but also to plastic manufacturing companies throughout Central, Eastern and Western Europe. The plastic products made from the raw materials supplied by TVK are essential for both industrial users and the broader public.

Along with Slovnaft Petrochemicals, s.r.o., located in Bratislava, TVK composes the Petrochemical Division within the MOL Group, which holds a leading position in petrochemical sector in Central-Eastern Europe and – in terms of its production capacities – is one of the ten largest polymer producers in Europe.

The structure of TVK's Sustainability Accounting System

The company is aware that nowadays the benchmarks of long-term success and social acceptance cannot be observed only in economic indicators. Its activity is increasingly evaluated in the light of the company's ability to reduce negative effects on both the environment and society. This goal is served by the development and operation of a sustainability accounting system.

1. The aim of TVK's sustainability accounting system:

TVK's sustainability accounting system contributes to the long-term realization of sustainability by providing a well-established and applicable planning, decision-making and operating process. On this basis, the operation of the system is annually reviewed by using such benchmark documents as the Dow Jones Sustainability Index and the expectations of the international conventions for the purpose of complying with industry best practices; furthermore, existing and missing elements are continuously identified in order to see "what progress the company has made".

Its sustainability accounting system evaluates the efficient implementation of the sustainability objectives; furthermore, it encourages continuous improvement efforts, and helps to increase the level of awareness and transparency.

2. The principles and requirements of operating TVK's sustainability accounting system:

Every industrial sector and every corporation have different objectives and, therefore TVK is not exceptional in individually identifying and defining its objectives and tasks in terms of sustainability, which reads as follows: Sustainable development is a corporate commitment for us that is aimed at equally integrating economic, environmental and social factors into our daily business operations, maximizing long-term value and keeping the license we received from society to carry on our operations (TVK 2013). As a chemical company, it has a significant impact on the environment and society; the negative consequences of its operations are reduced by applying the principles of precaution and responsible care.

The company marks the boundaries of its sustainability accounting system following the guidelines made by is the UN's Global Compact and the GRI. In practice, it means that the company defines its objectives within the three dimensions of sustainability, and evaluates its sustainability performance. The economic aspects primarily mean value creation, but the increase of customer satisfaction, the development of the local economy and infrastructure as well as reducing the possibility of corruption are also included. The social dimension is filled with the involvement of stakeholders, the organization of social investment programs, the improvement of employability, the development of human capital, ensuring the society's health and safety conditions and raising customers' environmental consciousness. The environmental aspects extend to energy use, water consumption, reduced pollution, waste management, the moderate use of hazardous materials, the use of recycled materials, the protection and rehabilitation of the land and the conservation of biodiversity.

The evaluation period of the company's sustainability performance is basically determined on a yearly basis. During product development, however, the "cradle to grave" concept also appears, that is, the health and environmental effects of these products are taken into account through the whole life cycle of the product.

The currency unit employed by TVK, according to its size and international influence, is expressed in million HUF or in thousand Euros. In addition, metric tons are commonly used as a natural unit of measure, partly for measuring the weight of the produced goods and partly for measuring environmental impacts.

3. Methods and devices for data collection, data record, measurement and analysis:

The nature of information its sustainability accounting system is required to collect is derived from TVK's sustainability objectives. In most cases, the indicators are based on measurement and calculations but sometimes it also happens that they are based on estimations, depending on the subject or on the premises. The operational environment and the company's performance are constantly analyzed and evaluated in order to fully meet the shareholders' expectations.

Economic performance is evaluated by the quantification of environmental and social costs and revenues, the application of risk matrices, life-cycle analyses and benchmarks. The impact on society is examined with the help of stakeholder analyses and social efficiency indicators. The company's environmental performance is monitored by applying condition test methods, eco-efficiency indicators, and input-output analyses. Since TVK pays special attention to developments contributing to sustainability, it measures the percentage of the realization of such investments together with their average level of preparedness.

For the integrated evaluation of corporate sustainability performance the Sustainability Balanced

Scorecard is used. Apart from this, the company examines its compliance with the requirements of the GRI, its position in the ranking of sustainability and corporate social responsibility, and it also appears in the definition of the Dow Jones Sustainability Index and the Oekom Research index.

4. TVK's sustainability accounts and reports:

From the above, it is obvious that TVK is committed to sustainability and communicates its achievements to the stakeholders. An annual report is issued on the company's sustainability performance. Although monthly and quarterly reports are issued for to the board of directors, they usually focus on the financial situation of the company, lacking any social and environmental information. The evaluation of sustainability investments and projects is an exception, provided that they report whether their realization is carried out in due time, in the required quality and below the originally approved budget.

The company developed a standard form for its reports, ensuring the comparability of its accounts. In terms of economic and financial issues, detailed information can be found in the Annual Report, while more can be read about the company's sustainability performance in its Report on Sustainable Development. It has to be emphasized that the company's Annual Report also includes data reflecting its sustainable performance in an integrated way.

5. The qualitative characteristics of information on sustainability:

By providing as much detailed and accurate industry-specific information as possible, TVK aspires to the greatest level of transparency in order to minimize the risks related to the anticipated economic, social and environmental changes and developments, and to ensure the comparability of the results. Therefore, the accounting information on its sustainability performance has to be relevant, complete, comparable, accurate, timely, clear and reliable and they equally have to be concerned with both the positive and negative effects (a balance should be sought after), they have to be in line with the stakeholders' expectations, and they have to present sustainability connections as well. As a summary of the above, a logical model of TVK's sustainability accounting system is shown in Figure 2.

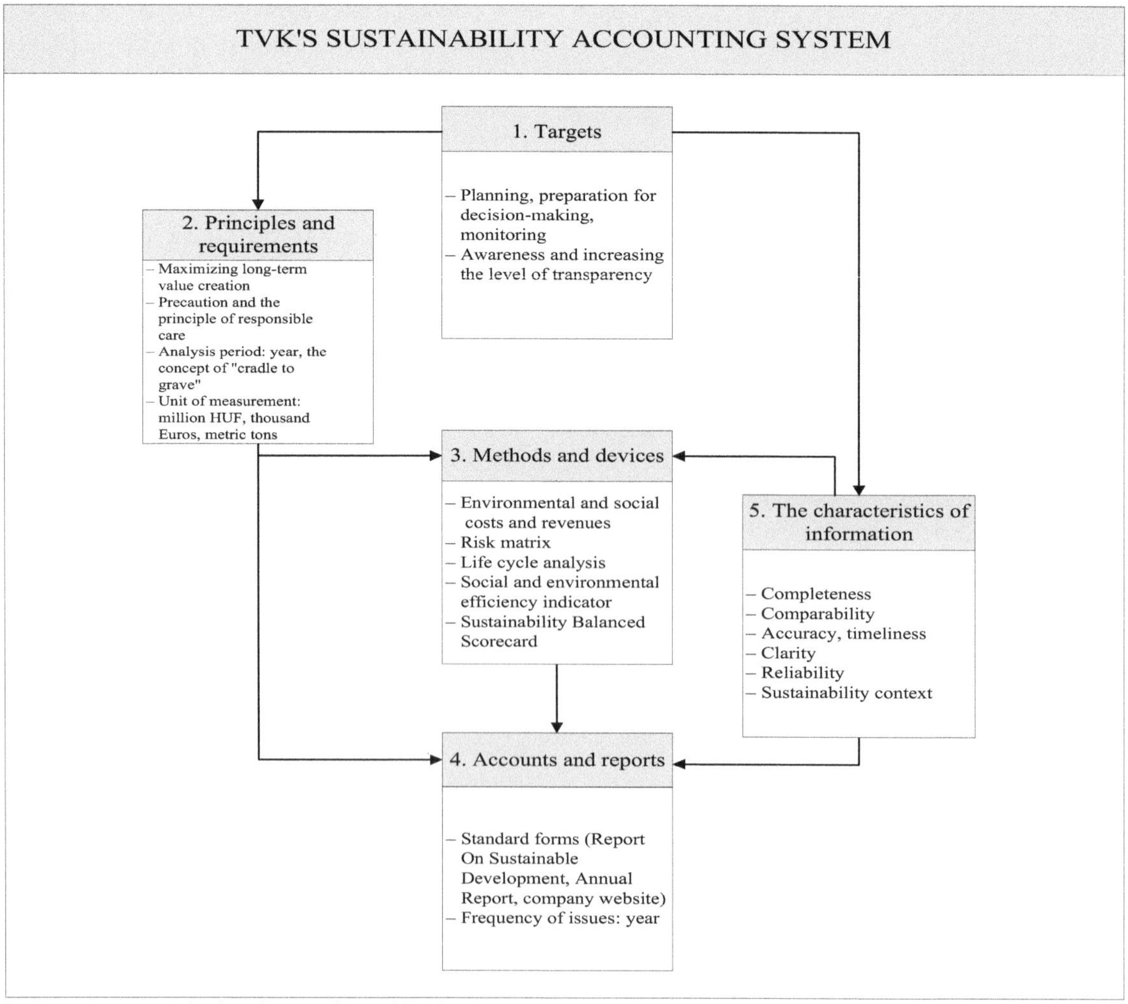

Source: own construction based on Lamberton (2005)

Figure 2. The logical framework of TVK's sustainability accounting system

The Benefits of Operating Sustainability Accounting Systems

Sustainability accounting systems must primarily meet the needs of those demanding the information. Accordingly, the function of a sustainability accounting system is to identify, collect, analyze, and communicate feedback on the company's economic, social and environmental performance. TVK's sustainability accounting systems provide appropriate, reliable and real information on the sustainability results of the company. Apart from supporting managerial decision-making, the information provided by sustainability accounting systems can also be utilized in other areas that give a basis for reports on sustainability. The major corporate as well as micro- and macro-environmental benefits resulting from operating the sustainability accounting system of the investigated company are summarized in Table 2.

Table 2
The benefits of operating sustainability accounting systems

Corporate benefits	Micro- and macro-environmental benefits
– Presents the impact of sustainability performance on balance sheet earnings – Maps cost-saving opportunities, revenues and financial advantages originating from sustainability -oriented operation – Evaluates, handles and reduces social and environmental risks, liabilities, cost and expenses – Creates more favourable conditions in the course of economic or investment negotiations, widens the range of potential investors – Helps to determine the cost of production as well as set the price of a product more accurately – Supports establishing cleaner production projects, the evaluation of investments (by mapping the social and environmental effects of investment decisions) – Facilitates appearance on the list of 'eco' suppliers – Facilitates tracing energy and material flows more accurately, contributing to increased resource efficiency – Helps the management to make responsible decisions – Fosters the social and environmental awareness of employees while performing their tasks and strengthens their commitment and motivation	– Satisfies the information needs of external users – Makes better relationships with the stakeholders – Ensures and improves the legitimacy, credibility and the reputation of the company – The public recognizes corporate accountability, transparency and trustworthiness in social and environmental issues, thus improving the company's general acceptance – Facilitates the comparability of the company's sustainability performance to other companies or industrial sectors – Promotes the application and improvement of sustainability accounting by acquiring knowledge on the best practices – Contributes to sustainable development on a corporate, national and global level

Source: Fülöp and Hódi Hernádi, 2013

RESULTS AND SUGGESTIONS FOR FURTHER RESEARCH

The novelty of the paper could be summarized as follows:

- The comprehensive overview of the developing phases of the accounting in the last two decades from the aspect of to what extent the system integrates the principles of the sustainability into itself: traditional accounting (economic factors), environmental accounting (economic and environmental factors), and sustainability accounting (economic, environmental and social factors).
- The comparison of the characteristics of the different accounting information systems (dimensions, target, field of application, method, unit of measurement, forms of accounts, regulation strictness) in order to support the selection of the measures and tools.
- The specification and introduction of a logical model of sustainability accounting system (targets, principles and requirements, methods and devices, form and content features of the information).
- The classification of the company, micro- and macro-environmental benefits of the system.

Obviously, all of this can contribute to complying with the different kinds of quality expectations the companies are facing.

These results, of course, can be regarded as the initial steps of a fresh research project that needs further specification on both theoretical and practical perspective in the future. The following research tasks are needed to achieve these goals:

- Practical application of the conceptual model of a sustainability accounting system.
- The clarification of the impact of the sustainability accounting information supply to the decision makers on the sustainability performance of the company.
- Carrying out further domestic and international case studies for the more explicit illustration of the interactions between quality and sustainability with the application of a sustainability accounting system.

Acknowledgements

This research was (partially) carried out in the framework of the Center of Excellence of Mechatronics and Logistics at the University of Miskolc.

REFERENCES

ACT C of 2000 on Accounting, Hungary, net.jogtar.hu/jr/gen/hjegy_doc.cgi?docid=A0000100.TV

ALMÁSSY, D.: Zöld számvitel (Green Accounting). In: PÁL, T. (Ed.) (2006): Számviteli rendszerek (Accounting Systems). Miskolc, Economix Kiadó

ARAS, G. & CROWTHER, D. (2008): Evaluating Sustainability: a Need for Standards. Social and Environmental Accounting, Vol. 2, No. 1, Pp. 19-35

BEBBINGTON, J. & GRAY, R. (2001). An account of sustainability: Failure, success and a reconceptualization. Critical Perspectives on Accounting, 12, 557-587.

BURRITT, R. & SCHALTEGGER, S. (2010): Sustainability Accounting and Reporting: Fad or Trend?, Accounting, Auditing & Accountability Journal, Vol. 23, No. 7, pp. 829-846.

BRUNDTLAND GH. (1987): Our Common Future. World Commission on Environment and Development, Brussels

CSUTORA, M. & KEREKES, S. (2004): A környezetbarát vállalatirányítás eszközei (Tools of Eco-friendly Business Management). KJK-KERSZÖV, Budapest

DEBNATH, S., BOSE, S.K. & DHALLA, R.S. (2012): Environmental Management Accounting: An Overview of its Methodological Development, International Journal of Business Insights and Transformation, Vol. 5, No. 1, pp. 44-57

DYLLICK, T. & HOCKERTS, K. (2002): Beyond the Business Case for Corporate Sustainability. Business Strategy and the Environment, No.11, pp. 130-141

FAMA, E.E. & JENSEN, M. C. (1983): Separation of Ownership and Control. Journal of Law and Economics, No.3, pp. 301-325

FREEMAN, R. E. (1984): Strategic Management. A Stakeholder Approach. Pitman, New-York

FÜLÖP, GY. & HÓDI HERNÁDI, B. (2012): Corporate Sustainability – Strategic Alternatives And Methodology – Implementation. Management, Knowledge and Learning International Conference, 20-22 June 2012, Celje, Slovenia, pp. 109-120

FÜLÖP, GY. & HÓDI HERNÁDI, B. (2013): Sustainability Accounting: A Success Factor in Corporate Sustainability Strategy. International Sciencific Conference "New Challenges of Economic and Business Development", 08-11 May 2013, Riga, Latvia, pp. 229-241

GLOBAL REPORTING INITIATIVE (GRI). (2002). Sustainability reporting guidelines. Boston.

GRAY, R. (1993): Accounting for the Environment. Chapman: London

HÓDI HERNÁDI, B. (2012): Green Accounting for Corporate Sustainability. Theory, Methodology, Practice Vol. 8., Nr. 2., pp. 23-30.

ILLÉS M. (2002): Vezetői gazdaságtan (Managerial Economics). Kossuth Kiadó, Budapest

INSTITUTE FOR DEVELOPMENT AND METHODOLOGY, STATE AUDIT OFFICE OF HUNGARY (2005): A környezettudatos gazdálkodás és a fenntartható fejlődés a szabályozás és az ellenőrzés tapasztalatinak tükrében (Environmental Management and Sustainable Development in the Light of Experience of Regulation and Control). Report., Budapest

JASCH, C. & LAVICKA, A. (2006): Pilot project on sustainability management accounting with the Styrian automobile cluster, Journal of Cleaner Production 14, pp. 1214-1227

KEREKES S. & WETZKER K. (2007): Keletre tart a „társadalmilag felelős vállalat" koncepció ("Socially Responsible Company" Concept Goes to East). Harvard Business Review, 4. sz.

LAMBERTON, G. (2005): Sustainability accounting - A brief history and conceptual framework. Accounting Forum, 29(1): 7–26.

MUSINSZKI, Z. (2012): Kontrolling (Controlling). Oktatási segédlet, Miskolc

NGWAKWE, C. C. (2012): Rethinking the Accounting Stance on Sustainable Development. Sustainable Development, 20, pp. 28–41

PÁL, T. (2011): Innovatív számviteli rendszerek (Innovative Accounting System), Miskolci Egyetemi Kiadó, Miskolc

SCHALTEGGER, S., BENNETT, M. & BURRITT, R.: Sustainability Accounting and Reporting: Development, Linkages, and Reflection. An Introduction. In: SCHALTEGGER, S., BENNETT, M. & BURRITT, R. (Eds.) (2006): Sustainability Accounting and Reporting. Dordrecht, Springer, pp.1-35

SCHALTEGGER, S., & BURRITT, R. L. (2000): Contemporary environmental accounting: Issues, concepts and practice. Sheffield: Greenleaf Publishing.
SCHALTEGGER, S. & BURRITT, R. (2010): Sustainability accounting for companies: Catchphrase or decision support for business leaders? Journal of World Business, 45, pp. 375-384
SIGMA (2003): The SIGMA guidelines—Toolkit. Stakeholder engagement tool. London: The SIGMA Project
SZLÁVIK J. (2007): Environmental Economics (Környezetgazdaságtan). Budapest: Typotex Kiadó.
TVK (2013): Sustainability Report, Annual Report. Tiszaújváros
YAKHOU, M. & DORWEILER, V.P. (2004): Environmental accounting: an essential component of business strategy. Business Strategy and Environment, Vol. 13, pp. 65-66.

3

Intellectual Capital Valuation and Stock Market Performance in an Era of Financial Turmoil: Blue Chip Banks Listed in Stock Exchanges of the Visegrad Countries

JAROSLAW GODYN

e-mail: jarekgodyn@gmail.com

SUMMARY

The core purpose of this empirical study is to investigate the influence of intellectual capital on stock market performance of the Visegrad countries in era of financial turmoil. This study is prompted by increasing evidence that the major drivers of value creation focus on a firm's intangible assets rather than its physical tangibles. In this quantitative analysis, nine listed large banks concentrated in particular national stock exchanges in Prague, Budapest, Warsaw and Bratislava are investigated. The study uses empirical data from Bloomberg Terminal Platform for data management that cover 2006-2012 and Intellectual Capital methods based on market capitalization.

Keywords: Banking sector, financial crisis, valuation, stock exchange, intellectual capital.

INTRODUCTION

The financial crisis emerged in the summer 2007, and a year later, with the bankruptcy of the investment bank Lehman Brothers, in the present decade the apogee of panic was reached. It was an unprecedented event in the history of the postwar economy, and had huge implications for the global financial environment. The financial crisis showed the weakness of financial institutions in most developed countries. Fundamental credit condition problems in the region led to pressure on bank capitalization and profitability. Banks had to face real financing problem and roll up their own short-term debt. The examples of financial institutions embroiled in the process of mortgage securitization and securities trading with negative consequences started to cross the geographical borders of the United States. The rapid drop in the US housing market was the trigger for spreading the influence of the crisis to other areas where assets were held. It became obvious that the subprime crisis had transformed into a banking crises and started to steadily infect other assets, not only in developed western countries but in emerging markets as well. The scale of the crisis reached a global dimension, no matter what kind of liberal or conservative policy was dominating in particular markets.

Aalbers (2009) pointed that crisis started in 2007 when credit indicators on the US real estate market began to creep up, accompanied by the fall of prices. The increasing interest rates bit by bit swept away the frontier of the solvency of households and over time they became massively insolvent. The subprime mortgage securities depreciated while more credit institutions went bankrupt or posted large losses. Large credit institutions of the United States such as Citigroup, Merrill Lynch, Goldman Sachs and Morgan Stanley suffered billions of dollars in losses by the end of 2007.

Then a dramatic turn occurred: in 2008 real estate prices in the US dropped by 20% and in some cities the fallen was up to 30%. According to Egedy (2012), another problem was that rating firms were closely intertwined with lending companies like banks, which led to the confusing situation that rating agencies often rated their own decisions. Financial speculation and panic due to deterioration of the situation also became factors in the outbreak of the global fiscal crisis. A similar point of view was presented by Akerlof and Schiller (2009), who pointed out that speculation on the financial markets was the main reason for the crisis. Bookstaber (2007) and Authers (2010) emphasized that problems caused by the crisis lie, on the one hand, in institutional structures and lack of control, and in the weaknesses of state institutions on the banking system and, on the other hand, in the wide-spread misconception that such long-established, large institutions do not go bankrupt.

THE INTELLECTUAL CAPITAL CONCEPT

There is increasing evidence that the major drivers of value creation in present decade focus on a firm's intangible assets rather than its physical tangibles. Over the last three decades the concept of intellectual capital has become popular among many researchers. Even today, after so many years of investigation, there is no universally accepted definition of Intellectual Capital (IC). For instance, Edvinsson and Sullivan (1996) define Intellectual Capital as knowledge that can be converted into value. From the perspective of Hunter et al. (2005), who categorize IC as a subset of Intangible Capital, the term intangible refers to assets that do not exist physically, and capital relates to assets retained by the organization to contribute to future profits. On the other hand Ross and Ross (1997) define IC as all the processes and the assets which are not normally shown on the balance sheet, as well as all the identifiable intangible assets which may be observed on balance sheets, like trademark, patents and brands.

It is often emphasized that the essence of intellectual capital is based on three pillars: human capital, organizational capital and relation capital with customers and business partners. False illusion lies in the belief that knowledge alone is sufficient to gain an advantage. Knowledge is just the source to achieve the possibility of transformation of potential included in the three pillars into real value for the company. Then we can assume that the formation of intellectual capital in that way becomes the most precious resource in the entire company's assets, making the possibility for the creation of a competitive advantage in the market.

In order to describe the role of IC, Edvinsson and Malone (1997) compared organizations to a tree, observing that both are living organisms with corresponding elements. Available financial documents are represented in the visible components of the tree like leaves and fruit. Assuming that this represents the true nature of the tree, or even of its future health, is misleading. In fact, the root system significantly determines the future health of the tree. According to Stewart (1991) IC is one part of a revolution. Within this radical era of transition to a knowledge economy, information replaces working capital, and intellectual assets replace physical ones. We are now in an era in which natural resources and physical labor have largely been replaced by knowledge and communication as the fundamental sources of wealth. Intellectual Capital is the most important value driver in companies. Additionally Nonaka and Takeuchi (1995), emphasize that a company cannot establish a sustainable competitive advantage without proper knowledge management.

THE CONCEPTUAL FRAMEWORK

The conceptual framework of the present study is to investigate the relationship between Intellectual Capital valuation and the stock market performance of large listed banks in the stock exchanges of the Visegrad countries during the global financial turmoil. Previous investigations and empirical results of studies exploring the connection of IC and stock market performance were inconclusive, as I will discuss later. The second aim of this study is to analyze how the global crisis has affected stock market performance and intellectual capital value. This research focuses only on large listed banks from Visegrad countries for various reasons: the banking sectors in these countries have undergone a major restructuring process in the transition from a centralized to a market economy system. Banking systems in these countries share high levels of foreign bank penetration due to strong economic and financial integration with the advanced European countries. Finally, during the crisis their banking systems became highly susceptible to deepening European debt and the banking crisis.

The basic ambition was to extend the actual empirical studies about IC and the stock exchange and focus particularly on some large banks from countries that are less penetrated and investigated. That is why my basic research question is whether the Intellectual Capital value change of listed banking blue chips from the Visegrad countries affects their stock market performance during global financial turmoil.

The first step in my research is to determine the appropriate indicators of IC valuation among all available that correspond to market capitalization and return on assets and then analyze the empirical results. The hypothesis was defined as follows:

H1: The Intellectual Capital value change of listed banking blue chips from Visegrad countries, affect their stock market performance during global financial turmoil.

For hypothesis-testing purpose I use methods that are based on market capitalization and return on assets. I decided to use the VAIC methodology (Pulic 2000), MVA methodology (Stewart 1990) and MV/BV ratio (Stewart 1997). All information for the application of these methodologies is available in the companies' accounts and public databases. This research uses quantitative analysis and is based on empirical data from Bloomberg Terminal Platform for data management that cover the period of time from 2006 to 2012.

The empirical analysis is undertaken for the four Visegrad banking sectors over the period 2006 to 2012 and involves nine listed blue chip banks: FHB Mortgage Bank Co Plc, OTP Bank, OTP Banka Slovensko, Všeobecná ůverová banka, Komerčni banka, Bank Handlowy S.A., Bre Bank S.A., Pekao S.A., and PKO BP S.A. A blue chip company refers to large and creditworthy company, well established that has financial strength, stability and good history of dividend payments to investors. According to New York Stock Exchange Gropu Inc. (2011) blue chip stock is stock in company with national reputation for quality, reliability and the ability to operate profitably in good times and bad.

RESEARCH METHODOLOGY

Bearing in mind that research is focusing on companies listed on the stock exchange from the banking sector, the research methodology needed to consider the specification of bank's financial statements and data availability. There is no universally accepted IC measurement and evaluation method. Sveiby (2007) categorizes the methods into four groups: market capitalization methods, direct IC measurement methods, scorecard approaches and economic value added approaches. Based on the research of Sledzik, Czerwinska et al. (2010), there is a group of IC valuation methods selected by experts as the most applicable and best suited to the purpose of research. Among them the highest scores were assigned to the following methods: MVA (190), KCE (170), MV/BV (140), VAIC (130), CIV (105) and EVA (65).

Market Value to Book Value Ratio

The Market Value to Book Value ratio (MV/BV) was proposed by Stewart (1997) and is based on conception that intellectual capital is the difference between a company's market value and its book value (Gutherie, 2001). According to the suggestions of Urbanek (2008), construction of the ratio is as follows:

$$MV/BV = \frac{price\_of\_shares\_x\_number\_of\_shares}{assets\_-\_debt\_capital} \quad (1)$$

$$MV/BV = \frac{market\_value}{book\_value} \quad (2)$$

Market value is calculated by multiplication of the actual market price of the shares and the total number of shares, whereas book value is calculated by looking at the firm's historical cost according to the financial statement, in line with accounting rules. This method has been criticized because IC value is determined by accounting policy and the volatility of market price of equity in some circumstances may reflect the mood of investors and be the results of panic. However, the ease of calculation and data availability is making this method one of the most used tools to evaluate IC among others. Further, Ghosh and Wu (2007) identify the market-to-book value ratio (MV/BV) as a proxy measure for measuring the investor response.

Market Value Added

The MVA concept was presented by Stern Stewart & Co. in the beginning of the 1990s. It measures the difference between the market value of the firm and the amount of capital invested. According to Shil (2009) when total market value of a company is more than the amount of capital invested in it, the company has managed to create shareholder value. If the market value is less than capital invested, the company has destroyed shareholder value. The construction of the ratio is as follows:

$$\text{Market Value Added} = \text{Company's total Market Value} - \text{Capital Invested} \quad (3)$$

With the simplifying assumption that market and book value of debt are equal, this is the same as:

$$\text{Market Value Added} = \text{Market Value of equity} - \text{Book value of equity} \quad (4)$$

Further, Thenmozhi (2000) identifies market value added as being identical in meaning to the market-to-book ratio. The difference is only that MVA is an absolute measure and market-to-book ratio is a relative measure. According to Stewart (1994), market value added tells us how much value the company has added to, or subtracted from, its shareholders investment. Successful companies add their MVA and thus increase the value of capital invested in the company. Unsuccessful companies decrease the value of the capital originally invested in the company. The biggest disadvantage of this method is the simplification that intellectual capital value is just the difference between market and book value and in some cases could be negative.

Value Added of Intellectual Coefficient

According to its founder, this methodology shows the abilities of a company in value creation and represents a measure for business efficiency in a knowledge-based economy (Pulic, 1998). VAIC was designed to provide a means by which to measure the efficiency of three types of inputs: physical and financial capital, human capital, and structural capital (Pulic, 2000).

The model has been explored and explained by various approaches to the research application of the model in various stages of the literature. For example, Bontis (2001), made an extrapolation on the theory of reasoned action with additional variables leading to an action theory model of consumption. Additionally, Wang and Chang (2005) classify intellectual capital into four elements – human capital, customer capital, innovation capital and process capital – and relate these elements to the performance of the firm. Further, Chen et al. (2004) found a significant relationship between the scores of the four IC elements and the business performance of firms, providing evidence of the validity and rationality of the VAIC model and the qualitative index system.

According to Sledzik, Czerwinska et al. (2010), the main advantage of the VAIC ratio is the simplicity of the calculation and the fact that all the necessary data are available in the financial statements of banks. In addition, the indicator allows a comparative analysis between companies operating in the same competitive sector and introduces basic standards for measuring the effectiveness of their activities. However, the VAIC ratio has been subjected to criticism. For example, Puntillo (2009) was unable to confirm the link between the variables involved. The only statistically significant correlation was found between CEE and business performance indicators. Further, Samiloglu (2006) found no significant relationship between the MV/BV coefficient and the VAIC model. The value added of intellectual coefficient can be written as follows (Pulic, 1998):

$$VAIC^{TM} = HCE + SCE + CEE \quad (5)$$

where VAIC = value added intellectual coefficient as an overall indicator of capital employed efficiency, HCE = indicator of human capital efficiency, SCE = indicator of structural capital efficiency and CEE = indicator of asset value efficiency.

The VAIC ratio is determined in five steps: (1) estimation of total value added VA, (2) determination of the human capital efficiency ratio HCE, (3) calculation of the efficiency ratio of structural capital SCE, (4) calculation of the capital employed efficiency ratio CEE, and finally (5) addition of the indicators listed in Steps 2, 3 and 4.

A company's value added VA is defined as a difference between sales outputs OUT, which represents sales, and inputs IN which includes all expenses except labor costs. The formula is as follows:

$$VA = OUT - IN \quad (6)$$

The next step is determining the human capital efficiency ratio HCE. It includes the company's value added and human capital HC, measured by yearly labor costs:

$$HCE = \frac{VA}{HC} \quad (7)$$

Later, we need to calculate the efficiency ratio of structural capital SCE, which includes structural capital SC and the company's value added. It can be written as follows:

$$SCE = \frac{SC}{VA} \quad (8)$$

where structural capital SC is defined as the difference between VA and HC.

The next to last step is calculation of the capital employed efficiency ratio CEE, which is the value added created by one unit of physical and financial capital of a company:

$$CCE = \frac{VA}{CE} \quad (9)$$

Last but not least, we add HCE, SCE and CEE in order to obtain the result of the VAIC ratio.

Research Results

The conceptual framework of the present study was to investigate the relationship between IC value and the stock market performance of nine listed companies in the banking sector of the Visegrad countries between 2006 and 2012. Based on the research question, three major methodologies were selected as best suiting the purposes of the research: MV/BV ratio, Market Value Added, and Value Added of Intellectual Coefficient.

Methodology Results of Measuring Intellectual Capital by MV/BV Ratio

The Market Value to Book Value ratio, calculated by multiplication of the actual market price of the shares and total number of shares by the book value of shares, is one of the most commonly used methods by researchers to present the evidence of intellectual capital in the company. Values of the MV/BV ratio for the nine investigated banks over the period of 2006-2012 are shown in Table 1.

In terms of ratio MV/BV value was the highest for the whole group of investigated banks in 2006 and 2007, before the global financial crisis had reached its apogee in 2008. Among the best performing in 2006 were PKO BP (4.66), Pekao (4.26) and FHB Mortgage Bank (4.17).

The lowest values in the same year were recorded for Bank Handlowy (2.09), Komercni Banka (2.37) and OTP Banka Slovensko (2.65).

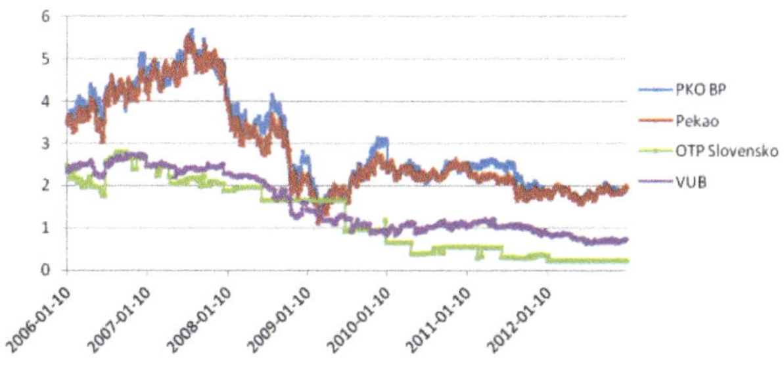

source: own calculations based on data from Bloomberg Terminal Platform

Figure 1. The best and worst performing banks by MV/BV ratio values in 2006-2012

Table 1
MV/BV values for investigated banks, 2006-2012

No.	Bank	Country	2006	2007	2008	2009	2010	2011	2012
1	FHB Mortgage Bank Co Plc	Hungary	4.17	3.81	1.11	1.09	1.06	0.57	0.50
2	OTP Bank	Hungary	2.92	2.76	0.77	1.29	1.08	0.64	0.79
3	OTP Banka Slovensko	Slovakia	2.65	1.86	1.64	1.17	0.53	0.32	0.20
4	Vseobecna Uverova Banka	Slovakia	2.71	2.27	1.57	0.84	1.06	0.87	0.72
5	Komercni Banka A.S.	Czech Rep.	2.37	3.34	1.82	2.21	2.25	1.60	1.55
6	Bank Handlowy S.A.	Poland	2.09	2.33	1.11	1.47	1.88	1.38	1.74
7	BRE Bank S.A.	Poland	3.92	4.50	1.50	1.87	1.85	1.29	1.42
8	Pekao S.A.	Poland	4.26	4.05	2.07	2.32	2.33	1.74	1.97
9	PKO BP S.A.	Poland	4.66	4.41	2.54	2.32	2.54	1.76	1.94
	mean		3.31	3.26	1.57	1.62	1.62	1.13	1.20
	standard deviation		0.89	0.93	0.51	0.54	0.66	0.51	0.62

source: own calculations based on data from Bloomberg Terminal Platform

The panic on the stock exchange occurred in 2008 due to financial instability related to mortgage credit, the growth of uncertainty and the bankruptcy of Lehman Brothers Bank in the US. The average MV/BV ratio in 2008 decreased by 52% compared to 2007, from 3.26 to 1.57. However the high volatility on the market and stock price drop did not yet result in the worst value of the ratio; the lowest MV/BV ratio was recorded in 2011 (mean 1.13) and for some banks one year later. Among the banks in 2011 with the weakest results over the whole period were OTP Bank (0.64), BRE Bank (1.29), Pekao (1.74) and PKO BP (1.76). In 2012 the weakest results over the period 2006-2012 were experienced by OTP Banka Slovensko (0.20), FHB Mortgage Bank (0.50), Vseobecna Uverova Banka (0.72) and Komercni Banka (1.55). There is only one example of a bank which recorded its lowest MV/BV ratio in 2008 compared to other years (Handlowy Bank, at 1.11).

After the peak of the financial crisis for all investigated banks, the value of MB/BV ratio was no higher than at the beginning of the research period in 2006-2007. Furthermore, the mean value of MV/BV ratio at the end of 2012 was lower by 64% than in 2006 and 63% lower than in 2007.

On examining the relationship between MV/BV ratio and share price it is found that all banks except for Komercni Banks ($r = 0.3922$) showed a high correlation with the average being $r = 0.7239$. Among banks with high correlation were: OTP Bank ($r = 0.8391$), Vseobecna Uverova Banka ($r = 0.8390$), OTP Banka Slovensko ($r = 0.8333$), Peako ($r = 0.7918$), FHB Mortgage Bank ($r = 0.7878$), Bank Handlowy ($r = 0.7557$), PKO BP ($r = 0.6712$) and BRE Bank ($r = 0.6045$).

Methodology Results of Measuring Intellectual Capital by MVA Ratio

Market Value Added is essentially the difference between the company's current market value, as determined by its stock price, and its economic book value. The MVA of selected banks shows that at the end of 2006 and 2007 all investigated banks had positive MVA, as given in Table 2.

Table 2
MVA values of selected banks in million EUR, 2006-2012

	2006	2007	2008	2009	2010	2011	2012
FHB Mortgage Bank	430.74	362.09	40.11	73.27	172.41	-3.90	-87.49
OTP Bank	6 662.85	6 314.11	-880.84	1 268.07	368.04	-1 624.35	-1 005.19
OTP Banka Slovensko	142.00	90.00	67.00	15.00	-41.00	-60.00	-91.00
Vseobecna Uverova	1 073.00	992.00	350.00	-156.00	59.00	-147.00	-320.00
Komercni Banka	2 474.97	4 461.15	2 104.99	3 334.42	3 672.82	1 850.93	2 389.07
Bank Handlowy S.A.	1 543.73	2 116.00	155.78	717.96	1 444.00	543.63	1 438.16
BRE Bank S.A.	1 920.09	3 268.82	467.58	877.04	1 484.11	516.76	1 120.88
Pekao S.A.	7 551.34	14 093.74	4 123.80	5 878.87	6 758.07	3 532.01	5 306.25
PKO BP S.A.	9 623.12	11 525.16	5 196.17	6 595.12	8 282.04	3 879.50	5 476.53
mean	3 491.32	4 802.56	1 291.62	2 067.08	2 466.61	943.06	1 580.80

source: own calculations based on data from Bloomberg Terminal Platform

The intellectual capital represented by MVA ratio was the highest in 2007, with the average value of 4.8 billion EUR. Pekao S.A., PKO BP and OTP Bank were the top three companies by MVA value, with more than 30bln of EUR. An year later the average value of MVA decreased by 73%, from 4.8 to 1.3 billion EUR. Each year in the period of 2008 and 2010 only one bank showed negative MVA each year, consecutively OTP Bank, Vseobecna Uverova Banka and OTP Banka Slovensko.

During the year 2011 and 2012 four banks – FHB Mortgage Bank, OTP Bank, OTP Banka Slovensko and Vseobecna Uverova Banka – had negative MVA and depreciated it's shareholder value. The lowest average value of MVA was recorded at the end of 2011, with the value of 943 million EUR, decreased by 80%, compared to 4.8 billion in 2007. There were five banks – Komercni Banka, Bank Handlowy, BRE Bank, Pekao and PKO BP – that experienced positive MVA value each year over the period 2006-2012. The biggest contributions to the total value of MVA were made by PKO BP, Pekao, Komercni Banka, BRE Bank, Bank Handlowy, as shown in Figure 2.

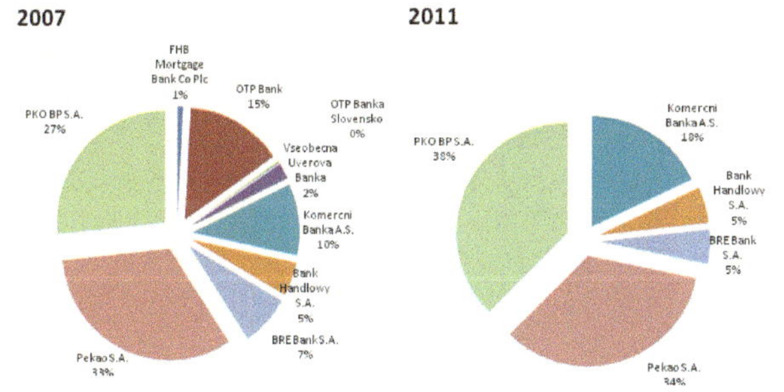

source: own calculations based on data from Bloomberg Terminal Platform

Figure 2. Percentage share of MVA values for investigated banks in 2007 and 2011

In 2007 all investigated banks participated in the creation of total MVA value, with the shares holding adequately by Pekao S.A. (33%), PKO BP (27%), OTP Bank (15%), Komercni Banka (10%), BRE Bank (7%), Bank Handlowy (5%) and the rest with less than 4%. The top three banks – Pekao S.A., PKO BP and OTP Bank – aggregated three quarters of the total MVA value in 2007, while in 2011 the top three held around 90% (PKO BP, Pekao S.A. and Komercni Banka).

The total MVA value between 2011 and 2007 decreased by 34.7 billion EUR, from 43.2 to 8.5 billion EUR. The biggest slumps were experienced by OTP Banka Slovensko (-167%), OTP Bank (-126%), Vseobecna Uverova Banka (-115%) and FHB Mortgage Bank (-101%). In contrast, the other banks kept a positive MVA value in 2011, despite decreases in MVA value: Komercni Banka (-58%), PKO BP (-66%), Bank Handlowy (-74%), Pekao (-75%), and BRE Bank (-84%).

On examining the relationship between MVA and share price of company it was found that share price is highly correlated to MVA, ranging from 0.6465 to 0.8491. For the investigated banks, the correlations were as follows: FHB Mortgage Bank (0.7987), OTP Bank (0.8415), OTP Banka Slovensko (0.8386), Vseobecna Uverova Banka (0.8491), Komercni Banka (0.6465), Bank Handlowy (0.8323), BRE Bank (0.7869), Pekao (0.7098), and PKO BP (0.8359).

Methodology Results of Measuring Intellectual Capital by VAIC Ratio

The biggest advantage of this method is that data for calculation can be found in financial statements. In general, the larger the size of VAIC ratio for the selected bank, the better efficiency in the use of capital employed, human capital, structural capital and better value added size. The results of VAIC ratio for the investigated banks in 2006-2012 are presented below.

Table 3

The Value Added of Intellectual Coefficient (VAIC) ratio for investigated banks in 2006-2012

No.	Bank	Country	2006	2007	2008	2009	2010	2011	2012*
1	FHB Mortgage Bank Co Plc	Hungary	4.09	3.72	7.08	7.80	12.01	9.51	5.22
2	OTP Bank	Hungary	4.45	4.08	3.79	3.29	3.14	2.96	-
3	OTP Banka Slovensko	Slovakia	2.56	2.64	2.85	1.94	1.58	2.08	1.64
4	Vseobecna Uverova Banka	Slovakia	4.13	4.37	4.42	3.80	4.10	4.28	-
5	Komercni Banka A.S.	Czech Rep.	4.87	5.21	4.95	4.35	4.66	3.61	4.45
6	Bank Handlowy S.A.	Poland	3.75	3.59	3.05	2.89	3.37	3.29	3.73
7	BRE Bank S.A.	Poland	3.53	3.74	3.95	2.28	3.35	4.11	4.07
8	Pekao S.A.	Poland	4.08	4.05	4.41	3.79	6.17	6.41	6.53
9	PKO BP S.A.	Poland	3.44	3.90	3.95	3.35	3.92	4.24	4.04
		mean	3.88	3.92	4.27	3.72	4.70	4.50	4.24

source: own calculations

* For 2012 two banks had not reported their audited annual reports by the point when data was gathered.

On examining the relationship between VAIC ratio and the share price of company it was found that share price is moderately correlated to the value of VAIC ratio, in a range from -0.4307 to 0.6653. Correlations for the investigated banks are as follows: FHB Mortgage Bank (-0.4307), OTP Bank (0.6473), OTP Banka Slovensko (0.6653), Vseobecna Uverova Banka (0.3704), Komercni Banka (0.1376), Bank Handlowy (0.6594), BRE Bank (0.1327), Pekao (-0.3153), and PKO BP (- 0.3067).

The leaders in terms of the efficient use of capital invested in the bank in 2006 include the PKO BP (CEE = 0.52), OTP Bank (CEE = 0.45) and BRE Bank (CEE = 0.46). The lowest values of CEE in the same year were recorded for Bank Handlowy (CEE = 0.27), OTP Banka

Slovensko (CEE = 0.32) and FHB Mortgage Bank (CEE = 0.36). The efficient use of capital invested for the period of research is shown in Figure 3.

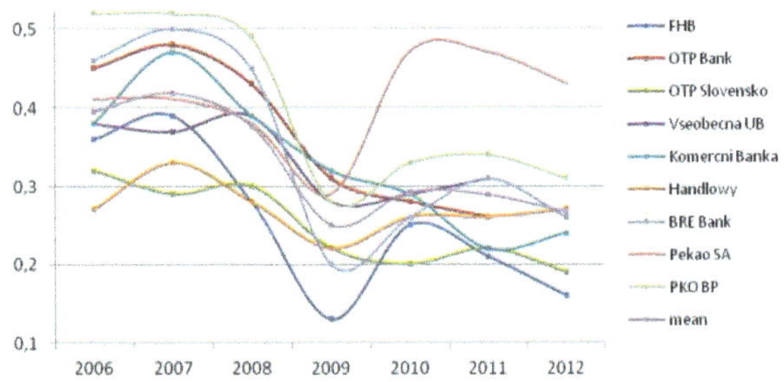

source: own calculations

Figure 3. Capital Employed Efficiency (CEE) ratio for investigated banks, 2006-2012

All tested banks recorded a decrease in the efficient use of capital invested from the peak of 2006-2007 to the bottom, in 2009. Some of the investigated banks have even continued the negative trend to the end of 2012, such as Komercni Banka and OTP Banka Slovensko, and OTP Bank to the end of 2011. The banks recording the biggest slump were FHB Mortgage Bank (-64%), BRE Bank (-56%), PKO BP (-46%), and Pekao SA (-29%) over the period 2006-2009. The major reason was due to the growth of capital employed over the value added between 2006 and 2009. The average value and median value of CEE over the period 2006-2012 amounted to 0.33 and 0.2, respectively.

The highest efficiency of human capital in 2006 was shown by Komercni Banka (HCE = 3.75), OTP Bank (HCE = 3.30) and Vseobecna Uverova (HCE = 3.08). The lowest HCE ratios in the same year were recorded by OTP Banka Slovensko (HCE = 1.80), PKO BP (HCE = 2.34) and BRE Bank (HCE = 2.47).

The values of the structural capital efficiency (SCE) ratio of the investigated banks in the period 2006-2012 are presented in Figure 4.

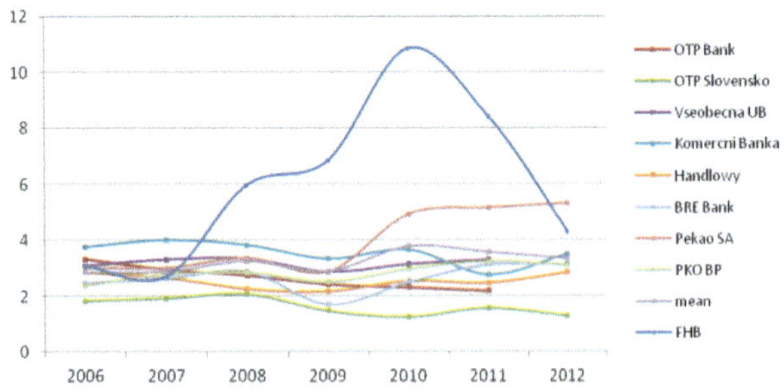

source: own calculations

Figure 4. Structural capital efficiency (SCE) ratio of investigated banks, 2006-2012

Regarding the HCE ratio, values have been stable and smooth for the majority of banks over the period 2006-2012 because of low volatile human capital values. The case of FHB Mortgage Bank is an exception, mainly due to a rapid decline of 58% in human capital between 2007 and 2008, but it began to rise again from 2011. The least volatile HCE ratio among banks were Vseobecna Uverova, with a coefficient of variation of 0.052, and Handlowy (CV = 0.098). The most volatile HCE ratios were found for FHB Mortgage Bank (CV = 0.455) and Pekao (CV = 0.264).

The highest efficiency of human capital in 2012 was found for Pekao SA (HCE = 5.29), FHB Mortgage Bank (HCE = 4.29) and Komercni Banka (HCE = 3.50). Most of the investigated banks improved their HCE ratio in 2012 compared to 2006.

A deterioration of HCE ratio was observed for OTP Bank of (-34%), OTP Slovensko (-30%), Komercni Banka (-7%) and Handlowy (below 1%). The mean value of the HCE ratio was the highest for all banks in last three years, between 2010-2012, and was HCE = 3.77, HCE = 3.56 and HCE = 3.33, respectively. Even if we exclude FHB Mortgage Bank, the mean value in the period between 2010 and 2012 will be the highest. The lowest value of average human capital efficiency ratio, HCE = 2.39, occurred in 2009.

The values of the structural capital efficiency (SCE) ratio of banks in the period 2006-2012 are presented in Figure 5.

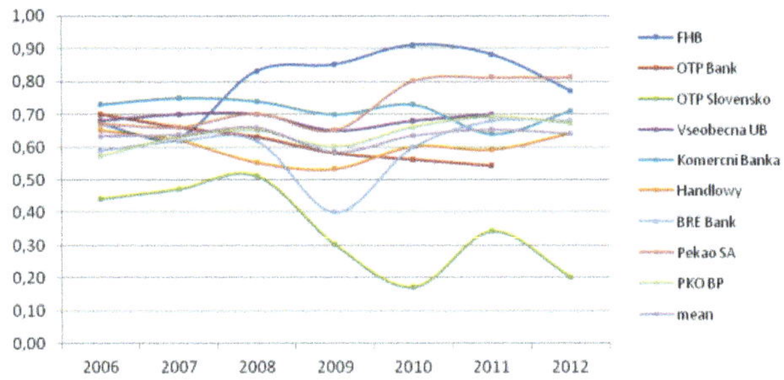

source: own calculations

Figure 5. Structural capital efficiency (SCE) ratio of investigated banks, 2006-2012

The highest SCE ratios in 2006 were noted for Komercni Banka (SCE = 0.73) and OTP Bank (SCE = 0.70). The lowest value of SCE was recorded in 2009 for OTP Slovensko (SCE = 0.30), BRE Bank (SCE = 0.40) and Handlowy (SCE = 0.53). The lowest average structural capital efficiency ratio, amounting to SCE = 0.35 over the period 2006-2012, was noted for OTP Slovensko due to its weak relation between value added and human capital value. In contrast, the highest average SCE ratios were recorded by FHB Mortgage Bank (SCE = 0.79) and Pekao SA (SCE = 0.73).

Most of the investigated banks noted a decrease in the SCE ratio between 2008 and 2009, except FHB Mortgage Bank, which reported a moderate growth of 2.41% year to year. On the other hand, BRE Bank and OTP Banka Slovensko noted the biggest drops in SCE ratio in 2009 compared to 2008, 35.48% and 41.18%, respectively.

CONCLUSIONS

This paper presents an investigation of the relationship between intellectual capital value and the stock market performance of nine companies listed on the stock exchange from the banking sector of the Visegrad countries between 2006 and 2012.

The methodology used in this study includes MV/BV ratio, MVA ratio and VAIC ratio for calculating IC. It was found that the relationship between the MV/BV ratio and share price is positively correlated between r = 0.3922 and r = 0.8391. All banks except for Komercni Banks (r = 0.3922) showed a high correlation with the average being r = 0.7239. The average MV/BV ratio in 2008 decreased by 52% compared to 2007, from 3.26 to 1.57. However the high volatility on the market and stock price drop did not yet result in the worst value of the ratio; the lowest MV/BV ratio was recorded in 2011 (mean 1.13) and for some banks one year later.

The intellectual capital represented by MVA ratio was the highest in 2007, with the average value of 4.8 billion EUR while an year later the average value of MVA decreased by 73%, from 4.8 to 1.3 billion EUR. Each year in the period of 2008 and 2010 only one bank showed negative MVA each year, consecutively OTP Bank, Vseobecna Uverova Banka and OTP Banka Slovensko.

Furthermore, the relationship between MVA and the share price of listed banks is even higher, correlated in a range from 0.6465 to 0.8491. In contrast, when testing the relationship between VAIC ratio and the share price of the bank, it was found that the share price is correlated to the value of VAIC ratio, ranging from -0.4307 to 0.6653. Those methods which correspond with market capitalization, like the MV/BV ratio and MVA, have shown a higher correlation in relation with intellectual capital value than the VAIC methodology. Negative correlations was investigated only for three banks as follows: FHB Mortgage Bank (-0.4307), Pekao (-0.3153), and PKO BP (-0.3067). All tested banks recorded a decrease in the efficient use of capital invested from the peak of 2006-2007 to the bottom, in 2009. Some of the investigated banks have even continued the negative trend to the end of 2012, such as Komercni Banka and OTP Banka Slovensko, and OTP Bank to the end of 2011. Regarding the human capital efficiency, values have been stable and smooth for the majority of banks over the period 2006-2012 because of low volatile human capital values. The case of FHB Mortgage Bank is an exception, mainly due to a rapid decline of 58% in human capital between 2007 and 2008, but it began to rise again from 2011. Most of the investigated banks noted a decrease in the structural capital efficiency between 2008 and 2009, except FHB Mortgage Bank, which reported a moderate growth of 2.41% year to year.

Nowadays, it is becoming clear that intellectual capital is a key hidden asset value of a company and represents the ability to obtain a competitive advantage.

REFERENCES

AALBERS, M. (2009).Geographies of the financial crisis. Area, 41 (1), pp. 34-42

AKERLOF, G., and SCHILLER, R. (2009). Animal Spirits: How human psychology drives the economy and why it matters for global capitalism. Princeton, N.J., Princeton University Press.

AUTHERS, J. (2010). The fearful rise of markets: Global bubbles, synchronized meltdowns, and how to prevent them in the future. Upper Saddle River, N.Y. FT Press.

Bloomberg Terminal Platform.

BONTIS, N. (2001). Assessing Knowledge assets: A review of the models used to meausure intellectual capital, International Journal of Management Reviews 2001, 3(1), pp. 41-60.

BOOKSTABER, R. (2007). A demon of our own design: Markets, hedge funds and the perils of financial innovation. New York, Wiley.

CHEN, J., ZHU, Z. and XIE, H.Y. (2004), Measuring intellectual capital: a new model and empirical study, Journal of Intellectual Capital, 5(1), pp. 195-212.

CZERWIŃSKA, M., SLEDZIK, K., WIERZBA, R. (2010).Intellectual capital as generator of competitive advantage for banks. Fundacja Rozwoju Uniwersytetu Gdanskiego, Sopot, pp.97

EDVINSSON, L., and SULLIVAN, P. (1996).Developing a model for managing intellectual capital. European Management Journal, 14, pp. 356-364.

EDVINSSON, L., and MALONE, M.S. (1997). Intellectual capital: realizing your company's true value by finding its hidden roots. Harper Business, New York.

EGEDY, T. (2012).The effects of global economic crisis in Hungary. Hungarian Geographical Bulletin, 61 (2), pp. 157-158.

GHOSH, D. & WU, A. (2007), Intellectual capital and capital markets: additional evidence, Journal of Intellectual Capital, 8(2), pp. 216-235.

GUTHERIE, J. (2001). The management, measurement, and the reporting of intellectual capital, Journal of Intellectual Capital. 2(1), pp. 27-41.

HUNTER, L., WEBSTER, E., and WYATT, A. (2005).Measuring intangible capital: a review of current practice. Australian Accounting Review, .15 (2), pp. 4-21.

New York Stock Exchange Group Inc. (2011). available at: www.nyse.com/content/faqs/1042235995602.html?cat=Listed_Company___General

NONAKA, I., and TAKEUCHI, H. (1995). The Knowledge Creating Company: How Japanese Create the Dynamics of Innovation. New York. Oxford University Press.

PULIC, A. (1998) Measuring the performance of intellectual potential in knowledge Economy.available at: www.measuring-ip.at.

PULIC, A. (2000), VAIC™ – an accounting tool for IC management, International Journal of Technology Management, 20 (5-8), pp. 702-714.

PUNTILLO, P. (2009). Intellectual capital and business performance from Italian banking industry. Electronic Journal of Corporate Finance, 4(2), pp. 97-115.

ROOS, G., and ROOS, J. (1997).Measuring your company's intellectual performance. Long Range Planning, 30(3), pp. 413-426.

SAMILOGLU, A. T. (2006). The performance analysis of the Turkish banks through VAIC and MV/BV ratio. Journal of Administrative Sciences, 4(1), pp. 207-226.

SHIL, N.C. (2009). Performance Measures: An Application of Economic Value Added, International Journal of Business and Management, 4(3), pp. 171.

STEWART, G. B. (1990). The Quest for Value: the EVA management guide, Harper Business, New York, pp. 153.

STEWART, T.A. (1991). Brainpower: How Intellectual Capital is Becoming America's Most Valuable Asset. Fortune. June 3, 1991. pp.44-60.

STEWART, T.A. (1994). Your company's most valuable asset: intellectual capital. Fortune. October 3, pp..68–74.

STEWART, G.B. III (1994). EVA™: Fact and Fantasy, Journal of Applied Corporate Finance, 7(2), pp. 71-84.

STEWART, T.A. (1997). Intellectual capital: the new wealth of organizations, Dell Publishing Group, Inc.

SVEIBY, K.-E.(2007). Methods for Measuring Intangible Assets.available at: www.sveiby.com/articles/IntangibleMethods.htm

THENMOZHI, M. (2000). Market value added and share price behaviour: an empirical study of BSE Sensex companies. Delhi Business Review, 1(1), pp. 1-10.

URBANEK, G. (2008). Valuation of company's intangible assets.PWE 2008, Warsaw.

WANG, W-Y. & CHANG, C. (2005), Intellectual capital and performance in causal models: Evidence from the information technology industry in Taiwan, Journal of Intellectual Capital, 6(2), pp. 222-236.

Outsourcing and Organisational Innovation: The Example of a Service Provider

HOLYEVÁCZ CSABA
PH.D. STUDENT

e-mail: holyevacz.csaba@tigaz.hu

SUMMARY

The history of the gas and oil industry in Hungary goes back to the mid-19th century. This industry and its participants have gone through an organisational structural transition that presents an exclusive example for establishing the modern corporate structure as well as ofvalue-creating opportunities in organisational development.

In the present paper the notion of modern corporate organisation, the reasons for its establishment and its stages are presented through the example of a Hungarian gas provider, supported by theoretical outlooks.

The organisational development of one of the largest Hungarian gas providers made since the market opening (2004) is an appropriate way of representing the economic and organisational benefit within the application of modern organisational theories and strategies. This development presents the effects of the implementation of modern efficiency measuring means and methods (Economic Value Added) in the management operation to meet the expectations of investors. Decisions and steps determining the changes in the corporate organisation give a good example of measures taken to improve the efficiency implemented by centralizing as well as by process optimizing restructurings according to LEANmanagement principles.

The frequent presentation of decisions in classical (IT, mass data management) and competence-assessment-based outsourcing provides examples for effects of cost-saving opportunities and efficiency-improving measures.

The main purpose of the paper is the presentation of organisational development based on the practical evidence of organisational theories and relationships through which theoretical conclusions are proved. In addition, the conception that the efficient practical application of relationships developed by theories means economic benefit for companies is also presented.

However, development is still in progress. On the basis of the practical examples of the past and their theoretical connections there are further challenges in the networking of organisations and the virtual organisational structure.

Keywords: outsourcing, organisational innovation and organisational effectiveness

INTRODUCTION

The history of the gas and petroleum industry in Hungary dates back to the mid-19th century. This sector of industry has a long history and its players have experienced favourable structural changes, which set businesses a good example of how to establish a modern corporate structure and offer value-creation opportunities hidden in developing an organisation.

HISTORY OF OUTSOURCING

A Brief History of Natural Gas Production in Hungary

By the 1840s and 1850s several European and overseas countries were involved in extracting petroleum. People had been using petroleum or crude oil and its products for a variety of purposes for years. The industrial-scale production of crude oil began when customers' demand for illumination and lubricants needed to be met. Later people started to use hydrocarbons and their compounds.

The first Hungarian natural gas deposit was discovered in the Transylvanian basin and described by Valentin Frank von Frankenstein, the royal judge from Nagyszeben (Sibiu), in 1690. The first research into petroleum in Hungary began in the 1850s. Several decades later, on 15 July, 1938, the Hungarian-American Petroleum Corporation (Hungarian acronym: MAORT) was founded, which was producing enough oil to fully meet the country's needs in 1940.

In the late 1950s the role of hydrocarbons increased rapidly in the energy sector, leading to the emergence of a hydrocarbon processing industry. The Hungarian Oil Trust was founded. The Hungarian gas industry joined the Trust in 1960 and the Hungarian Oil and Gas Trust (Hungarian acronym: OKGT) was established.

After several re-structuring processes, the Hungarian Oil and Gas Company Plc (known as MOL), was founded in 1991 as a legal successor to OKGT. The Hungarian petroleum industry currently operates within the framework of this company. With the establishment of MOL, an integration of the entire Hungarian hydrocarbon industry was performed after a carefully considered selection process (Vince, YEAR). (Vince: 2009)

This stage in the history of this industry can be considered to be preparation for privatisation and market liberalisation, both from a Hungarian and a European prospective. The European Union opened its natural gas market in compliance with Directive 98/30/EC and its amendments, which entered into force on 8 October 2000 and have been in force for eligible consumers since then. The market opening resulted in the following phenomena (Index, 2008)

- competition on the energy marketwas created;
- service provision was concentrated;
- complex energy services were provided when a service provider had a right to offer several energy and various services.

Since Hungary did not apply for derogation in the energy sector, Act XLII of 2003 on natural gas supply stipulated some business activities, as a result of which MOL lost its monopoly in January 2004. Any holder of the 'licence for the access to the cross-border natural gas transmission pipeline' had the right to import natural gas to Hungary. (Borbély, 2006)

Tigáz, the Largest Regional Gas Distributor Company in Hungary

Natural gas was discovered in 1925 in Hajdúszoboszló when thermal water was being searched for. It was primarily used for generating electric power for trams and illuminating train compartments, and later it was compressed, stored in cylinders and sold. The members of the city council of Hajdúszoboszló formed the Hajdúszoboszló Natural Gas Production and Distribution Public Company, a company that produced gas filled in cylinders, on 13 June 1950. This small public company was integrated into the Hungarian Oil and Gas Trust in 1967 and began its activity under the new name of Transtisza Gas Provider and Maintenance Company (Tigáz). Tigáz was the first company in the EU that applied gas pipes made from polyethylene, a very advanced, durable and safe material.

In the late 1980s and early 1990s Tigáz acquired a stake in the Schlumberger plant in Hungary, which produced gas meters. This move considerably contributed to further development of the Hungarian gas network. In the early 1990s, the company became suitable for the implementation of the privatisation programme announced by the Hungarian government. By spring 1994 the national government had elaborated the basic privatisation principles of special strategic sectors.

On 22 November 1995 the Italgas-SNAM consortium acquired a majority stake in Tigáz Plc and Tigáz became a member not only of the Italgas group, but of Eni, an Italian multinational oil and gas company as well. A small gas supplier company operating in two settlements with nearly one hundred consumers in 1957 had by 2000become one of the largest regional gas suppliers in Hungary and a recognised member of Eni group, one of the major energy companies in the world.

Organizational Strategy and Challenges of ENI, a Multinational Company

Eni is a universal, open and dynamically developing company, whose principle values lie in sustainability, corporate culture, partnership, innovation and efficiency. The main elements of Eni's corporate culture and success are as follows:

- placing people and their wellbeing in the centre of attention;
- developing people's skills and expertise;
- ensuring employees do their job effectively and allowing them to fully exploit their hidden potential and creativity;
- creating a working environment that ensures everybody equal and discrimination-free opportunities and complies with 'value' community norms; (eni Strategic Plan:2012)

In order to achieve the implementation of these fundamental principles, Eni continuously elaborates organisation development projects that ensure adaptability, growth and sustainability. Special attention is paid to human resource management. In 2001 Eni further developed the new organisational model that was suitable for providing efficient support to develop strategic directions of the company group. This move involved delegation of decision-making processes and responsibilities to operative units. The company prepared a basis for the renewal of corporate management, the integration of the Eni Corporate University (www.eni.com) and launched the Internal Communication project. In the following years the direction of organisational development shifted towards controlling centralisation and targeted equilibrium between management and control. In 2003 Eni reviewed the role of the Board of Directors, the corporate governance system, adopted the regulations of Internal Control Committee and Compensation Committee and reviewed several other issues related to corporate governance.

The Board of Directors defined Strategic Guidelines for sustainable development for the period encompassing 2007 and 2010 and set up a special unit for their implementation. The principles of these guidelines can be seen on the Tigáz website. (www.tigaz.hu)The first sustainability report was published and a sustainability organisational model was elaborated. The Welfare Project and the Health Project were also introduced. Since currently the main objective of the company is to fight against corruption, the New Eni Regulatory System has been adopted.

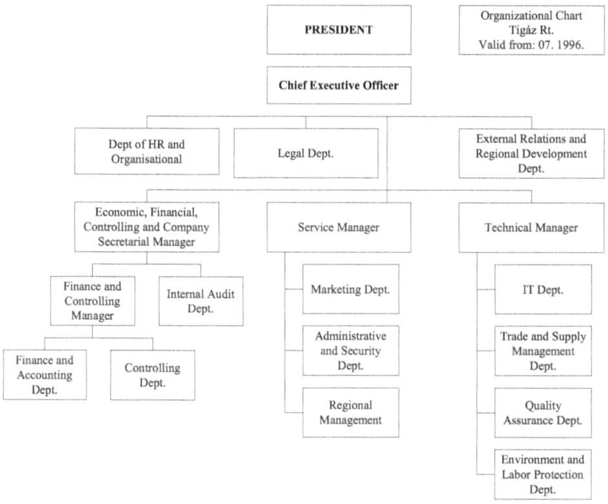

Figure 1. Tigáz organisational structure in 1996

ORGANISATION INNOVATION AT TIGÁZ

The evolution process of a modern corporate structure can be observed at Tigáz. The organisation development process presented in this paper follows the corporate structural and theoretical modernisation trends in an eclectic way, illustrating and justifying the basic principle of the 20th and 21st centuries.

The Conventional Organisational Model

In 1996 -- at the time of its privatisation -- Tigáz was the largest natural gas service provider in Hungary, employing 5,370 people, and had a vertical structure with a broad spectrum of separate departments and directorates involved in great variety of activities. The main activities of the company encompassed the provision of natural gas to the general public (not to the public sphere) and its distribution through natural gas pipelines within distribution areas belonging to the company. The company operated in the form of a public limited company. It had a Directorate General with a president CEO who managed the company's operations. Under the CEO there were directorates and main departments that directly reported to him (see Figure 1).

The territorial units that directly belonged to the Director of Services performed the main activities of the company. However, all territorial units operated completely independently. They were 'autonomous companies'. The term 'line of business' may be used for characterising the operation and clearing system of the territorial units of that time. The territorial directorates within the company structure were independent clearing units. This organisational structure resulted in a broadly vertical and decentralised company operation (see Figure 2).

After the company's privatisation, the corporate objectives – which already included investors' needs and expectations – were incorporated in the company's operation and became one of the inductive factors of high priority in the motivation elements for innovation. However, investors' expectations were primarily aimed at achieving increase in the invested capital. This increase in value could be measured by share prices. However, the changes in share prices did not always reflect the company's performance. Realising this fact, the company management looked for a model for measuring the company's performance. In the early 1980s, the Economic Value Added (EVA) model was adopted, which measured companies' performance more accurately than the natural value of share prices. The EVA metric offered by Stern Stuart Management Services creatively linked the corporate accounting data and performance with the company's performance on the Stock Exchange. Unlike share evaluations, EVA is continuously applicable to performance evaluation.

EVA is calculated from the net operating profit after tax minus 'suitable' alternative costs of the invested capital (WACC x invested capital). Contrary to market-based evaluations like MVA (market value added), EVA is calculated at division or sector levels (a strategic economic level). Contrary to the accounting-based profit like EBIT, Net Income and EPS (earnings per share), EVA is an economic indicator that covers both operating and capital costs.

The Economic Added Value calculations at Tigáz presented in this paper have always produced negative numbers since the company's privatisation. This economic indicator proves that the corporate management has faced serious challenges in order to improve efficiency and increase business results. The reason for such an extremely negative EVA was the high financing costs invested by shareholders during and after privatisation of the company. The return on this huge investment does not seem to be ensured even at present, which makes the current management face exciting challenges (see Table 1).

A positive value for EVA in the examined period was achieved only in 2007, which was the period of legal separation. However, this value is not relevant if the available Tigáz-DSO Ltd data are taken into consideration, since this figure shows the effect of capitalregrouping between the two companies.

Another aspect of the investors' approach is the increasing market competition and globalisation, which has placed corporate adaptability and initiative skills in the focus of attention through turbulent market, technical and environmental changes in order to stay competitive. Thus, since 1990 the term ‘innovative organisation’ has been linked with the company’s ability to change, rapidly adapt and take the initiative. The direction of structural changes can be considered to be systematic efforts made towards decentralisation, which involve reduction of organisational levels, setting up divisions and using market-based external and internal services. Special attention is paid to integration processes, mainly to the systems supporting company management (VIR, ERP, BSC). Organisational processes have changed since the company became both vertically and horizontally integrated, which is primarily experienced in IT and process management.

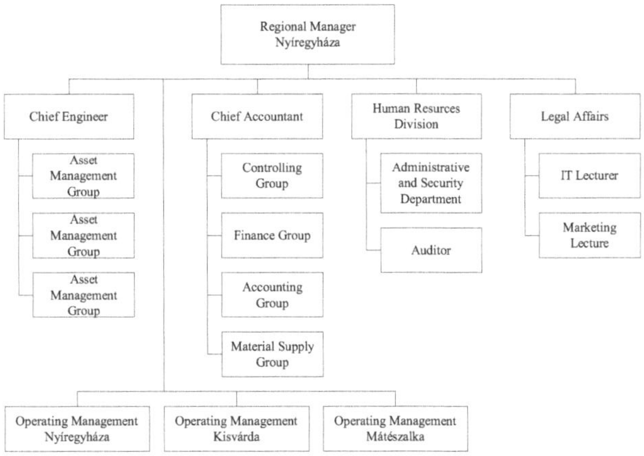

Figure 2. Tigáz territorial directorate organisation in 1996

Table 1
Tigáz’s derived economic value added

Data in million HUF	1996	2006	2007	2009	2010	2011	2012
Revenue+other revenue	46 834	234 037	294 564	325 770	312 714	292 598	287 618
Total cost	45 795	234 503	273 859	322 681	310 739	294 529	304 739
EBIT	1 039	-466	20 705	3 089	1 975	-1 931	-17 121
Tax	185	0	0	0	38	0	0
Earnings after taxes net income	854	-466	20 705	3 089	1 937	-1 931	-17 121
WACC	n.a.	6,0%	6,6%	8,5%	8,0%	7,5%	7,9%
Equity	27 228	35 118	158 603	144 498	145 077	138 083	62 191
Cost of Capital [WACC*(Equity+Debt)]	n.a.	2 104	10 420	12 282	11 606	10 356	4 913
EVA (million HUF)	n.a.	-2 570	10 285	-9 193	-9 669	-12 287	-22 034
Staff	3 572	1 814	586	567	583	585	563

In the past a division or a department was operated for strategic reasons and acted as a potential source of development or flexibility, or for historical or sentimental reasons, as in the case of Tigáz. At present this policy does not fit in with tough financial pressures.

The First Steps of Privatisation and the Evolution of a Modern Corporate Form

Since the investors’ objectives changed, the company with its vertical structure concentrated its efforts on implementing disintegration. The company’s profile was changed to increase the company’s profitability. The activities were redesigned to recoup the losses. The organisation was streamlined and middle managerial and some other positions were eliminated. The amount of the long-term tied-up capital was decreased. The profitability was improved. Due to modularization of services, the logistics and ITsystems rapidly developed. The scarce resources were concentrated on the activities which were drivers of real competitive advantages. As Arun Maira, a product manager at Arthur D. Little, Inc., formulated, “structure is an old paradigm and we have to forget the description of an organisation. Weare actually speaking about organisation – organisation of a process and not about the structure.”(Szintay, 2011:4)

Centralization and Cost Efficiency

In terms of organisational optimisation processes, the main objectives are as follows:

- establishing independent sectors of industry for operating natural gas distribution;
- separating natural gas trading and service provision from the organisational structure
- establishing an independent ‘Customer Service Directorate’ to meet the existing and emerging market and customer needs more effectively in a very competitive environment (see Figure 3).

After reviewing the business activities of the gas industry, it becomes clear that trading with natural gas starts from purchasing the gas through selling it to consumers and finishes with its distribution, which means ‘transmitting’ the natural gas to consumer points. This process encompasses two completely different business activities in terms of character and content. Trading activities are of service character, whereas distribution activities have a considerable technical content since they involve operation, development, measuring and gas meter reading activities. The listed main activities provided bases for measuring their value- added skills and establishing independent organisations to perform these activities.

The priority given to trading with natural gas resulted from the core character of this activity. The company’s fundamental activity was determined and separated from the other core sectors, namely from distribution as well as from supporting units (HR, legal and financial activities).

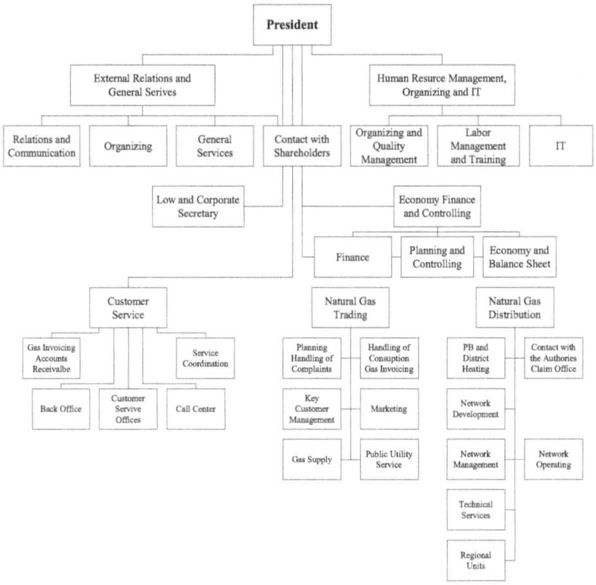

Figure 3.Organisational structure of Tigáz Plc. in 2007

Putting a 'Customer' in Corporate Objectives is a Response to Market Competition

Liberalisation of the natural gas market and increase in market competition resulted in a new need, namely the need to provide 'modern' services to customers. New natural gas service providers operating in a competitive market are not only trying to set customer-friendly prices in order to increase their own sales, turnover and customer base, but they also attempt to provide a broader range of services to achieve higher customer satisfaction and convenience and to ensure customers a better access to more information as well. Thus, a Customer Services Directorate was formed to respond to customer enquiries and provide customer service related to the following areas:

- ➢ invoicing and collecting the outstanding dues on the accounts,
- ➢ offering back office functions,
- ➢ operating customer service offices,
- ➢ operating call centres.

Another aspect of increasing efficiency of an organisation is to promote centralisation and cost efficiency. In order to achieve this goal, the activities supporting and assisting the work of core organisations are concentrated and delegated to directorates which directly report to the president.

Model Changes in the Natural Gas Market and Legal Separation

The Model Oil and Gas Conservation Act entered into force in 2004 and was facilitated by Act XLII of 2003 on natural gas supply. The fundamental principles and the model change formulated in the Model Act were further amended by a new Gas Act in 2008. Thus, the regulations of the Hungarian natural gas sector complied with the EU directives. Following this Act, the Tigáz Group shifted from vertical integration towards networking and strategic outsourcing processes, which triggered the development of the organisation in a completely new legal environment.

Customer Services Directorate, as a Supporting Organisation and Lean Management

Both the ever increasing and diversified competition and the competitive market environment made Tigáz review its internal processes and organisational structure in 2008 and 2009 in order to improve its operation and to adapt the lean management practices.

LEAN management is a strategy which helps organisations operate more efficiently and optimize processes. LEAN management means 'creating value with no waste'. Its objective is to optimize all the activities required for value creation and eliminate *muda*, a Japanese word for waste. LEAN thinking results in creating customer-oriented processes. Descriptions of processes and interface, clearly-defined responsibilities, early reactions to committed mistakes and application of simple organisational methods promote stable processes resulting in offering high quality products. (Szintay, 2008)

Organisations fundamentally rethink processes of corporate operations and form a new supporting organisation in order to operate more flexibly, faster and in a more standard way, which leads to increase in efficiency and lays bases for making the first step towards corporate modernization.

New ideas in companies' lives are taking shape. Apart from a 'customer' who is actually a consumer in the core corporate business activity, a 'partner' is emerging. The 'partner' is an organisational unit which uses the services of another organisational unit. An internal service provision emerges since services are ordered and provided; partners' needs are identified and met within corporate processes and operation.

One of the tasks of the new supporting organisation is to ensure services and provide assistance to core organisations in the areas which do not belong to a non-direct core activity. As for Tigáz, its core organisations are Sales and Distribution (DSO). As for the supporting organisation, it is Customer Service, since this organisation was engaged in performing activities related to customers after a great variety of changes had been introduced in the company. Thus, the processes which were centralized after the core areas had been identified were integrated the most efficiently.

The company restructured these functions and integrated customer services in the organisation (see Figure 4). A new supporting organisation was established with the following activities:

- managing customer accounts starting from taking the reading of gas meters to billing customers,
- ensuring uniform collection of outstanding dues on the accounts starting from managing customer accounts through collecting outstanding dues to terminating services,
- promoting customer and communication areas (Office of Complaints, Back Office, Front Office, and Contact Centre),
- establishing an advanced technical and IT background and service coordination.

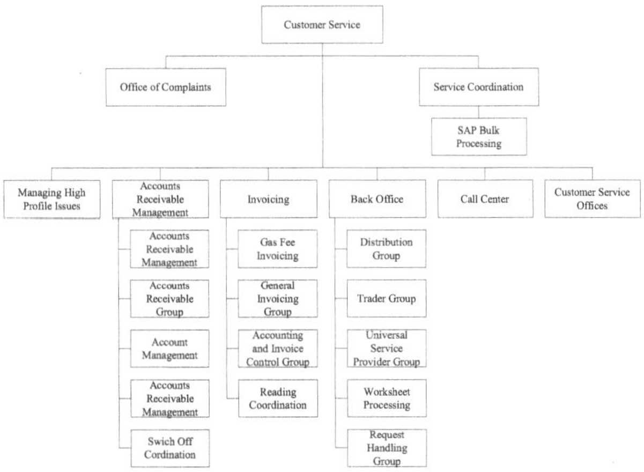

Figure 4. Organisational chart of Customer Services Directorate at Tigáz Plc. in 2009

Outsourcing, a New Organisation Development Method at Tigáz

Tigáz is dedicated to preserving its traditions and corporate culture, which are rooted in large organisational structure, direct management and organisational principles in terms of 'remaining within the boundaries of a sleeve'. As for the further development of the company, there were favourable signs showing that the company still had some activities and processes under its sleeve. There were inefficient business operations and unprofitable investments that caused the company to incur significant expenses and other costs. The return and the efficiency of these activities were not measurable (see Figure 5). At first, Tigáz concentrated on in-company skills, on its strengths and on the 'what are we strong at?' category. Then the company shifted towards external or market factors in order to remain competitive within the national grid. An accurate systematisation of outsourcing objectives was done on the basis of internal and external competencies. The Insigna-matrix provided an outsourcing strategy that the company adopted.

According to most researchers, outsourcing has been given much attention in the past few years because it has been realised that 'it is not the possession of capabilities that counts, but rather the company's ability required to control and build majority of critical capabilities'. Instead of possession companies must strive for capability outsourcing to strengthen their market position, cut costs, streamline the organisation and improve quality. (Szintay, 2011) Outsourcing at Tigáz followed the classical outsourcing processes and was performed in two phases.

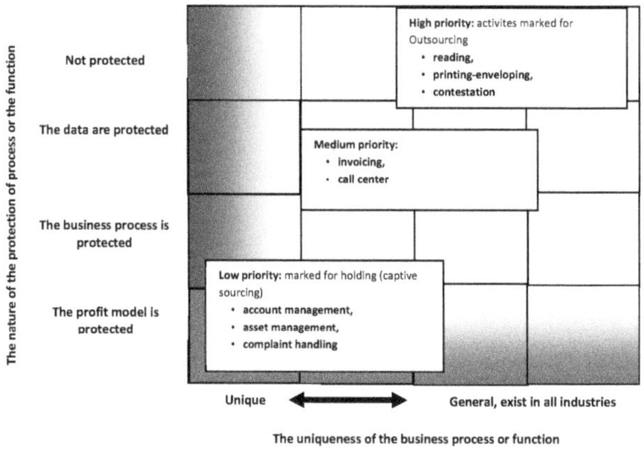

Figure 5. Protection assessment of functions and processes in customer service offices at Tigáz

Classical Outsourcing Practices at Tigáz

Informatics operations and data processing services were the first areas that were outsourced by Tigáz. Tigáz, being a natural gas service provider with the largest area coverage in Hungary, served over 1,200,000 customers. The informatics operations and data processing services of such a huge number of customers involved tasks related to mass data processing (SAP MM, SAP ISU), which could be resolved by ensuring back support. Thus, the Customer Master Data Management as a support to Back Office organisations was outsourced.

Another huge task of mass data management was to handle fact sheets which contained the nature of the work carried out at the consumers' place, such as taking the reading of gas meters, inspecting and exchanging them, etc. All data were registered on paper fact sheets by workers at territorial units and forwarded to the headquarters. The company generated about 450,000 fact sheets a year. Transferring the information from the fact sheet to the SAP business system also belonged to the company's basic activities which were not of strategic importance. Thus, the operation activities related to shipping the fact sheets from territorial units to the processing centre on a daily basis and uploading the information on the fact sheets to the VIP system were also outsourced and supported by an outsourcing agreement. This outsourcing decision resulted in saving costs (see Table 2). In addition, the time that the fact sheets spent in the pipeline was decreased; since they were delivered to the processing place faster, their processing time became shorter, their processing was performed in a concentrated way and the data required for billing were uploaded to the SAP system in a shorter period of time. This resulted in a more efficient billing procedure and revenue generation for the company.

Table 2
Impacts of Master Data Outsourcing on cost effectiveness

Cost before outsourcing (fictive figures		
Master data management	number of staff	15
	number of worksheets	350 000
	specific human cost (HUF/person/year)	4 208 800
	overhead (HUF/person/year)	162 400
	total cost amount (HUF/year)	65 568 000
Work order processing	number of staff	20
	number of worksheets	600 000
	specific human cost (HUF/person/year)	4 208 800
	overhead (HUF/person/year)	162 400
	total cost amount (HUF/year)	87 424 000
Total (HUF/year)		152 992 000
Cost of the outsourcing activities (HUF/year)		118 250 000
Total cost reduction (HUF/year)		34 742 000

Outsourcing Decisions Improving Cost Effectivenessat Tigáz

In 2007 the second phase of outsourcing decisions targeted such non-strategic business operations as optimization of processes and promotion of organisational efficiency. Reading gas meters represented a key challenge to Tigáz since utility workers carried out the reading of the gas meter and inspected it on site each monthly billing cycle. Before 2007 this work was done by people who had valid temporary contracts with Tigáz and were directly managed by the company. This work was extremely labour intensive and was not really efficient. Outsourcing gas meter readings could be considered to be an attractive decision of business process management. The contracted external parties, whose core activities involve visiting consumers, carry out meter readings cost-effectively. The outsourced reading activities ensure that the contracted parties actually physically visit and read the meter and prove this by taking photos of the meters, which are uploaded to the SAP system and improve process efficiency. In addition, photos of gas meters help discourage utility theft and enable the company to inspect actual natural gas usage. The natural gas provider would like to concentrate its activities on inspection and not on execution of it. However, the company pays special attention to liaising with strategic partners who generate the company revenues by providing accurate and reliable gas meter reading services (see Table 3).

Table 3
Comparison of meter reading services before and after outsourcing

Indicators of meter reading effectiveness		
	Before Outsourcing	After Outsourcing
Status of readers	self-employed trustee	entrepreneur
Reading frequency	monthly	yearly
Documentation of reading	data sheet (meter balance)	data sheet (meter and consumer data) + photo
Effectiveness of reading - meter	100%	97%
Effectiveness of reading - photo	0%	97%
Checking of reading	telephone (based on a sample)	documented with photos

Future Directions in Organisational Development- Integration of Processes

The primary objective of Tigáz Group is to further develop by adapting to the ever changing internal and external challenges and to optimize its operations to achieve sustainable development. The current economic and market environment imposes strict requirements on natural gas industry and natural gas service providers. The current difficult economic situation requires that Tigáz continually focus on customer retention and broadening the customer base. The serious deterioration in the economic situation makes the collection of the outstanding depts on customers' accounts extremely difficult. Tigáz should develop special incentive programmes to motivate customers to meet their contractual requirements and in this way to generate more stable company revenue. Apart from these extrovertal interactions, the company also concentrates on intra-company processes, cutting costs and further increasing efficiency to achieve sustainable development.

Tigáz is making every effort to nurture and grow customer relationships and reacts to this challenge by integration tools and organisational development. The primary aim of integration is as follows:

- implementing integration of tasks and human resource management to improve performance, maximize efficiency and cut costs,
- showing more flexibility in delegating tasks while taking into consideration workload to increase work efficiency,
- setting customer service standards in customer service operations and performance measurements to foster customer satisfaction,
- introducing technological developments to provide support to the aforementioned operations. Customer Services is aimed at establishing two interactive units (see Figure 6):
- the Contact Centre will manage tasks related to 'external customers' (consumers) through both

electronic and face-to-face communication channels,

- back offices supporting business processes will be integrated in a single organisation to improve efficiency.

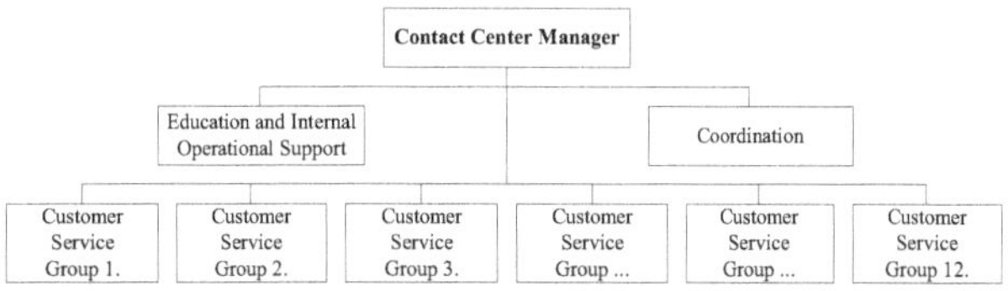

Figure 6. Contact Centre in 2012

The planned measures are expected to result in a more optimal utilization of available resources, flexible delegation of workloadand saving resources and costs.

The development of IT management and governance will provide a basis for implementation of integration to enable the organisational units and groups to perform their work supported by electronic communication and a work-flow system.

CONCLUSION

An organisation of the future is an integrated organisation that has sophisticated IT support, continuously measures performance and keeps the organization in balance to achieve the best performance. The future vision of the integrated organisation formulated in the objectives places Tigáz Group among modern companies and channels it into paths where the company can fully meet the requirements of sustainable development.

This analysis is a basis for further research work aiming to identify and analyse corporate synergies. Identifying and defining the benchmarks and synergies will lead to determining the potential benefits of further integration of the organisation.

REFERENCES

BKL Kőolaj és Földgáz 140. 2007/3: 70 years of the Hungarian oil and gas mining,

BORBÉLY SZILVIA (2006:) EU: gas market liberalization and unbundling, MARMOL,

SZINTAY ISTVÁN (2011): The theoretical limit - Unlimited organizations

SZINTAY ISTVÁN (2008): Network and Cluster

SZINTAY ISTVÁN (2011): The outsourcing as one of the defining trends of innovative organizations streamline Start of the competition in the gas market, Index 2008. január 30.

VINCE PÉTER (2009): Model Changes in gas supply

Tigáz Zrt.: internal documents, studies

eni Strategic Plan (2012): www.eni.com

www.tigaz.hu

www.eni.com

www.hungas.hu

Technological Audit as a Method of Evaluation of the Commercial Attractiveness of the Objects of Intellectual Property

ALEKSANDRA KOSENKO, Ph.D.
ASSOCIATE PROFESSOR

e-mail: a.kosenko@rambler.ru

SUMMARY

Considered in this paper are the questions used to assess the commercial potential of intellectual property objects in the theory and practice of the technological audit. A mechanism for the valuation of the level of commercial attractiveness of intellectual technologies is proposed, and the theoretical provisions of principles, objectives, and outcomes of technological audit are discussed. The features of the technological audit of the results of intellectual activities of industrial enterprises are determined.

INTRODUCTION

In modern society intellectual products are traded as purchases of global importance in the background of the rapid and comprehensive development of science and industry. Sustainable success in business and development can be achieved by the enterprise or country that closely follows technological novelties and is at the forefront of scientific and technical progress. Analysis of products of the machine-building industries allows to assert that any firm that does not use the achievements of the past five years in their field of activitybecomes uncompetitive and is much less effective than companies paying due attention to scientific achievements.

Evaluation of the commercial attractiveness of the objects of intellectual property (OIP) is the most important task in the innovation strategy of the economies of developed countries of the world (Abramov A.A., 2012).This is due to the fact that the solution of this problem directly affects the international competitiveness of national production. The object of the cognitions of objects of intellectual property goods is the commercial realization of forming a new feature of industrial organizations (Allen K., 2007). Intellectual property consists in the creation of a specific product which can be introduced into the economic turnover (Brett A., 1995; Zabelina I.N, 2006).

A STUDYOF THE EXISTING SITUATION

In an innovationeconomy, the competitiveness of an organization is determined not only by its ability to satisfy the public demand for production and realization of products, but also the ability to create, implement legal protection and to implement intellectual property on the domestic and the world market (Allen K., 2007). Today the majority of domestic organizations are in the typical situation where the composition of their assetsincludes the objects of intellectual property, which for many years not only were "dead weight", but which even at the stage of creation were not intended for actual use (Zabelina I.N, 2006).The company regularly continues to bear the costs for maintaining a patent in force, despite the absence of any economic effects of it (Kletkina Y.A., 2008). However, the realities of the modern Ukrainian economy are such thatthe need to protect the innovations which are able to improve the efficiency of production and generate income should be put in first place.This is necessary because of the diversity of the results of scientific-technical activities, so that promising objects of intellectual property with the greatest commercial potential need to be highlighted.

THE ADVANTAGES OF THE PROCESS OF COMMERCIALIZATION

The commercialization of intellectual property is the process of the involvement of the objects of intellectual property in economic turnover, using intellectual property in the business activities of enterprises. We list here a number of practical advantages of commercialization (Kozyrev, A.N., 2003; Pestunov M.A., 2006; Rodionova E.M., 2009; Spiridonov E.A., 2009; Kocziszky G., 2012; Rogers E.M., 1995):

- owners of intellectual property to be founders of companies without paying real money: money replacing the intellectual property contributed to the share capital of the company;
- additional income can be received for the transfer of the right of use of intellectual property;
- intellectual property can be used as collateral for obtaining credit;
- intellectual Property secures new products from competitors in the early stages of its life cycle, as well as protection against unfair competition;;ó
- intellectual property contributes to the creation of the advertising image in providing information about the legal protection of the products or work on the license of a well-known manufacturer;
- intellectual property enables the reduction of the tax on profits by reducing the taxable base by the amount of depreciation of intangible assets and the amount of expenses for creation of objects of intellectual property;
- intellectual property allows to reduce the tax to the added cost, if the transaction is executed as a patent, license or acreator's agreement.

THE SOURCES OF THE EFFECTIVENESS OF THE OBJECTS OF INTELLECTUAL PROPERTY

The economic sense of the commercial realization of intellectual property relations is in receipt of income. The form of the receipt of income is determined by the dual nature of intellectual property objects (Zabelina I.N., 2006; Kocziszky G., 2012; Rosenberg N., 1982). On the one hand, the objects of intellectual property may serve as a factor of production, representing a part of the resource potential of the enterprise or its intangible assets. On the other hand, objects of intellectual property may be a separate object of purchase, that is, the goods. Moreover, another option may be equally effective, to use the results of intellectual activity. The scheme of receiptof income from the commercial realization of intellectual property is represented in Figure 1.

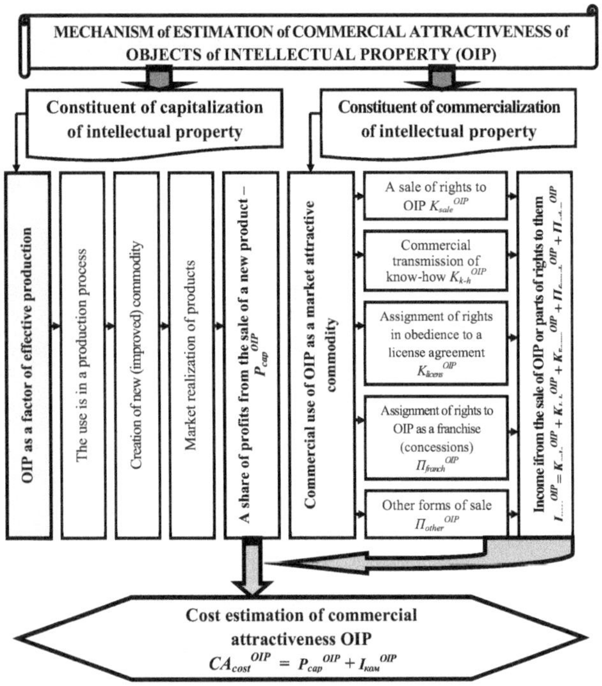

Figure 1. The mechanism of reception of the income from commercial realization of intellectual property

In the process of commercialization of objects of intellectual property as a factor of production there is a gradual transfer of value of intangible objects based on the value of the products produced, the so-called process of capitalization. In this case, the income is a part of the profit from the sale of the finished product, created with the use of innovations.

The implementation of the economic interests of the owner of the results of intellectual creative activity is possible not only at the stage of production, but also in the process of exchange through the commercialization of intellectual property, when the transfer of the rights to the income arises in the form of revenue from sale of the object or of some powers from the range of intellectual property rights. Capitalization and commercial use of intellectual property objects have a significant economic effect (Zabelina I.N., 2006).

TECHNOLOGICAL AUDIT AS A METHOD OF EVALUATING THE COMMERCIAL POTENTIAL OF OIP

Studies have shown (Brett A., 1995; Kletkina Y.A., 2008; Kocziszky G., 2012) that a technological audit is an important method of assessing the prospects of innovative development of an organization and its current technological condition and health.

In a general sense an audit is a process of accumulation and evaluation of information related to a particular economic system, in order to compare it with the established criteria. A technological audit is a variation of the operational audit and is an examination of the OIP, technological processes, methods, techniques, and procedures used in the organization, with the aim of evaluating their performance and effectiveness (Kocziszky G., 2012).

The implementation of the operational audit is, as a rule, a more complex task than that of other types of audit, as the efficiency of operations is usually much more difficult to evaluate objectively than, say, the financial statements based on generally accepted accounting principles. The criteria for the assessment of technological information are less stringent than in the case of financial statements, and are more subjective in nature. Therefore, an operational audit (and in particular, a technologicalaudit) is to a certain extent similar to a consulting company's administration (Table 1).

Table 1
Comparative characteristics of a technological and a financial audit

Aspect of comparison	Financial audit	Technological audit
The main objective of the audit	Tests for compliance of the financial statements with generally accepted accounting principles	Assessment of the efficiency of production and management technologies
References to the time period	Largely retrospective character; focused on the past	For the prospects of economic activity; focused on the future of the business entity
The main users of the information obtained in the course of the audit	Informing external counterparties (creditors, shareholders, tax and statistical bodies, etc.) and managers of the organization	Designed mainly for managers of the organization

Clarifying the essence of the technological audit is assisted by its comparison with the audit of the financial statements on a number of characteristics. While in an audit of financial statements the auditor focuses on whether the economic operations are reflected in the financial statements, in the technological audit emphasis is placed on efficiency and productivity technologies. The audit of financial statements is focused on the past (has a retrospective character),while the technological audit for the prospects of economic activity is focused on the future of the organization. In the audit of the financial statements auditor's report, as a rule, is intended for many users (shareholders, bankers), while the technological auditing is intended first of all for managers (administration) of the organization.

A technological audit is in operation an objective assessment of the capacity of OIP as an object of commercialization. In view of the fact that the commercialization of technologies is a long and expensive process, then, before a lot of time and financial resources are spent, it is necessary to appreciate the feasibility of the sale of the idea or invention or of its successful transformation into a market product. A study of the existing definitions of the technological audit has allowed the author to develop her own definition of this economic category. The technological audit allows us to understand the analysis of the object of intellectual property, new technologies (technology), the state of production equipment, which are involved in the production or, potentially, may be introduced in production or sold on the market. In other words, it is an evaluation of intellectual and industrial potential, as well as the technological capabilities of the enterprise from the point of view of the possibility of their promotion on the market, the economic effect of scientific and technical results, selection of optimal ways of using new technologies and the accumulated scientific developments.

The objects of the technological audit of the industrial enterprises are likely to become:

- objects of intellectual property;
- technologies;
- innovative programs and development plans or reorganization of production;
- production equipment;
- technological regulations and instructions;
- technological road maps;
- cost;
- investment projects.

As a result of these multiple objects, the technological audit of the enterprise can produce very different results. Their composition and priority depends on the tasks set. The author proposes that the main objectives of the technological audit should include the following:

- allocation of new intellectual technologies with commercial potential;
- the allocation of opportunities for their application at the enterprise (sale on the market and increasing the efficiency of production facilities;
- definition of the most probable ways to realize each opportunity;
- identification of opportunities to maximize the profit from the existing scientific development or technology;
- formation of a source of information for the elaboration of the strategy of management of the production potential of the enterprise;
- definition of ways of combining the existing production facilities with new production directions of activity;

- definition of stages of the introduction of new production areas and their value;
- definition of the reasons for instability of enterprises and over-consumption of resources. Development of a plan of activities ensuring a stable production process;
- examination of conformity with requirements of process regulations,such as for production equipment; identification of causes of non-compliance with expenditure norms;
- development of measures for management of the cost price of the technological process.

The process of conducting a technological audit in organizations can be divided into three main stages.

The first step is to review the technologies being used at the enterprise, and evaluation of opportunities of the enterprise in respect of the application of these technologies.

The second phase is an overview of the technologies used in other organizations, primarily those of competitors, and the identification of technological standards, i.e. the best technology usedin practice. The main management tool for solving these tasks is benchmarking.

The third step in the audit process is to compare the use of technology in the organization with the technological standards, which allows to evaluate the effectiveness, and hence the market perspective. The main tool for solving problems of the third stage is the analysis of the technological portfolio of the organization.

To evaluate the commercial potential of the idea (invention) or other object of intellectual property it is necessary to conduct research and search for answers to many questions. The author proposes a methodology for technological audit of the OIP that includes the most important provisions, the essence of which can be reduced to the following provisions.

1. Authorship. In carrying out a technological audit first of all it is necessary to find out:

- who is the author of the object of intellectual property;
- who funded the creation of this object.

Unfortunately, the authors of the invention often do not attach due importance to the issue of financial sources of their development. However, if the invention was made in the course of implementation of scientificresearch, experimental design or technological work under contract, then according to Ukrainian legislation, the customer has the right to use the results of the work provided to it by the executor, including those capable of legal protection, and the contractor shall have the right to use the work results obtained by him for his/her own needs. This means, if the contract did not specify the distribution of the ownership of the treaty in the course of work results, all rights to inventions made during the execution of the work and transferred to the customer, the customer owns and authors can get a return on their invention with the consent of the customer (the usually - written).

2. Patent search. This is carried out with a view to:

- the search for similar inventions;
- search of alternative decisions of task the technological audit of which is conducted.

The existence of a patented identical invention invalidates the further development of the idea (invention). The presence of other solutions to this problem leads to the need to assess the prospects of an idea (invention), not only from the point of view of competition with existing products on the market, but also to the possible competition from another unsold on the market as a product of the invention. Moreover, due to lack of information on the authors of these inventions intention, evaluation must be conducted in any case, even if the invention in the future will not be converted into a marketable product.

A patent search can be done:

- independently, using the available database of patents, the search systems, the Internet, etc.;
- on the server Ukrpatent to conduct a search of Russian patents (a search is partly paid, partly free of charge);
- on the servers of the European patent organization, with the help of the free search engine system Espacenet;
- on the network server Espacenet, which provides access to the interface in Russian language to the world databases of patent information and to patent funds of different countries and international organizations;
- using the services of a patent attorney.A complete list of patent attorneys in Ukraine can be founded on the site Ukrpatent;
- order the carrying out of a search organization, rendering services on conducting a patent search.

3. Inspection of technical feasibility. The method of obtaining the results consists of two consecutive stages:

- checking the reliability of the concept;
- assessment of the performance of the product in the real world.

Validation of the concept is often quite a time-consuming process, because there are only "general considerations" on the reliability of the concept, so it is necessary to confirm the calculations and test them in practice by experiments (in some cases, by simulations). A successful practical proof-of-concept should evaluate the performance of the product (technology) under real conditions of operation, which will be created on the basis of the proposed concept. This assessment will help:

- identify some obvious obstacles to the use of an intellectual product by the end user;
- approximately evaluate the technical characteristics of a possible intellectual product;
- find new areas of application of the intellectual product (technology).

4. Definition of technologies for comparison. To assess market prospects of the intended product (technology) it is necessary to conduct a search of products and technologies existing on the market that solve the same problems and meet the same needs of the buyer. Such a search is best carried out with the help of search engines, which allow you to specify the parameters of search queries. Researches show that the authors of ideas on objective reasons often over-estimate the nicety of the idea, therefore in descriptions of projects, offered for practical realization, a phrase is present "unique technology, not having analogues in the world". In the vast majority of cases (although, of course, there are exceptions), this phrase means only that the authors did not conduct a patent search and search of similar technologies and products, or a search was conducted but not thoroughly. The results of the search should contain the following information:

- products and technologies available on the market and similar in purpose;
- their technical characteristics;
- their cost characteristics (including maintenance).

5. Determination of the market benefits of technology. Assessment of the market advantages of the intellectual product or technology is made up of several components.

In the case when the product has no analogs on the market, the potential market of a product may be very extensive. In this case, the manufacturer most likely will need a substantial investment of financial resources for the advertising campaign of a new product in order to convince the buyer that he (the buyer) must satisfy hisneed (of which he had not known) for a new product. In such a situation it is necessary to carefully assess the market of the intended product.

In the case of analogs of the prospective product being already on the market, we should:

- compare the prices of the intended product and analogs;
- assess the degree of improvement of technical and consumer properties in comparison with the analogs;
- compare the value of the intended product and analogs;
- compare the estimated operating costs and the operating costs of the analogs.

6. Evaluation of market prospects. In evaluating the market prospects of the intended product (technology) it is necessary to take into account the following factors:

- actual presence of market of this object of intellectual property (whether there is a requirement in this commodity);
- the size of the market and its dynamics. Studying the market of any products and forecast of its dynamics over the next few years is a very difficult task and thebest solution is to contact the experts. It is quite possible that the size of the market for the new product is restricted, or negative dynamics mean that by the time of the release of the new product demand will be very small.
- competition in the market. The existence on the market of active competition and large companies–competitors with significant resources–significantly reduces the likelihood of successful commercialization of ideas or inventions.

7. Practical feasibility. Evaluation of the practical feasibility of the idea (invention) is carried out in the following directions:

- the availability of specialists, both in the technical and the commercial realization of the idea;
- estimation of the cost of ideas and the availability of funding;
- availability of materials for realization of the idea;
- term of realization of the project for the commercialization of ideas and a payback period of invested funds;
- procedural restrictions on the production of the intended product.

Now let us consider what is evaluated during the technological audit, how and according to what criteria. Selection of evaluation criteria directly depends on the purpose of the audit and can quite vary greatly depending on the branch of industry, on the situation in the business sphere of a region or country, and on the specifics of the object of evaluation. In general, though its development innovative technology can act on the various aspects of the existence and activities of both the company and its particular enterprise. Therefore, the emphasis and the importance of the criteria for the evaluation of technologies can vary considerably. Table 2 shows the main parameters for carrying out an assessment of the commercial potential and the capacity of transfer of technologies (Brett A., 1995). Comparison of the identified technologies usually begins with such a table. In the cells of the table in the mode of active discussion a score is given for each of the technologies identified in the course of technological audit. Various systems of scoring occur In different countries. In this case either a five-point system (modeled on schools)or some other five-point evaluation system (for example, from -2 to +2) seems convenient with the semantic content of each assessment:

- +2 - excellent,
- +1 - good, acceptable,
- 0 - satisfactory, medium (as well as vague, unknown),
- -1 - poor, significantly below the average,
- -2 - verypoor.

Table 2
Matrix calculation for capacity for commercialization and building technology transfer

Potential for commercialization of intellectual property objects		intellectual property objects		
		№1	№....	№ N
1	The reasonable cost of the commercial establishment of the OIP			
2	The opportunity to obtain not one, but a family of products or applications			
3	The existence of a market			
4	Competitive advantages			
5	Industrial elaboration already carried out or being conducted at the present time			
Final assessment of potential commercializationof the OIP				
The potential transfer of the OIP				
1	OIP is sufficiently prepared to transfer			
2	There is a group that can help in the development or transfer of intellectual property objects			
3	OIP is worthy of attention from a market point of view			
4	Terms of commercialization are reasonable			
5	Actual or potential buyers of technology or license have been identified			
Final assessment of the potential transfer of the OIP				
Total assessment				

In addition, it is possible to go beyond these interval estimates, if any parameter of technology is fundamentally unacceptable (for example, from an environmental point of view, or by reason of dual-use prohibited by specific agreements), or promises such high profits that it may outweigh minor flaws in the other dimensions.

According to the results of completion of the summary matrix for all technologies identified by the customer in the course of the audit, the sum of the points are simply calculated as total points characterizing separately the commercial potential and the potential of the transfer, as well as the final score given as the sum of these two summary points. By the result of audit and there is a report of these three marks on all technologies, on the basis of what recommendation is formulated about the preference of work on the transfer of technologies, collecting maximal marks, and on occasion – and recommendation about the most preferable strategy of transfer or commercialization.

CONCLUSION

The results of the study showed that technological auditing is one of the essential conditions of successful implementation of the results of innovation activities in any country. The individuality of innovative products requires each of the enterprisesto develop their own approach to this process. Therefore, for the effective commercialization of objects of intellectual property enterprises need to pay particular attention to the selection of a method of commercialization. The enterprise which can not only develop an innovation, but also the right to implement it, is able to preserve its competitiveness and increase the efficiency of its activities.

REFERENCES

ABRAMOV A.A. Analysis of the innovation capacity of the new production of industrial enterprises / A.A.Abramov // Bulletin of the Taganrog State University.- Issue 11 (115).- 2012.- P. 90-95 .

ALLEN K. Promotion of new technologies to the market / K.Allen. - Moscow: BINOM. Knowledge Laboratory , 2007. – 455p.

BRETT A. Evaluation of the commercialization of technology / A. Brett // In the book . "Technology Commercialization . Global experience - the Russian regions".- M.: Moscow News, 1995. - P.78 -93 .

ZABELINA I.N. Socio-economic content and the role of intellectual property in innovative economy: the thesis abstract on competition of a scientific degree of candidate of economic sciences: 08.00.01 / I.N. Zabelina. - Eagle 2006. – 24 p.

KLETKINA Y.A. Evaluation of the commercial potential of intellectual property / Y.A. Kletkina // Russian Entrepreneurship.- 2008. - №12.- Issue.1 (124). - P. 70-75.

KOZYREV A.N. Valuation of intangible assets and intellectual property / A.N. Kozyrev, V.L. Makarov.- Moscow: World charts, 2003.- 352 p.

PESTUNOV M.A. The management of intellectual property / M.A.Pestunov.- Chelyabinsk : Publishing House of the CSU, 2006.- 409 p.

RODIONOVA E.M. Comprehensive assessment of the commercial potential of product innovation university / E.M.Rodionova // Bulletin of the Chelyabinsk State University.- 2009.- №19 (157).- Economy. - Vol. 21.- P.147-155.

SPIRIDONOV E.A. The economic rationale for commercialization strategy intellekutalnoy property : Dis. candidate ... ekon.nauk . - St. Petersburg , 2009.- 24 p.

DODGSON M. and Rothwell R. (Eds.).The Handbook of Industrial Innovations. – Aldershot: Brookfield, 1994. – P. 78-93.

NELSON R. The Simple Economics of Basic Research / R.Nelson // The Journal of Political Economy, Vol. 67, No. 3 (Jun., 1959), The University of Chicago Press. – P. 297-306.

KOCZISZKY G. Technology transfer / G.Kocziszky, P.G.Pererva.- Kharkiv-Miskolc, 2012.- 668p.

ROGERS E.M. Diffusion of innovations (4th ed.) / E.M.Rogers // New York: The Free Press, 1995. – P. 367.

ROSENBERG N. Inside the Black Box / N.Rosenberg.- Cambridge: Cambridge University Press, 1982. – P. 304.

6

Forming the Strategic Potential for Development of Machine-building Enterprises: The Balanced Scorecard in Use

ROMAN POBEREZHNYI
ASSOCIATE PROFESSOR

e-mail: pobrom@gmail.com

SUMMARY

The methodological approaches to strategy development for engineering companies using balanced scorecard are described in the article. The results are given of an analysis of strategic potential of modern Ukrainian machine-building enterprises. An indicator of the current state of the base potential and integral index of the potential of the enterprise forinnovative development is proposed that characterizes the use of the strategic potential of Ukrainian machine-building enterprises.
Keywords: strategic potential, internal and external environment

INTRODUCTION

The long-term effective operation of any company, including an engineering firm, requires that its growth and development are determined by the right choice of strategic guidelines that allow the best way to realize the potential human capital and other resources of the enterprise. The strategy that the company selects must ensure sustainable economic growth and development of the company, increasing its competitiveness. Therefore, engineering firms are now faced with the task of development of effective management, including strategic management, in order to take the lead.

The problems of strategic management, how to evaluate and formulate strategic directions of development potential, and problems of methodological of predicting outcomes of development strategies are important for modern enterprises and are analyzed through various aspects in a number of scientific works.In particular, Kaplan and Norton studied the causal relationships between strategic objectives of enterprises and structural units and functional services based on the Balanced Scorecard. Marytnenko andIgnatieff described the basic principles of strategic management. Rampersad paid attention to the formation of the mission and strategic goals based on the concept of a universal system performance of the enterprise. Fedulova, Ivakina, and Malyarets described and studied a modern criteria balanced scorecard (BSC) for defining and shaping an effective strategy for avcompany. Shekhovtsova, Mizyuk, Shershneva, Thompson and Strickland explored the nature of management and its place in the management system,ad analyzed the content management objective laws governing the functioning and development of the organization's management system in market conditions.

The basis for practical calculations is primarily statistical and financial information of machine-building enterprises of the Kharkov region in 2007 to 2011. To achieve this goal a system of general and special methods was used.

POTENTIAL DEVELOPMENT OF MACHINE-BUILDING ENTERPRISES

It must be noted that modern enterprises for sustainable development should be considered as a condition of the internal environment, as well as constant and variable conditions of an unstable external environment. At the same time we believe that the strategic development of the company has properties as shown in Figure 1:

- cyclicity - a property that is to move from quantity to quality, new quality gives the further development, etc.;
- helicity - the property that is the change of the spiral, with different influences in the development of the object. Direction can be positive or negative for object development. There are both upward and downward spirals of development.

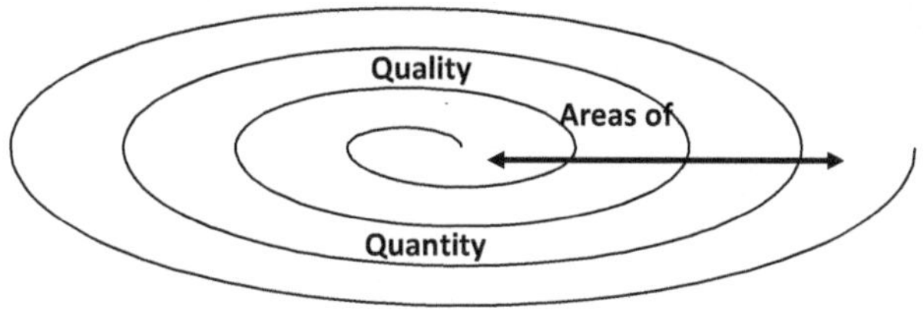

Source: own development

Figure 1. Properties of strategic development of industrial enterprises

Consider the development of the organization as a positive impact of development, so that a negative effect or a negative development will lead, ultimately, to the liquidation of the company.

The overall system organization as shown in Figure 2 represents a set of elements of the internal environment that characterize the capabilities and limitations of a company, which through the development and implementation of strategic and operational decisions form the elements of the scope of the enterprise, describing the organization's activities in the environment of operation.

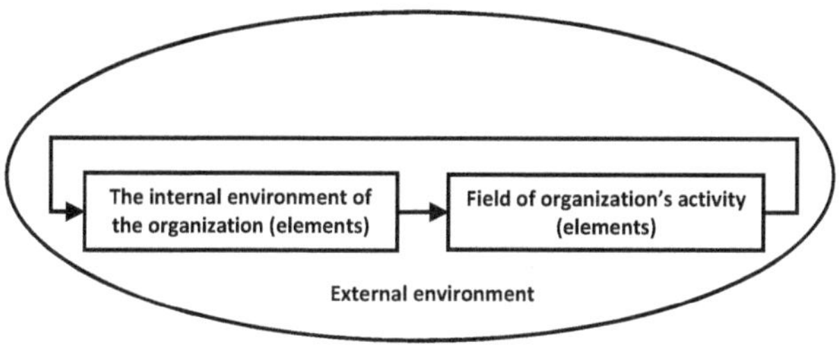

Source: own development

Figure 2. General system of the organization

Internal elements of the enterprise environment affect the formation of element areas that allow for better internal environment elements. The properties of the organization reflect the cyclical and helical development.

The elements of internal environment that characterize the capabilities and limitations of this company, in our view, should include:

- Raw materials (their quality, quantity, price, etc.);
- Technology (existing in the enterprise);
- The means of labor (fixed assets, their characteristics);
- Company personnel (structure, quantity, quality characteristics, etc.);
- Financial resources (equity and debt, generating funds, investment, etc.);
- Structure of the enterprise (the division of responsibilities and work, hierarchy, degree of freedom in decision making, etc.);
- Management system (principles and tools of management, planning, organization, control, motivation, and coordination);
- System information (documents, characteristics, information security, etc.);
- The process of converting raw materials into a finished product (value chain, cost, etc.).

Development of the elements of the internal environment of the organization increases the possibilities and reduces limiting on the activity of the company, and thus contributes to the development of reasonable and timely strategic and operational decisions, which in turn creates and develops the scope of activity of the enterprise.

The scope of the enterprise, which characterizes the activities of the organization in its environment functioning includes, in our opinion, the following elements:

- Finished product (the quality, price, consumer value, etc.);
- The market and consumers (market share, new markets, old and new customers, etc.);
- Position within the industry (competitors, suppliers, distribution system and sales, etc.);
- Technology (technology applied, innovation, novelty, etc.).

Development of the elements of the business sector enables a company to more effectively set strategic and operational objectives, increase productivity and efficiency of activities of the organization, and provides opportunities for the development of its internal environment.

Strategic management is now seen as not only a set of strategic management decisions that determine the long-term development of the enterprise, but also concrete action to ensure rapid response to changes of the external environment that may require strategic maneuvering, revision of goals and choosing a new direction of development (Ivakina I., 2007).

For their existing conception about the state of the implementation of selected goals for objective measurement of the results of implementation strategy, the management of many Ukrainian machine-building enterprises has used the traditional system of financial-accounting indicators. In our opinion, in today's conditions of development, which has replaced the earlier industrial competition, now it is the time of information competition, meaning that reconsideration is needed of approaches to the formation, control and efficient allocation of financial, industrial, intangible and labor assets of the company. Enterprises need an additional evaluation system, which is linked to accurate and reliable financial evaluation of such intangible assets as market promotion of new products and services, potential ability, experience, interest in employee flexibility, customer loyalty, innovation projects, investment in production and workers, and other assets.

In order to satisfy the needs of Ukrainian enterprises, we are proposing to use the method of Balanced Scorecard (BSC) (Kaplan R. and Norton D., 1992). BSC complements the financial parameters system which reflect the results of grading the development prospects system of enterprises. Objectives and indicators of the system are formed depending on the ideology and strategy of each organization and consider its activities on four criteria: financial, customer relationship, internal business processes, as well as training and staff development (Kaplan R. and Norton D., 2003).

Figure 3 shows the relationship and subordination between the components of BSC by shaping the strategy of development of a modern engineering enterprise. This vision is based on the proposed dual structure of potential strategic development of industrial enterprises (including engineering), which combines the current state of the underlying potential and the ability of companies to develop, i.e. the effectiveness of innovative potential.

Thus, in our view, the modern industrial enterprise faces two major tasks: first, creation of a system of indicators, and second, its use as an integrated system of strategic control for their development.

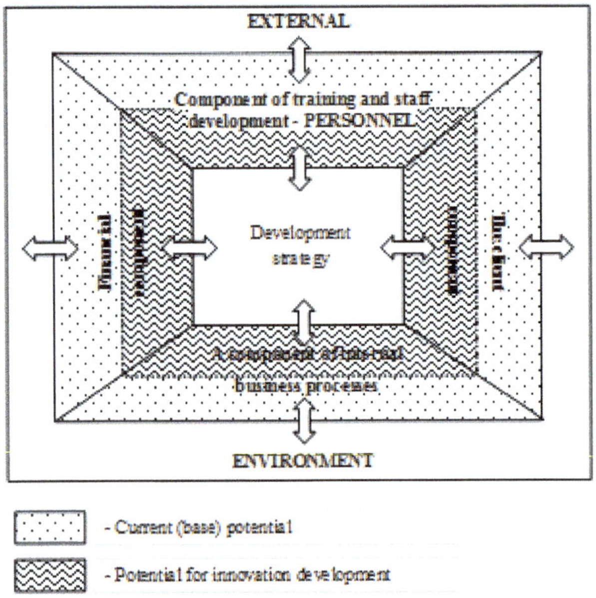

Source: own development

Figure 3. Subordination and the relationship between components of BSC in the formation of development strategy

One of the main methods of management for the development potential of industrial enterprises is to develop a system of evaluation and development of methods of assessment on development potential and its prediction to identify the priority capacity of a development enterprise environment.

As a result, there is a need for quantitative and qualitative assessment of the current (base) potential and capacity for innovation development to guide the process of formation of competitive advantage and provide evaluation and formulation of strategic directions of engineering enterprises.

Analysis of Development Potential

For solving the problems that relate to the company's further development and creating the most effective strategy, tabulated lists of indicators that are part of the BSC are given for assessing the current potential (Table 1) and the potential for innovative development (Table 2). Application of the proposed system performance will, in our view, take into account their integrated impact on the competitive advantages of machine-building enterprises.

Table 1
Indicators for evaluation of the current (base) potential of machine-building enterprises

Indicator	Symbol
1.1 The financial component	
1.1.1 Ratio of general (current) liquidity	$X_{1.1.1.}$
1.1.2 Return on equity	$X_{1.1.2.}$
1.1.3 Net return on sales	$X_{1.1.3.}$
1.1.4 Share of labor costs in operating expenses	$X_{1.1.4.}$
1.1.5 Share of social transfers in operating costs	$X_{1.1.5.}$
1.2 Staff	
1.2.1 Rate of utilization of time	$X_{1.2.1.}$
1.2.2 Share of workers aged 18 to 55 years	$X_{1.2.2.}$
1.2.3 Proportion of employees with university degrees	$X_{1.2.3.}$
1.2.4 Proportion of additional salary	$X_{1.2.4.}$
1.2.5 Share of administrative costs in the cost of goods sold	$X_{1.2.5.}$
1.3 The client component	
1.3.1 Net profitability on sales	$X_{1.3.1.}$
1.3.2 Rate of turnover of receivables	$X_{1.3.2.}$
1.3.3 Rate of credit turnover payable	$X_{1.3.3.}$
1.3.4 Share of cost of marketing in the cost of goods sold	$X_{1.3.4.}$
1.4 Business processes	
1.4.1 Coefficient of autonomy	$X_{1.4.1.}$
1.4.2 Coefficient of financial stability	$X_{1.4.2.}$
1.4.3 Coefficient life of fixed assets	$X_{1.4.3.}$
1.4.4 Reduction factor for fixed assets	$X_{1.4.4.}$
1.4.5 Share of production costs in the cost of goods sold	$X_{1.4.5.}$
1.4.6 Average annual outputper worker, thousandUAH/person	$X_{1.4.6.}$
1.4.7 The share of investment in fixed assets of own capital	$X_{1.4.7.}$

Source: author

A development strategy for machine-building enterprises involves finding out the current strategy and analysis of the current (base) potential and efficiency in using the company's potential for innovation development.

Table 2

Indicators for evaluation of the potential for innovative development of engineering enterprises

Indicator	Symbol
2.1 The financial component	
2.1.1 Share of investments in intangible assets in total assets	$X_{2.1.1.}$
2.1.2 Share of investment in informatization of the total investment in intangible assets	$X_{2.1.2.}$
2.1.3 Share of domestic investors investment in total spending on innovation	$X_{2.1.3.}$
2.1.4 Share of investments of foreign investors in the total expenditure on innovation	$X_{2.1.4.}$
2.2 Component of training and staff development	
2.2.1 Share of workers with knowledge of new professions	$X_{2.2.1.}$
2.2.2 Share of workers who raised their qualification within the last year	$X_{2.2.2.}$
2.2.3 Share of workers who are inventors and innovators	$X_{2.2.3.}$
2.3 The client component	
2.3.1 Image resource	$X_{2.3.1}$
2.3.2 S of expenditure on participation in trade shows and other image events in total costs of product sales	$X_{2.3.2.}$
2.3.3 Share of spending on marketing and advertising	$X_{2.3.3.}$
2.3.4 Share of shipped innovative products in total sales of products	$X_{2.3.4.}$
2.3.5 Share of new products set for export in total new products	$X_{2.3.5.}$
2.3.6 Proportion of new technologies transferred abroad in the total transferred technology	$X_{2.3.6.}$
2.4 Business - Processes	
2.4.1 Share of investment in innovation in total capital	$X_{2.4.1.}$
2.4.2 Share of investment in innovation in equity	$X_{2.4.2.}$
2.4.3 Share of expenditure on research and development (excluding depreciation) of the total expenditure on innovation	$X_{2.4.3.}$
2.4.4 Share of expenditure on machinery, equipment and software associated with the introduction of innovations in the total expenditure on innovation	$X_{2.4.4.}$
2.4.5 Share of own investments in technological innovation in the total cost of innovation	$X_{2.4.5.}$
2.4.6 Proportionof products shipped that underwentsubstantialtechnological changein the totalshippedproducts	$X_{2.4.6.}$
2.4.7 Proportion of products shipped produced using an improved process of manufacture in total products shipped	$X_{2.4.7.}$
2.4.8 Proportion of transfer of new technologies in Ukraine in total transferred technology	$X_{2.4.8.}$

Source: author

Implementation strategy associated with conducting strategic changes should lead to three challenges: 1) the prioritization of administrative tasks in accordance with the strategy adopted, 2) to establish whether the chosen strategy and development processes of resources are a potential component of selected components of BSC, 3) reduction in accordance with the chosen strategy management capabilities of the enterprise.

For the study we selected 19 leading, famous engineering companies in Ukraine, Kharkov. Among them the most competitive companies are: Open Joint Stock Company(OJSC) "Turboatom" which is manufacturer of enginesand turbinesfor nuclearand electricpower plants, Joint Stock Company(JSC) "Kaharkov Bearing Plant" which is manufacturer ofball androller bearingsand theirparts, Public Joint Stock Company (PJSC) "FED" which is manufacturer of aircraft and spacecraft, PJSC "Volchansky Aggregate Plant" which is of aircraft and spacecraft, cars, it is a researcher inthe field of engineering, JSC "Kharkiv Machine Building Plant "Light Miner" which is manufacturerof machinesand equipment formining and construction industries, research in technical sciences, JSC "Plant. Frunze" which is manufacturerof pumpsand compressors, JSC "Kupyansky Engineering Works" which is manufacturerof machines and equipmentfor processingagricultural products, JSC "Izymsky Locomotive Works" which is manufacturerof railway rolling stock.

Financial and statistical reports of enterprises for 2007 - 2011 years were obtained for the analysis. Requiredand mostinfluentialparameterswere obtainedbymultivariatefactor analysisusing the package STATISTICA 6.0.The integral parameters of the current (base) potential and efficiency potential of innovative development of engineering enterprises were calculated based on the performanceevaluationsystem(Table1 and2) andthe relevant data.

Analysis of the use of strategic development potential was carried out for 2007 to 2011. The overall results of the analysis are shown in Figures 4.

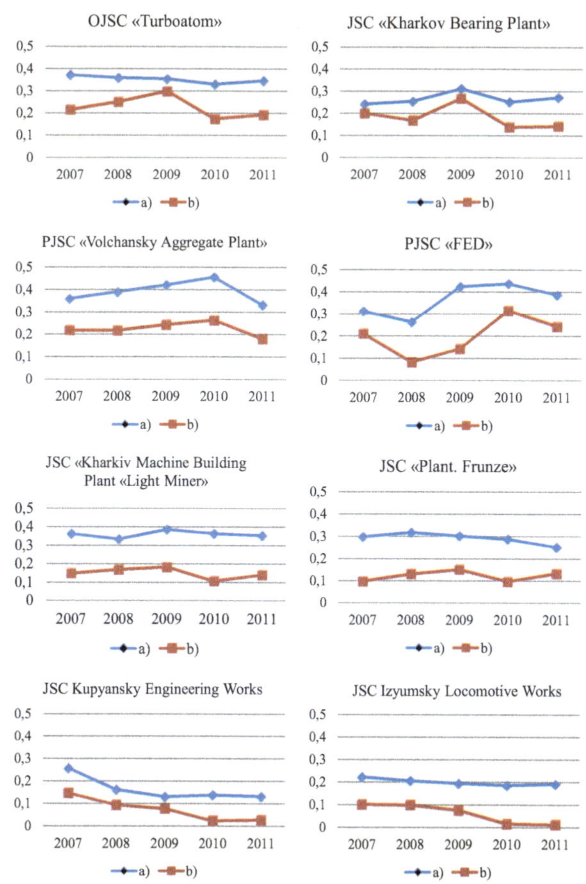

Source: own development

Figure 4. Dynamics of integral parameters of (a) the current (base) potential and (b) efficiency potential of innovative development of four engineering enterprises

The effectiveness of strategic development potential should be basedon an analysis ofthe calculated integral index ofthe current state of basic capabilities and the integrated parameterpotential of the enterprise for development andinnovation.

Graphically presented information shows insufficient effectiveness use of basic capabilities and potential of innovative development for 2007 - 2011 years of selected companies. The largest integral parameter of the current (base) potential reaches 0.36 in 2007 and 0.35 in 2011 in the JSC "Kharkiv Machine Building Plant "Light miner". The smallest integral parameter of the current (base) potential reaches 0.13 in the JSC "Kupyansky Engineering Works". The calculated indicators do not reach1 or 100%. Currentpotential of thesecompaniesis used only13%-40%. This indicates theexistence of problemsin the managementof enterprises,the lack ofstrategicplanning,the shortcomingsin personnelpolicies andweakmarketing.

Presented graphically dynamic potential of innovative development is evidence of itssmallsize andtendency tosmall changes. The largest integral parameter of potential of innovative development reaches 0.21 in 2007 and 0.19 in 2011 in the OJSC "Turboatom". The smallest integral parameter of potential of innovative development reaches 0.09 in 2007 and 0.13 in 2011 in the PJSC "FED". The calculated indicators do not reach1 or 100%. Potential of innovative development is used only13%-40%. This suggests the need for additional investment in these enterprises for development of innovative activity. Also it required staff training, updating of material and production base, the introduction of new technologies, the usage of progressive forms and methods of management.

CONCLUSIONS

The analysis of the dynamics of integrated indicators characterizing the use of strategic capacity development for local engineering industry indicates the following:

- the existence of negative trends, which is evident in the decline of manufacturing engineering products that are competitive on the domestic and foreign markets;
- formation of negative trends associated with the influence of a rapidly changing external environment and the lack of a clear strategic program for long-term business development in machine-building enterprises and of strategic management of its potential;
- strategic development potential is the most important factor for the economic and strategic security of an engineering enterprise and defines the base for creating a long-term competitive advantage.
- the balanced scorecard approach can provide accurate and timely information about the current (base) potential and the potential for innovative development of engineering enterprises. We believe that this information will allow for more efficient shaping of competitive advantages and improve strategic decision making at engineering companies.

REFERENCES

FEDULOVA, L. (2007): Current concepts of management. Kyiv: Center educational literature.

RAMPERSAD,H.(2004):A universal systemperformance: How to achieve results, while maintaining the integrity of the(translated from English.). Moscow:Harvard Business Review.

IVAKINA, I. (2007): The Balanced Scorecard. Kharkov: Factor.

KAPLAN, R., NORTON, D. (2003):The Balanced Scorecard(Translatedfrom English.). Moscow:Olympus -Businesss

MALYARETS, L. (2008): The Balanced Scorecard in the evaluation of the enterprise. Kharkiv: Abstract.

MARTYNENKO, M., IGNATIEV, I. (2006): Strategic Management. Kyiv: Caravel.

MIZYUK, B. (2006): Essentials of Strategic Management. Lviv: Magnolia.

SHEKHOVTSEVA, L. (2006):Strategic Management.Kaliningrad:IzdRSUthem.Kant.

SHERSHNEVA, S. (2004) Strategic Management. Kyiv: MBK.

THOMPSON, A., STRICKLAND, A. (1998): Strategic Management. Art of strategy development and implementation (translated from English.). Moscow: Unity.

7

Optimizing the Number and Location of Warehouses in Logistics Networks Considering the Optimal Delivery Routes and Set Level of Reserve Stock

VOLODYMYR V. SYSOIEV, Ph.D.
ASSOCIATE PROFESSOR
e-mail: sysoevvv@ukr.net

SUMMARY

Forming the optimal structure of a warehouse network is one of the main strategic tasks in arranging an efficient logistics network. The suggested mathematical model and iterative method allow an optimal number and location of warehouses (in the area served by the logistics network) to be defined – with the minimum of total logistics costs for shipping of goods from suppliers through warehouses to customers. The focus is on optimal delivery routes and the optimal level to set for reserve stock contained in the storage network.
Keywords: logistics network, warehouse, optimal warehouse location, logistics costs, optimaldelivery route.

INTRODUCTION

The globalization of business requires efficient management in the movement of goods between manufacturers, resellers, and consumers, which can only be ensured by the establishment of large multi-format logistics networks. At the heart of setting up any logistics network (dealing with distribution of material flows in the field of supply and distribution logistics), there is the complex task of arranging the optimal structure for its most important subsystem – the warehouse network, which includes defining the number of warehouses and their geographical location in the service area. The solution of this task requires a large amount of initial data: the scope of supply and demand for goods, locations of suppliers and consumers, estimated capacity of warehouses, features of transportation services, logistics costs, etc., which requires the use of economic-mathematical methods and models.

The urgency of the task is due to the fact that the number of warehouses and their locations in the logistics network (with extensive transport infrastructure) have a significant effect on costs involved in the delivery of goods to consumers, thus affecting the final cost of sold products. Given that transport and storage costs show different responses to a change in the number of warehouses and their locations (with regards to producers and consumers), the dependence between total costs for the operation of a logistics network and the number of warehouses is parabolic, i.e., the task can be formulated as a search for an optimal or sub-optimal (close to optimal) solution.

ANALYSIS OF EXISTENT METHODS

The complexity and multi-factor character of this complex task have led to (in the majority of cases) separate solutions for its two components.

The first task – defining the number of warehouses – is solved by the method of economic compromises, regarding the totality of all costs associated with their maintenance. This task is a basis for the establishment of centralized and decentralized distribution of goods. The best-known approach to its solution is based on the qualitative dependence between various logistics costs and numbers of warehouses, which assumes the selection of their optimal number – in the absence of formulas and quantitative characteristics, based on logic and common sense (Coyle et al., 1985). The analytical method of solving this task assumes selecting the number of warehouses with use of a linear programming model, which optimizes the general costs (including the costs for construction of warehouses, costs for shipping of goods to consumers, and costs for warehouse handling) (Dybskay, 2008).

The second task (choosing the warehouse location) was first reviewed within the theory of labor forces siting (production companies) – by German scientist A. Weber, who formulated it as mathematical problem of choosing the lowest transportation costs for shipping of goods between warehouse and a group of spatially distributed consumers (while considering the distance factor only) (Weber, 1929).

With development of logistics as an economic science, there was an increase in the importance of tasks aiming to define the location of warehouses (when forming a spatially distributed logistics network). While formulating the three basic strategies of positioning the distribution warehouses (depending on the principle of their arrangement: near markets, near production sites, or in an intermediate location), well-known "golden rules" of sales logistics still require some mathematical calculations (to determine the specific areas of their placement) (Hoover, 1948).

Later, the methodology of solving a task on defining the location of warehouses (distribution centers) in logistics networks developed towards a combination of economic-mathematical models – due to more complete accounting of influencing factors and economization of its optimizing criteria.

A conceptual vision of the task (spatial location of warehouses in logistics network) and the main approaches to its solution (regarding the possible restrictions, optimizing and multi-purpose nature of the task) are presented in Tansel et al. (1983a, 1983b). A typology of tasks (placing the objects in a logistics network depending on management objectives), parameters affecting their solution, and performance indicators were reviewed in Brandeau and Chiu (1989).

Depending on the nature of variation, they distinguish the methods of solving a continuous and discrete task (defining the location of warehouses). In one case, the warehouse may be located anywhere (in the area under review); in the second case it should be at pre-defined locations, which is more realistic (given the actual transportation services of logistics networks).

Methods of solving the continuous task have included the center of gravity method for cargo flows (Bowersox, 1974) and,,based upon it, the method of the equilibrium system center, which accounts for transportation costs (serving as weight factors) (Coyle et al., 1985; Mirotin, 2002), as well as the method of searching for minimum transport work (Sergueyev, 1997). In methods based on the "mass center of a physical body", distances (even average-weighted) are determined by coordinate axes (considered in straight lines), which requires the imposition of a coordinate grid on the map of potential warehouse locations and is effective only if the area under review is provided with a developed network of transportation services. The fundamental difference of a method searching for minimum transport work lies in defining the distance between objects as a "hypotenuse", as well as in applying the iterative algorithm of combined search, which allows the detection of optimal warehouse location (through successive evaluation of options).

The majority of methods for solving a discrete task (defining the warehouse location) are not optimizing methods. The method of factor-rating systems lies in a point-based assessment of factors affecting the choice of warehouse location; despite the possibility of accounting for qualitative indicators, this method has the significant drawback of all expert methods – subjectivity in defining the point scale and in assessment of factors (their weight ratios) (Wild, 1995). The autoregressive method, which enables more strict definition of the most important features (during selection of warehouse location), requires a large scope of statistical material and does not allow the dependence of variables (multicollinearity of factors) (Chase et al., 1998). In some scientific papers, the solution of a discrete problem is viewed using a method of defining the zones of influence (on consumers), which are used in marketing: the method of isochronous lines (Engel, 1995), method of potential sales areas (Tjapuhin, 2001), method of identifying and segmenting the trade zones (Yager, 1982). However, all of these are characterized by a high degree of subjectivity and do not ensure an optimal solution.

The majority of the above-mentioned methods can solve either the task of defining the number of warehouses or the task of defining their location; at that, the warehouse is usually viewed only as a source of material flow, which does not reflect the specifics of arranging the logistics networks, where the warehouse is a link between suppliers and consumers (both in the field of supply and sales).

In this view, particular interest is caused by methods for solving a complex task which consider the interaction of warehouses with all members of a logistics network. As a rule, such methods assume the shared use of optimization models and heuristic methods, which adjust the obtained theoretical solutions based on actual network infrastructure, transportation services, features of vehicles, possible variations in demand, level of reserve stock, time restrictions, etc.

There are several approaches to the formulation of a complex task, which differ in optimization criteria: the first one focuses on distance characteristics (Wilson, 1974); the second on cost characteristics, while using the full cost of the storage network (Giddings et al., 2000) or total transport work (Lukinskiy (Ed.), 2007) or total transport and storage costs as indicators (Khumawala and Kelly, 1974); the third one considers time characteristics (O'Kelly, 1986); and the fourth (complex) one simultaneously considers multiple characteristics (Cheong et al., 2007; Salihov, 2007).

Among the main drawbacks of actual approaches to solving a complex task, we should distinguish among one-criterion character of models, two-stage optimization of the delivery process (before/after the warehouses), and a snap-to-coordinate grid, which, apart from additional heuristic procedures required to specify the location of warehouses, also cannot consider the diversity of actual transportation services (in the area served by the logistics network) or define the optimal routes for door-to-door delivery of goods (from suppliers, through warehouses, and to consumers).

The purpose of this paper is to develop a model and method for optimizing the number and location of warehouses – regarding optimal routes of cargo delivery in the logistics network, storage costs, andthe set scope of reserve stock of goods at warehouses.

MODEL

Let us review the logistics network comprising of suppliers I and consumers J (for a certain kind of goods) and having geographical pointsMpossible locationsof warehouses (for their storage and handling).

Initial data for the task:

$W_i(i=\overline{1,I})$ – scope of supplying the goods from the i-th supplier;

$V_j(j=\overline{1,J})$ – scope of demand in goods of the j-th consumer, while $\sum_{i=1}^{I} W_i \geq \sum_{j=1}^{J} V_j$;

$\mu_i(i=\overline{1,I})$, $\beta_j(j=\overline{1,J})$ – weight factors of the i-th supplier and j-th consumer, respectively (reflecting the additional factors that affect the plan on optimal attachment of consumers to suppliers – e.g., impossibility of direct transit (warehouse) supplies or their priority with regards to other supplies);

$d_{ij}(i,j=\overline{1,M})$ – distance between all points of the logistics network (linked by relevant transportation services);

Z – scope of total stock reserve for certain type of goods, which must always be maintained in warehouses of the logistics network under review.

It is necessary to determine the optimal number of warehouses and their locations in potential points of logistics network at the smallest possible total of logistics (transportation and storage) costs. Cost indicatorsare shown inconventional monetary units (CMU).

Regarding the minimizing nature of optimality criterion, it would be appropriate to convert and normalize the weight factors:

$$\mu_i' = \frac{1}{\mu_i}; i=\overline{1,I}; \qquad \beta_j' = \frac{1}{\beta_j}; j=\overline{1,J};$$

$$\bar{\mu}_i = \frac{\mu_i'}{\sum_{i=1}^{I}\mu_i'}; \qquad \bar{\beta}_j = \frac{\beta_j'}{\sum_{j=1}^{J}\beta_j'}.$$

A mathematical model of the task (defining the number and location of warehouses in the logistics network, based on actual transportation services and the need to maintain reserve stocks in the warehouse network) looks like:

$$B(X,Y) = [\sum_{i=1}^{I}\sum_{k=1}^{N} d_{ik}\bar{\mu}_i x_{ik} + \sum_{k=1}^{N}\sum_{j=1}^{J} d_{kj}\bar{\beta}_j y_{kj}]T_0 + \varphi[G_{k_1}^{(N)}; G_{k_2}^{(N)};...; G_{k_N}^{(N)}] \rightarrow \min,$$

$$\sum_{k=1}^{N} x_{ik} \leq W_i; i=\overline{1,I};$$

$$\sum_{i=1}^{I} x_{ik} \leq G_k; k=\overline{1,N}; \qquad (1)$$

$$\sum_{i=1}^{I} x_{ik} - \sum_{j=1}^{J} y_{kj} \geq \frac{Z}{N}; k=\overline{1,N};$$

$$\sum_{k=1}^{N} y_{kj} = V_j; j=\overline{1,J};$$

$$x_{ik} \geq 0; i=\overline{1,I}; k=\overline{1,N};$$

$$y_{kj} \geq 0; k=\overline{1,N}; j=\overline{1,J},$$

where B(X,Y) – total logistics costs for transportation of goods from suppliers to warehouses and from warehouses to suppliers (including the storage costs);

N – required number of warehouses in points of the logistics network;

d_{ik}, d_{kj} – distances between suppliers and warehouses, warehouses and consumers (accordingly);

$X = \|x_{ik}\|_{I,N}$ – matrix – scopes of goods transported from suppliers to warehouses;

$Y = \|y_{kj}\|_{N,J}$ – matrix – scopes of goods transported from warehouses to suppliers;

T_0 – freight rate, CMU/t·km;

$\varphi[G_{k_1}^{(N)}; G_{k_2}^{(N)};...; G_{k_N}^{(N)}]$ – function of storage costs (depends on number and capacity of warehouses);

$G_k^{(N)}; k=\overline{1,N}$ – capacity of the k-th warehouse (at N-th number of warehouses).

Ratios – equations and inequations of the model include:

- limitations on the total export of goods from each supplier (to warehouses);
- limitations on the total import of goods from suppliers (to each warehouse);
- limitations on the size of reserve stock (at each warehouse);
- limitationson the needsof consumers andnon-negativityconditionson thequantity ofthe goods transported.

Task (1) assumes mathematical programming; its solution would cause no trouble if the location and number of warehouses (N) were known. For large logistics networks, determining a solution via sorting the possible number of warehouses and their locations is unacceptable (due to the inevitably large number of solution options).

METHOD

We suggest an iterative method of solving the task (the algorithm is shown in Fig. 1).

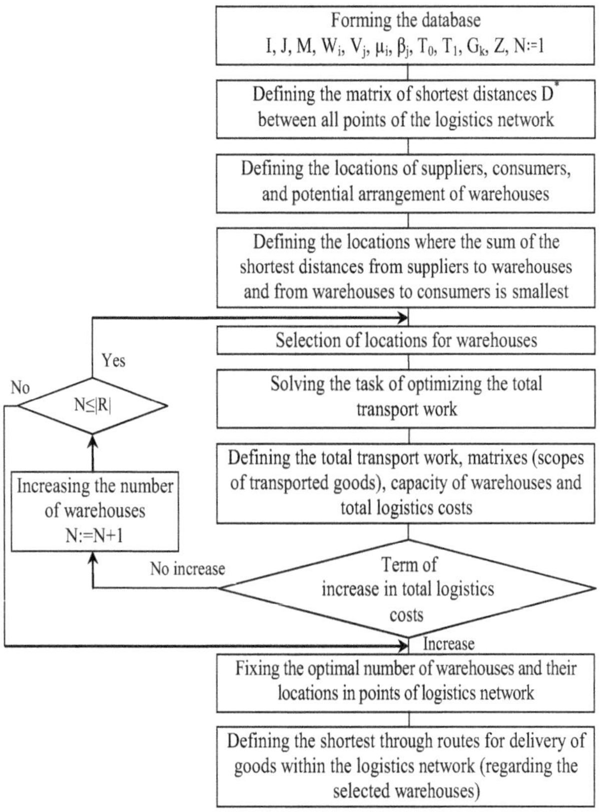

Figure 1. Algorithm of optimizing the number and location of warehouses in logistics network

Let us review in detail the main stages of the suggested task-solving procedure:

First stage. Let us define the matrix of distances between points of logistics network $D = \|d_{ij}\|_{M,M}$ as follows:

d_{ij}, if points i and j are directly linked to each other;
$D_{ij}= \infty$, if points i and j are not directly linked;
0, if $i = j$.

Second stage. Let us define the matrix of shortest distances between all points of the logistics network $D^* = \|d^*_{ij}\|_{M,M}$, while using a Bellman–Shimbel algorithm of search for the shortest path (Golstein, 1966):

$$d_{ij}^{2r} = \min_{1\le\lambda\le M} [d_{i\lambda}^{r} + d_{\lambda j}^{r}],\ r = 1,2,... \qquad (2)$$

For convenience of recording the expressions, let us assume that suppliers are located in points: 1,2,…,I and consumers – in points: M-J+1,M-J+2,…,M.

Let us define the set R as a subset of logistics network points {I+1,I+2,…,M-J} (possible locations of candidate warehouses) regarding the various constraints: geographic, economic, technical, social, etc. Thus, the warehouses can be placed in locations: $R \subseteq \{I+1, I+2,..., M-J\}$.

Third stage. Let us define the points of logistics network $k_s \in R; s = \overline{1,|R|}$, where the sum of the shortest distances (from suppliers to warehouses and from warehouses to consumers) is minimal:

$$k_1 = \arg\min_{k_s \in R} [\sum_{i=1}^{I} d^*_{ik_s} + \sum_{j=M-J+1}^{M} d^*_{k_s j}];$$

$$k_2 = \arg\min_{\substack{k_s \in R \\ k_s \ne k_1}} [\sum_{i=1}^{I} d^*_{ik_s} + \sum_{j=M-J+1}^{M} d^*_{k_s j}];$$

$$\vdots \qquad (3)$$

$$k_{|R|-1} = \arg\min_{\substack{k_s \in R \\ k_s \ne k_1; k_s \ne k_2,..., \\ k_s \ne k_{|R|-1}}} [\sum_{i=1}^{I} d^*_{ik_s} + \sum_{j=M-J+1}^{M} d^*_{k_s j}];$$

$$k_{|R|}.$$

Fourth stage.The total transportation work can be applied as the objective function instead of the total logistics costs in order to avoid the nonlinearityof the Task (1). The total transportation work is the essential characteristic of the carriage of goods process from suppliers to consumers via warehouses as well. Thus, the solution of the Task (1) can be similarly provided as a solution of the linear programming task:

$$F_1(X, Y) = \sum_{i=1}^{I}\sum_{k=1}^{N} d_{ik}\bar{\mu}_i x_{ik} + \sum_{k=1}^{N}\sum_{j=1}^{J} d_{kj}\bar{\beta}_j y_{kj} \to \min,$$

first, at N=1 ($k = k_1$), let us assume that the initial value of storage capacity is large enough (e.g. $G_{k_1} = \sum_{i=1}^{I} W_i$) and determine (for this case) the total transportation work $F_1^{(1)}$, matrixes (scopes of goods transported from suppliers to warehouse $X^{(1)} = \| x_{ik}^{(1)} \|_{I,1}$ and from warehouse to consumers) $Y^{(1)} = \| y_{kj}^{(1)} \|_{1,J}$, as well as capacity of the warehouse: $G_{k_1}^{(1)} = \sum_{i=1}^{I} x_{ik_1}^{(1)}$.

In this case, the minimum total (average-weighted) logistics costs (storage and transportation) will be:

$$B^{(1)} = [\sum_{i=1}^{I} \overline{\mu}_i L_{ik_1}^{(1)} d_{ik_1}^{*} + \sum_{j=1}^{J} \overline{\beta}_j L_{k_1 j}^{(1)} d_{k_1 j}^{*}] T_1 + \varphi(G_{k_1}^{(1)}) \quad (4)$$

where $L_{ik_1}^{(1)}, L_{k_1 j}^{(1)}$ are the number of cargo trips from the i-th supplier to the warehouse and from the warehouse to the j-th consumer, respectively, defined as:

$$L_{ik_1}^{(1)} = [\frac{x_{ik_1}^{(1)}}{q\gamma}]; \quad L_{k_1 j}^{(1)} = [\frac{y_{k_1 j}^{(1)}}{q\gamma}],$$

where q – rated carrying capacity of vehicle used for transportation;

γ – factor of utilizing the carrying capacity of vehicle;

T_1 – freight rate, CMU/km;

$\varphi(G_{k_1}^{(1)})$ – function of storage costs at one warehouse.

Then, while solving Task (1) for its objective function (total transportation work), where N=2 ($k = k_1, k = k_2$), let us define the total transportationwork $F_1^{(2)}$, matrixes (scopes of goods delivered from suppliers to two warehouses: $X^{(2)} = \| x_{ik}^{(2)} \|_{I,2}$ and from warehouses to consumers: $Y^{(2)} = \| y_{kj}^{(2)} \|_{2,J}$), as well as capacities of both warehouses: $G_{k_1}^{(2)} = \sum_{i=1}^{I} x_{ik_1}^{(2)}$, $G_{k_2}^{(2)} = \sum_{i=1}^{I} x_{ik_2}^{(2)}$.

In the case of two warehouses, the minimum total (average-weighted) logistic costs (storage and transportation) will be:

$$B^{(2)} = [\sum_{i=1}^{I} \sum_{s=1}^{2} \overline{\mu}_i L_{ik_s}^{(2)} d_{ik_s}^{*} + \sum_{s=1}^{2} \sum_{j=1}^{J} \overline{\beta}_j L_{k_s j}^{(2)} d_{k_s j}^{*}] T_1 + \phi[G_{k_1}^{(2)}; G_{k_2}^{(2)}] \quad (5)$$

where $L_{ik_s}^{(2)}, L_{k_s j}^{(2)}; s = \overline{1,N}$ are the number of cargo trips from the i-th supplier to the two warehouses and from the two warehouses to the j-th user, respectively, defined as:

$$L_{ik_s}^{(2)} = [\frac{x_{ik_s}^{(2)}}{q\gamma}]; s = \overline{1,N}; \quad L_{k_s j}^{(2)} = [\frac{y_{k_s j}^{(2)}}{q\gamma}]; s = \overline{1,N};$$

$\varphi[G_{k_1}^{(2)}; G_{k_2}^{(2)}]$ is thefunction of storage costs at the two warehouses.

Fifth stage. If total logistics costs for one warehouse are less than total logistics costs for two warehouses:

$$B^{(1)} \leq B^{(2)},$$

then one warehouse should be enough for the logistics network under review.

Otherwise, there is a transition to the fourth stage of the algorithm and Task (1) is solved for its objective function (total transportation work), where N=3 ($k = k_1$, $k = k_2$, $k = k_3$), etc., with relevant checks at the fifth stage, either till meeting the term of increase in total logistics costs or till having tried all items in the logistics network (subsets R from I+1 to M-J), which is practically improbable.

Sixth stage. Let us assume that optimal number of warehouses N and their locations in logistics network: $k_1, k_2, \dots, k_N$ have been defined. Following the solution of Task (1) for this set of warehouses, we obtain the optimal values of total transportationwork $F_1^{(N)}$, matrixes (scopes of goods transported to/from the warehouses $X^{(N)} = \| x_{ik}^{(N)} \|_{I,N}$, $Y^{(N)} = \| y_{kj}^{(N)} \|_{N,J}$), and capacity of all warehouses in logistics network:

$$G_{k_1}^{(N)} = \sum_{i=1}^{I} x_{ik_1}^{(N)}, \quad G_{k_2}^{(N)} = \sum_{i=1}^{I} x_{ik_2}^{(N)}, \dots, \quad G_{k_N}^{(N)} = \sum_{i=1}^{I} x_{ik_N}^{(N)}.$$

In this case, the minimum total (average-weighted) logistic costs (storage and transportation) will be:

$$B^{(N)} = [\sum_{i=1}^{I} \sum_{s=1}^{N} \overline{\mu}_i L_{ik_s}^{(N)} d_{ik_s}^{*} + \sum_{s=1}^{N} \sum_{j=1}^{J} \overline{\beta}_j L_{k_s j}^{(N)} d_{k_s j}^{*}] T_1 + \phi[G_{k_1}^{(N)}; G_{k_2}^{(N)}; \dots; G_{k_N}^{(N)}] \quad (6)$$

where $L_{ik_s}^{(N)}, L_{k_s j}^{(N)}; s = \overline{1,N}$ are the number of cargo trips from the i-th supplier to N warehouses and from N warehouses to the j-th user, respectively, defined as:

$$L_{ik_s}^{(N)} = [\frac{x_{ik_s}^{(N)}}{q\gamma}]; s = \overline{1,N}; \quad L_{k_s j}^{(N)} = [\frac{y_{k_s j}^{(N)}}{q\gamma}]; s = \overline{1,N};$$

$\varphi[G_{k_1}^{(N)}; G_{k_2}^{(N)}; ...; G_{k_N}^{(N)}]$ – function of storage costs at the N-th number of warehouses.

Seventh stage. Using the values of distance matrix D and shortest distance matrix D^*, let us define the optimal through routes for delivery of goods $\{i, \lambda_1, \lambda_2, ..., \lambda_s, j\}$ (from suppliers, through warehouses, and to consumers):

$$l_{i\lambda_1} = \min_{i \le \lambda \le M} [d_{i\lambda} + d^*_{\lambda j}];$$

$$l_{\lambda_1\lambda_2} = \min_{i \le \lambda \le M} [d_{\lambda_1\lambda} + d^*_{\lambda j}]; \quad (7)$$

$$\vdots$$

$$l_{\lambda_s j} = \min_{i \le \lambda \le M} [d_{\lambda_s\lambda} + d^*_{\lambda j}]$$

for $i = \overline{1, I}$; $j = k_1 k_2, ..., k_N$, and then for $i = k_1, k_2, ..., k_N; j = \overline{M - I + 1, J}$.

An Example of Application of the Model and Method

Let us imagine the implementation of developed the model and method on the example of logistics network consisting of a six consumers, three suppliers (A, B and C) and four pointspossible location ofthe warehouse (I, II, III and IV) (Fig. 2).

Initial data for modeling the supply processare presented in Table 1.

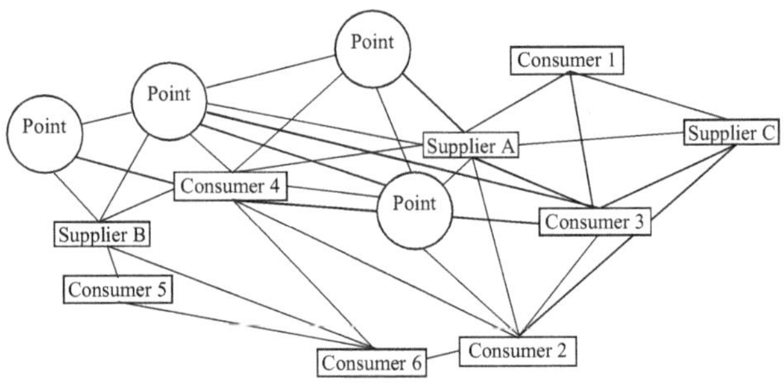

Figure 2.Graphic location scheme elements of logistics network (example)

Table 1

Initial data for modeling the supply process (example)

Parameters	Supplier A	Supplier B	Supplier C	Consumer 1	Consumer 2	Consumer 3	Consumer 4	Consumer 5	Consumer 6
W, t	2500	4000	1600	-	-	-	-	-	-
μ	0,5	0,3	0,2	-	-	-	-	-	-
V, t	-	-	-	800	1200	1500	700	1400	2300
β	-	-	-	0,14	0,18	0,1	0,3	0,08	0,2
q, t	20	20	20	10	10	10	10	10	10
γ	0,87	0,87	0,87	0,9	0,9	0,9	0,9	0,9	0,9
T_0, CMU/t·km	7	7	7	10	10	10	10	10	10

The scope of total stock reserve of goods, which should always be maintained in warehouses of the logistics network, is equal to 60 tons.

Storage costsconsist ofcosts relatedthe Exploitationthe warehouse,the cost of maintainingstocksand administrativecosts.Suppose that the functionstorage costsisdiscrete. Change instorage costs, depending on the capacity of warehouse for four possibleoptions shown in Table 2.

Table2

Change instorage costs, depending on the capacity of warehouse, CMU (example)

Capacity of warehouse, t	15	20	30	60
Costs relatedthe Exploitationthe warehouse, CMU	52000	57000	67000	146000
Costs of maintainingstocks, CMU	20000	24000	34000	68000
Administrativecosts, CMU	24000	27000	36000	64000
Storage costs, CMU	96000	108000	1370000	278000

The matrix of distances between the points of logistics network $D = \|d_{ij}\|_{13,13}$ is shownin Table 3.

The matrix of shortest distances between all points of the logistics network $D^* = \|d^*_{ij}\|_{13,13}$ is shownin Table 4.

Table 3
The distances between the points of logistics network, km

The participants logistics network	Supplier A	Supplier B	Supplier C	Point I	Point II	Point III	Point IV	Consumer 1	Consumer 2	Consumer 3	Consumer 4	Consumer 5	Consumer 6
Supplier A	0	∞	76	111	40	41	∞	42	121	51	106	∞	∞
Supplier B	∞	0	∞	70	∞	∞	68	∞	∞	∞	45	29	72
Supplier C	76	∞	0	∞	∞	∞	∞	68	∞	39	∞	∞	∞
Point I	111	70	∞	0	95	108	22	∞	∞	160	50	∞	∞
Point II	40	∞	∞	95	0	51	∞	∞	∞	∞	84	∞	∞
Point III	41	∞	∞	108	51	0	∞	∞	97	∞	97	∞	∞
Point IV	∞	68	∞	22	∞	∞	0	∞	∞	∞	69	∞	∞
Consumer 1	42	∞	68	∞	∞	∞	∞	0	∞	63	∞	∞	∞
Consumer 2	121	∞	∞	∞	∞	97	∞	∞	0	151	90	∞	31
Consumer 3	51	∞	39	160	∞	∞	∞	63	151	0	156	∞	∞
Consumer 4	106	45	∞	50	84	97	69	∞	90	156	0	∞	73
Consumer 5	∞	29	∞	∞	∞	∞	∞	∞	∞	∞	∞	0	81
Consumer 6	∞	72	∞	∞	∞	∞	∞	∞	31	∞	73	81	0

Table 4
The shortest distances between the points of logistics network, km

The participants logistics network	Supplier A	Supplier B	Supplier C	Point I	Point II	Point III	Point IV	Consumer 1	Consumer 2	Consumer 3	Consumer 4	Consumer 5	Consumer 6
Supplier A	0	151	76	111	40	41	133	42	121	51	106	180	152
Supplier B	151	0	227	70	129	142	68	193	103	201	45	29	72
Supplier C	76	227	0	187	116	117	209	68	190	39	182	256	221
Point I	111	70	187	0	95	108	22	153	140	160	50	99	123
Point II	40	129	116	95	0	51	117	82	148	91	84	158	157
Point III	41	142	117	108	51	0	130	83	97	92	97	171	128
Point IV	133	68	209	22	117	130	0	175	159	182	69	97	140
Consumer 1	42	193	68	153	82	83	175	0	163	63	148	222	194
Consumer 2	121	103	190	140	148	97	159	163	0	151	90	112	31
Consumer 3	51	201	39	160	91	92	182	63	151	0	156	230	182
Consumer 4	106	45	182	50	84	97	69	148	90	156	0	74	73
Consumer 5	180	29	256	99	158	171	97	222	112	230	74	0	81
Consumer 6	152	72	221	123	157	128	140	194	31	182	73	81	0

The model was implemented in Solver Add-In for MS Excel 2010.

As a result of the modeling, the optimum variant of a storage facilities organization for logistics network was determined. It is the variant with two warehouses located at the points III and II.

The values of the traffic volume indicators between the logistics network elements and storage capacity for three variants considered within the research are shown in the Table 5.

Table 5
Indicatorstraffic volumes andcapacityof warehouses, tons

The elements ofthe logistics network	Onewarehouse (Point III)	Two warehouses		Three warehouses		
		(Point III)	(Point II)	(Point III)	(Point II)	(Point I)
Supplier A	400	400	-	390	10	-
Supplier B	600	-	600	-	-	600
Supplier C	260	260	-	-	260	-
Consumer 1	80	-	80	-	80	-
Consumer 2	250	250	-	250	-	-
Consumer 3	170	-	170	-	170	-
Consumer 4	150	-	150	-	-	150
Consumer 5	50	-	50	-	-	50
Consumer 6	500	380	120	120	-	380
Capacity of warehouse	1260	660	600	390	270	600

The dynamics of change of the transportation work values for the considered variants of the logistics network construction are shown in Fig. 3.

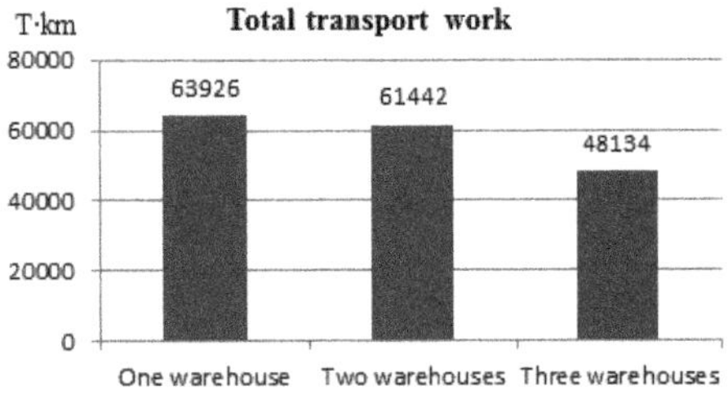

Figure 3.Dynamics ofchanges in the valuesof the transportwork

The dynamics of change of the logistics costs values for the considered variants of the logistics network construction are shown in Fig. 4.

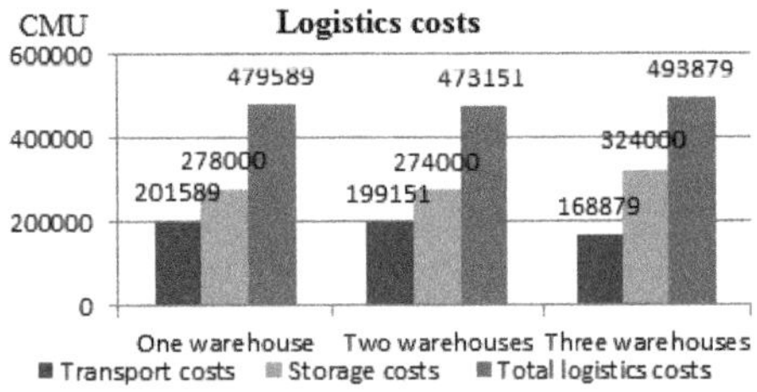

Figure 4.Dynamics ofchanges in the valuesof logistics costs

The best routes of cargo delivery from suppliers to customers through warehouses for the selected option of constructing a logistics network shown in Fig. 5.

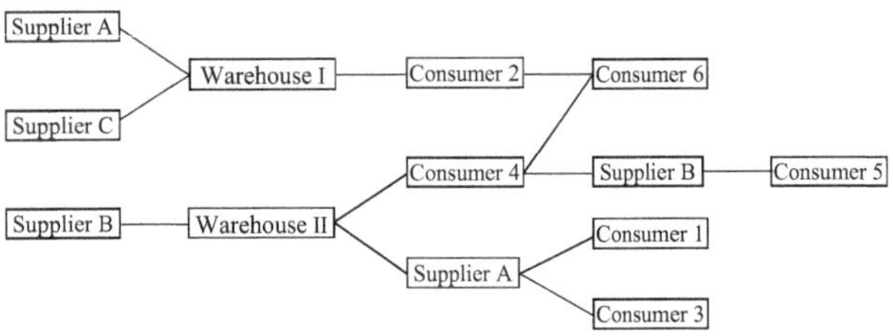

Figure 5.The best routesof cargo delivery tologistics network

CONCLUSIONS

The best logistics network (serving a larger territory with a larger number of spatially distributed links – providers, warehouses/distribution centers, consumers) is a network ensuring a high level of customer service at minimum total logistics costs.

The mathematical model and method suggested in the paper allow the definition of:

- the optimal number of warehouses for the logistics network under review, with set locations for suppliers and consumers;
- the optimal location of warehouses in points of logistics network, based on actual transportation services and a set level of total reserve stock at network warehouses;
- the optimal number of warehouses and their locations regarding the other influencing factors (reflected by weight factors of suppliers and consumers);
- total logistics costs, total transportation work and capacity of network warehouses;
- the shortest through routes for delivery of goods (in the logistics network).

This method can serve as a basis for development of methods defining the optimal number of warehouses and their locations in multi-format logistics networks (with developed transportation services), with additional restrictions on location of warehouses and regarding the multi-nomenclature character of goods, diverse nature of vehicles, and other factors influencing the optimal arrangement of a warehouse network.

REFERENCES

BOWERSOX, D. (1974). Logistical Management. New York: Macmillan Company.

BRANDEAU, M., CHIU, S. (1989).An Overview of Representative Problems in Location Research. Management Science, Vol. 35. No. 6, pp. 645-674.

CHASE, R., AQUILANO, N., & JACOBS, R. (1998).Production and operations management: manufacturing and services. Bloomington: Irwin/McGraw-Hill.

CHEONG, M.L.F., BHATNAGAR, R., & GRAVES, S. (2007). Logistics Network Design with Supplier Consolidation Hubs and Multiple Shipment Options.Journal of Industrial and Management Optimization.AIMS, Vol. 3, No 2, pp. 51-69.

COYLE, J., BARDI, E., & LANGLEY, J. (1985).The Management of Business Logistics. St. Paul: West Publishing Company.

DYBSKAY, V. (2008).Skladirovanie i gruzopererabotka (Warehousing and material handling).In V. SERGUEYEV (Ed.), Korporativnay logistika. 300 otvetov na voprosy profesionalov (Corporate Logistics. 300 Answers to the Questions of Professionals), pp. 564-674. Moscow: INFRA-M.

ENGEL, J., BLACKWELL, R., & MINIARD, P. (1995). Consumer Behavior, (8th ed.), Chicago: The Dryden Press.

GIDDINGS, A., BAILEY, T., & MOORE, J. (2000).Optimality analysis of facility location problems using response surface methodology. International Journal of Physical Distribution and Logistics Management, Vol. 31, No. 1, pp. 38-52.

GOLSTEIN, E., YOUDINE, D. (1966). Novye napravleniy v lineynom programirovanii (New Directionsin Linear Programming).Moscow: Nauka.

HOOVER, E. (1948). The Location of Economic Activity. New-York: McGraw-Hill.

KHUMAWALA, B., KELLY, D. (1974). Warehouse Location with Concave Costs. Infor, Vol. 12, No. 1, pp. 55-65.

LUKINSKIY, V.S., LUKINSKIY, V.V., MALEVICH, J., PLASTUNYAK, I., & PLETNEVA, N. (2007).Opredelenie kolichestva i koordinat skladov v regione (Determination of the numberand the coordinatesof warehousesin the region). In V.S. LUKINSKIY (Ed.), Modeli i metody teorii logistiki (Models andMethods of Logistics), pp. 383-407. (2th ed.). Saint-Petersburg: Piter.

MIROTIN, L. (2002). Transportnay logistika (Transport Logistics).Moscow: Exam.

O'KELLY, M. (1986).The Location of Interacting Hub Facilities. Transportation Science, Vol. 20, No. 2, pp. 92-106.

SALIHOV, R. (2007). Razrabotka algoritma proektirovaniy logisticheskih setey (Development of algorithmdesignlogistics networks). BulletinENGECON. Ser.: Economy, Issue5 (18), pp. 246-248.

SERGUEYEV, V. (1997).Menedgment v biznes logistike (Management inBusinessLogistics).Moscow: Feelyn.

TANSEL, B., FRANCIS, R., & LOWE, T. (1983a). Location on Networks: A Survey. Part I: The p-Center and p-Median Problems. Management Science, Vol. 29. No. 4, pp. 482-497.

TANSEL, B., FRANCIS, R., & LOWE, T. (1983b). Location on Networks: A Survey. Part II: Exploiting Tree Network Structure. Management Science, Vol. 29. No. 4, pp. 498-511.

TJAPUHIN, A. (2001). Raspredelitelnay logistika (Distribution logistics).RISK, No. 1, pp. 3-16.

WEBER, A. (1929). [translated by Carl J. Friedrich from Weber's 1909 book]. Theory of the Location of Industries. Chicago: The University of Chicago Press.

WILD, R. (1995). Essentials of Production and Operations Management: Text and Cases. (5th ed.). London: Cassell.

WILSON, A. (1974). Urban and Regional Models in Geography and Planning. Chichester and New York: John Wiley.

YAGER, R. (1982).[Russian Translation, 1986]. Fuzzy Set and Possibility Theory: Recent Developments. New York: Pergamon Press.

Problems of Corporate Governance in the Practice of Machine Building Enterprises of Ukraine

IULIIA FADIEIEVA
ASSOCIATE PROFESSOR

e-mail: julia_klb@rambler.ru

SUMMARY

This paper presents an analysis of the current state of corporate governance for mechanical engineering in Ukraine, and the main problems and features of corporate governance. It focuses on the current situation with corporate governance machine building enterprises in the Kharkov region. The objectives of the study are to identify the basic problems in the activity of corporate governance machine building enterprises in the region.as well as the features and limitations of corporate governance.
Keywords: Ukrainian machine building, corporate governance

INTRODUCTION

The transition of Ukrainian enterprises to a market economy was accompanied by the processes of privatization and corporatization. The most common form of business organization has become shareholder, due to its many advantages over other forms (the ability to transfer property rights and, at the same time, control of the company; capital increase through an additional share issue, while maintaining the financial stability of the company, etc.) .

This process did not pass over engineering industries. Thus, the most common form of ownership in the modern engineering industry is corporate. This is attested to by statistics. According to the State Property Fund of Ukraine, between 1998 and 2012, the number of joint stock companies in Ukraine has increased markedly. Overall, since the beginning of the privatization process, and as of July 1, 2012, 127901 enterprises in Ukraine changed ownership. With the development of the market environment, the functioning of these units has been directed towards the search for a niche market. Companies that were weak, usually unable to compete, ceased to exist.

However, the current state of corporate governance in the Kharkov region of Ukraine is characterized by a low level of corporate culture, a discrepancy between the existing corporate governance practices and generally accepted principles, lack of coordination of government in the regulation of corporate relations, poor management of state corporate law, etc. "On Joint Stock Companies" (2008).

Therefore, in the present conditions the development of corporate relations, especially in the machine-building industry, is important in order to attract investments to the Ukrainian economy, stock market development and the growth of national wealth.

Until recently, the privatization and corporatization in Ukraine was aimed at promoting the effectiveness of the individual entities and the revenue of the state budget. Now the emphasis should shift towards an integrated, systemic solution for how to increase the competitiveness and efficiency of basic industries and the economy in general, and on this basis people's livelihoods.

METHOD

Studies of corporate governance of enterprises in Ukraine conducted by the example of machine-building enterprises of Kharkov region. Among them, OJSC "ROSS" (OJSC "Kharkov plant modular machines"), OJSC "Plant Frunze", OJSC "Kharkov plant dies and pressform", OJSC "Kharkov Bearing Plant", OJSC "Kharkov Tractor Plant. S. Ordzhonikidze", OJSC "Turboatom", OJSC "Light Miner", OJSC "Potential", OJSC "Hidropryvid Kharkov Plant", OJSC Factory "Index", JSC "HZEMI", JSC "Electric machine", JSC "Ukrelectromash HELZ", OJSC "Teploavtomat", OJSC "Tochprybor", OJSC "Volchansky aggregate Plant", OJSC "Lozovskii forging-Mechanical Plant", OJSC

"Avtramat", CJSC "Finprofile" ("Stock market infrastructure" , 2012).

The main directions of research and implementation of corporate governance in selected enterprises include reorganization, the election of the chairman and members of the Supervisory Board, the decision to terminate their mandate as possible reasons for convening the extraordinary meetings of the past in 2012, the availability and variety of committees of the supervisory board, the competences of shareholders in the definition of the strategy, the existence of the internal documents of the company, including its own corporate code, etc. ("Stock market infrastructure", 2012) (Figure 1).

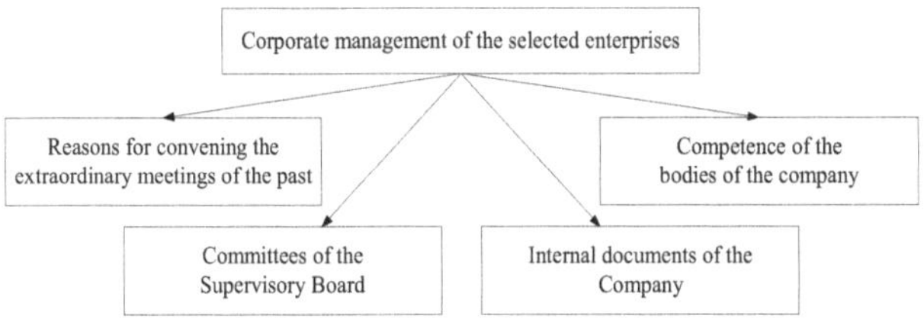

Figure 1. The main directions for studying corporate management of the selected enterprises

RESULTS

Analyzed companies is not a classical company created by combining capital and the privatization of the practice of their development as a joint-stock companies. It is this fact that determines the characteristics of corporate governance in Ukrainian enterprises. One such feature is the combination of management and ownership. However, among the studied companies the tendency is to reduce the share of management in equity.

The most effective form of corporate governance is provided by enterprises owned by foreign investors. Scientists of the Institute for Economy in Transition "Russia" conducted research in enterprises in the Czech Republic, Hungary, Russia, and Bulgaria, and found that the transformation of the enterprises with foreign capital is the best way, but the share of foreign capital should not be less than 30%.

In research conducted in Ukrainian enterprises, foreign investors are present in manufacturing plants in a small amount (less than 35%). This result means that the enterprises studied here have low attractiveness to foreign investors In addition, none of the companies quotes its shares on the stock market. This means that the management of enterprises is not trying to go for external financing through the sale of their shares.

Another important issue is the concentration of ownership in enterprises. The presence of a shareholder (or group of shareholders) in the company owning 70% of shares or more may mean a lack of mutual respect in the decision-making capabilities of minority shareholders to participate in management (decisions on all issues, including those which require a qualified majority, are taken by one person or a group of related persons). In fact, the minority shareholders become passive investors, and their shares essentially cease to be voting. This reduces the motivation of minority shareholders to participate in enterprise management, the effectiveness of management decisions and, consequently, the efficiency of the company. On the other hand, the greater the share of the largest shareholder-manager in a company, the less advantageous to him to withdraw the company's resources for personal consumption ("Industrial of Ukraine", 2013).

A significant lack in corporate relations in the engineering sector in Ukraine is the almost complete absence of committees of the supervisory board, although the Ukrainian and international principles of corporate governance consider it appropriate to consider the existence of such structures, and recommend implementation of the supervisory board of the Corporate Secretary. Up to the end of 2012 the Committee had been established in none of the studied companies, In the structure of the supervisory board of other engineering enterprises of Ukraine, along with the corporate form of governance there are such committees as the committee for strategic planning, audit committees, the appointment and remuneration and investment committees, but the position of corporate secretary has been not enough implemented.

Among the requirements for the members of the Supervisory Board, as shown in internal documents, in the researched companies the most common are industry knowledge and experience in the area (47% of surveyed companies) and personal qualities such as honesty and responsibility (46% of surveyed companies). In addition, there are claims for knowledge in the field of finance and management, and it is specified that there must be no conflict of interest. Requirements as to the age of members of the Supervisory Board were not detected. Of the enterprises, 13% did not have any requirements set in their documents. This low set of requirements for the members of the Supervisory Board indicates a lack in the level of development and implementation of corporate relations in the engineering sector in the Kharkov region (Figure 2).

Not enough attention is paid by the management of companies to internal corporate documents. However, these documents are often a means of resolving disputes and internal conflicts. Such documents may include Provisions on the General Meeting of Shareholders, the Supervisory Board of the executive body (Management Board) of the company officials, the audit committee, the company's shares, reports on the distribution of profits, etc. But among the studied companies domestic regulation documents are not used, which indicates the underdeveloped corporate relations.

Another important aspect of the activities of Ukrainian joint stock companies is the disclosure of information about their activities. The essence of the disclosure is to ensure access by interested parties, including the shareholders, to complete and accurate information about the industrial, economic and other activities of the company.

Almost all of the financial statements and the results of activities of the investigated engineering companies extend to the general meeting published in the press, as well as a public information database of the Securities Commission on the Securities Market. In addition, for the documents available for inspection joint-stock company, a copy may be obtained on the request of the shareholder, and the information made available on the website of the company.

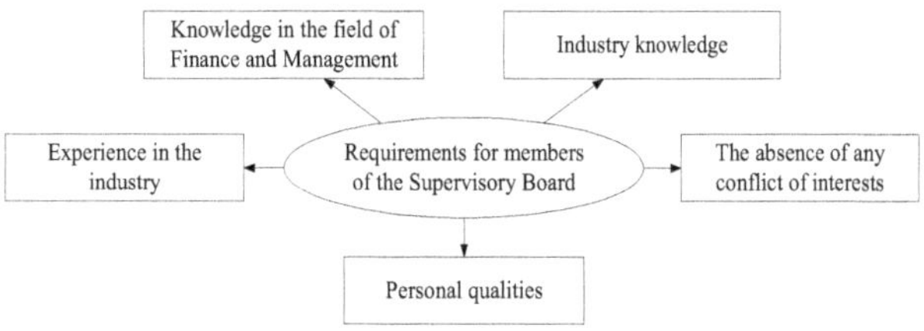

Figure 2. Requirements for members of the Supervisory Board

Furthermore, they published information oo shareholders holding 10% or more of the authorized capital, the composition of management bodies, the charter and by-laws (in their own web page on request of shareholders), minutes of general meetings of shareholders after meetings. Information on the remuneration of company officers is not made public.

Among Ukrainian joint stock companies it is not common to refer to consultants in the field of corporate governance and financial management. The enterprises surveyed have not received paid services of such consultants within the last few years, reflecting stagnation in the development of domestic corporate relations ("Industrial of Ukraine", 2013).

Recently, many foreign companies have corporate governance codes. The practice of multinational corporations suggests that the availability of its own code provides help in dealing with a wide range of applications. Corporate codes have been widely used in developed countries since the 1980s. Now 80% of the companies on the list of the 500 best companies in the world have such codes. But among the studied domestic engineering companies with the corporate form of management, there is no enterprise that has set up its own corporate code.

Thus, as the results of the study it can be concluded that the main problems of the corporate engineering enterprises in the Kharkov region associated with ownership are:

1. Low corporate culture;
2. Lack of investment attractiveness of enterprises;
3. The need to increase capitalization;
4. The need to improve the access of joint stock companies to the capital markets and reduce the cost of their involvement;
5. The poor reputation of the company in the domestic and international markets, as well as of its directors and managers;
6. Complicated control systems for corporate rights;
7. Lack of balance between the interests of the minority and majority shareholders;
8. Vague definition of the objectives of the corporation and how to motivate its owners;
9. The choice of organizational structure, inadequate goals;
10. Incompetent directors from the joint Soviet era;
11. Weak legal framework (particularly in the context of the interaction between business entities);
12. Low rate of market infrastructure facilities (stock and commodity exchanges, consulting and design firms, developed infrastructure of the labor market, etc.);
13. Conflicts of interest in government;
14. Low awareness of entrepreneurs and managers of the basic elements of corporate governance;
15. Ability to manipulate the composition and content of internal regulations;
16. Insufficient degree of transparency.

CONCLUSION

Thus it is clear that the current situation in the corporate sector of engineering enterprises in Ukraine requires the implementation of specific measures at the level of corporate enterprises. The quality of corporate governance is an important factor in the effectiveness of a company. During the financial crisis the cost of debt remains high, and outsourcing by the issue of shares is virtually nonexistent. Therefore, improving the level of corporate governance can provide a quick and significant financial effect, reducing the cost of capital to ensure the company and the growth of its market capitalization.

One source of constraints on the effective implementation of corporate management in engineering enterprises in Ukraine, as in other countries, is that the interests of shareholders and, for example, those of managers disagree. Despite recent interest in increasing the size of the corporation, its power and prestige, managers are often paid by a fixed salary (company income has no effect on the salary), thus the fate of the manager depends on the stability of a company and he/she aims to minimize risky investments in order to avoid bankruptcy and layoffs. But the majority of shareholders want to take risks in order to obtain large dividends. On the contrary, lenders may not be particularly interested in the high profits of the company – they are much more interested in the presence of these revenues. Therefore, they are skeptical of what they perceive of as very profitable but very risky operations. The topic chosen for this article is relevant to large complex corporate enterprises in Ukraine and requires further research.

REFERENCES

"Stock market infrastructure" (2012) Database of Stock market infrastructure development agency of Ukraine: March 2012: www.smida.gov.ua.

"Industrial of Ukraine" (2013) Ministry of Industrial Policy of Ukraine: February 2012: industry.kmu.gov.ua.

"Statistics Committee of Ukraine" (2013) Official site of the State: May 2008: www.ukrstat.gov.ua

"On Joint Stock Companies" (2008) The Law of Ukraine: September 2008: www.zakon.rada.gov.ua.

9

The Link between Firm-Level Productivity and Decisions to Export – The Case of Lodz Voivodeship

PIOTR GABRIELCZAK
PH.D. STUDENT
e-mail: pgabrielczak@uni.lodz.pl

TOMASZ SERWACH
PH.D. STUDENT, ASSISTANT PROFESSOR
e-mail: serwachtomasz@uni.lodz.pl

SUMMARY

The aim of this article is to test whether there are differences in productivity between exporters and non-exporters among manufacturing firms from Lodz Voivodeship. Not only do we look for a correlation, but also we verify two main hypotheses about the causality of the postulated relation: self-selection and learning-by-exporting (LBE). We use microeconomic data from the Central Statistical Office of Poland and the Olley-Pakes algorithm to estimate the total factor productivity (TFP) of firms. Then we apply that data to probit and logit estimations of export status and examine TFP increments of new exporters. We did not find sound evidence for self-selection among firms in Lodz Voivodeship. We managed, however, to prove the existence of an LBE effect, though this effect seems to be weak and restricted to certain sectors with comparative advantages. One should keep in mind that our research was limited by data availability and further studies are required. However, this study is a rare example of a regional analysis of international trade and deals with main New New Trade Theory postulates in a complex manner.
Keywords: productivity, internationalisation, export, Lodz Voivodeship

INTRODUCTION

Since the establishment of the New Trade Theory (NTT) it has been acknowledged that monopolistic competition under internal scale economies and consumers' love for variety can be seen as the environment within which international trade occurs (Krugman 1979, 1980; Helpman & Krugman 1985). However, NTT models were based on the assumption of a representative (typical) firm, which led to conclusion that if such a firm exports, then empirically one should see that all firms within the same narrowly defined industry do so. Casual observation violates that theoretical conclusion, raising question about characteristics distinguishing exporters from firms operating only domestically.

The new theoretical revolution, giving rise to the so-called New New Trade Theory (NNTT), started in the early 2000s. Melitz (2003) proved that firm-level productivity is the most crucial factor affecting the decision of whether to export or not. Only the most productive firms are competitive enough (due to low marginal costs) to make such high revenue from exporting that they can cover the sunk fixed costs of exporting (arising, for example, from the formation of distribution channels or promotion activities). Specifically, in every industry there exists a productivity threshold of exporting – if a firm's efficiency is below that value, then it is unable to start or continue exporting. Similar results were obtained in other theoretical models (Bernard et al. 2003; Melitz & Ottaviano 2008).

The phenomenon in which firm-level productivity influences the decision of exporting is called self-selection. This hypothesis is based on an empirically found correlation between firms' efficiency and their export status. However, correlation does not indicate causality, hence another direction of the link between productivity and exporting has been proposed. In the so-called Learning-by-exporting (LBE) hypothesis, engagement in international trade boosts a firm's efficiency[1]. Yeaple (2005) showed that in order to export, firms must adopt better technology and more skilled workers – the ultimate result being an increase in firm-level productivity. In a similar model Verhoogen (2008) demonstrated that foreign customers' preferences for high quality forces exporting firms to hire more skilled workers. Bernard et al. (2010) built a model in which engagement in export leads to concentration on the firm's core competence. The LBE hypothesis has also been tested in numerous empirical papers with mixed results (see Wagner 2005).

[1] *See De Loecker (2013) on empirical issues connected with detecting the LBE effect.*

The empirical literature shows that self-selection is a more common phenomenon than LBE. For instance, using simple VAR models Hagemejer (2006) found no evidence of LBE but at the same time proved the existence of self-selection among Polish manufacturing firms. In probit regression he also found that firm-level productivity affects the probability of exporting.

In this article we present the results of our research on the impact of productivity on the exporting activities of firms from Lodz Voivodeship. The choice of that voivodeship is motivated by the fact that it is a representative region with average economic power and sophistication compared to other regions of Poland. In the next section we compare the distributions of exporters' and non-exporter's productivity. Then we verify the self-selection and LBE hypotheses. The last section states our conclusions.

Exporters and Non-Exporters – Main Differences in Distribution of Productivity

Productivity in general is a feature that describes how well a given company performs or, in other words, how efficiently it uses its resources in order to maximise its product. Particularly, the Total Factor Productivity (TFP) is a measure of how effectively all inputs on production components are converted into economic outcomes[2]. However, technically it can be difficult to estimate TFP, as simple measures often suffer from serious biases which make conclusions based on them far from real.

Olley and Pakes (1996) proposed a semi-parametric method of estimating TFP, which we incorporated in our research. Their method is suitable for estimation of firm-level productivity as it resolves two main problems arising when dealing with panels of firm-level data: simultaneity and selection bias (Yasar et al. 2008, p. 221). The former refers to the fact that observed inputs, such as labour or capital, may be correlated with unobserved inputs or productivity shocks, such as quality of materials, management skills, technical wear of capital, etc. The latter refers to the problem of subjects falling out from the data set. Moreover, these endogenous exits are often correlated with other variables, most often with size (Aguirregabiria 2009, p. 2). The Olley-Pakes algorithm (OPA) copes with these issues by employing investment as a proxy for the unobserved, time-varying productivity shocks and using estimates of survival probability (Yasar et al. 2008, p. 222).

In our research we measured firm-level productivity (using OPA on Central Statistical Office data) of companies from Lodz Voivodeship (Poland), dividing them into two groups: exporters and non-exporters. We repeated our calculations for the years 2005 (the aftermath of Polish EU accession), 2008 (the verge of the subprime crisis) and 2011 (latest available data, global crisis entering its fadeout). We expected to obtain higher productivity measures for exporters in all the research periods. Table 1 contains the results.

Table 1
Results of TFP estimations

TFP estimates	Number of companies					
	Exporters			Non-exporters		
	2005	2008	2011	2005	2008	2011
(0.0 - 5.5]	17	21	26	59	52	58
(5.5 - 6.0]	140	97	96	162	148	134
(6.0 - 6.5]	170	165	163	173	180	143
(6.5 - 7.0]	120	108	107	80	78	66
(7.0 - 7.5]	56	58	85	17	28	23
(7.5 - 8.0]	34	46	33	4	11	15
(8.0 - 8.5]	7	13	17	1	4	3
(8.5 - 9.0]	6	4	6	0	0	1
(9.0 - 9.5]	0	0	1	0	0	0
9.5 <	0	1	4	0	1	1
Total number (% of all comp.)	550 (53%)	513 (51%)	538 (55%)	496 (47%)	502 (49%)	444 (45%)
Avg. TFP	6.45	6.53	6.59	6.09	6.18	6.18
St. deviation	0.66	0.72	0.78	0.51	0.59	0.65

Source: own calculations based on Central Statistical Office data

The most important observation is the fact that the average productivity of exporters was higher than that of non-exporters in all years of calculation. It is worth stressing that our calculation was based on a set of information about all production companies from Lodz region, so our averages are in fact expected values of complete discrete distributions given in Table 1. That is why there is no necessity for testing the significance of differences in averages if we wish to provide conclusions referring only to Lodz Voivodeship. Should we, however, wish to widen our inference, we could treat our sets as subsets of productivity distribution among exporters and non-exporters in general (or at least in Poland) and our averages as estimates of expected values. In that case one would also find, based on simple statistical testing, that these differences are significant at $\alpha=0.01$.

When referring to dynamics of average productivity, two pieces of information seem to be crucial. Firstly, exporters' TFP was growing in the entire period, whereas non-exporters' productivity grew in 2008 in comparison to 2005, but in 2011 the average TFP was exactly the same as in 2008. Secondly, although the crisis at its beginning brought a drop in the number of both exporters and non-exporters, leading even to an increase of the non-exporters' share in the amount of all companies, in 2011 the number of exporters began to rise again, while more and more non-exporters dropped out of the market. That is why it is safe to point out that when the first shock of global crisis had passed, it was the group of exporters that managed to recover more efficiently.

[2] *The basic idea of TFP is to present the relation of output value to sum of all costs of inputs incurred during the production process. TFP over 1 means that the value of enterprise's production (usually – sold production) exceeds its costs. In general, the higher TFP, the better, as it indicates more effective performance.*

Since all averages belong to the (6.0 – 7.0) range, let us fix 7.0 as the threshold for extraordinarily high productivity and 6.0 as the threshold for extraordinarily low productivity. For non-exporters, the shares of companies with low productivity were 45%, 40% and 43% for 2005, 2008 and 2011, respectively, and the share of companies with high productivity was 4%, 9% and 10%. As for exporters, the share of companies with low TFP (for 2005, 2008 and 2011, respectively) was 29%, 23% and 23% again, while the shares of exporters with high productivity were 19%, 24% and 27% respectively. This again shows that the productivity gap between the group of exporters and non-exporters is increasing with time.

THE SELF-SELECTION HYPOTHESIS

According to standard NNTT models (Bernard et al. 2003; Melitz 2003) exporters are more productive than non-exporters[3]. That view has been proved by numerous empirical studies (e.g. Bernard & Jensen 2004, Mayer & Ottaviano 2007, to name but a few). Hagemejer (2006) investigated the case of Poland. He found that self-selection characterises Polish manufacturing firms – more productive firms are more likely to become exporters. Bearing that result in mind, we tried to find whether such a phenomenon is present among firms from Lodz Voivodeship.

Our research was based on logit and probit estimations with export status (1 for exporter, 0 for non-exporter) playing the role of dependent variable. The sample consists of 5,373 observations. Table 2 enumerates independent variables used in the estimations.

Table 2
List of independent variables

Symbol	Description
ht	Olley-Pakes estimation of firm-level TFP (ratio)
lt	log of i-th firm workforce (people)
at	log of i-th firm age (years)
st	dummy for Treasury in ownership structure
jt	dummy for local government in ownership structure
zt	dummy for foreign capital in ownership structure
pt1	dummy for PKD (Polish Business Classification) divisions 10, 11 or 12
pt2	dummy for PKD divisions 13, 14 or 15
pt3	dummy for PKD divisions 16, 17 or 31
pt4	dummy for PKD divisions 18, 26 or 32
pt5	dummy for PKD divisions 19, 22 or 23
pt6	dummy for PKD divisions 20 or 21
pt7	dummy for PKD divisions 24 or 25
pt8	dummy for PKD divisions 27, 28 or 33
pt9	dummy for PKD divisions 29 or 30
mt	dummy for being an importer of capital goods
bt	dummy for investing abroad in the form of FDI

Source: own elaboration based on Central Statistical Office data

Both logit and probit estimations lead to the same qualitative conclusions (see Table 3). Surprisingly, we find no evidence of self-selection. Not only is the marginal effect of change in productivity negligible, but also firm-level efficiency appears in estimated equations with negative coefficients. That result can be interpreted as proof that the competitive edge of firms from Lodz Voivodeship is based on characteristics other than productivity (intuitively, high quality or uniqueness of products, high financial liquidity and access to vast networks of contacts can be seen as these traits). Low values of R-squared (McFadden R-squared or adjusted R-squared) indicate that factors other than productivity play a key role when firms decide whether to enter foreign markets through export.

The lack of self-selection is of paramount importance from policymakers' point of view. Without such a phenomenon there are no intra-industry reallocations in the direction of the most productive firms. Those reallocations are seen as a serious contributor to aggregate productivity gains (Pavcnik 2002; Melitz 2003). It seems that in Lodz Voivodeship the only productivity-connected effect of exporting resulting from the behaviour of individual firms may be LBE.

The results of logit and probit estimations also indicate that the probability of exporting increases with firm size (proxied by workforce) and age. It seems that the bigger the firm is, the more human resources it can devote to conducting international operations. The result for age can be seen in two different ways. Firstly, according to sequential internationalisation theories (like the Uppsala model) only firms successful enough on the domestic market can start international activities. Gaining such success requires time, hence older firms are more likely to become exporters. Secondly, there is probability of the so-called hysteresis effect – firm actively exporting in previous periods remain exporters. In such a situation age can be seen as a proxy for past exporter status.

Apart from that, the results show that ownership is another important aspect of firm-level decisions on international operations. Treasury-owned or local-government-owned firms are less prone to engage in exporting. At the same time foreign ownership increases the probability of exporting. What is more, if the firm is an importer of capital goods or invests abroad (FDI), then it is also more likely to enter foreign markets via export. The effects of foreign ownership and engagement in other forms of internationalisation lead to the conclusion that firms belonging to international production networks are more likely to be exporters.

Our results also indicate that the industry in which the firm operates has an effect. Having divided the industries into nine categories, we used eight of them in estimations (we skipped one to avoid the problem of collinearity). However, each of the coefficients was negative, meaning that belonging to the non-included (ninth) sector

[3] *Self-selection can be found in importing as well. See also Bernard et al. (2013) with two-sided firm heterogeneity.*

increases the probability of exporting. In general, that industry is connected with production of vehicles. It seems this is where the (static) comparative advantage of Lodz Voivodeship lies.

Table 3
Results of probability estimations

Var.	Logit estimation				Probit estimation			
	Coef.	Stand. error	z	Marg. effect	Coef.	Stand. error	z	Marg. effect
const.	-1.816	0.458	-3.96	---	-1,016	0,256	-3,97	---
ht	-0.012	0.076	-0.16	-0.003	-0,023	0,044	-0,54	-0,009
lt	0.469	0.045	10.51	0.112	0,278	0,026	10,65	0,108
at	0.116	0.045	2.61	0.028	0,065	0,026	2,48	0,025
st	-0.176	0.186	-0.95	-0.042	-0,093	0,109	-0,86	-0,036
jt	-1.632	0.983	-1.66	-0.390	-1,014	0,573	-1,77	-0,393
zt	1.323	0.102	12.92	0.316	0,761	0,057	13,24	0,295
pt1	-1.517	0.241	-6.31	-0.362	-0,864	0,133	-6,50	-0,334
pt2	-0.562	0.236	-2.38	-0.137	-0,297	0,130	-2,29	-0,116
pt3	-0.864	0.251	-3.44	-0.212	-0,468	0,140	-3,34	-0,185
pt4	-1.248	0.259	-4.83	-0.301	-0,708	0,144	-4,92	-0,276
pt5	-0.929	0.243	-3.82	-0.228	-0,527	0,134	-3,94	-0,208
pt6	-1.304	0.264	-4.94	-0.313	-0,732	0,148	-4,93	-0,285
pt7	-0.847	0.248	-3.42	-0.208	-0,476	0,137	-3,47	-0,188
pt8	-0.921	0.245	-3.76	-0.226	-0,512	0,136	-3,77	-0,202
bt	0.627	0.287	2.18	0.137	0,821	0,043	19,26	0,314
mt	1.337	0.071	18.84	0.315	0,364	0,156	2,33	0,133
Stat.	Dependent var. – mean			0.571	Dependent var. – mean			0.571
	Dependent var. – SD			0.495	Dependent var. – SD			0.495
	McFadden R-squared			0.226	McFadden R-squared			0.226
	Adjusted R-squared			0.222	Adjusted R-squared			0.222
	Log likelihood			-2842.8	Log likelihood			-2844.7
	Akaike crit.			5719.6	Akaike crit.			5723.4
	Schwarz crit.			5831.7	Schwarz crit.			5835.4
	Hannan-Quinn crit.			5758.8	Hannan-Quinn crit.			5762.5

Source: own calculations based on Central Statistical Office data

THE LEARNING-BY-EXPORTING HYPOTHESIS

The LBE hypothesis is one of the views referring to a link between productivity and engagement in international trade, according to which, companies that enter foreign markets by exporting manage to benefit from it not only due to increases in sales, but also thanks to being exposed to new technologies, more demanding customers, higher competition, different management styles and operational standards, etc. as well as through joining production chains and networks. This may enable them to specialise either in a narrower range of goods or in just a part of production process, leading to investment in more advanced and specialised human resources and equipment and benefiting from economy of scale (see Redding 2010). All of this helps them to develop and thus become more productive. In other words, supporters of the LBE hypothesis claim that TFP productivity shift is a result of establishing contacts with foreign markets and international partners.

Whether the LBE effect is an existing real phenomenon or just a theoretical construct remains uncertain. Some results support its existence (see i.e. Isgut 2001 or Maggioni 2010), others stand against it (see i.e. Bernard 1995; Delgado et al. 2002; Wagner 2002). As for research on the LBE effect in Poland, the situation is very similar. Out of three main research projects on that issue, one showed the existence of LBE (Hagemejer & Kolasa 2008), one found that export was insignificant for productivity changes, so there is no LBE (Bukowski et al. 2006), and one was inconclusive (Hagemejer 2006).

In our research we tried to find out if firms entering foreign markets (new exporters) note any productivity increases during the first three years of their international activities. We analysed increments of the variable ht – the OPA productivity estimator (see Table 4).

Table 4
Productivity gains in the first three years after engaging in exports

	Productivity (ht) gain after		
	1 year	2 years	3 years
Mean	0.019	0.029	0.032
St. deviation	0.085	0.101	0.121
25th percentile	-0.018	-0.025	-0.037
50th percentile	-0.003	0.005	0.014
75th percentile	0.037	0.066	0.087

Source: own calculations based on Central Statistical Office data

Firstly, the average increases in productivity are positive and growing with time, though with falling dynamics. However, they are also very small. With an average of ht about 6.5, the gain of more or less 0.03 is only about 0.5%, which is not much. Moreover, in the first year half of new exporters suffered from a negative productivity change and in the following years at least 25% maintained that condition. To make matters worse, the standard deviation is almost four times the mean, which only proves that effects of becoming an exporter (in terms of TFP changes) were soundly heterogeneous. However, though it would be hard to treat these results as strong arguments in favour of the LBE hypothesis, one should also consider that our research period, 2005-2011, mostly coincided with a crisis, which strongly increases volatility and negative production dynamics.

LBE effects are also not equal in all sectors. Table 5 shows our results for average productivity gains with sectoral filtration imposed.

Table 5
Sectoral differences in averages of the productivity gains within the first three years of exporting

	Avg. productivity (ht) gain after		
Sector	1 year	2 years	3 years
pt1	0.018	0.035	0.043
pt2	0.012	0.025	0.018
pt3	0.026	0.017	0.014
pt4	0.026	0.022	0.013
pt5	0.040	0.055	0.072
pt6	0.028	0.027	0.039
pt7	0.006	0.006	0.001
pt8	0.001	0.012	0.014
pt9	0.019	0.058	0.077

Source: own calculations based on Central Statistical Office data

As appears from gathered data, the strongest learning benefits were observed in two general sectors. The first one, marked as pt5, stands for production of non-metallic raw materials, especially oil refining products, gums and plastics. The second, marked as pt9, is the production of vehicles and other transportation equipment. This sector was already identified as the sector in which the exporting probability – in the sense of self-selection for reaching and maintaining positive exporting status – is the highest. Now it is also clear that the LBE effect is the strongest in that industry. Again it would seem, then, that it should be one of the most strategic sectors for Lodz Voivodeship.

What is more, a traditionally and historically important sector for the Lodz region, the textile industry (pt2), turned out to place among the least promising in terms of productivity stimulation via export. Moreover, one of the strategic ideas of the local government to boost development of the region was to encourage business process outsourcing (BPO) services in Lodz. However, production of IT technology, marked as pt4, which is complements the BPO services production industry, was also one of the sectors with the lowest LBE effects. The very lowest learning benefits from exports were noted for the production of metallic raw materials, marked as pt7. Based on our results, these sectors should not be backed by local business support institutions.

CONCLUSIONS

According to the new theoretical models regarding international trade there is a strong link between firm-level productivity and export status. The results of our research contrast with that view. We found that there is no self-selection characterising the exporting behaviour of firms from Lodz Voivodeship (at least not favouring the most productive establishments). At the same time the results proved that the extent of learning-by-exporting (LBE) in the region is highly limited. Those results are of great importance. It seems that the only export-related mechanism causing total factor productivity (TFP) growth within sectors is LBE (though the strength of that mechanism may be rather scant), and not self-selection.

Probably the most important conclusion refers to the sectoral aspect of the link between efficiency and the export status of firms. It seems that firms operating in the transport vehicle industry are not only more likely to engage in trade but also benefit the most in terms of increases in productivity. Bearing that in mind, rational policymakers should be able to save scarce resources by limiting trade promotion to that sector. By supporting firms from that industry (in which Lodz Voivodeship apparently has a comparative advantage) the region would enhance its growth potential.

One must be also aware of the limitations of our research. Especially, introduction of access to the credit market or proxies for quality of goods in the logit regression could shed light on other determinants of firm's decision to export. Due to lack of data we were unable to do so, hence we recommend it for future research on the topic.

Acknowledgement

This article is a result of the research project Wpływ produktywności na aktywność międzynarodową przedsiębiorstw z województwa łódzkiego (Impact of productivity on international activity of enterprises from Lodz Voivodeship), conducted in cooperation with the National Science Centre (3812/B/H03/2011/40) of Poland.

REFERENCES

AGUIRREGABIRIA, V. 2009, Econometric Issues and Methods in the Estimation of Production Functions, MPRA Paper 15973, University Library of Munich, Germany.

BERNARD, A.B. 1995, Exporters and trade liberalization in Mexico: Production structure and performance, mimeo, Massachusetts Institute of Technology, Cambridge, MA.

BERNARD, A.B. & JENSEN, J.B. 2004, 'Exporting and productivity in the USA', Oxford Review of Economic Policy', vol. 20, pp. 343–357.

BERNARD, A.B., EATON, J., JENSEN, J.B. & KORTUM, S. 2003, 'Plants and Productivity in International Trade', American Economic Review, vol. 93, No. 4, pp. 1268-1290.

BERNARD, A.B., MOXNES, A. & ULLTVEIT-MOE, K.H. 2013, Two-sided Heterogeneity and Trade, CEPR Discussion Paper 9681, London.

BERNARD, A.B., REDDING, S.J. & SCHOTT, P.K. 2010, Multi-product firms and trade liberalization, mimeo, Tuck School of Business at Dartmouth College, Hanover, NH.

BUKOWSKI, M., MAGDA, I., MARĆ, Ł. & ZAWISTOWSKI, J. 2006, Źródła i perspektywy wzrostu produktywności w Polsce (Sources and prospects of the productivity growth in Poland), Institute for Structural Research, Warsaw, Poland.

DELGADO, M.A., FARINAS & J.C., RUANO, S. 2002, 'Firm productivity and export markets: a non-parametric approach', Journal of International Economics, vol. 57(2), pp. 397-422.

DE LOECKER, J. 2013, 'Detecting Learning by Exporting', American Economic Journal: Microeconomics, vol. 5(3), pp. 1-21.

HAGEMEJER, J. 2006, 'Czynniki wpływające na decyzję przedsiębiorstw o eksporcie. Analiza danych mikroekonomicznych' ('Factors Driving the Firms Decision to Export. Firm-level Evidence from Poland'), Bank i Kredyt, vol. 37, No. 7, pp. 30-43.

HAGEMEJER, J. & KOLASA, M. 2008, Internationalization and economic performance of enterprises: evidence from firm-level data, National Bank of Poland Working Papers 51, National Bank of Poland, Warsaw, Poland.

HELPMAN, E. & KRUGMAN, P.R. 1985, Market Structure and Foreign Trade, MIT Press, Cambridge.

ISGUT, A. 2001, 'What's Different about Exporters? Evidence from Colombian Manufacturing', Journal of Development Studies, vol. 37(5), pp. 57-82.

KRUGMAN, P.R. 1979, 'Increasing Returns, Monopolistic Competition, and International Trade', Journal of International Economics, No. 9, pp. 469-479.

KRUGMAN, P.R. 1980, 'Scale Economies, Product Differentiation, and the Pattern of Trade', American Economic Review, vol. 70, No. 5, pp. 950-959.

MAGGIONI, D. 2010, Learning by exporting in Turkey: an investigation for existence and channels, MPRA Paper 37157, University Library of Munich, Germany.

MAYER T. & OTTAVIANO G.I.P. 2007, The Happy Few: New Facts on the Internationalisation of European Firms. New facts based on firm-level evidence, Bruegel Blueprint Series, vol. III, CEPR, Brussels, Belgium.

MELITZ, M.J. 2003, 'The Impact of Trade on Intra-industry Reallocations and Aggregate Industry Productivity', Econometrica, vol. 71, No. 6, pp. 1695-1725.

MELITZ, M.J. & OTTAVIANO, G. 2008, 'Market Size, Trade, and Productivity', Review of Economic Studies, vol. 75, pp. 295-316.

OLLEY, G.S. & PAKES, A. 1996, 'The dynamics of productivity in the telecommunications equipment industry', Econometrica, vol. 64, pp. 1263–1297.

PAVCNIK, N. 2002, 'Trade Liberalization, Exit, and Productivity Improvement: Evidence from Chilean Plants', Review of Economic Studies, vol. 69(1), pp. 245-76.

REDDING, S.J. 2010, Theories of Heterogeneous Firms and Trade, CEP Discussion Paper No. 994.

VERHOOGEN, E.A. 2008, 'Trade, Quality Upgrading and Wage Inequality in the Mexican Manufacturing Sector', Journal of International Economics, vol. 65, pp. 1-20.

WAGNER, J. 2002, 'The causal effects of exports on firm size and labor productivity: first evidence from a matching approach', Economics Letters, vol. 77(2), pp. 287-292.

WAGNER, J. 2005, Exports and Productivity: A Survey of the Evidence from Firm Level Data, University of Luneburg Working Paper Series in Economics, Nr 4.

YASAR, M., RACIBORSKI, R. & POI, B. 2008, 'Production function estimation in Stata using the Olley and Pakes method', Stata Journal, vol. 8(2), pp. 221-231.

YEAPLE, S.R. 2005, 'A simple model of firm heterogeneity, international trade, and wages', Journal of International Economics, vol. 65(1), pp. 1-20.

10

Entrepreneurship in Relation to the Competitive Potential and Position of Economies – A Regional Approach Based on Polish Provinces

ALEKSANDRA GAWEŁ, DR HAB.
ASSOCIATE PROFESSOR

e-mail: aleksandra.gawel@ue.poznan.pl

SUMMARY

The aim of this study was to determine the influence of entrepreneurship on the competitiveness of regional economies, in particular on the competitive potential and position of regions. In order to do this, an empirical study of the Polish provinces was conducted. In order to achieve the aim of the study, regression function parameters were estimated by means of three methods: the classic method of least squares, the panel method with fixed effects and the panel method with random effects. Empirical confirmation was obtained for the first hypothesis, which assumed a positive impact of entrepreneurship on the competitive potential of a region. In particular, the findings lend support to the two related secondary hypotheses, which indicated a positive impact of the enterprise start-up rate (Hypothesis 1A) and enterprise density rate (Hypothesis 1B) on the competitive potential of a region. The issue of the impact of entrepreneurship on the competitive position of a region is less clear. One of the secondary hypotheses, which assumed a positive impact of the enterprise density rate on the competitive position (Hypothesis 2B) was confirmed by the findings. However, the enterprise start-up rate was found to have an adverse influence on the competitive position of regions, thus Hypothesis 2A has to be rejected.

Keywords: entrepreneurship, regional competitiveness, Poland

INTRODUCTION

This article examines the determinants of regional competitiveness. Because in the vast majority of cases companies begin their business operations in a local market and later expand their activities to other markets, an analysis of local economic conditions seems to be extremely important.

Among the different factors that have an impact on regional competitiveness, the analysis concentrates on entrepreneurship understood in its narrow meaning as the process of creating and running a business enterprise. This issue is relatively rarely discussed, although according to the literature the relationship between entrepreneurship and competitiveness can be bidirectional (Audretsch & Pena-Legazkue 2012) and the findings of earlier research do not provide definitive answers regarding the direction and strength of those dependencies. Some studies indicate that entrepreneurial opportunities appear in the environment, whereas others argue that it is entrepreneurs who shape the environment (Edelman & Yli-Renko 2010).

To address this research problem, the article differentiates between competitive potential and competitive position. Entrepreneurial capital is an important regional asset (Audretsch & Pena-Legazkue 2012) and it can be considered as a factor which affects the competitive potential of a region. At the same time, a properly conducted entrepreneurial process influences a region's competitive position.

The article is divided into four sections. The first section explains the essence and meaning of competitiveness. The second contains a theoretical discussion of the role of entrepreneurship in shaping the competitive position and potential of a region. The third part presents the adopted research assumptions, including the research hypotheses and methods of empirical analysis. The final section includes the findings of the research, followed by concluding remarks.

THE ESSENCE AND MEANING OF COMPETITIVENESS

Competitiveness is a multifaceted concept, which can be discussed on a national level or on an industry, enterprise or product level (Buckley et al. 1988; Flanagan et al. 2007), and each of those levels is significantly different from the others (Flanagan et al. 2007).

The multidimensionality of competitiveness means that many different definitions of it can be found in the literature, none of which having been universally accepted (Flanagan et al. 2007; Balkyte & Tvaronaviciene 2010). Some prominent global institutions adopt the following definitions (Fischer & Schornberg 2007):

- The OECD defines competitiveness as the ability of companies, industries, regions, nations or supra-regional economies to generate relatively high factor income and employment levels on a sustainable basis while being exposed to international competition,
- In the definition of the European Commission, competitiveness is the ability of an economy to provide a sustained rise in the standards of living for all the people who are willing to work,
- According to the definition adopted in the Global Competitiveness Report prepared by the World Economic Forum, competitiveness is a set of institutions, policies and factors which affect the level of productivity of a country (World Economic Forum 2011-2012, p. 4).

Competitiveness is also understood as a dynamic comparison between enterprises, industries or sectors in which the goods or services they produce can complement or compete with each other at certain points in order to achieve specific commercial or financial objectives. This comparison is continuous and dynamic, and it shows the evolution in the advantages of enterprises, industries or sectors over their competitors (Lombana 2011).

In another approach competitiveness is defined in the following ways, depending on the level of analysis (Buckley et al. 1988; Balkyte & Tvaronaviciene 2010):

- Competitiveness at the company level – a company is competitive if it is able to provide products or services of high quality and at lower prices than its national and international competitors,
- Competitiveness at the regional level – the ability of a region to use its competitive potential in order to achieve and maintain a competitive position over other regions,
- Competitiveness at the national level – the ability of a country to generate the resources necessary for fulfilling its national needs.

A particular form of national competitiveness is the international competitiveness of a country, traditionally explained on the basis of the theory of international trade (Balkyte & Tvaronaviciene 2010), or in a narrow sense as export competitiveness (Gorynia et al 2007b).

The concept of competitiveness is used to try and explain why some countries develop faster than others (Vares et al. 2011). The primary role of a nation is to create local conditions for the operation of companies. In the initial stages of existence, companies are usually dependent on local economic conditions, which shape their identity and determine access to resources (Grant 1991).

National competitiveness can be considered in two meanings (Thompson 2004):

- A narrow meaning, relating to cost conditions as determined by the exchange rate,
- A broader meaning, comprising the institutional and systemic circumstances of a business environment, for example the legal or political factors which influence business activities.

Another dimension of competitiveness is regional economies. The competitiveness of companies and the competitiveness of regions are interdependent concepts (Huggins 2003). The competitiveness of a region, both at the local and the regional level, is the ability of a specific sub-national economy to attract and retain companies which have a stable and/or growing market share, and to sustain a stable or growing standard of living for the population of the region (Huggins 2003). Regional competitiveness should also indicate the relative position of the companies from a given region in external markets, as well as the productivity and utilisation of local resources (Turok 2004). Additionally, regional competitiveness relates to how successfully regions compete against one another in order to win a share of the national or international markets (Kitson et al. 2004).

It is assumed that the foundations of regional competitiveness, measured by regional productivity, employment and the standard of living, comprise the manufacturing capital, human capital, social and institutional capital, cultural capital, infrastructure and knowledge (Kitson et al. 2004). The concept of competitiveness involves both efficiency, understood as the ability to achieve goals; and effectiveness, which means that goals are achieved at the lowest possible cost (O'Farrell et al. 1993).

There are several approaches and models for explaining competitiveness. The models derived from the works of Porter are considered to be mainstream models in the study of competitiveness although their critics point to some limitations such as a restricted possibility of widening the spectrum of analysis, focusing on the domestic sphere or the role of the government (Lombana 2011). Michael Porter's Five Forces model assumes that competitiveness is influenced by five forces and that basic competitive strategies exist (Porter 2006, pp. 31 and subsequent). On the other hand, Porter's National Diamond model enumerates the following pillars of competitiveness: factor conditions, demand conditions, related and supporting industries as well as company strategy, structure and rivalry (Prasad 2011; Balkyte & Tvaronaviciene 2010; Ozgen 2011).

Other models of competitiveness are presented in the work of Ormanighi and Stringa (2008). The Structure-Conduct-Performance SCP) model assumes the impact of the structure of an industry on the conditions of conducting business, which affects the performance of companies. From the perspective of game theory, competitors are engaged in a specific game. The resource-based approach suggests that the efficiency of companies varies due to their different access to resources. And market process economics indicates that competitive advantage stems from a subjective assessment of profit potential, the creation and use of uncertainty as well as the coordination of learning and knowledge.

Another model of competitiveness, the 3P model, assumes the existence of three dimensions of competitiveness (Taggart & Taggart 1998):

- potential competitiveness – describes the inputs that can be made,
- process competitiveness – includes all the aspects of business operations through which competitive potential can change into competitive position,
- performance competitiveness – indicates the results of competitiveness.

With the introduction of aspects related to potential, process and position, competitiveness has become a coherent concept which can be integrated with management studies, economics or operations research (Flanagan et al. 2007).

The three dimensions of competitiveness interact with one another. Competitive potential influences the competitive position by making it permanent, and it influences the competitive process through generating resources which are necessary for management. Competitive process influences the position through managing the competitive potential, and it influences the potential through managing the decisions which determine the competitive potential. Finally, competitive position makes it possible to improve the competitive potential and the competitive process (Buckley et al. 1990). Competitive potential is connected with the inputs and competitive position is connected with the outputs (O'Farrell et al. 1993). Another study (Gorynia et al. 2007a) distinguishes between competitive potential and competitive position, just as in the 3P model, but the term competitive process is replaced by competitive strategy.

In the literature various measures are suggested to describe the dimensions of competitiveness as described by the 3P model; for example, the following measures can be used (Taggart & Taggart 1998; Buckley et al. 1990):

- potential competitiveness – labour costs, productivity, prices, research and development expenditure, commercialisation of research and development activities,
- process competitiveness – involvement in international business, marketing skills, economies of scale, internal and external relations,
- performance competitiveness – market share, share in exports market, dependence on exports, increase in exports, profitability.

Research findings also indicate that some measures of competitiveness seem to have values which are specific for given sectors, such as, for example, the volume and value of sales, sales growth, profitability and time- and cost-effectiveness as measures of competitive position; the quality of a product as a measure of competitive potential; and international orientation, management content or market orientation as measures of process competitiveness. Other measures may have a more universal nature, for instance employee's skills or relationships in key markets as measures of competitive potential, and the organisational structure, management styles and systems as measures of process competitiveness (Coviello et al. 1998). For a company to achieve a stable and balanced competitive situation it should be competitive in all the aspects of the 3P model (Taggart & Taggart 1998).

THE ROLE OF ENTREPRENEURSHIP IN SHAPING THE COMPETITIVENESS OF A REGION – A THEORETICAL APPROACH

The present study focuses on the competitiveness of a regional economy. This dimension has been adopted because of the importance of local conditions for the operations of business enterprises. Typically, companies start to operate in local markets and only later do some of them begin the process of internationalisation (Grant 1991). Therefore, regional competitiveness is a phenomenon which is important in terms of both theory and practice.

One of the key dimensions of effective regional competitiveness is sustainable growth in employment. A key factor in achieving sustainable growth is maintaining a critical number of firms, measured by the saturation of an economy with enterprises, which helps generate new entrepreneurs and innovators in emerging sectors and markets as well as creating new jobs (Huggins, 2003).

There are two perspectives of regional competitiveness. The first is a microeconomic perspective, which involves the companies operating in a given region and their ability to produce goods in a stable and profitable manner, making it possible to meet the demand in an open economy. The second perspective is the result of macroeconomic competitiveness (Dimian & Danciv 2011).

This article assumes that entrepreneurship is a factor which influences regional competitiveness. Entrepreneurship, just like competitiveness, is a multi-faceted concept which remains outside the mainstream of neoclassical economics. Although research into entrepreneurship has been conducted for over half a century, there is still no single universally accepted definition or theory of this concept (Bygrave & Hofer 1991; Campbell 1992; Zachary & Mishra 2010); however, entrepreneurship is becoming an increasingly legitimate area of research (Hoskisson et al. 2011).

One problem of entrepreneurship studies is thought to be that fact that there is no clear conceptual basis; instead, research is based on various concepts derived from neoclassical equilibrium, psychology, and the Austrian school, as well as economic, cultural and socio-political schools (Murphy 2011). Entrepreneurship is analysed in historical, time, institutional, spatial and social contexts (Welter 2011). There are three principal research trends, in which entrepreneurship is understood as innovativeness (Schumpeter 1960; Hoskisson et al. 2011), risk-taking (Emmett 1999), or noticing and exploiting market opportunities (Kirzner 1997; Douhan et al. 2007). In the literature, entrepreneurship is equated with starting a business, innovation, seeking business opportunities, taking risks, seeking profit, making a new use of resources, obtaining and managing resources, creating value, company existence, taking initiatives, ownership, as well as the strategic development of an enterprise (Morris et al. 1994; Hoskisson et al. 2011). In a narrow sense, entrepreneurship is connected with the creation and development of an enterprise (Griffiths et al. 2012), whereas in a broad sense it is connected with its attributes and resources (Bridge et al. 2009, pp. 39-44].

This article has adopted a narrow definition of entrepreneurship, being the process of creating and running a company. Creating a new business is a complex process that involves a range of activities, such as identifying market opportunities, preparing a plan of action, and obtaining resources, as well as formalising the company and its further development through successive stages of growth (Gorzelany-Dziadkowiec & Gorzelany, 2007). In the course of the entrepreneurial process an idea is transformed into an operating company (Bratnicki 2008).

The relationships between entrepreneurship and regional competitiveness are not often analysed in the literature and they require further study (Audretsch & Pena-Legazkue 2012). Studies which examine the relationships between entrepreneurship and the environment present two opposing views: some claim that entrepreneurial opportunities emerge in the environment, whereas others argue that entrepreneurs shape the environment (Edelman &Yli-Renko 2010); sometimes it is said that a two-way relationship exists between these two categories (Audretsch & Pena-Legazkue 2012). Previous study has looked for a relationship between the location of new enterprises, the place of an entrepreneur's operations and entrepreneurship support policies (Trettin & Welter 2011). Moreover, it is indicated that the characteristics related to the location of businesses, especially access to local resources, affect their ability to implement innovation (Karlsen et al. 2011).

This study assumes that the level of entrepreneurship in a given region affects regional competitiveness, so entrepreneurial activity influences the environment. Adopting such an assumption stems from the observation that entrepreneurship is embedded in the social structure, and enterprises are part of a larger system consisting of other enterprises as well as society as a whole. A local community can be regarded as an important basis for developing entrepreneurial activity. Entrepreneurs are agents of change and organisers of the community development process (Spilling 2011). Entrepreneurial capital is a significant regional asset which can accelerate the transformation of a local economy through increased competition and regional productivity (Audretsch & Pena-Legazkue 2012). A region's greater capability of generating new knowledge and creating new enterprises are positively correlated with its level of competitiveness (Gonzalez-Pernia et al. 2012).

Market entries of new enterprises and the activity of the existing ones can influence the level of regional competitiveness through several channels. The appearance of new market entrants increases competition between companies and creates demand for skilled workers (Kitson et al. 2004), which has a positive impact on the competitiveness of the region. This positive impact can be attributed to two causes. The first one is a selection mechanism which prevents inefficient companies from surviving on the market, thus enabling new companies to enter. The second mechanism indicates that competition between enterprises forces existing companies to improve technologies or the organisation of their operations (Turok 2004). Thus, possible entries of new firms increase the efficiency of existing companies, which raises the competitive potential of a region.

Such a relationship can also be linked to the type of technological regime in a region, which affects the ways of introducing innovation to the market. There are two types of regimes: an entrepreneurial regime and a routinised regime. An entrepreneurial regime is characterised by a high number of new enterprises that introduce innovation into the market. In routinised regimes the start-up rate is relatively low, and innovation is implemented by existing companies (Audretsch & Fritsch 2002; Lin & Huang 2008; Peneder 2008). In an entrepreneurial regime there is creative destruction, which means that new companies enter the market and replace existing businesses; and in a routinised regime there is creative accumulation, which is characterised by a relatively stable number of companies. It is easier for new businesses to enter entrepreneurial regime markets because of lower entry barriers (Lin & Huang, 2008). It is believed that entrepreneurial regimes are characterised by a greater increase in value added and in employment; however, labour productivity is lower than in routinised regimes (Peneder 2008).

The saturation of an economy with enterprises, which promotes the generation of new entrepreneurs and innovators, is considered to be one of the key factors for achieving effective regional competitiveness (Huggins 2003).

THE IMPACT OF ENTREPRENEURSHIP ON THE POTENTIAL AND THE COMPETITIVE POSITION OF A REGION – RESEARCH ASSUMPTIONS

In view of what has been said above, the business environment can be regarded as one of the elements of the economic system of a region. Taking into account the bi-directionality of the possible interactions between entrepreneurship and competitiveness, it has been assumed that the entrepreneurial process connected with the appearance of new market entrants and the growth of existing firms affects the potential and the competitive position of economies at a regional level.

To justify this one can refer to the assumptions of neoclassical economics, especially the processes which shape the long-term situation in perfect competition (Mankiew & Taylor, 2009 pp. 386-388; Czarny & Nojszewska 2000, pp. 129-132; Varian 2001, p. 408 and subsequent). The more companies operate in a market and the lower their concentration, the easier it is for new companies to enter the market. This is because such a market more closely resembles the structure of perfect competition and consequently entry barriers are lower, there are better conditions for companies to make their mark, and the regional market is more open to new business enterprises. New market entrants affect the form of the supply function, which in the long term leads to the decline in prices to a level where profit is reduced to zero. Simultaneously, such a situation prompts companies to implement new solutions and look for the most efficient methods of utilising their resources in the search for profit. Competition between existing enterprises and the threat of new entries can thus affect the competitive potential and competitive position of a region.

Existing and newly created companies help improve the competitive potential of the region in which they operate through their influence on the inputs that can be made and utilised in the region's economy. On the one hand, enterprises obtain the factors of production which are necessary for their operations; on the other hand, they decide how to use them. It can therefore be assumed that the more developed entrepreneurship is in a region, the higher the region's competitive potential. The above dependencies lead to formulating the first research hypothesis.

Hypothesis 1: Entrepreneurship has a positive impact on the competitive potential of a region.

Existing and emerging businesses influence the competitive position; that is, the results that a region achieves in comparison to other regions. Through managing their resources, companies generate economic benefits both for themselves and for cooperating groups of stakeholders. This is reflected in the overall economic performance of the region. The greater the number of efficient companies which operate in a region, the better the region's economic performance. The above observations lead to formulating the second research hypothesis.

Hypothesis 2: Entrepreneurship has a positive impact on the competitive position of a region.

An empirical study was conducted in order to verify the research hypotheses relating to the positive impact of entrepreneurship on the competitive potential and position of regional economies. The study analysed the economies of 16 Polish regions. Based on data availability, for each of the economies the course of the variables was examined for the years 2003-2009 in yearly data. This means that for each region a time series of seven years was analysed. Altogether, 112 observations were used for each of the variables .

The impact of entrepreneurship on the competitive potential and position of economies was determined on the basis of the estimated parameters of regression function. It was assumed that the regression function is represented by the following regression equation

$$K = a_0 + a_1 MP_1 + \ldots + a_n MP_n \quad (1)$$

where:

K – measures of competitiveness, including measures of both competitive potential and competitive position,

$MP_1 \ldots MP_n$ – measures of entrepreneurship from 1 to n,

$a_0, a_1 \ldots a_n$ – regression function parameters.

Because this study has adopted the narrow meaning of entrepreneurship as a process of enterprise creation and development, appropriate measures were applied which illustrate these processes. Initially, four measures of entrepreneurship were adopted:

- enterprise start-up rate (SR) – calculated as the percentage of newly registered enterprises in a given year in the total number of enterprises in each region,
- enterprise closure rate (CR) – measured as a percentage of deregistered companies in a given

- year in the total number of enterprises in each region,
- enterprise net rate (NR) – calculated as a percentage of the difference between new and deregistered companies in a given year in the total number of enterprises in each region,
- enterprise density rate (DR) – calculated as the number of enterprises per 1,000 inhabitants in each region.

In the absence of consensus with regard to competitiveness measures, this study refers to entrepreneurship studies which use the indicator approach. These include the Global Competitiveness Report produced by the World Economic Forum (Fischer & Schornberg 2007).

The Global Competitivness Report includes the Global Competitivness Index (GCI), which is influenced by 12 pillars, each indicating the determinants of competitiveness. These pillars depict such aspects of competitiveness as institutions, infrastructure, macroeconomic environment, health and primary education, higher education and training, goods market efficiency, labour market efficiency, financial market sophistication, technological readiness, market size, business sophistication, and innovation (Global Competitiveness Report 2011-2012). Although the GCI is a comprehensive measure for competitiveness assessment, it presents an international perspective and there is no data relating to individual regions of a country. That is why the GCI could not be used for the purposes of this study.

It can be noted that the measures of entrepreneurship adopted in this study can be linked to the sixth pillar of competitiveness – the efficiency of the goods and services market. In the GCI one of the components of this pillar is domestic competition, which includes the number of new manufacturing enterprises and the time required to start a business. The measures of entrepreneurship adopted in this study (enterprise start-up rate, closure rate, net rate and density rate), although not entirely corresponding to the components used in the GCI, can be considered to present a broader picture of competition between enterprises.

Although Porter's five forces model evaluates the profitability of an industry and not of a region (Porter 2006, pp. 31 and subsequent; Prasad 2011), it can be seen that the adopted measures of entrepreneurship as determinants of competitiveness are associated with the threat of new market entries, which is one of the forces analysed in the model. Additionally, with regard to Porter's diamond of national advantage, the determinants adopted in this study relate to the part of the diamond which comprises the strategy of companies, their structure and rivalry (Balkyte & Tvaronaviciene 2010; Prasad, 2011).

To determine the competitive potential of individual regions, which involves the resources that can be utilised, the present study used the potential measures proposed in the 3P model (Taggart & Taggart 1998; Buckley et al. 1990). In particular, the following three measures were taken into account:

- Labour costs in PLN per one inhabitant (LC),
- Price dynamics, where the previous year is considered to be 100 (PD),
- Research and development expenditure in PLN per inhabitant (RDE).

Competitive position, in turn, which indicates the performance competitiveness of regions, was measured by means of two parameters: GDP per capita and disposable income. In the literature, net national income per capita, measured by purchasing power, is considered to be the most synthetic indicator of economic performance (Kowalski & Pietrzykowski 2010, pp. 30-31); however, in the Polish economy the differences in price levels are not very significant so correcting GDP with purchasing power is not necessary. GDP per capita is often used in studies as a measure of regional competitiveness (e.g. Dimian & Danciv 2011) which indicates the results and thus the competitive position of regions.

In the case of competitiveness measures this study took into account the ranking of regions' effectiveness, that is the relationship of GDP per capita and disposable income in a region to the level of these values in Poland, with the average value for Poland being 100. Thus, the following two measures for the competitive position of regions were adopted:

- A percentage deviation of GDP per capita in a given region from GDP per capita in Poland (GDP per capita, Poland = 100) (GDP)
- A percentage deviation of disposable income in a given region from disposable income in Poland (Disposable income, Poland = 100), (DI).

The denominator for most of the adopted indicators describing the competitive potential and position (LC, RDE, GDP, DI) is the population of a given province. This stems from the desire to obtain a common denominator for competitiveness measures and the enterprise density indicator (DR).

Because one of the adopted variables, the enterprise net rate (NR), can have both positive and negative values, it cannot be converted to natural logarithms. Therefore, to achieve the comparability of variables at this stage of the study, the decision was taken to keep the raw data; if only linear dependencies were to be analysed when creating regression functions, all the variables should be converted to natural logarithms.

In order to eliminate the collinearity of independent variables, correlations between the variables were examined (see Table 1).

Table 1
The correlation coefficient between variables

	GDP	DI	LC	PD	RDE	SR	CR	NR	DR
GDP		0.954	0.808	-0.021	0.807	-0.134	-0.185	0.155	0.732
DI	0.954		0.766	-0.027	0.707	-0.126	-0.137	0.098	0.757
LC	0.808	0.808		0.333	0.830	0.281	0.152	-0.022	0.605
PD	-0.021	-0.027	0.333		0.127	0.206	0.296	-0.252	0.043
RDE	0.807	0.707	0.830	0.127		0.076	-0.018	0.070	0.459
SR	-0.134	-0.126	0.281	0.206	0.076		0.643	-0.209	0.053
CR	-0.185	-0.137	0.152	0.296	-0.018	0.643		-0.883	-0.117
NR	0.155	0.098	-0.022	-0.252	0.070	-0.209	-0.883		0.182
DR	0.732	0.757	0.605	0.043	0.459	0.053	-0.117	0.182	

Source: own compilation

From the point of view of estimating the regression function parameters, it is important to exclude those variables which have a high correlation. Out of the four independent variables adopted (SR, CR, NR, DR), there is a high positive correlation between the start-up rate (SR) and the closure rate (CR) (0.643). Therefore, enterprise closure rate (CR) was discarded as an independent variable and only three measures of entrepreneurship were used in further research procedures: enterprise start-up rate (SR), enterprise net rate (NR) and enterprise density rate (DR).

The Impact of Entrepreneurship on the Competitiveness of Regions – Research Findings

The next research step, following the correlation analysis (see Table 1), was the estimation of regression function parameters according to Equation (1). The dependent variables were the measures of competitive potential and competitive position, and the independent variables were the measures of entrepreneurship. First, the classic method of least squares was used to estimate the level of significance (p value) for each of the parameters (see Table 2).

Out of the 5 regression functions (see Table 2) estimated during the second research step, in 4 cases the parameters for the independent variable enterprise net rate (NR) turned out to be not statistically significant (for the dependent variables GDP, DI, LC and RDE), and for the fifth function (dependent variable PD) this parameter was again significant with a lower level of significance than the level adopted in this study (the threshold of significance adopted in this study is at the value of $p<0.01$, whereas in the analysed case the value was $p=0.016$). Therefore it was concluded that there is no basis for adopting the enterprise net rate as an independent variable influencing competitiveness, and this variable was excluded from further analysis.

Table 2
Regression function parameters calculated by means of the classic method of least squares using raw data

Dependent variable	Independent variables	Parameter value	Standard error	t-distribution	p value
GDP	Constant	24.805	11.794	2.103	0.038
	SR	-3.163	1.169	-2.706	0.008
	NR	-0.191	0.728	-0.262	0.794
	DR	0.991	0.086	11.480	0.000
DI	Constant	52.712	6.799	7.753	0.000
	SR	-2.002	0.674	-2.972	0.004
	NR	-0.549	0.419	-1.309	0.193
	DR	0.631	0.050	12.67	0.000
LC	Constant	-4439.980	1743.390	-2.547	0.012
	SR	538.332	172.754	3.116	0.002
	NR	-120.471	107.549	-1.120	0.265
	DR	105.030	12.764	8.228	0.000
PD	Constant	100.802	1.020	98.780	0.000
	SR	0.164	0.101	1.626	0.107
	NR	-0.154	0.063	-2.446	0.016
	DR	0.006	0.007	0.830	0.409
RDE	Constant	-245.301	90.850	-2.700	0.008
	SR	5.324	9.002	0.591	0.556
	NR	-0.172	5.604	-0.031	0.976
	DR	3.484	0.665	5.238	0.000

Source: own compilation

On completion of the second research stage, two variables were finally adopted as independent variables, the enterprise start-up rate (SR) and the enterprise density rate (DR). This allows us to analyse the influence of entrepreneurship both from the point of view of entrepreneurial potential, measured by the start-up rate (SR), and from the point of view of entrepreneurial results, measured by enterprise density (DR).

Adopting these two dependent variables makes it possible to refine the research hypotheses. Hypothesis 1, which concerns the positive impact of entrepreneurship on the competitive potential of a region, has been modified by adding two specific hypotheses.

Hypothesis 1A: Enterprise start-up rate has a positive impact on the competitive potential of a region.

Hypothesis 1B: Enterprise density rate has a positive impact on the competitive potential of a region.

By analogy, the second research hypothesis, which concerns the positive impact of entrepreneurship on the competitive position of a region, has been modified by formulating two specific hypotheses.

Hypothesis 2A: Enterprise start-up rate has a positive impact on the competitive position of a region.

Hypothesis 2B: Enterprise density rate has a positive impact on the competitive position of a region.

After enterprise closure rate and enterprise net rate had been excluded from the set of analysed variables, it was possible to convert all the remaining variables to natural logarithms. When this had been done, the parameters of the regression function were estimated according to the initial form of Equation (1) by means of three consecutive methods: the classic method of least squares, the panel method with fixed effects, and the panel method with random effects.

Table 3

Regression function parameters for GDP per capita as a dependent variable

Independent variables	Parameter value	Standard error	t-distribution	p value
Classic method of least squares				
Constant	0.671	0.337	1.988	0.049
SR	-0.221	0.078	-2.817	0.006
DR	0.947	0.067	14.040	0.000
Panel method with fixed effects				
Constant	4.025	0.317	12.700	0.000
SR	-0.050	0.016	-3.148	0.002
DR	0.127	0.073	1.744	0.084
Panel method with random effects				
Constant	3.559	0.319	11.170	0.000
SR	-0.060	0.017	-3.582	0.001
DR	0.235	0.073	3.230	0.002

Source: own compilation

When analysing the results of estimating the parameters of the regression function for GDP per capita as a dependent variable by the use of three methods, it can be observed that irrespective of the method of estimation, the enterprise start-up rate (SR) is inversely proportional and the enterprise density rate is directly proportional to GDP. In all the methods of estimation, both the independent variables have a statistically significant impact on the dependent variable (see Table 3).

Comparing the absolute values of the estimated parameters, it can be assumed that the enterprise density rate of an economy has a greater impact on GDP per capita than the start-up rate.

Table 4

Regression function parameters for disposable income (DI) as a dependent variable

Independent variables	Parameter value	Standard error	t-distribution	p value
Classic method of least squares				
Constant	2.097	0.216	9.717	0.000
SR	-0.126	0.050	-2.507	0.014
DR	0.599	0.043	13.880	0.000
Panel method with fixed effects				
Constant	3.823	0.187	20.500	0.000
SR	-0.030	0.009	-3.175	0.002
DR	0.173	0.043	4.038	0.000
Panel method with random effects				
Constant	3.618	0.185	19.540	0.000
SR	-0.034	0.010	-3.536	0.001
DR	0.221	0.042	5.226	0.000

Source: own compilation

Another dependence which was examined, using the same three methods of estimating regression function parameters, was the influence of entrepreneurship on the disposable income of the population (see Table 4). In all three cases it was found that the start-up rate (SR) inversely influences and the density rate (DR) directly influences the disposable income of the population. The DR variable turned out to be statistically significant in all the analysed cases with the adopted level of significance ($p<0.01$). The ST variable is statistically significant at the adopted level of significance ($p<0.01$) in the case of the panel method with random and fixed effects; however, in the case of the classic method of least squares this variable is significant at a lower threshold of significance ($p=0.014$).

The absolute values of the estimated parameters indicate that the enterprise density rate is a factor which has a greater influence on the disposable income of the population than the business start-up rate.

Next, the influence of entrepreneurship on labour costs per capita (see Table 5) was analysed using the three methods of estimating the parameters of the regression function. Both measures of entrepreneurship, enterprise start-up rate (SR) and enterprise density rate (DR), in the case of all the regression functions, turned out to have a directly proportional and statistically significant influence on labour costs.

Table 5

Regression function parameters for labour costs per capita (LC) as a dependent variable

Independent variables	Parameter value	Standard error	t-distribution	p value
Classic method of least squares				
Constant	3.889	0.516	7.537	0.000
SR	0.549	0.120	4.586	0.000
DR	0.907	0.103	8.797	0.000
Panel method with fixed effects				
Constant	-1.463	1.237	-1.183	0.240
SR	0.925	0.062	14.840	0.000
DR	1.921	0.284	6.759	0.000
Panel method with random effects				
Constant	1.280	0.834	1.535	0.128
SR	0.960	0.063	15.34	0.000
DR	1.298	0.190	6.833	0.000

Source: own compilation

A comparison of the absolute values of the estimated parameters indicates that, similarly to the previous regression functions, business density rate is a factor which exerts a greater influence on labour costs than does the business start-up rate.

Table 6

Regression function parameters for price dynamics (PD) as a dependent variable

Independent variables	Parameter value	Standard error	t-distribution	p value
Classic method of least squares				
Constant	4.588	0.034	135.200	0.000
SR	0.015	0.008	1.946	0.054
DR	0.002	0.007	0.324	0.747
Panel method with fixed effects				
Constant	4.054	0.213	19.020	0.000
SR	0.016	0.011	1.448	0.151
DR	0.120	0.049	2.459	0.016
Panel method with random effects				
Constant	4.588	0.034	135.200	0.000
SR	0.015	0.008	1.946	0.054
DR	0.002	0.007	0.324	0.747

Source: own compilation

The next research step was to determine the influence of entrepreneurship on the price dynamics in each region (see Table 6). However, in none of the three methods for estimating the parameters of the regression function did the parameters of both measures of entrepreneurship, enterprise start-up rate (SR) and enterprise density rate (DR), reach the adopted level of significance ($p<0.01$). Thus there are no grounds for confirming the influence of entrepreneurship on price dynamics.

The final stage of the research was to examine the impact of entrepreneurship on research and development expenditure per inhabitant (see Table 7) using the three adopted methods of estimating regression function parameters. All the regression functions showed that both measures of entrepreneurship – the start-up rate (SR) and the density rate (DR) – have a directly proportional influence on research and development expenditure. However, the statistical significance of this relationship is unclear. In half of the cases (three out of six) the assumed significance threshold was reached, in two other cases the p values marginally exceeded the target level ($p=0.019$; $p=0.018$), and in the last case the significance level was at the value of $p=0.059$. This means that if a lower level of significance ($p=0.1$) is accepted, all the variables can be considered significant, but with the assumed threshold in half the cases the variables did not reach the target level.

Table 7

Regression function parameters for research and development expenditure (RDE) as a dependent variable

Independent variables	Parameter value	Standard error	t-distribution	p value
Classic method of least squares				
Constant	-5.822	2.136	-2.725	0.008
SR	1.183	0.496	2.386	0.019
DR	1.731	0.427	4.052	0.000
Panel method with fixed effects				
Constant	-7.697	4.363	-1.764	0.081
SR	1.683	0.220	7.654	0.000
DR	1.918	1.003	1.913	0.059
Panel method with random effects				
Constant	-7.345	3.313	-2.217	0.029
SR	1.679	0.210	8.006	0.000
DR	1.842	0.757	2.432	0.017

Source: own compilation

Similarly, as in the case of the dependencies which were analysed earlier, on the basis of the absolute values of the estimated parameters it can be stated that the impact of enterprise density on research and development expenditure is greater than the impact of start-up rate. This time, however, the difference in the strength of the impact is smaller than it was in the previous instances.

In conclusion, it is evident that the results of the analyses have confirmed the impact of the two measures of entrepreneurship, enterprise start-up rate and enterprise density rate, on both the potential and the competitive position of regions.

Both the adopted measures of entrepreneurship exert a positive influence on the competitive potential of regions. The start-up rate, which depicts the scale of new businesses entering the market, has a directly proportional influence on labour costs and on prices, as well on as research and development expenditure. A greater number of new market entrants increases competition for resources, including human capital. This produces an increase in labour costs, resulting from salary-based forms of attracting new employees, as well as an increase in price dynamics. At the same time, a higher start-up rate forces all the market operators to look for innovative solutions, which leads to an increase in research and development expenditure.

The rate of enterprise density also has a favourable influence on the competitive potential of a region. The greater the enterprise density in a given economy, that is the greater the number of businesses per 1,000 inhabitants, the more intense the competition between them for the factors of production, including human capital. This results in higher labour costs and greater price dynamics. At the same time, a greater density of enterprises prompts them to look for new solutions, which increases the level of research and development expenditure.

It is worth noting that the adopted measures of entrepreneurship exert the strongest influence on research and development expenditure and the weakest on price dynamics.

Consequently, the findings of this part of the research provide confirmation for the first research hypothesis, which assumed a positive impact of entrepreneurship on the competitive potential of a region. The findings also provide support for accepting the two specific hypotheses, which assumed a positive impact of enterprise start-up rate (Hypothesis 1A) and enterprise density rate (Hypothesis 1B) on the competitive potential of a region.

The situation is somewhat different as regards the influence of entrepreneurship on the competitive position of regional economies. It was discovered that during the analysed period one of the measures of entrepreneurship, the enterprise start-up rate, had an adverse effect on the competitive position, whereas the second measure, the enterprise density rate, had a positive effect on the competitive position of regions.

The enterprise start-up rate depicts the scale of new market entries. Thus it is a form of human, especially entrepreneurial, and financial capital investment in new business activity. However, not all new companies are able to survive in the market, and enterprise closure rates (see Table 1) show what proportion of new business enterprises fail. In the short term a large scale of new entries can be a burden on the economy of a region and can lead to a deterioration in its competitive position, and only the activity of businesses that manage to survive in the market – depicted in the form of the enterprise density rate – has a positive impact on the competitive position of a regional economy.

The above findings do not provide sufficient grounds for accepting in its entirety the second hypothesis, which assumed a positive impact of entrepreneurship on the competitive position of a regional economy. As regards the secondary hypotheses, there are no grounds for accepting Hypothesis 2A, which assumed a positive impact of the enterprise start-up rate on the competitive position of a region. However, empirical findings provide confirmation for Hypothesis 2B, which assumed a positive impact of the enterprise density rate on the competitive position of a region.

Conclusions

The aim of this study was to determine the influence of entrepreneurship on the competitiveness of regional economies, in particular on the competitive potential and position of regions. In order to do this, an empirical study of the Polish provinces was conducted. The study used yearly data pertaining to the subject of the research for the years 2003-2009. Panel data were created, which showed the value of the adopted indicators for 16 regions over the period of 7 years, which produced 112 observations for each of the variables. In order to achieve the aim of the study, regression function parameters were estimated by means of three methods: the classic method of least squares, the panel method with fixed effects and the panel method with random effects.

The findings of the research were then related to the research hypotheses. Empirical confirmation was obtained for the first hypothesis, which assumed a positive impact of entrepreneurship on the competitive potential of a region. In particular, the findings lend support to the two related secondary hypotheses, which indicated a positive impact of the enterprise start-up rate (Hypothesis 1A) and enterprise density rate (Hypothesis 1B) on the competitive potential of a region.

The issue of the impact of entrepreneurship on the competitive position of a region is less clear. One of the secondary hypotheses, which assumed a positive impact of the enterprise density rate on the competitive position (Hypothesis 2B) was confirmed by the findings. However, the enterprise start-up rate was found to have an adverse influence on the competitive position of regions, thus Hypothesis 2A has to be rejected.

The above findings provide a basis for further research. It seems essential to verify the findings obtained in this study with regard to the regional economies of other countries. An important aspect for future research also seems to be the issue of a time delay in the impact of entrepreneurship on regional competitiveness, particularly on the competitive position. It seems possible that entrepreneurship, especially as expressed through new firm creation, affects the competitive position of a region with a certain time lag, resulting from the fact that new businesses need time before they are able to produce economic results.

REFERENCES

AUDRETSCH, D.B. & FRITSCH, M. (2002). Growth Regimes over Time and Space. Regional Studies, vol. 36(2), 113-124.

AUDRETSCH, D.B. & PENA-LEGAZKUE, I. (2012). Entrepreneurial activity and regional competitiveness: an introduction to the special issue. Small Business Economics, 39(3), 531-537.

BALKYTE, A. & TVARONAVICIENE, M. (2010). Perception of Competitiveness in the Context of Sustainable Development: Facets of 'Sustainable Competitiveness'. Journal of Business Economics and Management, 11(2), 341-365.

BRATNICKI, M. (2008). Konfiguracyjne ujęcie przedsiębiorczości organizacyjnej [Configurational approach to organisational entrepreneurship]. Ekonomika i Organizacja Przedsiębiorstw, 6(701), 17-22.

BRIDGE, S., O'NEIL, K., & MARTIN, F. (2009). Understanding Enterprise: Entrepreneurship and Small Business. 3rd Edition, Palgrave Macmillan.

BUCKLEY, P.J., PASS, C.L., & PRESCOTT, K. (1988). Measures of International Competitiveness: A Critical Survey. Journal of Marketing Management, 4(2), 175-200.

BUCKLEY, P.J., PASS, C.L., & PRESCOTT, K. (1990). Measures of International Competitiveness: Empirical Findings from British Manufacturing Companies. Journal of Marketing Management, 6(1), 1-13.

BYGRAVE, W.D. & C.W. HOFER (1991). Theorizing About Entrepreneurship. Entrepreneurship Theory and Practice, 16, 13-22.

CAMPBELL, C.A. (1992). A Decision Theory Model for Entrepreneurial Acts. Entrepreneurship Theory and Practice, 17, 21-27.

COVIELLO, N.E., GHAURI, P.N., & MARTIN K.A-M. (1998). International Competitiveness: Empirical Findings from SME Service Firms. Journal of International Marketing, 6(2), 8-27.

CZARNY, E. & NOJSZEWSKA, E., (2000). Mikroekonomia [Microeconomics]. Polskie Wydawnictwo Ekonomiczne, Warszawa.

DIMIAN, G.C.& DANCIV, A. (2011). National and Regional Competitiveness in the Crisis Context. Successful Examples. Theoretical and Applied Economics, XVIII (21), 67-78.

DOUHAN, R., ELIASSON, G. & HENREKSON, M. (2007). Isreal M. Kirzner: An Oustanding Austrian Contributor to the Economics of Entrepreneurship. Small Business Economics, 29, 213-223.

EDELMAN, L. & YLI-RENKO, H. (2010). The Impact of Environment and Entrepreneurial Perceptions on Venture-Creation Efforts: Bridging the Discovery and Creation Views of Entrepreneurship. Entrepreneurship Theory and Practice, 34 (5), 833-856.

EMMETT, R.B. (1999). The Economist and the Entrepreneur: Modernist Impulses in Risk, Uncertainty, and Profit. History of Political Economy, 31 (1), 29-52.

FISCHER, C. & SCHORNBERG, S. (2007). Assessing the Competitiveness Situation of EU Food and Drink Manufacturing Industries: An Index-Based Approach. Agribusiness, 23(4), 473-495.

FLANAGAN, R., LU, W., SHEN, L. & JEWELL, C. (2007). Competitiveness in construction: a critical review of research. Construction Management and Economics, 25, 989-1000.

World Economic Forum, Global Competitiveness Report, 2011-2012,. http://www.weforum.org/reports/global-competitiveness-report-2011-2012, access: 05-12-2012

GONZALEZ-PERNIA, J.L., PENA-LEGAZKUE, I. & VENDRELL-HERRERO F. (2012), Innovation, entrepreneurial activity and competitiveness at a sub-national level, Small Business Economics, 39 (3), 561-574.

GORYNIA, M., JANKOWSKA, B. & OWCZARZAK, R. (2007a). Clusters – an attempt to respond to the globalisation challenge? The case of furniture cluster in Wielkopolska, Poznan University of Economics Review, 7(2), 5-28.

GORYNIA, M., NOWAK, J. & WOLNIAK, R. (2007b). Multinational Enterprises and the Competitiveness of Transitional Host Economies: The Case of Poland. Journal of Transitional Management, 12(2), 23-42.

GORZELANY-DZIADKOWIEC, M. & GORZELANY, J. (2007). Zarządzanie przedsiębiorcze w sektorze małych i średnich przedsiębiorstw [Entrepreneurial management in the SME sector]. Ekonomika i Organizacja Przedsiębiorstwa, 11 (694), 51-56.

GRANT, R.M. (1991). Porter's 'Competitive Advantage of Nations': An Assessment, Strategic Management Journal, 12, 535-548.

GRIFFITHS, M., KICKUL, J., BACQ, S. & TERJESEN, S. (2012). A Dialogue With William J. Baumol: Insights on Entrepreneurship Theory and Education. Entrepreneurship Theory and Practice, 36(4), 611-625.

HOSKISSON, R.E., COVIN, J., VOLBERDA, H.W. & JOHNSON R.A. (2011). Revitalizing Entrepreneurship: The Search for New Research Opportunities. Journal of Management Studies, 48 (6), 1141-1168.

HUGGINS, R. (2003). Creating a UK Competitive Index: Regional and Local Benchmarking. Regional Studies, 37 (1), 89-96.

KARLSEN, J., ISAKSEN, A. & SPILLING O.R. (2011). The challenge of constructing regional advantages in peripherial areas: The case of marine biotechnology in Tromso, Norway, Entrepreneurship and Regional Development, 23 (3-4), 235-257.

KIRZNER, I.M. (1997). Entrepreneurial Discovery and the Competitive Market Process: An Austrian Approach. Journal of Economic Literature, XXXV, 60-85.

KITSON, M., MARTIN, R. & TYLER, P. (2004). Regional Competitiveness: An Elusive yet Key Concept? Regional Studies, 38 (9), 991-999.

KOWALSKI, T. & PIETRZYKOWSKI, M. (2010). The economic and monetary union vs. shifts in competitiveness of member states. In: B.Jankowska, T.Kowalski, M.Pietrzykowski (eds.) Dimensions of Competitiveness, Poznan University of Economics Press.

LIN. P.-Ch. & HUANG D.-S. (2008). Technological Regimes and Firm Survival: Evidence Across Sectors and Over Time. Small Business Economics, 30, 175-186.

LOMBANA, J. (2011). Looking for a Distinctive Model with which to Analyze Competitiveness. Advances in Competitiveness Research, 19 (3-4), 32-44.

MANKIEW, N.G. & TAYLOR, M.P. (2009). Mikroekonomia [Microeconomics]. Polskie Wydawnictwo Ekonomiczne: Warsaw.

MORRIS, M.H., LEWIS, P.S. & SEXTON D.L.(1994). Reconceptualizing Entrepreneurship: An Input – Output Perspective. SAM Advanced Management Journal, Jan., 21-31.

MURPHY, P.J (2011). A 2x2 Conceptual Foundation for Entrepreneurial Discovery Theory. Entrepreneurship Theory and Practice, 35(2), 359-374.

O'FARRELL, P.N, HITCHENS, D.M. & MOFFAT, L.A.R. (1993). The Competitive Advantage of Business Service Firms: A Matched Pairs Analysis of the Relationship Between Generic Strategy and Performance. The Service Industries Journal, 13(1), 40-64.

ORMANIGHI, O. & STRINGA, O. (2008). Porter's Model of Generic Competitive Strategies, Business Economics, 43(3), 55-64.

OZGEN, E. (2011). Porter's Diamond Model and Opportunity Recognition: A Cognitive Perspective. Academy of Entrepreneurship Journal, 17(2), 61-76.

PENEDER, M.R. (2008). Firm entry and turnover: the nexus with profitability and growth. Small Business Economics, 30, 327-344.

PORTER, M.E. (2006). Przewaga konkurencyjna [Competitive advantage]. Wydawnictwo Helion: Warsaw

PRASAD, A. (2011). The Impact of Non-Market Forces on Competitive Positioning. Understanding Global Industry Attractiveness through the Eyes of M.E. Porter. Journal of Management Research, 11(3), 131-137.

SCHUMPETER, J. (1960), Teoria rozwoju gospodarczego [Theory of economic development]. PWN: Warsaw.

SPILLING, O.R. (2011). Mobilising the entrepreneurial potential in local community development. Entrepreneurship and Regional Development, 23(1-2), 23-35.

TAGGART, J.M. & TAGGART, J.H. (1998). Stable Currency and International Export Competitiveness: A test of Buckley's 3-P Model. Journal of Marketing Management, 14, 487-502.

THOMPSON, E.R. (2004). National Competitiveness: A Question of Cost Conditions or Institutional Circumstances? British Journal of Management, 15, 197-218.

TRETTIN, L. & WELTER, F. (2011). Challenges for spatially oriented entrepreneurship. Entrepreneurship and Regional Development, 23(7-8), 575-602.

TUROK, I. (2004). Cities, Regions and Competitiveness. Regional Studies, 38(9), 1069-108.

VARES, H., PARVANDI, Y., GHASEMI, R. & ABDULLAHI, B. (2011). Transition from an Efficiency-Driven Economy to Innovation-Driven: A Secondary Analysis of Countries Global Competitiveness. European Journal of Economics, Finance and Administrative Sciences, 31, 123-132.

VARIAN, H.R. (2001). Mikroekonomia [Microeconomics], Wydawnictwo Naukowe PWN: Warsaw.

WELTER, F. (2011). Contextualizing Entrepreneurship – Conceptual Challenges and Ways Forward. Entrepreneurship Theory and Practice, 35(1), 165-184.

ZACHARY, R.K. & MISHRA, C.S., 2010, Entrepreneurship Research Today and Beyond: Hidden In Plain Sight! Journal of Small Business Management, 48(4), 471-474.

11

Fisher's Rate and Aggregate Capital Needs in Investment Decisions

MÁRIA ILLÉS, Ph.D.
UNIVERSITY PROFESSOR
e-mail: vgtilles@uni-miskolc.hu

SUMMARY

Fisher's rate means the interest rate where the net present values of two mutually exclusive projects become equal. The paper examines the background and the circumstances of conformation of Fisher's rate in connection with the aggregate capital needs. Aggregate capital needs is a new conception and gives a new viewpoint to investment project decisions. The paper defines the special content of aggregate capital needs, and compiles an index number for it. The analysis widens knowledge regarding the content of net present value, and highlights the importance of taking the aggregate capital needs into consideration. Fisher's rate only means useful information in practice if the ranking is made based on the net present value. However, this principle of ranking is in contradiction with the concept of long-term profit maximization. The transformed net present value, which is free of distorting effects (and assuming equal required rates of return,) gives the same ranking list as the internal rate of return. Therefore, Fisher's rate has no importance in business decisions.

Keywords: aggregate capital needs; investment project decisions; net present value; internal rate of return; ranking; Fisher's rate

INTRODUCTION

Fisher's rate (or intersection) is nowadays an often quoted and illustrated category in financial books. This rate shows the interest rate that would provide the same net present value for two mutually exclusive projects. The relating intersection is that point where the two net present value curves drawn according to the series of interest rate intersect each other. The illustration covers a range of rates from zero interest rate to a rate slightly higher than the internal rate of return of the two projects. The value of the intersection on the x axis gives the rate; on the y axis it shows the same net present value of the two projects. In the range of interest rates where the interest rate is smaller than the Fisher's rate, the ranking based on the net present value differs from the ranking based on the internal rate of return. After the intersection the ranking of net present values changes, and the rankings based on the net present value and on the internal rate of return become equal. The literature mainly deals with the demonstration and ranking-changing role of this rate; (to my best knowledge) there has been no substantive mapping of the background of these relationships yet.

The financial literature recommends net present value as a tool of ranking. Since the middle of the 20th century, financial recommendations say that the ranking of investment alternatives must support the maximization of shareholder wealth, which means the realization of projects with the highest net present value. The authors usually refer to the work of Fisher. Illés (2012b) gives a brief literary overview on this topic.

If net present value (NPV) is used as a ranking indicator, the intersection can mean important decision-making information, as this is the point where the net present value based ranking of the two projects changes order. However, net present value is not suitable for ranking. After removing distorting effects from the net present value method (and assuming equal required rate of return) this ranking list leads to the same ranking as the internal rate of return (IRR). Illés (2012a) proves this relationship. Based on this article doubt is cast upon several statements of the literature, including the role of Fisher's rate in the process of investment project decisions.

The main objectives of this paper are:

1. To discover the causality relationships between net present value and required rate of return from a business economics perspective.
2. To define and analyze the concept of aggregate capital needs.
3. To compile an index number of aggregate capital needs.
4. To discover and explain the mechanism and internal coherences of the formation of Fisher's rate and Fisher's intersection.

5. To discover the causality-based pre-conditions of appearance of this rate and intersection.
6. To highlight that this rate should not be treated as substantive information in investment project decisions.

The paper analyzes the net present value and its internal relationships by using an economic detour approach. The analysis applies in principle a business economics view and system of conditions that makes it fundamentally different from any financial analyses. Illés (2012b) works out the most significant differences between the financial and the business economics approach.

One of the basic categories of examinations is the yield, which means the difference between the total revenues and total expenditures of a year. (In the literature yield is used in different contexts and so can mean different things. In this paper the yield always means the difference of the total revenues and total expenditures of a year.)

In this paper investment decisions concern investment projects with orthodox cash flow patterns. (The well-known criteria of orthodox cash flow patterns are: a series of the difference of annual revenues and expenditures starts with negative amount or amounts and the sign of these differences changes only once. That is, from a point in time where this difference first turns into positive, this positive sign does not change.)

In order to be clear, the paper only calculates with the usage of equity capital and defines profit as pre-tax profit and at project level. (At company level a loss-reducing investment does not give profit, therefore at this level it is not taxable.)

The Original Name of the Rate

The name Fisher's rate refers to the work 'The Theory of Interest' of Irving Fisher published in 1930. This study was issued more than eight decades ago. Its significance is indisputable. Besides its financial hypotheses, another significant benefit of this work is that it is one of the establishers of the methodology of dynamic profitability calculations. The terminology has changed with time. For example, the expression 'net present value' is not mentioned in Fisher's book.

Fisher actually examines the interest rate according to which the income streams of two mutually exclusive projects will be equal. "That is, this equalizing rate is such that the present values of the two options would be equal" (Fisher 1930:155). This equality has an implicit assumption that the two projects have equal initial investments.

The author names the interest rate where the present values of two projects are equal 'the rate of return over cost'. This expression is used altogether 77 times in the book. The denomination does not refer to the real content. Scientific articles and studies of the last century refer to the category according to Fisher's denomination (for instance: Alchian 1955; Renshaw 1957; Dudley 1972; Keane 1975; Meyer 1979; Hirst & Ma 1983). The economic content of the rate would be slightly better described by the expression "equalizing rate", also used by the author; however, this expression is only mentioned three times in his book.

There are several misunderstandings in the contemporary literature due to the novelty of Fisher's topic and to the rather specific denomination of the category. One of the biggest and most often referred to misunderstandings can be found in the work of Keynes (1936). Several authors quote and analyze this oversight (for instance Alchian 1955; Carlson et al. 1974; Keane 1975). The substance of this is that (in today's terminology) Keynes defines in his work the internal rate of return that he has drawn up as equal to "the rate of return over cost" developed by Fisher. Although considering Fisher's denomination this misunderstanding is not surprising, it is still remarkable because besides the significant differences in content – with some simplification – two projects are necessary to calculate Fisher's rate, while for the internal rate of return only one project is needed (Alchian 1955).

It should be noted, however, that in some cases a different interpretation of the rate of return over cost is also possible. For instance: "In general, the rate of return over cost has to be derived by more complicated methods. As already indicated, the rate of return over cost is always that rate which, employed in computing the present worth of all the costs and the present worth of all the returns, will make these two equal. Or, as a mathematician would prefer to put it, the rate which, employed in computing the present worth of the whole series of differences between the two income streams (some differences being positive and others negative) will make the total zero." (Fisher 1930:168-169.) The second sentence of the quote is a clear explanation of the type of misunderstanding seen in Keynes.

Dudley (1972), as well as Hirst & Ma (1983), finds it important to highlight that according to Fisher's examples the initial investment of the two projects (implicitly) is the same. In fact, this fisherian solution can be the reason that in the related examples of financial literature, the initial investment of the two examined projects is always the same. The equality of the initial investment in the examples is basically uninteresting; the information about the aggregate capital needs would be relevant. Fisher gave preference to the project, from the mutually exclusive projects, with the highest present value, because he thought that this could make the highest contribution to the growth of shareholders' wealth. This view of Fisher that prefers (net) present value even in case of ranking is referred to in the recommendations of the mainstream of today's financial studies.

Furthermore, according to Fisher's approach it is worth mentioning the explanation of the rate at the intersection as the relevant re-investment rate (Dudley1972; etc., critical analyses: Keane 1975; orthodox micro-economic approach: Meyer 1979).

Today in most cases only the name of the rate and of the intersection refers to the scientist. Besides these general references there is usually no concrete literature reference (for instance Van Horne & Wachowicz 2008; Baker & Powell 2009). In business economics publications it is mostly typical that the categories related to the intersection of the net present value curves do not use his name, not even in their denomination (e.g., Adelberg et al. 1986; Arnold & Hope 1990). Among the financial publications there are also some where neither the denomination of the intersection nor the name of the related rate refers back to Fisher (for instance Brealey & Myers 1988, or Firer & Gilbert 2004).

THE BACKGROUND OF THE NET PRESENT VALUE CURVE

The plotting of the curve of the net present value is a regularly appearing topic within the related literature. (This curve is illustrated by Figure 1.) The authors consider this figure well-known and widely used in this form; therefore do not use any professional reference. The figures and related explanations can be introduced from different perspectives: once a general theoretical relationship (Arnold & Hope 1990:254), another time as a solution of an exercise or an introduction of a problem through an example (Brealy & Myers 1988:79; Van Horne & Wachowicz 2008:329).

The literature usually illustrates that the higher the interest rate is, the smaller the net present value. As a result of increasing interest rate, this decrease first reaches the zero net present value, then further increasing results in higher and higher negative net present values. The interest rate that is at the intersection of axis x and that results in zero net present value is, as we all know, the internal rate of return. I am aware of no literature sources on the pre-conditions and detailed content background of the illustrated relationship.

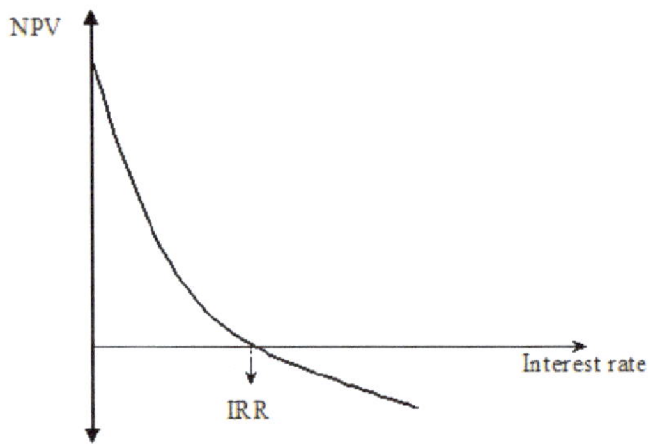

Source: Widely–used illustrations of the relationship

Figure 1 The sum of the net present value in the function of interest rate

In order to specify the problem it must be laid down that the curve in Figure 1 is valid for most but not all projects in question. The relationship is only valid for profitable projects with orthodox cash flow pattern. The illustrated relationship can also be applied for protracted investments. In this case, at the beginning of the duration the initial investment contains the compound interest as well. Hereinafter, in order to simplify modeling, that sort of model will be examined where the payment of initial investment occurs at the same time as operation is started. This is date zero. The first revenues will occur one year later, by this time the annual revenues exceed the annual expenditures.

The survey starts from the content background of economic correspondence. In this way the causality relationships may come to be evident. Related topics:

- to discover the process of the yield requirements formation,
- to analyze the changing content structure of the yield in function of interest rate,
- to show that when the yield requirements are fulfilled then all of the further yields become surplus profit, the discounted sum of which is the net present value.

The net present value method is applied to orthodox cash flow pattern projects, where the initial investment occurring at the zero point of time is the following:

$$NPV = \sum_{t=1}^{n}(B_t - K_t)\frac{1}{(1+i)^t} - E_0 \qquad \big|\, B_t - K_t > 0 \qquad (1)$$

where

B_t = revenues in year t,
K_t = expenditures in year t,
E_0 = initial investment,
i = required rate of return,
t = serial number of years ($t > 0$),
n = duration of the project.

The illustrated net present value curve starts from zero percent interest rate. When the required rate of return is zero, then the net present value is calculated as follows:

$$NPV = \sum_{t=1}^{n} B_t - \sum_{t=1}^{n} K_t - E_0 = M \qquad \big|\, i = 0 \qquad (2)$$

M= Total accounting profit that is the difference of the nominal value of total revenues and total expenditures including initial investment arising during the whole duration of the project.

As Equation (2) shows, at zero percent interest rate the net present value is the difference between the nominal value of total revenues and total expenditures including initial investment. This difference can also be considered as an accounting profit summed up in nominal value for the total duration of the project. This gives the conclusion that if no profit is gained at nominal value, the starting point of net present value curve cannot be in a positive range. Because of this the figure is not valid for projects that do not generate accounting profit

In this calculation, which considers the nominal value and the whole duration of the project, the problem caused by accounting not defining the profit as a difference between revenues and expenditures but as annual differences between revenues and total costs disappears. (Nevertheless, the profit of a project only means profit at the company level when the company itself is not in an accounting loss.)

The profit calculated at nominal value for the whole duration means the coverage of the profit requirements according to the required rate of return. In fact, the content mechanism of net present value method subtracts the amount of profit requirements – that can be calculated for the not yet returned investment using compound interest calculation – from this nominal profit sum. If the profit requirements are smaller than the sum of all accounting profits, the mechanism of the calculation discounts and summarizes the surpluses for the years concerned. This content mechanism is difficult to recognize because of the calculation is made on the basis of yields.

In case of an interest rate of 1 percent, in the first year this method calculates 1 percent interest-like profit requirements for the initial investment. The yield in the first year first of all covers the profit requirements and the remainder part of the yield covers a part of the initial investment. In the following years, the 1 percent profit requirements will be calculated for the sum of the not yet returned capital. (This way compound interest will be realized.) When all of initial investment and profit requirement is returned then all of the further yields become surplus profit. The higher the interest rate used in the calculation, the smaller surplus will remain from the total accounting profit, and then, when this does not provide coverage for the requirements any more, a yield lack arises. Discounting the surplus profit (or the lack of yield) for the date zero gives the net present value.

In the case of investment projects with orthodox cash flow patterns the net present value shows the sum of the surplus yield above the required one (or lack of that), discounted for present value. (The definition is in Illés 1990 and its mathematical proof can be found in Illés 2012a.) Consequently, increasing the rate of interest continuously decreases the surplus sum of accounting profit, then, after equality, it gradually increases the yield lack compared to the requirements.

The capital recovery process is not illustrated in Figure 1. In order to identify the relationships, it is practical to clarify that the annual difference of revenues and expenditures, that is, the annual yields of examined investment project, first of all are expected to cover the profit requirements according to the required rate of return and the possible part of not yet returned capital. The yearly profit requirements are calculated by multiplying of the not-returned capital and the interest rate.

Considering that the return of capital and profit requirements must be covered by the annual yields, and furthermore that the return of the nominal value of the initial investment and the profit requirements are not differentiated, the essence of the method does not become clear. The essence is that the profit requirements calculated with compound interest should be returned from the sum of the total accounting profit. This latter part of the relationship is illustrated by the amount of net present value at zero percent interest rate. (The details will come later.)

Assuming otherwise constant conditions, the higher the interest rate is, the higher the amount that needs to be returned. The interest rate of which the required profit sum is just covered by the sum of all accounting profit is the factual profit rate of the time-varying tied- up capital. At this interest rate there is no surplus profit or lack of yield (and this interest rate is named as internal rate of return). A profit requirement that is higher than the factual profit rate cannot be fulfilled according to the project's database, thus the calculation will show lack of yield. In such cases, the value of the yield lack at the end of the period after discounting will be the net present value with negative sign.

Of course, net present value can be defined as a difference between the present value of future yields and the initial investment. From the aspect of management process, this seems to be only a theoretical approach; it does not give sufficient information about the content background.

Calculation of the Profit Requirements According to the Not Returned Part of Capital

The profit requirements calculated for the duration of the project are the following:

In the first year: $$M_{s1} = E_0 i \qquad (3)$$

In the second year:
$$M_{s2} = E_1 i\text{ ; where } E_1 = |H_1 - E_0 i - E_0| \qquad (4)$$

In the third year:
$$M_{s3} = E_2 i\text{ ; where } E_2 = |H_2 - E_1 i - E_1| \qquad (5)$$

For the $t > 1$ year, where the payback period (in years) is not smaller than the duration of the project:

$$M_{st} = E_{t-1} i\text{; where } E_{t-1} = |H_{t-1} - E_{t-2} i - E_{t-2}|\text{ ; } |\ 1 < t \leq z \qquad (6)$$

H_t = the yields (that is the difference of revenues and expenditures) in year t, where the value of H_t is always positive for years $0 < t \leq n$ by the terms of orthodox cash flow pattern projects, and the initial investment occurring at the zero point of time,

E_t = the not returned part of capital at the end of year *t,*

M_{st} = the profit requirement in year *t* according to the not returned part of capital and required rate of return,

z = the number of years of the dynamic payback period.

In order to show the content relationships, in Equation (6) the following mathematical merger of the components is not included: $H_{t-1} - E_{t-2}\, i - E_{t-2} = H_{t-1} - E_{t-2}(1+i)$

Between the first and the z-1-th years the yield has two content components. These are profit requirement and certain capital return (provided that the yield is greater than the profit requirement). If the yearly profit requirement is larger than the current year's yield, then the difference is added to the capital still to be returned. In the *z*-th year the yield has a third content component as well, provided that the return cannot be met at the end of the year. This third component is a surplus profit.

The total profit requirements that arise during the lifespan of the project (as an accounting approach) can be defined as follows:

$$\sum_{t=1}^{n} M_{st} = \sum_{t=1}^{n} E_{t-1}\, i \;\; \Big| \, n \leq z; \tag{7}$$

where

$$E_{t-1} = \left| H_{t-1} - E_{t-2}\, i - E_{t-2} \right| ; \qquad \Big| \, t > 1$$

If the payback period is not shorter than the project duration in years, then the present value of surplus profit is the net present value itself:

$$NPV = \left[M - \sum_{t=1}^{n} M_{st} \right] \frac{1}{(1+i)^n} \qquad \Big| \, n \leq z \tag{8}$$

If the payback period is shorter than the project duration in years, there will be some years without capital and profit requirements. In this case the yields of the additional years are surplus profits as well. (The number of these years is *n-z*.) According to the continuance of the conformity with net present value method, these surplus profits can be compounded to the end of the duration. The amount of nascent quasi interest will disappear when discounting. (See Table 2 and the following calculation.)

Example for Calculating Interest Rate Dependent Profit Requirements

The above statements are illustrated by a simple example. The basic data of a project – let us call it Project S – are the following: at date zero, 240 units of expenditure arise (as an initial investment), and then for 4 years a100-unit yield (revenues minus expenditures) is gained annually.

According to the database, during the total lifespan of Project S an accounting profit of the nominal value of 160 units is gained. (400-240=160) This amount can be divided between the return based on profit requirements and surplus profit, or in case of higher profit requirements, the difference means a lack of yields.

The relevant data are summarized in Table 1. The detailed and explaining calculations can be found in Tables 2 to 4. For the better identification of relationships, the results of these calculations are presented as rounded numbers.

Table 1

The total profit requirements and surplus profits according to different interest rates of Project S

Measurement unit: unit

Interest rate as a required rate of return	0 %	8 %	20 %	24 %	30 %
Nominal value of the total profit requirements	0	38	121	160	219
Surplus profit /lack of yield at the end of Year 4	160	124*	39	0	- 59
NPV (present value of the surplus profit /lack of yield at the end of Year 4)	160	91	19	0	-21

*This amount contains 2 units of technical (quasi) surplus profit. See details in Table 2.

In Table 1, the sum of profit requirements and the nominal value of surplus profit always add up to 160 units as the sum of all of accounting profits. (In case of yield lack, the difference of profit requirements and yield lack gives the accounting profit of 160 units.) The 24 percent is at the same time the internal rate of return as well. In this case there is no surplus profit or yield lack. The sum of the profit requirements is 160 units. (This is the whole accounting profit of the project.)

As is visible in Table 2, the annual amounts of profit requirements are accounted by multiplying the amounts of the not yet returned capital and the required rate of return. The annual yield of 100 units on the one hand covers the profit requirements of the current year, then, on the other hand its remaining part decreases the not yet returned capital until the total amount of capital is returned. In the payback year, the yield that remains over the profit requirements and not yet returned capital is the surplus profit. The yields in the following years mean clear surplus profit.

Table 2
Details of the economic calculation in the case of 8 percent required rate of return

Measurement unit: unit

Year	Capital to be returned at the beginning of the year	Amount of profit requirements (8 %)	The structure of 100 units annual yield		Capital still to be returned (-)/ surplus profit at the end of the year (+)
			Profit requirements	For capital return	
1.	240	19	19	81	- 240 + 81 = - 159
2.	159	13	13	87	- 159 + 87 = - 72
3.	72	6	6	94	- 72 + 94 = + 22
4.	surplus profit 22	2*	Surplus profit in the current year 100 + 2*		+22 + 102 = +124

*In order to ensure the consistency of the net present value method, the surplus profits gained before the end of the duration need to be compounded to the end of it. $(22 \times 0.08 = 2)$ This is only a technical solution and only concerns those cases where the payback period in years is shorter than the duration of the project. The calculated quasi-surplus profit disappears when compounded surplus profit will discounted to date zero.

Below is a control calculation of net present value where the required rate of return is 8 per cent: $-240 + \frac{100}{0.30192} = -240 + 331 = 91$, and $124 \times 0.73503 = 91$

Table 3
Details of the economic calculation in the case of 20 percent required rate of return

Measurement unit: unit

Year	Capital to be returned at the beginning of the year	Amount of profit requirements (20 %)	The structure of 100 units annual yield		Capital still to be returned (-)/ surplus profit at the end of the year (+)
			Profit requirements	For capital return	
1.	240	48	48	52	- 240 + 52 = -188
2.	188	38	38	62	- 188 + 62 = -126
3.	126	25	25	75	- 126 + 75 = - 51
4.	51	10	10	90	- 51 + 90 = + 39

Table 4
Details of the economic calculation in the case of 24 percent required rate of return

Measurement unit: unit

Year	Capital to be returned at the beginning of the year	Amount of profit requirements (24 %)	The structure of 100 units annual yield		Capital still to be returned (-)/ surplus profit at the end of the year (+)
			Profit requirements	For capital return	
1.	240	58	58	42	- 240 + 42 = -198
2.	198	48	48	52	- 198 + 52 = -146
3.	146	35	35	65	- 146 + 65 = - 81
4.	81	19	19	81	- 81 + 81 = 0

THE AGGREGATE CAPITAL NEEDS

The method of net present value only considers the amount and period of capital investment up to the level of required rate of return in a correct way. Any surplus profit over this level is simply being discounted and summed up. The amount remaining as a surplus profit is not affected by the capital-focused corporate efforts that are what was the average tied-up capital and how long it was needed to gain a certain surplus profit. In practice, from an economic viewpoint, this means the main deficiency of the information content of this category and this is the main reason that net present values cannot be compared on the merits.

A net present value with positive sign has the following message for the decision-maker: the profit requirements according to the required rate of return will be fulfilled and in present value a surplus profit of a certain amount will also be gained. If the question is whether the profit requirements are fulfilled, this answer is satisfactory. But it is not easy to tell what advantage this amount exactly means. A quite ordinary example: for an individual who is fixing 300,000 euro in a bank for one year, it is more meaningful to do so at an interest rate of 4.5% than to be told that he will get 3% interest on his deposit plus 4,500 euro more. This special sort of deposit is more difficult to see through with a long-term commitment (Illés 2012b).

The literature that deals with net present value is not concerned about the aggregate capital needs. However, it is absolutely evident that if a higher capital sum is needed for a longer time, then the aggregate capital needs will be higher. Knowledge of the aggregate capital needs can help in the comparison of net present values. In the clarification process it can be considered as a step forward when the aggregate capital needs may help us to see that the net present values (with their original content), and the net present values divided by initial investment or multiplied by the loan repayment factor cannot be compared. These recommendations can be found in various literary sources. (On the latter in more detail see Illés 2012a.)

The project's aggregate capital needs means the amount of capital needed for the operation of the project during its full duration. For investments with an orthodox cash flow pattern, the capital needs are basically determined by three factors: the amount of initial investment, the duration of the project and the rapidity of capital payback. The latter depend on the required rate of return as well. As illustrated in the example of Project S, the higher the required rate of return is, the larger the part of the annual yield that is used to cover the profit requirements and the less remains to cover the not yet returned capital. By increasing the interest rate, the return of nominal value of the capital will be delayed, and the aggregate capital needs of the project increase.

The exact calculation of aggregate capital needs for investment projects is not a simple task. This issue has not arisen; no correct method of calculation has been discovered yet. As mentioned above, there are three reasons for the differences in aggregate capital needs of the project variants: different initial investment, different duration of the project and the different rapidity of capital payback. According to this, main manifestations of the higher aggregate capital needs – higher initial investment, longer time of return, lower rapidity of return – and different combinations of these. In the case of one-way differences, it might be obvious which variant has the higher aggregate capital needs. However, in reality, these three factors can appear in different combinations and at the same time can have effects in different directions. For example, one variant has a higher initial investment that will return in a shorter time but at with slower capital payback, etc.

The series of annual tied-up capital are built up in the Equations (3)-(6). According to these, the not yet returned capital concerning the payback period of the project can be calculated as the following:

In the first year of operation, the full amount of initial investment tied up in the projects is: E_0

In the second year, the amount of the tied-up capital is decreased by the capital returned as the result of the first year's operation: $E_1 = |H_1 - E_0\, i - E_0|$

In the third year, the tied-up capital is decreased by the capital returned during the second year's operation: $E_2 = |H_2 - E_1\, i - E_1|$

During $1 < t \leq z$ years the amount of tied-up capital is:

$$E_{t-1} = \left|H_{t-1} - E_{t-2}\, i - E_{t-2}\right| \; ; \quad \left|\, 1 < t \leq z \right. \tag{9}$$

The index number of the aggregate capital needs should be worked out on the basis of yearly tied-up capital and the duration of the project. Tied-up capital is a state indicator, and therefore the tied-up capital of different years cannot be summed up from this aspect. However, in consideration the income-producing potential needs to take into account simultaneously the tied-up capital and tied-up time. The solution is to sum up the yearly tied-up capital, that is, the not-returned parts of the capital for each year. To do this correctly as a measurement unit may be one unit tied-up capital for one year. According to the calculation method used above a three-year tie up of one capital unit is equal to three capital units tied up for one year. This solution is considered to be correct because the tied-up capital is computed with a database where the profit requirements are subtracted from the yields. (In the general case a three-year tie up of one unit of capital would be more burdensome than a one-year tie up of three units. This is because of using the compound interest method.)

Based on all these, the index number of aggregate capital needs (E_{ACN}) is as follows:

$$F_{ACN} = \sum_{t=1}^{n} E_{t-1} \tag{10}$$

This index number reflects the effect of initial investment, the duration and the rapidity of capital payback in the aggregate capital needs rather well, but concerning the content it means a capital amount which is tied up for one year.

In case of equal lifetimes the index number of annual average capital needs ($E_{average}$) can also provide useful information.

$$E_{average} = \frac{\sum_{t=1}^{n} E_{t-1}}{n} \tag{11}$$

The average tied-up capital shows how much tied-up capital is used in average during the lifetime of the project. This average index number is comparable only if the projects' duration is the same. (The rapidity of capital payback is taken into account as well.)

The category of the aggregate capital needs has a significant opinion-forming role in the sphere of using the net present value method. For the evaluation of the relative amount of surplus profit this index number is also necessary. When using the internal rate of return, the aggregate capital needs are important information as well; because of this the index number shows the real comparable capital amount which results in this profitability.

As was mentioned above, the required rate of return can also have a great effect on the aggregate capital needs. The higher the required rates of return, the smaller the part of the annual yields for capital return. Consequently, when the required rate of return is higher the return of the capital takes longer and the index number of the aggregate capital needs will be higher. This is illustrated through the calculations related to

Project S (see Tables 2-4). In regard to the fact that when calculating the annual tied-up capital, the profit requirements were already considered, the examination concerns the nominal value of capital to be returned. The results of the calculations related to the capital needs are summarized in Table 5.

Table 5
The effect of interest rate on the capital needs for Project S

Measurement unit: unit

Year	Yearly capital needs depending on the interest rate				
	0 %	8 %	20 %	24 %	30 %
1	240	240	240	240	240
2	140	159	188	198	212
3	40	72	126	146	176
4	-	-	51	81	99
Aggregate capital needs					
Aggregated	420	471	605	665	727
Annual average capital needs calculated for the duration of the project					
Average	105	118	151	166	182

The analysis of Table 5 refers to Project S, where the duration is 4 years. This is the relevant information for calculating the annual average capital needs. In the case when the average calculation refers to the real tie-up period of the capital instead of the whole duration of the project, the index number does not show comparable information. (As Table 5 shows applied interest rates of 0 and 8 percent, the tied-up capital only lasts 3 years, while at 10 and 24 percent this would be 4 years. In case of an interest rate of 30 percent the profit requirements are not covered.)

THE RATE AND THE INTERSECTION

As was mentioned above, the finance literature usually calls the interest rate Fisher's rate when the net present values of the two investment projects are equal. The intersection of the net present value curves of the two projects is called the Fisher's intersection. The intersection and the rate are illustrated by Figure 2. The names of the projects are: Project A and Project B. The rate that belongs to the intersection on the x axis is the Fisher's rate, while the intersection reflected on the z axis gives the same net present value of the two projects.

In Figure 2, the net present value of Project A considering zero percent interest rate (i.e. the accounting profit of the whole duration of the project) is significantly higher than that of Project B. The aggregate capital needs of Project A must be significantly higher so that the gradually increasing profit requirements according to the rate of interest will use up higher amounts of the accounting profit than in the case of Project B. Under certain capital and profit conditions, the intersection comes into being as a result of the differently decreasing surplus profits. At the interest rate that belongs to the intersection, the net present values of the two projects are equal.

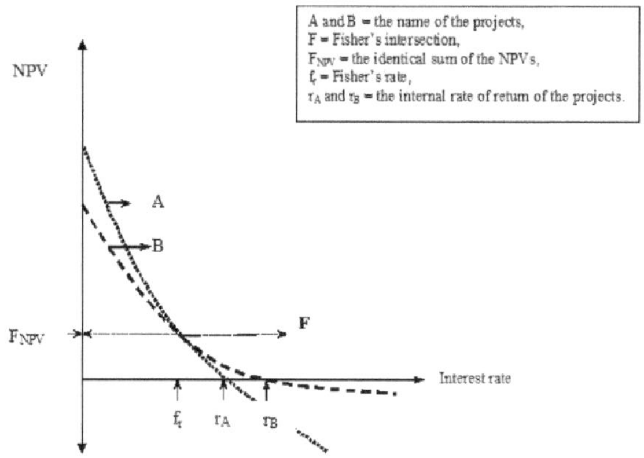

Source: Edition by the author, based on commonly used figures in the related literature (For instance, Keane 1975:22; Adelberg et al. 1986:708; Brealey & Myers 1988:83; Arnold & Hope 1990:257; Firer & Gilbert 2004:42; Van Horne & Wachowicz 2008:332; Crundwell 2008:189; and Baker & Powell 2009:259)

Figure 2 The intersection of NPV curves and the related Fisher's rate

At interest rates over the intersection, the project variant with lower capital needs will have the higher net present value. Where the surplus profit disappears, there is the internal rate of return. The surplus profit of the variant with lower capital needs lasts up to higher interest rates, which shows higher profitability of capital. The profit requirements of the variant with higher aggregate capital needs 'uses up' the total surplus profit faster, thus the internal rate of return will be lower. (The capital invested in this variant will have a lower average profitability.) This is the main reason that above the intersection the rankings based on the net present value and the internal rate of return are the same.

But it cannot be a question whether in terms of equal net present values the two projects can be considered economically equal. The aggregate capital needs are significantly higher for Project A. By investing the difference into another project, further net present values could be gained. We cannot leave out of consideration whether the same surplus profit can be gained with lower aggregate capital needs. This relationship can only be disregarded in case of unlimited capital resources and under other special conditions (Illés 2012b).

THE CAUSALITY BASED PRE-CONDITIONS FOR EMERGENCE OF INTERSECTION

Keane (1975) highlights that the existence of Fisher's rate is not necessary, furthermore when illustrating two net present value curves, even more intersections can emerge. The latter means that the net present values of two projects can be equal at several interest rates.

Keane (1975:23) cites the findings of Mao (1969) about the conditions that are necessary for existence of the Fisher's rate:

"There will be no Fisher intersection in the interval (0, rm) where rm = the smaller of the two rates of return, if

(1) a) A's NPV > B's NPV at zero discount rate, and
    b) A's NPV decreases at a greater rate than B's, in response to a given increase in k
    c) A's IRR > B's IRR.

(2) a) A's NPV > B's NPV at zero discount rate, and
    b) A's NPV decreases at a lesser rate than B's in response to a given increase in k.

There will be a unique intersection between the two NPV functions where:

a) A's NPV > B's NPV at zero discount rate, and
b) A's IRR < B's IRR
c) A's NPV decreases at a greater rate than B's in response to a given increase in k."

In their study Hirst & Ma (1983) look for the explanation of the emergence of Fisher's intersection. They built upon the fact that Fisher (implicitly) used equal initial investments in his calculations; therefore this can be excluded as a possible reason. Further root causes can be the duration of a project and the rapidity of capital payback. In order to consider the common effect of the two factors, the authors introduced the category of weighted duration, which can be used as an explanation for the intersection. They say that the net present value of the variant with higher weighted duration is more sensitive to changes in interest rate. (According to the terminology of the current study the reasons for the longer weighted duration are the longer duration and/or the slower rapidity of capital payback.) For the calculation of weighted duration Hirst & Ma (based on the works of other authors) use the present values of annual yields as weights. (In the numerator of the fraction there is a sum that is calculated by multiplying the ordinal numbers of operating years with the annual discounted yields. The denominator contains the sum of all discounted yields. The authors also analyze the effect of applied interest rate on the weighted duration.) Hirst & Ma (1983) show some interesting examples in the field of intersections in context of weighted duration. It must be emphasized that this weighted duration can only be accepted as a root cause if the initial investment is the same in both projects.

According to the related thesis of Descartes (1596–1650), the maximum number of internal rate of return of an investment project is determined by the number of sign changes in the yield series. The project may have as many internal rates of return as the number of yield series sign changes. A lower number of internal rates of return than this are possible, but no more. In our days this basic relationship can be considered as generally known. Having more than one internal rate of return is the characteristic of unorthodox cash flow pattern projects only. The number of internal rates of return means how many times the net present value function intersects the x axis.

The Fisher's rate – from this aspect – is the interest rate that makes the series of yield differences of the two projects zero. The internal rate of return of the series of annual yield differences will be equal to the same interest rate where the net present value of the two projects becomes equal. So at the Fisher's intersection the present value of the yield differences of the two projects becomes zero. Consequently the Fisher's rate is the internal rate of return of yield differences as well.

If the criterion of an orthodox cash flow pattern is fulfilled for both variants and the sign change of the yield differences occurs only once, there can be no more than one point of intersection. However, several occurrences of intersections of two projects with orthodox cash flow patterns are possible as well when the sign of yield-differences changes on several occasions. This is illustrated in Figure 3.

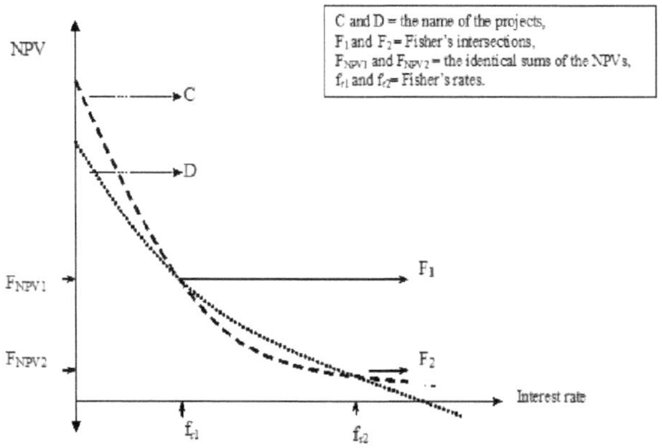

Source: This sort of illustration can be found in the study of Hirst & Ma (1983:169) according to another conception. Illustration in this context is the author's work.

Figure 3 The possible occurrence of Fisher's rates and intersections of two projects with orthodox cash flow patterns where the yield differences changed sign twice

The several sign changes in the yield difference series do not necessarily mean several intersections. If intersections of the net present value curves of arbitrary type investment projects (e.g. with unorthodox cash flow patterns) are examined, then general quantifying of these intersections may become very complicated.

The classical Fisher's rate defines only one intersection. The majority of recent (English) financial books do not deal with the possibility of more than one intersection, either. A causality-based comprehensive background of this is not analyzed in the literature.

The simultaneous fulfillment of the following six conditions is necessary to have one and only one intersection:

1. The criterion of orthodox cash flow pattern must be fulfilled in case of both variants.
2. The sign change of the difference of the two series of yields occurs only once.
3. Both projects must have an accounting profit.
4. The sum of all accounting profits and the aggregate capital needs must be different for the two projects.

5. The variant with the higher sum of all accounting profits must have higher aggregate capital needs.
6. The variant with lower capital needs must have a higher internal rate of return.

The illustration of net present values of the two project variants starts with a discounting by zero percent interest rate (Figure 2). If the accounting profit sums differ, the starting points on the y axis will also be different, thus one requirement of the intersection is already fulfilled.

The variant with higher sum of all accounting profits must have higher aggregate capital needs, so that by increasing the interest rate, the net present value of this variant would decrease faster. The different rapidity of decrease is also a requirement of the intersection.

In addition, to have equality besides a positive net present value, it is also necessary that the variant with lower capital needs must have a higher internal rate of return. (The first and second conditions are necessary so that only one internal rate of return of yield differences may come into being.)

The Importance of the Internal Rate of Return of Yield Differences

In his quoted work, Fisher deals a great deal with the question of internal rate of return of the series of annual yield differences of the two projects. He attaches very great importance to it.

As mentioned in detail above, the internal rate of return of the yield differences means exactly the same interest rate where the net present values of the two projects are equal. This is obvious, as this interest rate has made the differences of yield series disappear.

According to my current knowledge, this is only a technical feature, it has no substantive significance. The literature on modern corporate finances uses the internal rate of return of the yield differences as a rather simple way of calculating the Fisher's rate. This method of Fisher's rate calculation is much simpler than calculating the net present values of the two projects starting from zero percent interest rate to higher percentages until the two net present values become equal (or this interest rate will determined in approaching from two sides).

Illustration and Explanation of the Intersection through an Example

The purpose of the example below is to illustrate and explain the Fisher's rate and the Fisher's intersection through numerical relationships. The most important data of the two mutually exclusive project variants are summarized in Table 6.

Table 6

Revenues, expenditures and yields of the two project variants (assuming equal initial investment, equal duration, but different aggregate capital needs)

Measurement unit: unit

Date	Project A_1			Project B_1			The difference of the two series of yields $A_1 - B_1$
	Expenditures	Revenues	Yields	Expenditures	Revenues	Yields	
0	350	0	-350	350	0	-350	0
1	552	557	5	771	1171	400	– 395.000
2	691	696	5	1017	1022	5	0
3	352	852	500	861.488	866	4.512	495.488

According to the database the main economic characteristics of the projects are the following. The initial investment and the duration of the two projects are equal but the rapidity of capital payback is significantly different. In case of Project B_1, the nominal value of the 350-unit initial investment is exceeded by the yield of 400 units already at the end of the first year. In the following two years – despite the fact that the sales revenues only decreased by 8-12 percent – only 4.5-5 units of yield are gained. In the same time, in the case of Project A_1, the yields of the first two years only support the return of capital needs and profit requirements with a rather small amount of yield, 5 units; 98% (500 units) of the yield is only gained at the end of the third year. At an interest rate of zero percent the total accounting profit of variant A_1 is 160 units, while of variant B_1 it is only 59.5 units.

Considering the fact that the two series of yields are orthodox cash flow patterns, the internal rate of return shows the average profitability of the projects. The aggregate tied-up capital shows how much capital operates with this profitability rate.

The internal rate of return for Project A_1: ~13.5 %, aggregate tied-up capital: 1182 units.

The internal rate of return for Project B_1: ~16.5 %, aggregate tied-up capital: 362 units.

Variant B_1 with its significantly lower capital sum results in the internal rate of return of 16.5 percent.

Variant A_1 with higher aggregate tied-up capital provides a capital profitability of 13.5 percent. For making a good choice between the two projects, it is practical to examine the profitability possibilities of re-investing the yield difference of 395 units for two years, and then compare this with the critical profitability rate of the re-investment. (Details are shown in Illés 2012a.) Table 7 contains the data necessary for the illustration of Fisher's rate and Fisher's intersection.

Table 7
The net present values of two project variants with different interest rates

Measurement unit: unit

Project	0 %	4 %	6 %	8%	10 %	12 %	15 %	20 %
A_1	160.0	103.9	79.0	55.8	34.3	14.3	-13.1	-53.0
B_1	59.5	43.3	35.6	28.2	21.2	14.3	4.6	-11.6

The net present values of the project variants can differ due to the different interest rates as well. When increasing the interest rate, due to the higher aggregate capital needs, the net present values of Project A_1 are decreasing more rapidly than those of Project B_1. The equality of net present values occurs at the interest rate of 12 %. The significant points calculated from the data of the above example are illustrated in Figure 4.

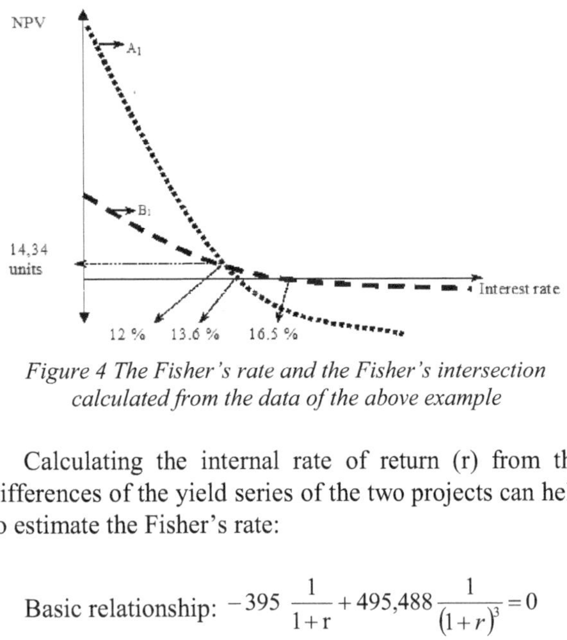

Figure 4 The Fisher's rate and the Fisher's intersection calculated from the data of the above example

Calculating the internal rate of return (r) from the differences of the yield series of the two projects can help to estimate the Fisher's rate:

Basic relationship: $-395\frac{1}{1+r}+495{,}488\frac{1}{(1+r)^3}=0$

After rearrangement: $\frac{495{,}488}{395}=(1+r)^2$

After executing the calculation: (1+r)2 = 1.2544; where r = 0.12

The internal rate of return calculated from the data series of yield differences is 12 %, which is equal to the Fisher's rate. As we can see, this rate of 12 % is irrelevant in the economic evaluation of projects.

SUMMARY

According to the approaches and recommendations of finance, the net present value has a primary importance in supporting investment decisions. Therefore the existence of Fisher's rate and the rate itself are significant business information in finance. The literature calls attention to the fact that conformation of the intersection is not necessary. This study works out the causal relationships that are necessary for existence of the intersection, in order to gain a better understanding of internal relationships of the net present value method.

The net present values of different projects cannot be compared in general; therefore the net present value is not suitable as a ranking indicator. Factors that cannot be disregarded are how much initial investment, for how long and how much tied-up capital is needed to gain a certain net present value. After eliminating the three main distorting factors, the net present value will be a sort of rate that gives the difference between the internal and the required rate of return (corrected by a calculation error factor). Thus this corrected net present value rate is approximately equal to the surplus profitability that exceeds the required rate of return (Illés 2012a).

If the risks of the projects are equal or risk management of the projects has been done in advance (e.g. decreasing the series of revenues or increasing the series of expenditures and so on), the ranking based on the net present value rate that is free of distorting effects and the ranking based on the internal rate of return will be the same. The surplus profitability over the required rate of return will be the highest for the project where the internal rate of return is the highest. Thus the same projects will gain the first, second, etc. place in both rankings. No change of ranking is possible with Fisher's rate.

In theory, the company can reach the best growth if the projects with the highest internal rate of return are carried out. (Provided, that is, that the required rate of return is equal.) Based on the rates of critical profitability and the real profit opportunities of the difference of initial investment and other capital need differences, the expedience of choice can prefer solutions that differ slightly from the ranking based on the internal rate of return. (This topic is showing in detail by work of Illés 2012a.) But even in these cases the decision criterion is still not the net present value. The relationship that in case of limited capital-investment opportunities at a certain risk level, the highest profitability can lead to the highest profit is still valid.

From this aspect, ranking based on the simple net present value is not relevant as well. The interest rate that would provide the same net present value for two projects is also irrelevant. In most cases when the net present values are equal, the aggregate capital needs are different.

The paper also defines the special content of aggregate capital needs, and elaborates an index number for this content. The project's aggregate capital needs means the amount of capital needed for the operation of the project during its full duration. It considers the income-producing potential necessary to take into account simultaneously the tied-up capital and tied-up time. The measurement unit is one unit tied-up capital for one year. The solution is to sum up the yearly tied-up capital that is the not-returned parts of the capital for each year. This solution considered to be correct because of the tied-up capital is computed with a database where the profit requirements are subtracted from the yields. The category of the aggregate capital needs has a significant opinion-forming role.

A highly important relationship is the following: profit requirements calculated with compound interest should be returned from the sum of the total accounting profit. The larger the aggregate capital needs of the project, the greater the profit requirement that arises.

Based on these conclusions, considering a real economic system of conditions and the purpose of long-term profit maximization (maximization of shareholder value), Fisher's rate and the Fisher's intersection can only have theoretical significance. Their analyses can give a better understanding of the content background of the net present value, but are irrelevant for making investment decisions.

REFERENCES

ADELBERG, A.H., FABOZZI, F.J. & POLIMENI, R.S. (1986). Cost Accounting: Concepts and applications for managerial decision making. McGraw-Hill Book Company, New York, St. Louis, San Francisco etc.

ALCHIAN, A.A. (1955). The Rate of Interest, Fisher's Rate of Return over Costs and Keynes' Internal Rate of Return. American Economic Review, 45(5), 938-943.

ARNOLD, J. & HOPE, T. (1990): Accounting for Management Decisions. Prentice Hall International (UK) Ltd.

BAKER, H. K. & Powell, G. (2009): Understanding Financial Management: A Practical Guide. John Wiley & Sons, USA, UK, Australia.

BREALEY, R. A. & MYERS, S. C. (1988): Principles of Corporate Finance. McGraw-Hill Publishing Company, New York, St. Louis, San Francisco etc.

CARLSON, C.R., LAWRENCE, M.L., WORT, D.H. (1974): Clarification of the Reinvestment Assumption in, Capital Analysis. Journal of Business Research. Volume 2, Number 2. (April) pp. 201-208.

CRUNDWELL, F. K. (2008): Finance for Engineers. Evaluation and Funding of Capital Projects. Springer, London.

DUDLEY, C. L., Jr. (1972): A Note on Reinvestment Assumptions in Choosing between Net Present Value and Internal Rate of Return. The Journal of Finance. Vol. 27, No. 4, pp. 907-915.

FIRER, C. & GILBERT, E. (2004): Investment Basics XLVIII. Common challenges in capital budgeting. Investment Analysts Journal, No. 59. pp. 41-45.

FISHER, I. (1930): The Theory of Interest. Macmillan, New York

HIRST, M. & MA, R. (1983): Duration and Fisher's Rate of Return over Cost. Abacus, Vol. 19, No. 2, pp 162-170.

ILLÉS, M. (1990): A gazdaságossági és jövedelmezőségi számítások alapjai. (Fundamentals of profit requirements and profitability calculations.) Szakszervezetek Gazdaság- és Társadalomkutató Intézete, Budapest.

ILLÉS, M. (2012a): Transforming the Net Present Value for a Comparable One. 'Club of Economics in Miskolc' TMP Vol. 8 Nr.1, pp. 24-32.

ILLÉS, M. (2012b): Links Between Net Present Value and Shareholder Value from a Business Economics Perspective. 'Club of Economics in Miskolc' TMP Vol. 8. Nr.2. pp 31-36.

KEANE, S. M. (1975): Investment selection criteria: an examination of the theory of the internal rate of return and of the investment discount rate under conditions of uncertainty. PhD thesis. University of Glasgow.

KEYNES, J. M. (1936): The General Theory of Employment, Interest and Money. Macmillan, London.

MEYER, R.L. (1979): A Note on Capital Budgeting Techniques and the Reinvestment Rate. The Journal of Finance. Vol. 34, No. 5, pp. 1251-1254.

MAO, J. C. T. (1969): Quantitative Analysis of Financial Decisions. Macmillan, New York.

RENSHAW, E. (1957): A Note on the Arithmetic of Capital Budgeting Decisions. Journal of Business. Vol. 30, No. 3, pp. 193–201.

VAN HORNE, J. C. & WACHOWICZ, J. M., Jr. (2008): Fundamentals of Financial Management. Pearson Education Limited.

12

Complex Evaluation Model of Corporate Energy Management

ÁGNES KÁDÁR HORVÁTH, Ph.D.
ASSOCIATE PROFESSOR
e-mail: vgthagi@uni-miskolc.hu

SUMMARY

With the ever increasing energy problems at the doorstep alongside with political, economic, social and environmental challenges, conscious energy management has become of increasing importance in corporate resource management. Rising energy costs, stricter environmental and climate regulations as well as considerable changes in the energy market require companies to rationalise their energy consumption and cut energy costs. This study presents a complex evaluation model of corporate energy management, which can be used for identifying corporate challenges resulting from global energy crises and for seeking possible answers to them as well as enabling companies to evaluate their current energy management practices and identify the level of their energy consciousness. This model enables companies to rethink their energy management tasks and identify the most acute problems of their energy management practices.

Keywords: energy management, corporate resource management, evaluation model

INTRODUCTION

From an operation perspective, it is of major importance for a company to ensure the resources required for its smooth operation at the lowest possible cost impact. An effective organisation of corporate resource management is a fundamental factor in terms of competitiveness. As for resources, apart from raw materials, assets, human resources and other resources, the energy used also plays an increasing role. The importance of conscious energy management is growing, since market processes pose challenges to companies. The rising energy prices and strict environmental and climate-protection requirements require companies to rationalise their energy consumption and decrease energy costs. The fact that companies assign different priorities to these issues should not be neglected. The efforts companies make for energy rationalisation depend on company size, the sector it is categorised in, energy intensity of the activities, and the proportion of energy costs compared with operating costs. Based on the information reviewed, it would be wise for companies to review their priority list in terms of energy rationalisation measures, evaluate their current energy management practices and level of their energy consciousness, set further tasks regarding their energy management and identify problem areas in their current practices. The complex evaluation model elaborated in this paper can provide assistance to companies in this endeavour.

THEORETICAL FRAMEWORK OF THE TOPIC

Before the complex evaluation model of corporate energy management was constructed, the available technical literature was thoroughly reviewed. The available literature on the topic of energy management has increased over the past few years. A number of sources deal with setting tasks in energy management, motivation factors and barriers of its application, and energy-management tools from different aspects and in various depths. (See among others: National Productivity Council, 2002; Zsebik & Czinege, 2003; Zsebik et al., 2003; Goebel, 2007; Diófási & Diófási, 2009; Carbon Trust, 2010, 2011a,b; Hirzel et al., 2011; Bihari, 2012; Thorpe, 2013). There have been several empirical studies on evaluating energy efficiency of particular sectors of economy (Önut & Soner, 2007; Pardo Martínez, 2009; Gordićat al., 2010; Sivill, 2011; Madlool et al., 2013). Apart from the above-listed studies, a number of other sources provided background for developing the approach used in this paper. As for the applied methodology, self-assessment models widely used in current practices (energy management matrix (EMM)[1], Energy Management Assessment (EMA)[2], Ecomapping[3], Ecostar methodology) and self-assessment questionnaires (Virtual Power Plant Programme, Gvozdenak & Morvay, 2008) were thoroughly reviewed.

This paper presents two self-assessment models which are most frequently applied: the Energy Management Matrix and the Energy Management Assessment. The Energy Management Matrix (Brescu, 1993) is a simple and easy-to-use self-assessment method of energy management. It analyses energy management performance in six areas. The ascending rows, on the scale from 0 to 4, represent the increasingly sophisticated, mature and formalised nature of energy management activities, which indicate increasingly good practices. The organisational profile received after the levels have been marked indicates the areas where additional efforts are required to further promote energy management efficiency. The advantage of this method lies in its simplicity.

The matrix enables companies to assess the operation of energy management functional areas without involving external experts. If this assessment is repeated after a certain period of time, progress can be measured. The priority areas are apparent; however, I think their number and contents could be expanded. The disadvantage of this model is that it is subjective, like any other method based on self assessment. However, the subjectivity is slightly decreased since relatively concrete requirements are assigned to each level and clear and accurate statements provide bases for choosing the right level. Yet I think that – apart from the lowest and the highest levels – the statements are a bit constrained at other levels and do not always show realistic 'stair steps'. The application of only this single matrix highly simplifies, even over simplifies the assessment. Thus, it is advisable to collect background information related to particular areas and perform in-depth studies, which makes the choice of levels better grounded. (To this end, there are propositions formulated in 'Energy Efficiency Guide for Industry in Asia' (www.energyefficiencyasia.org). Unfortunately, the guide fails to list the cases and areas where a weaker performance can be considered acceptable.)

The Energy Management Assessment (EMA) provides a more detailed appraisal of energy management performance than the Energy Management Matrix. The Carbon Trust Guide (2011a, b) serves as a basis for introducing the method. The method distinguishes twelve key areas across five area groups and analyses each key area according to several criteria (with variable numbers). Particular criteria are weighed in different ways. Each key area is assigned a maximal reachable score and an actual reached score. After all the key areas are assessed, a summary table is compiled illustrating actual scores, maximal scores, and performance in percentage. The achieved results are illustrated in a cobweb diagram. The areas which require further improvement can be identified from the diagram (Carbon Trust 2011a, b). The advantage of the EMA is that it analyses several key areas according to several criteria. Since the criteria have different weight, the relevance of particular criteria can be distinguished. The disadvantage of the EMA is that the determination of the evaluation criteria and variables of particular areas results in superficial evaluation. Thus, the content lying behind the evaluation of particular areas requires further consideration. The EMA is not suitable for comparing companies.

After the secondary research was conducted, a comprehensive summary of the motivations, toolbars and main barriers of corporate energy management were prepared (Kádárné Horváth in Szakály (szerk.) 2012), which provided a basis for identifying the main directions of further research and compiling questions for a corporate questionnaire and the elements of an empirical model. The reviewed research studies were considered to be guidelines when the model was created. However, none of them was really suitable for performing the role of a complex evaluation method. When the complex evaluating model was elaborated, the methodological framework of the EMA self-assessment method was particularly inspiring. Its framework was mostly followed but its content was considerably changed when the complex model of corporate energy management evaluation was created.

Complex Model of Corporate Energy Management Evaluation

The starting point of the complex evaluation model was the most important task in corporate energy management, namely, to identify the corporate activities to be assessed. It was followed by grouping the identified tasks and establishing the pillars of the model. When the task groups making up the pillars of the model were determined, a principle of gradation was applied. On particular pillars, the energy management activities reflect tasks which require higher level and more corporate efforts and a more sophisticated and energy-conscious approach. The pillars (task groups) constitute main tasks of energy management (the sub-pillars) and main criteria for task evaluation. These criteria are assessed with a variable of different numbers.

The complexity of the model is experienced in several areas. First, the areas being evaluated cover almost all of the most important tasks, toolbars and motivating and hindering factors of energy management. Second, the model can be applied in several areas. Our aim was to construct a complex model with a double function which provides an informative evaluation of corporate energy management, mapping the areas for improvement and allows comparing companies. This double function can be fulfilled by the two evaluation tools applied in parallel in the model. The evaluation is performed on the basis of a detailed questionnaire in which there are questions related both to topics corresponding with the model elements and to background information in order to have a better insight into the issue. This method enables companies to identify the areas for improvement in their energy management, since companies have to think over what responses to give to the questions and utilise the opportunities provided by the individual evaluation of the responses. The scoring system developed on the basis of the model pillars makes individual assessment possible. This is the second tool for evaluation besides the questionnaire. Figure 1 shows the complex evaluation model.

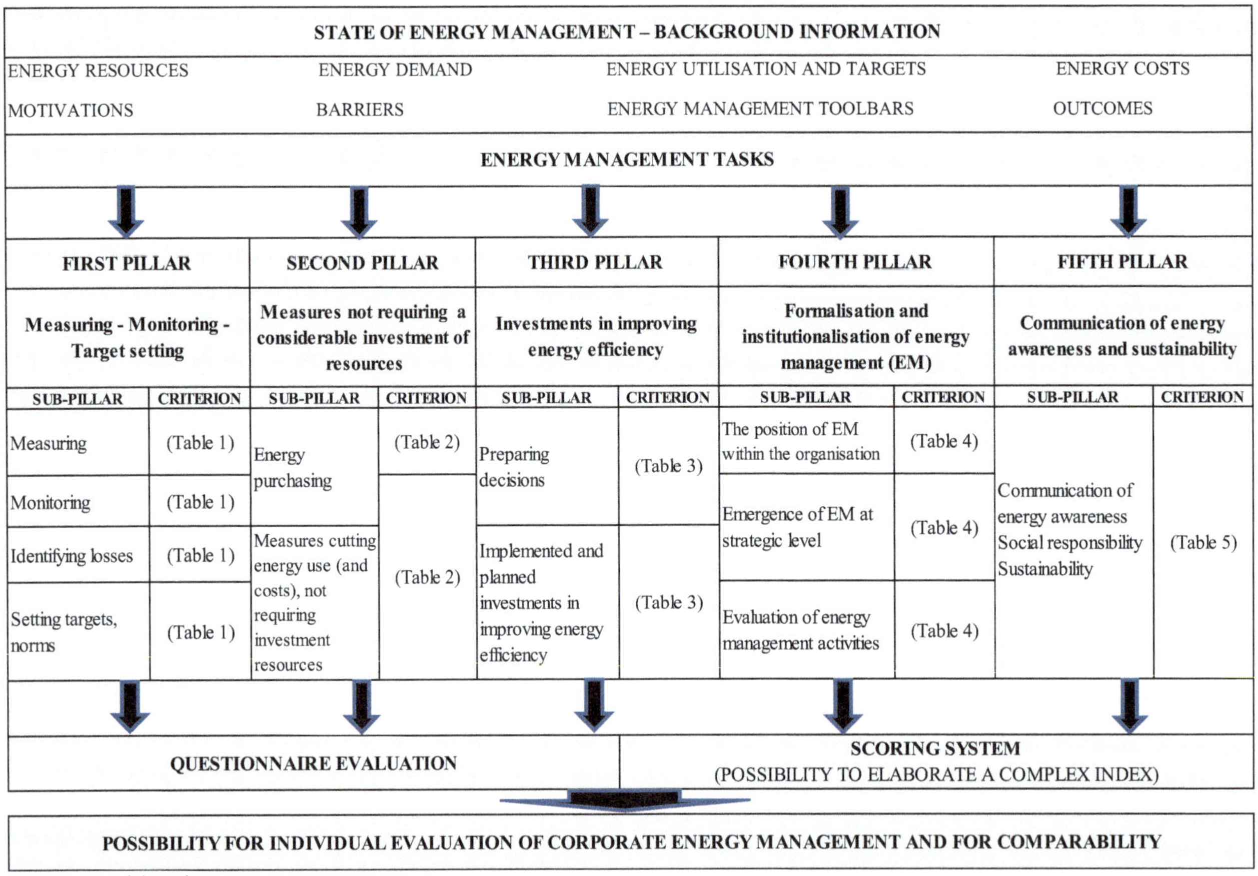

Source: own elaboration

Figure 1 Complex evaluation model of corporate energy management

In the next part of the study the pillars of the model are introduced.

The First Pillar: Measuring – Monitoring – Target Setting

The first pillar includes four tasks, which are measuring, monitoring, identifying energy losses, and setting norms and objectives (Table 1). They make up the first level of energy management tasks, where there is neither energy nor cost savings. However, these tasks are crucial from an efficient energy management perspective. Sustainable energy savings cannot be achieved without knowing where and with what purpose the energy is used, the amount of energy used, factors influencing it, where and at what points intervention is required, and what measures should be taken to achieve energy rationalisation. Major energy consumers, energy loss sources and the amount of lost energy are to be identified as well.

Without measuring, monitoring and controlling energy consumption, energy rationalisation measures cannot be accomplished. Identification of sources of energy losses and target setting are also important tasks. The assessment of the certain tasks should be carried out according to the following criteria:

- Measuring energy consumption. A company can estimate the amount of the energy used in several ways. One is to collect data from utility bills and suppliers' invoices. Another way is to read the utility meters. The latter provides more accurate information. As for the measurements, the first evaluation criterion is to identify the presence of measurement conditions, namely, to map whether the company has enough utility meters and sub-meters and in what state of maintenance they are; and whether the company has energy supervision and information systems that are suitable for analysing and evaluating the collected data. The other evaluation criterion is to identify the levels where the accurate measurements of energy consumption are performed and to examine the frequency of these measurements.

- Monitoring. Monitoring and analysing the energy consumption and energy costs are of vital importance from an energy management perspective. As for evaluation criteria of activities, it is also critical to know at what levels the measurements are carried out and with what frequency they are performed. Apart from monitoring at the corporate level, performing monitoring at the site, category, plant, building, process, equipment and shift levels also provides useful information for analyses. Accurate measurement data and the data available on the utility bills, as well as different calculation methods, provide bases for information. Another important move is to analyse and monitor energy costs. Accurate and detailed analyses also allow reliable evaluation of activities. It is not sufficient to examine only the trends in energy usage and energy costs – the reasons lying behind these trends are also worth considering when energy consumption and energy costs are evaluated. This is because several factors have a considerable impact on energy consumption and energy costs. Thus, the identification of these factors and the analysis of each impact are essential. The savings resulting from energy rationalisation measures, should be distinguished from the savings that result from changes in the weather, in the production structure, in the organisational structure (organisational changes, changes in work schedules, outsourcing or insourcing activities), in the production volume, in costs, in purchasing strategies and in energy prices.
- Identifying energy losses. Energy losses can be experienced at several levels. Apart from shipping, distribution and transformation losses, there may be technological and overhead-nature losses (in technological process or in lighting, heating). It is of utmost importance whether companies identify the main sources of energy losses or quantify the losses in some way. The quantification of monetary losses makes companies sensitive to these losses and helps them overcome their vulnerability.
- Setting goals and norms. Taking into account the outcome of analyses, a company sets goals related to energy savings. The assessment of the suitability and elaboration precision of these goals may be another evaluation criterion. The goals should be clear, realistic, relevant to the specific features of the area under analysis, and measurable. An additional criterion of evaluation is the presence of concrete action plans including resource, cost and timescale analyses, a list of names of responsible persons with set deadlines, and evidence for goal implementation, feedbacks and regular reviews.

Table 1
Structure and evaluation criteria of the first pillar

THE FIRST PILLAR	
Measuring – Monitoring – Target setting	
SUB-PILLAR	EVALUATION CRITERIA
Measuring	Presence of measurement conditions
	Measurement levels, frequencies
Monitoring	Monitoring frequencies
	Precision, detailedness of analysis
Identifying energy losses	Identification of sources of energy losses
	Quantification of energy losses
Setting targets, defining norms	Conformance of targets
	Extent of objective elaboration

Source: own elaboration

THE SECOND PILLAR: MEASURES NOT REQUIRING A CONSIDERABLE INVESTMENT OF RESOURCES

Measures not requiring a considerable investment of resources constitute the second pillar of energy management tasks (Table 2).

Table 2
Structure and evaluation criteria of the first pillar

THE SECOND PILLAR	
Measures not requiring a considerable investment of resources	
SUB-PILLAR	EVALUATION CRITERIA
Energy purchasing	Bargaining power in the energy market
	Performing operative tasks
	Elaborating the energy purchasing strategy
Measures for reducing energy use without requiring a considerable investment of resources	Energy saving measures
	Energy efficiency measures

Source: own elaboration

The first task among the measures is energy purchase which is not accompanied by considerable additional costs. When the energy is purchased, there are no energy savings; however, considerable energy costs can be saved by adopting appropriate energy purchasing strategies. Apart from purchasing tasks, the second pillar encompasses company measures resulting in reducing energy use and not requiring a considerable investment of resources.

The assessment of the certain tasks should be carried out according to the following criteria:

- Energy purchasing. The role of energy purchasing in saving corporate energy costs has increased in the past few years, especially after the liberalisation process of energy markets. Different types of contracts have been concluded in the free market, which requires better preparedness and knowledge from energy management. Comparing tenders submitted by energy traders competing in the energy market is also a complicated process. Apart from the negotiated prices and the grid fees, there are several other contractual terms and conditions (tolerance bands, surcharges, penalties, currencies, exchange rates, payment deadlines and timeframes) that should be taken into account. It is by no means certain that the contract offering the lowest price is really that cheap. Energy can be purchased from different vendors and places in various ways (OTC markets, energy stock exchanges, energy tenders and grouped purchases). There are also several ways to rationalise energy costs while purchasing energy. Whilst evaluating the utilisation of the opportunities lying in purchasing energy, the company's bargaining power, the performance of such basic tasks as checking energy bills, and the presence of professional competences used for developing purchasing strategies are also worth considering.
- Measures reducing energy usage and not requiring a considerable investment of resources. Energy usage can be reduced in two ways: by introducing measures targeting energy savings and through increased energy efficiency. The fundamental difference between the two ways is that in the first case energy can be saved by placing consumers in a worse situation (providing heating at a lower temperature). In the latter case, energy consumption is reduced; however, the original degree of comfort remains. The available options arising from this should be examined. This idea involves such simple actions as turning off machinery and interrupting power, eliminating the standby mode, encouraging employees' conserving behaviour, setting appropriate lightning levels, or identifying and utilising natural lighting options.

THE THIRD PILLAR: INVESTMENTS IN IMPROVING ENERGY EFFICIENCY

The third pillar is a considerable jump in terms of corporate energy management. The tasks on this level have financial implications since decision making involves financial considerations. In order to implement investments, a financial basis is to be established. As for energy- efficient investments, two sub-tasks are worth giving priority (Table 3). First, it should be analysed how much caution and prudence was exercised when the decision about investing in energy project was made and processes were prepared. Second, it should be investigated whether the company has already performed any investment activities or planned investments aiming at improving energy efficiency.

Table 3
Structure and evaluation criteria of the third pillar

THE THIRD PILLAR	
Investments in improving energy efficiency	
SUB-PILLAR	EVALUATION CRITERIA
Preparing decisions on investments improving energy efficiency	Priority to energy investments
	Support of energy investments
	Decision-making methodology
	Ways of raising resources
Executed and planned energy efficiency investments	Energy investment in corporate processes
	Energy investment in building energetics
	Reduction of energy loss
	Incorporation of energy efficiency criteria into other investment processes

Source: own elaboration

The assessment of the certain tasks should be carried out according to the following criteria:

- Preparing decisions. It is essential to analyse priorities a company has given to energy investment projects from the perspective of implementing different energy investments and their support in a company. Its mapping is important because some companies lack solid justification of investment projects in energy and the conditions of their implementation. Another evaluation criteria can be to identify the applied decision-making methodology and to evaluate the calculations a company has made before deciding for or against investing in a project. It is also worth examining whether minimum criteria (for instance, the return on the investment) are set when evaluating a project and whether all investments in energy are given the same considerations or each investment project is evaluated according to seperate criteria. The method of financing investment projects is also of great importance.

- Implemented and planned investments in improving energy efficiency. Mapping implemented and planned investments in improving energy efficiency is an important evaluation criterion. It is worth examining in what areas investments in energy efficiency were implemented and with what objectives, whether they targeted corporate main and support processes or building energetics or they were aimed at reducing losses. Another critical element is the presence of energy efficiency critera in other investment processes of a company (for instance, in purchasing office machines).

The Fourth Pillar: Formalisation and Institutionalisation of Energy Management

The fourth pillar analyses the level of formalisation and institutionalisation of energy management (Table 4). Formalisation and institutionalisation mean how energy management is addressed by a company, whether the company has an official framework for pursuing this activity and whether the functional area plays any role in corporate strategic visions. The fundamental tasks at this level are to identify the position of energy management within the organisation, to map its place at a strategic level and to evaluate corporate activities in energy management.

Table 4
Structure and evaluation criteria of the fourth pillar

THE FOURTH PILLAR	
Formalisation and institutionalisation of energy management	
SUB-PILLAR	EVALUATION CRITERIA
The position of energy management within the organisation	Emergence of energy management functional areas in the organisational structure
	The number of employees responsible for the energy management, their job duty areas and organisational position
	Harmonisation of competencies, powers of decision and responsibilities
Emergence of energy management at the strategic level	Emergence of energy management in the corporate strategy
	Energy strategy, energy policy
	Energy management system
Evaluation of energy management activities	Evaluation of outcomes of energy efficiency policy measures
	Identification of energy management tasks

Source: own elaboration

The assessment of the certain tasks should be carried out according to the following criteria:

- The position of energy management within the organisation. Energy management tasks can be positioned within the corporate hierarchy in a different way. Because of the character of energy management, it can be considered to be a border area between technical and economic areas, so its position in the organisation structure is not clearly defined. For this reason, the emergence of energy management functional areas in organisational structure is worth analysing. The focus should be laid on determining whether a company employs a person whose job duty areas are related solely to energy management; how many persons are responsible for performing energy management tasks; whether competencies, powers of decision and responsibilities are harmonised; whether the company has an Energy Management Department; whether the energy management tasks are present at middle and top management levels and the performance of this activity is indicated in the management's and other employees' payrolls; and whether energy efficiency is included in the performance evaluation as a criterion.
- Emergence of energy management at strategy level. Important evaluation criteria can be whether energy management issues are present in the corporate strategy within a formalised framework; whether the company has elaborated independent energy strategy and energy policy and whether they are in harmony with each other and with the corporate strategy; whether the company has implemented an energy management system certified by an international standard; and whether a regime of energy audits is introduced on a regular basis. The above-listed issues emerge at a more sophisticated level of a corporate energy management policy.
- Evaluation of energy management activities. It is worth examining whether a company performs a regular efficiency evaluation of energy management, strives to quantify the outcomes of energy efficiency policy measures, identifies the areas in energy management practices requiring improvement, and has professional competences to perform energy management tasks. The methods applied by the company when conducting the evaluation should also be examined.

THE FIFTH PILLAR: COMMUNICATION OF ENERGY AWARENESS AND SUSTAINABILITY

The fifth pillar is the most sophisticated level of performing energy management tasks (Table 5).

Table 5
Structure and evaluation criteria of the fifth pillar

THE FIFTH PILLAR	
Communication of energy awareness and sustainability	
SUB-PILLAR	EVALUATION CRITERA
Communication of energy awareness, emergence of sustainable energy management	Communication of energy awareness
	Participation in energy efficiency initiatives
	Further expansion of an energy-aware purchasing policy to materials, equipment and buildings
	Further expansion of energy-aware purchasing policy to the complete supply chain
	Emergence of energy efficiency criteria in product development
	Social and environmental responsibility
	Emergence of sustainable energy management

Source: own elaboration

The assessment of the certain tasks should be carried out according to the following criteria:

- Communication of energy awareness and emergence of sustainable energy management. Information about the following issues is to be collected at this level, namely whether the company communicates energy awareness inside and outside the company, is a participator or an active initiator of energy efficiency initiatives (for instance, the Virtual Power Plant Project), expands energy efficiency criteria to the whole purchasing process (including material, equipment and building purchases), expands energy aware purchasing concept to the complete supply chain, applies energy efficiency criteria in product development, undertakes social and environmental responsibility in corporate activities and includes sustainability and sustainable energy management in the corporate strategy.

OPERATION OF THE MODEL

As a result of the research work, a research questionnaire and the first draft of the scoring system have been created. Pre-testing has already been carried out. After pre-calculations are made a final version of the questionnaire will be developed.

According to the initial concept, the evaluation of the five pillars was performed along several sub-pillars on the basis of several (a variable number) evaluation criteria. Variables used for measuring particular elements were developed in every evaluation criterion. The set of variables used in the scoring system was compiled on the basis of the questions in the questionnaire. The questionnaire was made up of questions thematised by the elements of the introduced evaluation model. On the basis of the scoring system, an equal obtainable total score could be reached in each pillar. However, the sub-pillars making up the pillars were weighted differently, since sub-pillars were assigned a different maximal reachable score. The variables of the criteria selected to evaluate the sub-pillars were also weighted depending on how much relevance they have compared to each other. (The variables may include not only specific questions, closed questions, specific data and information but also scale-type questions, which involve some subjectivity.) There is a maximal reachable total score for each pillar and sub-pillar. After the evaluation is completed, the score reached by the company is established. As a quotient of the reached score and the maximal reachable total score, the percentage rate of the potential of a particular task group exploited by the company can be defined for each pillar.

The following concrete example presents the application of the model. As has already been mentioned above, the first draft of the research questionnaire and the scoring system built on it have been pilot tested. The responses given by 8 companies to the pilot questionnaire were evaluated and calculations related to eight companies were performed. On the basis of obtained results, the scoring system is currently under elaboration (clarification) and the circle of variables to be included in the scoring system is being worked on. Although only the results of the tentative calculations are available, they do not hinder the understanding of the theoretical operation of the model.

One of the concrete examples of test calculations illustrates the application and interpretation of the complex evaluation model. The information known about the company is as follows. The company's business activities belong to the sector of 'manufacture of wood and of products of wood and cork','manufacture of articles of straw and plaiting materials' and 'manufacture of furnitures'. As for the size, it is a small-sized company with five employees. It has been successfully operating as a family enterprise for 20 years. The business has been growing; its activities have expanded and changed. A new wood manufacturing company, a carpentry and wood machining plant, was founded to meet the increased consumer demand. The plant is involved in both trading and manufacturing activities and is a service provider, too. The plant has advanced machines (a wood drying machine, different types of circular saws, a milling machine, and a pressing machine) and technology, which enables the management to handle wood waste efficiently and use wood residues for further purposes. From an energy aspect, the purchasing of a biomass boiler was a major investment in enhancing the energy efficiency of the business. It is used for heating the workshop and burning wood waste and chips. The wood waste generated during production is made into useful briquettes, which are sold alongside with logs as a heating fuel. The company is thinking of further investments in modernising and expanding its machine park and plants to deploy solar panels with the objective of reducing and covering electricity demand. The return on these investments is estimated at 10-12 years. The management is not planning to hire an energy expert to perform energy management tasks. The company uses most of the purchased electricity for operating machines (60%), lighting (32%), and supporting processes (8%). They do not purchase any heating fuels for heating buildings or operating drying machines. The purchased biomass boiler, operating on logs and wood waste, is used for generating the required amount of heat. In addition, the company has two gas-powered forklifts. The proportion of energy costs in the revenue amounts only to 1.71% and together with fuel costs this figure accounts for 2.1%. The company is attempting to take an advantage of the liberalised electricity energy market and is planning to change its supplier. The management constantly strives to cut energy consumption. By rationalising the production processes, modernising lightning (using energy-efficient lamps), replacing old doors and windows and improving insulation, the company has saved a considerable amount of energy. The company lacked an explicit and written energy strategy and an energy management system. Their energy losses were assessed by an external expert. Nevertheless, the company adopted good energy management practices. On the basis of the new model and the results obtained from the tentative calculations, a summary table was elaborated (Table 6), which illustrates the points obtained, the maximal reachable score and the percentage performance.

Table 6
Summary table of the complex evaluation model (on a basis of a real company)

Evaluated areas	Reached scores	Maximal scores	Percent of points (%)
FIRST PILLAR: Measuring-Monitoring-Target setting	12.5	40	31.3
Measuring	0.25	8	3.1
Monitoring	6.75	16	42.2
Identifying losses	3.5	8	43.8
Setting targets, norms	2	8	25
SECOND PILLAR: Measures not requiring a considerable investment of resources	16.98	40	42.4
Energy purchasing	5.38	20	26.9
Measures cutting costs, not requiring investment resources	11.6	20	58
THIRD PILLAR: Investments in improving energy efficiency	16.48	40	41.2
Preparing decisions	1.48	10	14.8
Implemented and planned investments in improving energy efficiency	15	30	50
FOURTH PILLAR: Formalisation and institutionalisation of energy management	4.88	40	12.2
The position of energy management within the organisation	0.25	10	2.5
Emergence of energy management at strategy level	1	15	6.7
Evaluation of energy management activities	3.63	15	24.2
FIFTH PILLAR: Communication of energy awareness, sustainability	4	40	10
Energy awareness, communication, social responsibility, sustainability	4	40	10
Total:	**54.83**	**200**	**27.4**

Source: own elaboration

The obtained results are shown in a cobweb plot (Figure 2 and Figure 3) where the areas which need improving can be easily identified.

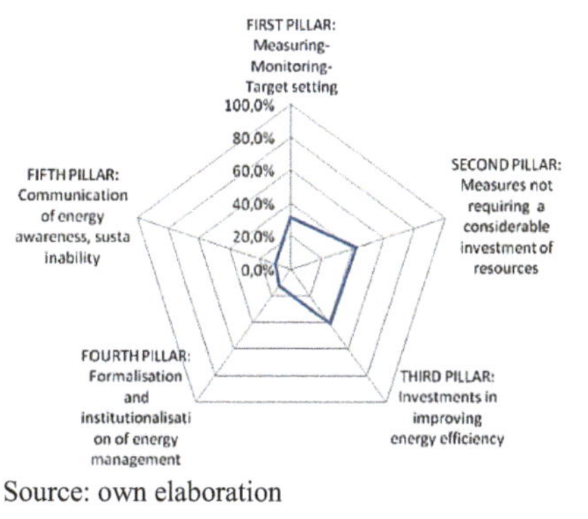

Source: own elaboration

Figure 2 Implementation of pillars in the company

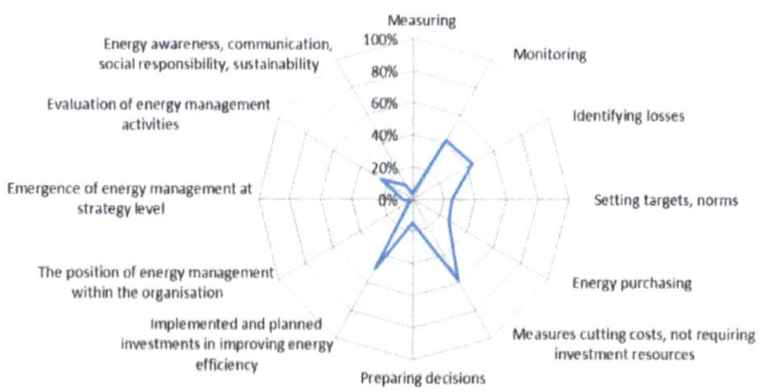

Source: own elaboration

Figure 3 Implementation of sub-pillars in the company

Although the obtained figures of the tentative calculations show that the company had some energy management areas where energy efficiency was low, it is invalid to draw negative conclusions from the outcomes themselves. First, taking into consideration the sectoral and corporate characteristics, low and high values need to be determined. If the value is low, the company's specific features are to be considered and the reasons for low performance in specific areas should be identified. It should be noted that not every company needs to have high values in every area. It may happen that a lower value in one group of companies shows better performance than a slightly higher value in another company group. This depends on what an acceptable level in specific cases is considered to be. In the case of the company under evaluation, the circle of issues related to strategy, formalisation, communication of energy awareness and sustainability will not play a very important role. This expectation is justified by the outcome. Taking into account that the rate of energy costs was relatively low related to their revenues, it can be stated that a 50% and a 58% performance reached in the components of investments in improving energy efficiency and measures not requiring a considerable investment of resources, respectively, is quite good.

After giving a serious consideration to these criteria and identifying causes, areas for energy improvement can be determined. The presented model makes it possible to perform an energy management analysis for each company separately. However, the model cannot be considered suitable for comparing energy management practices of companies.

POSSIBILITIES FOR CREATING A COMPLEX EVALUATION INDICATOR

The complex evaluation model was constructed with the objective of performing specific and individual evaluations as well as comparing companies. There is a growing requirement for establishing comparability of countries and companies. In cases where the comparison is done not only for one factor, but considering complicated and complex correlations, factors influencing each other and requiring identification of complex impacts, comparison is considerably more difficult. As a compromise solution to individual cases, composite indices have widely been used in the past few years. Both at a macro level (see OECD 2008, Bartha et al. 2013 among others) and at a micro level (Sasvári, 2008) complex indices are applied (country and corporate competitiveness index, sustainability index and so on).

The comparison of corporate energy management practices and energy awareness is not possible along one single dimension. The analysis should be done according to several criteria. In addition, in order to create bases for comparison, it is important to recognise the distortions arising from unique features of sectors and companies. In this regard, an idea of constructing a composite indicator used for comparing energy management and energy awareness of companies may be raised which combines impacts of numerous factors that influence each other into a complex indicator.

Table 7

*Theoretical possibilities for taking into account unique features of sectors and companies**

		COMPANY GROUPS (based on sectoral energy intensity and/or company size, and/or rate of energy costs)							
		DIVERGENT WEIGHTING (decrease of weight rate of less relevant factors)		APPLICATION OF MULTIPLIERS (by multiplying scores of less relevant factors)		APPLICATION OF DIVERGENCE TOTAL SCORES (by deducting scores of less relevant factors)		APPLICATION OF DIVERGENCE THRESHOLD (defining good performance threshold)	
		GROUP 1*	GROUP 2**	GROUP 1*	GROUP 2**	GROUP 1*	GROUP 2**	GROUP 1*	GROUP 2**
1st PILLAR	Measuring-Monitoring- Target setting	20%	40%	1	1	40	40	75%	50%
2nd PILLAR	Measures not requiring a considerable investment of resources	20%	30%	1	1	40	40	90%	70%
3rd PILLAR	Investments in improving energy efficiency	20%	15%	1	1.3	40	25	70%	40%
4th PILLAR	Formalisation and institutionalisation of energy management	20%	10%	1	1.3	40	25	80%	25%
5th PILLAR	Communication of energy awareness and sustainability	20%	5%	1	1.4	40	20	70%	15%
	TOTAL:	100%	100%			200	150		

*Group 1: energy intensive sector/ large companies/high energy cost rate
** Group 2: not energy-intensive sector/ SMEs/low energy cost rate
*** Figures in Table 7 are used for demonstration purposes only and require further research

Source: own elaboration

The complex indicator can be made up of the weighted summary of the total scores reached on each pillar or a weighted summary of the percentage performance (it could be interpreted on sub-pillar levels as well). Identifying unique features of sectors and companies is more important when a comparison is done than when individual cases are analysed. The company size, what sector it is categorised in, how energy intensive its activities are, the proportion of its energy costs and the company's rank on the vertical value chain all make a considerable contribution to determining the energy management priority levels and the tasks which are less relevant to the energy management of a particular company. Numerous possible methods can be used for determining these issues, four of which are shown in Table 7. In each case, the starting point is that the criterion of grouping of companies should be chosen, by which the differences in the importance of energy management activities are reflected. Then companies are divided into groups. In each company group, the sub-pillars that play the most important role and the ones that are the least relevant to the company group are identified. Table 7 offers some theoretical possibilities for how to take into account less relevant factors. It is important to note that the weights and multipliers in the Table 7 are indicated for demonstration purposes only and require further research.

CONCLUSIONS

The complex evaluation model described in this paper offers a theoretical approach which provides possibilities for measuring the efficiency of corporate energy management after conducting an analysis based on several evaluation criteria listed in the sub-pillars and the scoring system that has been created. By applying this model, corporate areas requiring further energy improvement can also be identified. The set target of establishing specific individual evaluation possibilities has been met. Apart from individual evaluation, there is also a growing need for establishing the comparability of companies. In some cases when the comparison of corporate energy management practices and energy awareness is not possible along one single dimension, an idea of constructing a composite indicator is raised, which combines impacts of numerous factors that influence each other into a complex indicator. The constructing of the composite indicator could be based on the complex evaluation model shown in this article. The complex indicator can be made up of a weighted summary of the total scores for each pillar or a weighted summary of the percentage performance. Weighting is needed because of the prerequisite of comparison, which identifies distortions resulting from unique features of sectors and companies.

The reception of composite indicators and their application varies greatly among scholars in the academic community. Indicators are criticised for their limited applicability, subjectivity in their creation, and loss of information. Indicators used at a micro-level raise further problems, namely, they lack 'hard' information, statistical data, measurable information, or collections of factual data: these are outweighed by 'soft' variables. Although the raison d'être of criticism is indisputable, the bias can be decreased by adopting a prudent approach to creating the indicators. There are strict fundamental criteria for developing composite indicators (establishing a theoretical framework, choosing data selection methods, handling missing data, conducting a multivariable analysis, performing normalisation, weighting and aggregation, addressing robustness and sensitivity issues) and if they are followed, the validity and reliability of indicators can be considerably improved (OECD 2008). The widespread application of composite indicators highlights the fact that there is a need for developing complex indicators which help evaluate reality, which is typically affected by several factors, and such indicators can simplify multidimensional correlations into a single index.

In conclusion it can be said that the complex evaluation model presented in this paper is suitable for meeting two objectives, namely it offers an informative evaluation about corporate energy management and shows areas for further improvement. In addition, it makes comparison of companies possible. Furthermore, it serves as a basis for constructing a composite type of indicator. The concept underlines the importance of background information, separate analyses of specific areas, specific features of companies, and the parallel application of evaluation tools to reduce information loss as much as possible.

Acknowledgement

This research was (partially) carried out in the framework of the Center of Excellence of Mechatronics and Logistics at the University of Miskolc.

REFERENCES

BARTHA, Z., SÁFRÁNYNÉ G. A. & TÓTHNÉ Sz. K. (2013): Intézményi megoldások, fejlődési modellek. (Institutional solutions, development models) GNR Szolgáltató és Kereskedelmi Bt, Miskolc

BIHARI, P. (2012): Energetikai alapismeretek. (Basics of energetics) Budapesti Műszaki és Gazdaságtudományi Egyetem. Retrieved: December 2013: ftp://ftp.energia.bme.hu/pub/energetikai_alapismeretek/Energetikai_alapismeretek_jegyzet.pdf

Brescu (Building Research Energy Conservation Support Unit) 1993: Organisational aspects of energy management. General Information Report 12. http://products.ihs.com/cis/Doc.aspx?AuthCode=&DocNum=85250

Carbon Trust (2010): Monitoring and Targeting: Techniques to help organisations control and manage their energy use. Carbon Trust, United Kingdom. Retrieved: January 2014: https://www.carbontrust.com/media/31683/ctg008_monitoring_and_targeting.pdf

Carbon Trust (2011a): Energy Management: A comprehensive guide to controlling energy use. Carbon Trust, United Kingdom. Retrieved: January 2014: http://www.carbontrust.com/media/13187/ctg054_energy_management.pdf

Carbon Trust (2011b): Energy Management Self-Assessment Tools. Carbon Trust, United Kingdom. Retrieved: January 2014: http://www.carbontrust.com/resources/tools/energy-management-self-assessment-tool

DIÓFÁSI Á. & DIÓFÁSI O. (2009): Energiamenedzsment. Energiamenedzsment az Egyesült Királyságban. Source: Energy Management in the UK, a Report on the Findings of BSI's July 2009 Energy Management Research Survey, 2009 October. Retrieved: January 2014: http://survive.hu/wp-content/uploads/2013/07/energiamenedzsment.pdf

Energy Efficiency Guide for Industry in Asia. Copyright© United Nations Environment Programme 2006. www.energyefficiencyasia.org Retrieved: January 2014

ENGEL, H.-W.: Translated into Hungarian by HERNER K.&TÓTH G.: Öko-térképezés. Szemléletes, egyszerű és gyakorlatias eszköz kisvállalkozások és kézműves üzemek környezeti teljesítményének felmérésére és javítására. (Eco-mapping. A visual, simple and practical tool to analyse and manage the environmental performance of small companies and craft industries) Eco-mapping © Heinz-Werner Engel 1998 Környezettudatos Vállalatirányítási Egyesület (KÖVET-INEM Hungária) Budapest, 2000 június. Retrieved: January 2014: http://www.14000registry.com/pdf/ecomaph.pdf

GOEBEL, D. (2007): Betriebliches Energiemanagement. PhD Dissertation, Universität Duisburg-Essen, Essen. Retrieved: December 2013: http://duepublico.uni-duisburg-essen.de/servlets/DerivateServlet/Derivate-16926/Endversion%20Dissertation%20Goebel.pdf

GORDIĆ, D., BABIĆ M., JOVIČIĆ, N., ŠUŠTERŠIČ, V., KONČALOVIĆ, D. & JELIĆ, D. (2010): Development of Energy Management System – Case study of Serbian car manufacturer. Energy Conversion and Management, 51, 2783–2790. www.elsevier.com/locate/enconman, Retrieved: December 2013

GVOZDENAK, D.D. & MORVAY, Z.K. (2008): Applied Industrial Energy and Environmental Management. Wiley-IEEE Press

HIRZEL, S.- SONTAG, B.- ROHDE, C. (2011): Betriebliches Energiemanagement in der industriellen Produktion. Kurzstudie. Fraunhofer-Institut für System- und Innovationsforschung ISI, Karlsruhe. Retrieved: December 2013 http://www.effizienzfabrik.de/sites/effizienzfabrik/files/dokumente/ISI_Kurzstudie_Energiemanagement.pdf

KÁDÁRNÉ HORVÁTH Ágnes (2012): A vállalatok energia-racionalizálási lehetőségei a globális energiaválság szorításában. (The opportunities of energy rationalization for companies in threat of global energy crisis) In: Fülöp, G. et al. (eds.). Vállalati kihívások - stratégiai válaszok. Miskolc: Miskolci Egyetem, 2012. pp. 15-43.

MADLOOL, N.A. – SAIDUR, R.- RAHIM, N.A.- KAMALISARVESTANI, M. (2013): An overview of energy savings measures for cement industries. Renewable and Sustainable Energy Reviews, 19 (2013) 18–29. www.elsevier.com/locate/rser Retrieved: February 2014

National Productivity Council (2002): Tisztább termelés és energiahatékonyság integrálása a vállalati gyakorlatban. (gyakorlati útmutató). (Integration of cleaner production and energy efficiency in corporate practice) National Productivity Council (2002): New Delhi, India, Adapted by: Tisztább Termelés Magyarországi Központja, Budapest, Retrieved: March 2013: http://hcpc.uni-corvinus.hu/exp_eng/cp-ee_manual_hungarian_pressoptimized_2.pdf

OECD (2008): Handbook on Constructing Composite Indicators: Methodology and User Guide. Retrieved: January 2014: http://www.oecd.org/std/42495745.pdf

PARDO MARTÍNEZ, C. I. (2009): Energy efficiency developments in the manufacturing industries of Germany and Colombia, 1998–2005. Energy for Sustainable Development, 13 (2009) 189–201

ÖNUT, Semih – SONER, Selin (2007): Analysis of energy use and efficiency in Turkish manufacturing sector SMEs. Energy Conversion and Management, 48, 384–394

SASVÁRI Péter (2008): Az információs és kommunikációs technológia fejlettségének empirikus vizsgálata (English title). PhD dissertation, University of Miskolc.

SIVILL, L. (2011): Success factors of energy management in energy-intensive industries: Energy performance measurement. PhD dissertation, Aalto University. Retrieved: November 2013

THORPE, David (2014): Energy Management in Industry. The Earthscan Expert Guide. Routledge: London and New York

Virtuális Erőmű Program. (Virtual Power Plant Programme) http://virtualiseromu.hu/ingyenes-onertekeles October 2013

ZSEBIK A.-FALUCSKAI N. J.-CZINEGE Z. (Editor) (2003): Energiagazdálkodás. (Energy management) Oktatási segédanyag. Kézirat. E.ON Hungária Rt. Budapest.

ZSEBIK A.-CZINEGE Z. (Editor) (2003): Energiaveszteség-feltárás. (Exploration of energy losses) Oktatási segédanyag. Kézirat. E.ON Hungária Rt. Budapest.

13

Changing Role of Industry in the Economy in the V4 Countries – A Regional Approach

WIOLETTA KILAR, Ph.D.
ECONOMIC GEOGRAPHER; LECTURER
e-mail: W.Kilar@up.krakow.pl

TOMASZ RACHWAŁ, Ph.D.
ECONOMIC GEOGRAPHER
e-mail: T.Rachwal@up.krakow.pl

SUMMARY

The theme of the article is the changing role of industry in the economy of the countries of the Visegrád Group, further referred to as V4. The goal of the research is to delimit the regularities in terms of changes of the importance of industrial activity in the economy of the region in the conditions of moving from the industrial to post-industrial to information phase of the development and building of a knowledge-based economy. The analysis is based on the NUTS-2 regions of the V4 countries against the general changes in the European Union states, based on selected measurements of industrial potential, i.e. employment and gross value added of industry, as well as indicators of spatial concentration, structure and dynamics in industrial activity, with a special focus on those related to the knowledge-based economy, such as employment in technology and knowledge-intensive sectors. The analysis is dynamic and refers to the years 2000-2012. The research is based on the following methods: comparative analysis, explanation, quantitative analysis and cartographic analysis, all with a regional approach.

The analysis indicates the diminishing role of industry in the V4 countries compared to the other EU states. However, the participation of employment in industry is relatively high in comparison with the rest of the EU states. Concentration of industry occurs in the earlier developed areas of concentration, i.e. industrial districts. As a result, there is a need for a new interpretation of the regional policy in the V4 states, where more attention should be paid to the role of industry in shaping the economic structure.

Keywords: industry, regional economy, the Visegrád Group, economic transformation

INTRODUCTION

Changes in the socio-economic system in the countries of Central and Eastern Europe, associated with the introduction of a market economy based on a competition mechanism, significantly affect the functioning of companies and different sectors of the economy. This also applies to industrial activities, which were growing in completely different conditions in the centrally controlled economy. As a result, a specific enterprise developed in which economic efficiency was not the main goal. The main aim of its operation was to serve the needs of the national economy and society, through the implementation of tasks planned and defined at the central level, not the company itself (Koźmiński 1998). In addition, these companies were usually characterised by excessive employment, large volume of production, mostly of not very modern products, unadjusted to the existing demand, outdated machinery equipment and the organisational structure adapted to the prescriptive-distributive system (Błaszkiewicz, 1994; Rachwał 2002; Rachwał 2006a). As a result, at the beginning of the economic transformation industrial enterprises found themselves in a difficult situation, which required them to undertake a restructuring process in order to increase their competitiveness on the domestic and international markets. Raising the competitiveness of these enterprises was carried out through means such as changes in the ownership structure, organisation and management structures, rationalisation of employment levels, adjusting the product portfolio to the expectations of buyers and the consequent modernisation of production assets, as well as the transformation of the sources of supply and, consequently, the sales structure (Rachwał 2002; Rachwał 2006a; Rachwał 2006b).

Today, in the era of the knowledge-based economy, improving competitiveness manifests itself primarily in the implementation of organisational, technological and product innovation: increased capital expenditures on fixed assets and innovative activities as well as intensive research and development (Kilar 2008). These changes reflect the participation of national industrial enterprises in the global economic processes and integration of industries of the countries of Central and Eastern Europe with the global industry, particularly through organisational, capital, technological, information and market links (Kilar 2010; Rachwał 2006a). They lead to the liquidation of the structural gap that occurred in connection with the implementation of fundamentally different models of industrialisation in the countries of Central and Eastern Europe and the countries of Western Europe, where the functioning of the national economy has been based on market rules. Corporate restructuring processes also affect the change in the role of industry in the national and regional economy.

OBJECTIVES, METHODS AND SOURCES OF STATISTICAL DATA

In the light of the above premises, the theme of the article is the changing role of industry in the economy of the Visegrád Group countries referred to as the V4. The aim of the study is to determine the regularity in terms of changes in the importance of industrial activities in the regional economy, in the conditions of transition from the industrial to post-industrial to information phase of the development and building a knowledge-based economy. The analysis is conducted in the system of the NUTS-2 regions of the V4 countries compared to the general trend of change in the European Union, based on the selected measures of industrial capacity, i.e. employment and gross value added (GAV) of industry, as well as indicators of spatial concentration, structure and dynamics relating to the industrial activities, with particular emphasis on those related to the knowledge-based economy, such as employment in technology- and knowledge-intensive sectors.

Achieving and maintaining a competitive position on the domestic and foreign markets requires considering – in the strategies of the industrial enterprises – the growing role of education and science, research and development and innovation, that is, everything that is the key to achieving a competitive advantage in the knowledge-based economy. Particular attention has been paid to the spatial variability of the phenomena; for this purpose the cartographic method of presentation of the phenomena was used. The analysis is conducted in a dynamic way and covers the period 2000-2012. In these years there was a change in the classification of activities from NACE 1.1 to NACE 2.0. It was considered, however, that due to the extent of aggregation this does not affect significantly the conclusions of the analysis, which was limited to an indication of the important regularity of the analysed phenomenon.

In total, 35 NUTS-2 regions from the Visegrád Group countries were analysed. They include 16 Polish, 8 Czech, 7 Hungarian and 4 Slovak regions. Due to the restrictions on access to data the research period for certain indicators may be shorter. The difficulties in accessing the data on the functioning of the industry, mainly due to the principles of statistical confidentiality and trade secrets of companies, were widely referred to in previous works by Rachwał (2008, 2010a). The study used data from Eurostat and the Central Statistical Office of Poland (GUS).

RESEARCH ISSUES IN THE LIGHT OF THE LITERATURE

The undertaken research problems were the subject of interest of various earlier authors. The themes undertaken in the 1990s mainly referred to the objectives and scope of the economic transition in the countries of Central and Eastern Europe (Bożyk 1999; Balcerowicz 1995; Kołodko 2000; Kornai 1997; Łukawer 1994a, b; Parysek 1998; Rosati 1998) and the privatisation of state enterprises, among which a prominent place was occupied by industrial enterprises (Bałtowski 2002; Karpińska-Mizielińska & Smuga 1995; Misztal 1993, 2000, 2003). A number of researchers undertook the problem of spatial adaptation (Stryjakiewicz 1999), restructuring (Jakóbik 1993) and structural changes of the industry in Poland and other countries of Central and Eastern Europe (incl. Abraham & Ese 1999; Domański 2003, 2006; Karpiński 2008; Lux 2010; Macias 2006; Paszkowski 1996; Rachwał 2009; Rochnowski 2001; Vishnevsky et al. 2011). A special place in these considerations is occupied by the issue of restructuring of selected industries (e.g. Czapliński 2011; Lizak 2009; Marszał,1993; Pakuła 1992; Rydz & Szymańska 2002; Tkocz 2006; Wiedermann 2002), and various industrial enterprises (Pełka 1994; Rachwał 2002, 2006a, 2006b, 2007; Sudoł & Karaszewski 1996). Under the conditions of the construction of the knowledge-based economy, researchers undertook the problem of the role of industry in the new conditions of economic development (Rachwał 2013; Zioło 2009), innovation and industrial competitiveness of Poland and other European countries (Doloreux & Parto 2005; Gierańczyk 2003, 2009, 2010; Gierańczyk & Rachwał 2012; Piras et al. 2012; Rachwał & Boguś 2012; Świadek 2006), as well as changes in the branch structure of the industry of Poland (Rachwał 2010b, 2011a) and the impact of the economic crisis on its functioning (Rachwał 2011b).

The issue of spatial diversity of industry in the regions of Poland and other European countries has been the subject of interest of, e.g., López-Bazo et al. (1999), Mikołajewicz (1995), Mrozińska (2013), Oort & Bosma (2013) and Rachwał et al. (2008a, 2008b, 2009), as well as other authors, who studied the issue of the transformation of industry in different regions (e.g. Malisiewicz & Zioło 1994; Pakuła 2003; Rydz & Jażewicz 2001; Tkocz 2001). In these works, however, there is no comparison of industrial regions in the V4 countries in recent years of the economic crisis.

We need to pay attention to the special place occupied by competitiveness and innovativeness of the V4 regional economy in the years 2001 to 2008, as presented in the work of Golejewska (2013). The results show that capital regions tend to develop faster and that there is a significant diversity of regional competitiveness and innovativeness across the V4 countries. The main conclusion from her cluster analysis is that the development of the regions in the Visegrád Group countries depends on their "nationality". The author also pointed to the correlation between innovation indicators (R&D expenditures and patent applications to the EPO) and the growth of the regional GDP per capita. She points out the fact that one of the factors affecting the innovativeness of regions is the structure of the industry, although she does not devote much space to the analysis of the role of industrial activity in the process.

Changing Role of Industry in the Economy of the V4 Countries Compared to Other EU States

According to the theory of the three sectors, whose authorship is attributed to A. Fisher, C. Clark and J. Fourastié (Czapliński et al. 2013, p. 176), industry, after a growth phase, loses its share in the structure of employment in favour of services. Today this regularity is observed in virtually all countries in the post-industrial stage of development. Also in the analysed period 2000-2012 in the V4 countries, as in other EU states, there was a decline in the share of industry in employment (see Fig. 1).

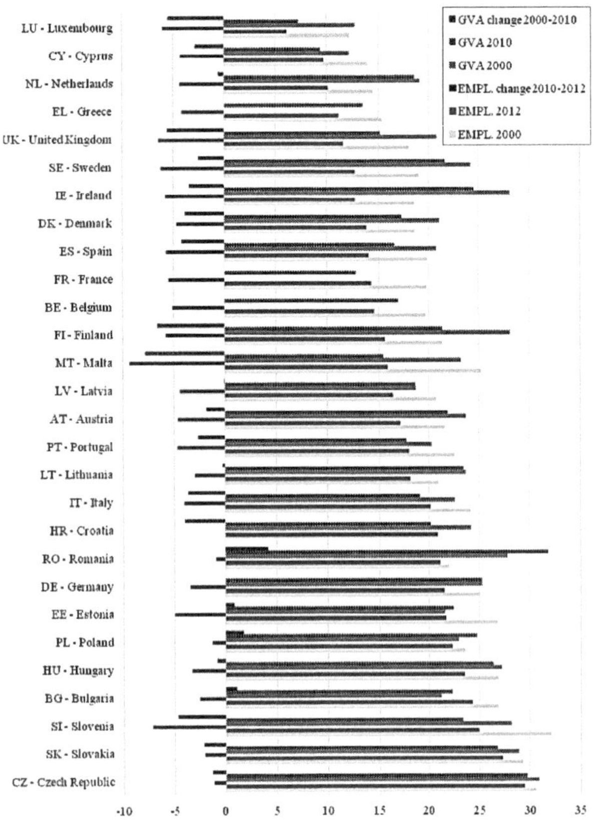

Source: own elaboration based on Eurostat data

Figure 1 Changes in the share of industry in employment (EMPL) and gross value added (GVA) in the EU states: 2000-2012 (pp).

It should be noted that the decrease was much smaller in the V4 countries (in the Czech Republic by 1.1 pp, in Poland by 1.3 pp, in Slovakia by 2.1 pp and in Hungary by 3.3 pp) than in the Western EU countries, although the shares of industry in employment in Central and Eastern Europe are far greater, amounting in 2012 from 18.1% in Lithuania to 29.4% in the Czech Republic. The largest drops - by more than 6 pp - were recorded in Malta, the UK, Sweden and Luxembourg.

Somewhat different is the variation in the case of the share of industry in the gross value added. Firstly, it should be noted that this participation is generally higher than in the case of employment, especially in Western countries and Scandinavia, which follows from the structure of the industry in these countries. The dominant role in this structure is not played by the traditional labour-intensive industries, but by more modern, high-value-added industries. Secondly, it should be noted that drops in the share of industry in the countries of Central and Eastern Europe are generally very small, and in some countries (e.g. Poland, Romania, Bulgaria and Estonia) the share of industry in GVA is up by 4.2 pp. In this situation it is difficult to speak of a universal deindustrialisation of Europe, but rather of only the confirmation of the thesis of the decline in the importance of industry in the mobilisation of labour resources and consistent reindustrialisation processes in the countries of Central and Eastern Europe in the context of economic transformation.

Industry Concentration in Regions of V4 Countries

The concentration of industrial activity, measured by the number of employees in industry per 1000 km^2, shows a high spatial diversity in the V4 regions (Fig. 2).

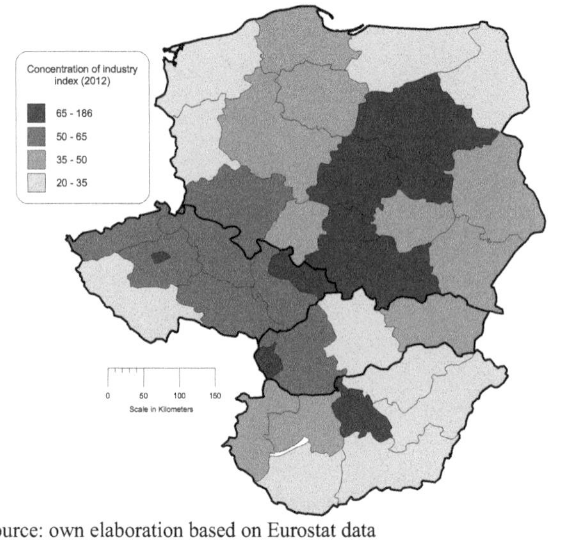

Source: own elaboration based on Eurostat data

Figure 2 Concentration of industry index in the regions of the V4 in 2012

The V4 regions with a high industrial concentration include the capitals of all countries (Bratislava, Budapest, Prague and Warsaw) as well as the region of Moravian Silesia (Moravskoslezsko) in the Czech Republic and the regions of the Śląskie, Małopolskie and Łódzkie Voivodeships in Poland. In addition, the regions of the Czech Republic have much higher concentration indexes than other regions of Hungary, central Slovakia and north-western and north-eastern Poland. This spatial concentration refers to the traditionally shaped industrial districts in these countries. In the analysed period of 2000-2012, this index, however, underwent significant changes (Fig. 3).

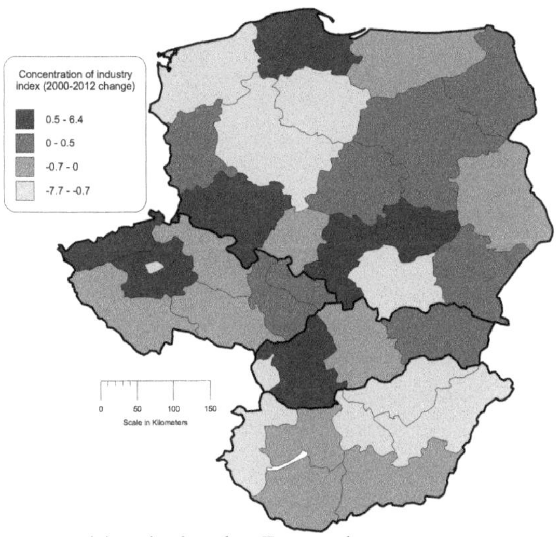

Source: own elaboration based on Eurostat data

Figure 3 Change of concentration of industry index in the V4 region in the years 2000-2012

High increases in the industry index's value were recorded in two north-western regions of the Czech Republic, Západné Slovensko in Slovakia and in four Polish regions: Śląskie, Dolnośląskie, Pomorskie and Świętokrzyskie Voivodeships. Noteworthy is the decrease in concentration in the capital regions of Prague, Bratislava and Budapest and other regions of Hungary. It should be noted, however, that this index was based on the number of employees in industry, and in the period considered Hungary witnessed the emergence of new and development of operating industrial enterprises that are far more technologically advanced (mainly in the automotive and consumer electronics), and also less labour intensive, which, as noted by Gierańczyk & Rachwał (2012), is probably one of the causes of dynamic growth in the participation of high-tech products in the export of Hungary in the first decade of the twentieth century. Of great importance among such changes of the spatial concentration are the investments in automotive companies in the regions of the V4 countries, belonging now among the world centres of production of cars and their components (Wójtowicz & Rachwał 2014).

Participation of Industry in Employment and GVA in the Regions of the V4 Countries

In order to capture the role of industry in the regional economy of the V4 countries indicators of industry participation in employment and GVA were used. They exhibit a large spatial diversity. The rate of participation of industry in employment in 2012 ranged from 10.6% in the region of Prague to 35.2% in the Moravian Silesia in the Czech Republic (Fig. 4).

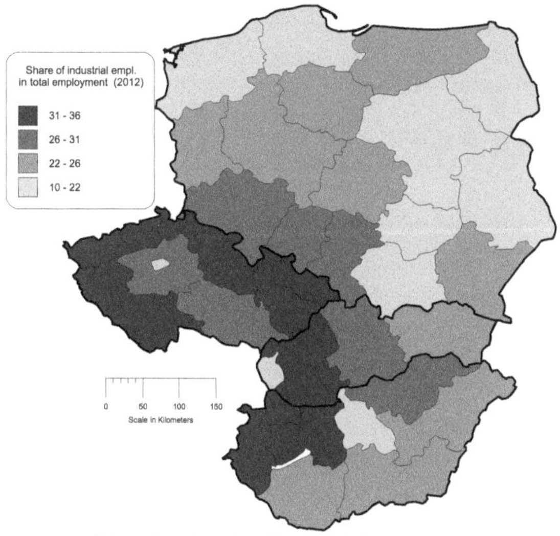

Source: own elaboration based on Eurostat data

Figure 4 Share of industry in total employment in the V4 regions in 2012 (%)

A high share of industry in employment, over 31%, is also seen in other regions of the Czech Republic, Západné Slovensko in Slovakia and the western regions of Hungary. The lowest rates, below 22%, are characteristic for the capital regions (besides the already mentioned Prague, also Bratislava, Budapest and Warsaw - the Mazowieckie Voivodeship) as well as the eastern (especially the Lubelskie and Podlaskie Voivodeships) and north-western regions of Poland. Although in the analysed period (2000-2012) in most regions of the V4 a drop was recorded in the share of industry in employment, even by almost 8 pp in the Śląskie Voivodeship (Fig. 5), it is worth noting that in 15 of the 35 regions an increase in employment in this sector was recorded. Assuming the base year as 100, the calculated index of dynamics ranged from 85.5 to 115.4. As a result, in some regions, mainly of eastern, central and south-western Poland, as well as the northern regions of the Czech Republic and in Západné Slovensko in Slovakia, a slight increase in the share of employment in industry was noted. In all the regions of Hungary there was a decline in the share of the industry in employment.

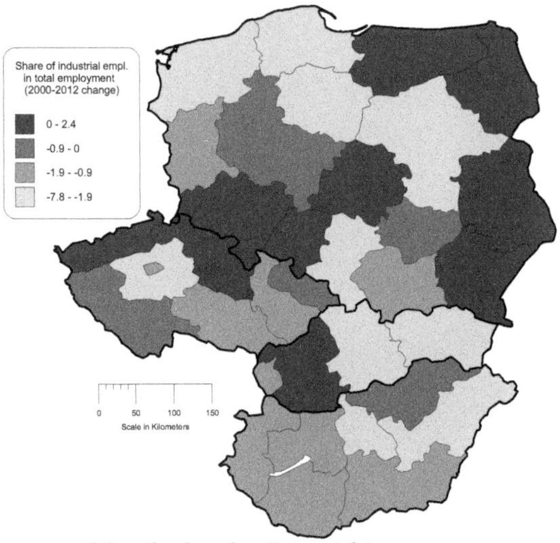

Source: own elaboration based on Eurostat data

Figure 5 Change in the share of industry in total employment in the regions of the V4 in the years 2000-2012 (pp)

The situation is somewhat different in the case of gross value added in the industry. The area with a large proportion, over 36%, includes the northern regions of the Czech Republic as well as Western Slovakia and Hungary (Fig. 6). The low shares are recorded in the capital regions, where service activities normally dominate, and in the southern and eastern regions of Hungary, eastern Slovakia and eastern Poland.

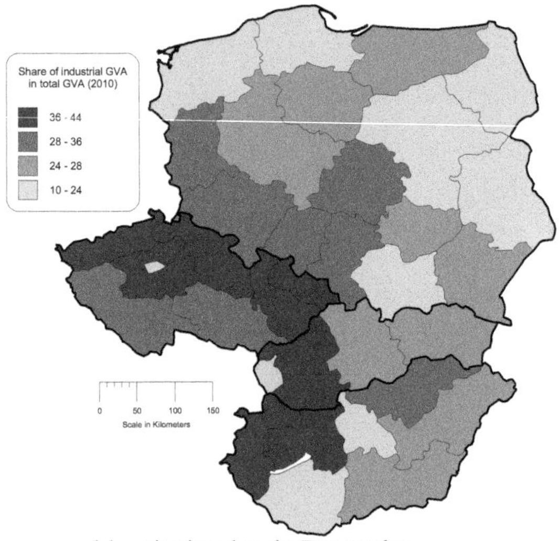

Source: own elaboration based on the Eurostat data

Figure 6 Share of industry in GVA in the V4 regions in 2010 (%)

In the period 2000-2010 in all the regions, growth was recorded in gross value added of industry at current prices, up to 3-fold. Large differences in the dynamics mean that the increase in the share of industry in GVA also applied to the regions where the share was low at the beginning of the study period (Fig. 7). Increases were recorded in 20 of 35 regions, and so twice as many as than the increases in the share of industry in employment. The highest increases in this share were recorded in the south-western provinces of Poland (including the Dolnośląskie Voivodeship, up by 9.4 pp), the Warmińsko-Mazurskie Voivodeship (PL) and the region of Észak-Alföld (HU).

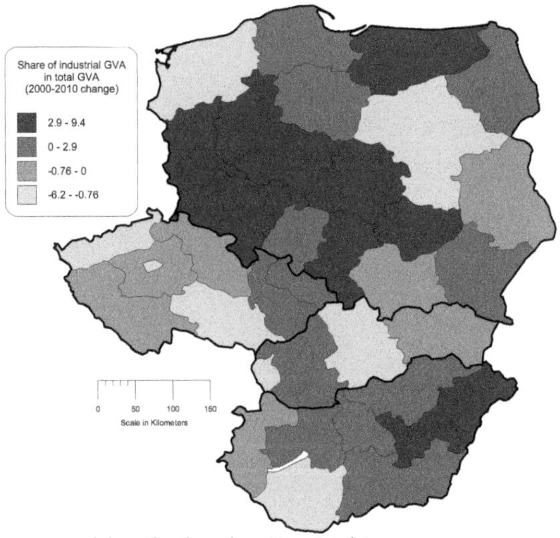

Source: own elaboration based on Eurostat data

Figure 7 Change in the share of industry in GVA in the regions of the V4 in the years 2000-2012 (pp)

DYNAMICS OF THE GROSS FORMATION CAPITAL AND HTEC[1] EMPLOYMENT IN THE V4 REGIONS

An expression of changes in industry associated with the construction of the knowledge-based economy is the employment in technology- and knowledge-intensive manufacturing. In the years 2004-2012 (for which the data is available), there was a significant increase in employment in this sector in the voivodeships of central and south Poland and the region Strední Cechy (CZ). The drop in employment mainly referred to the regions of Hungary and Slovakia, as well as certain voivodeships of Poland (Fig. 8).

Competitiveness of industry is also affected by the level of capital investment. The analysis of the gross fixed capital formation indicates that in the years 2000-2012 the largest increases in expenditures were recorded in some regions of Poland and the Czech Republic (including the region of Prague) and in the Bratislava region (Fig. 9). Low increases were observed in the regions of Hungary, two regions of the Czech Republic and two largest voivodeships of Poland, the Mazowieckie and Wielkopolskie Voivodeships.

[1] *HTEC: high-tech industry and knowledge-intensive manufacturing*

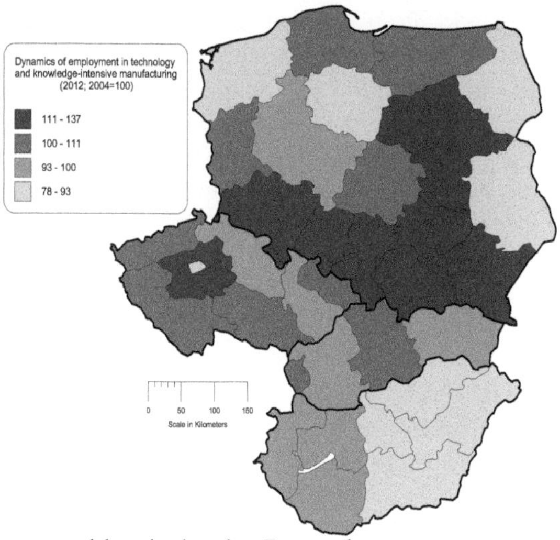

Source: own elaboration based on Eurostat data

Figure 8 Growth of employment in technology- and knowledge-intensive manufacturing in the regions V4 in the years 2004-2012 (2004=100)

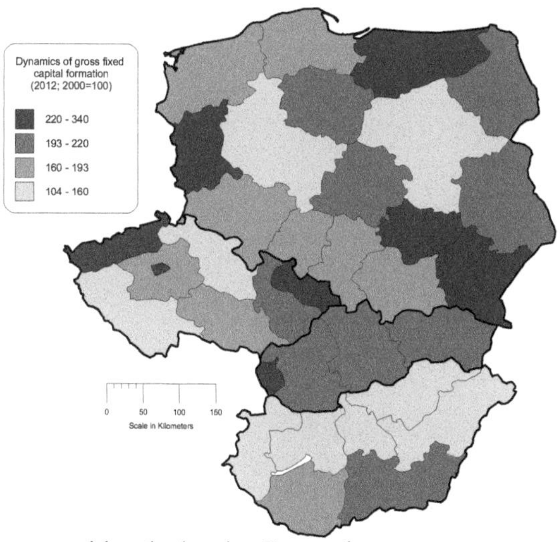

Source: own elaboration based on Eurostat data

Figure 9 Dynamics of gross fixed capital formation in the regions V4 in the years 2000-2012 (2000=100)

CONCLUSIONS AND RECOMMENDATIONS

The analysis points to the declining role of industry in the total employment in the V4 countries against other European countries, although the rate of decline of the participation of industry is much lower than in the countries of Western Europe. Still, the share of industry in employment is relatively high compared to other EU countries. In contrast, the shares of industry in gross value added are higher than in the case of employment, because of the increased importance of modern industries in the structure of GVA, generating high added value tax. Importantly, the regions with a high concentration of industry still include the capital regions of all the Visegrád countries and regions of the Moravian Silesia (Moravskoslezsko) in the Czech Republic as well as the Śląskie, Małopolskie and Łódzkie Voivodeships in Poland. Concentration of industry, therefore, refers to the pre-shaped areas of concentration (industrial districts).

It seems, therefore, that the traditional industrialised regions occurring in the area of the Visegrád countries, being subject to intense changes as a result of the increasing globalisation in terms of shaping the knowledge-based economy, should seek to strengthen the role of modern industries. Both employment and gross value added indicate that in the study area there are regions which have significant industrial potential, which is often the driving force behind their socio-economic development as a result of the occurrence of the multiplier effect. Conclusions from the analysis indicate the need for continued research on the changes of the regional economy in these countries because their development path differs from that of the regions of Western Europe. The results of the research can be used in the formulation of goals and objectives of regional policy in the V4 countries, in which a significant place should be taken by the goals related to industrial activities, the importance of which is still large in the economic structure.

REFERENCES

ABRAHAM, T. & ESE, T.W. 1999. Regional development in Central and Eastern Europe: Between transformation and integration. The example of Poland. Raumforschung und Raumordnung, 57(2-3), 83 – 95.

BALCEROWICZ, L 1995, Socialism, capitalism, transformation Central European University Press, Budapest.

BAŁTOWSKI, M 2002, Przekształcenia własnościowe przedsiębiorstw państwowych w Polsce (Ownership transformation of state enterprises in Poland), WN PWN, Warszawa.

BŁASZKIEWICZ, K 1994, 'Przeobrażenia strukturalne w przemyśle polskim' ('Structural changes in Polish industry'), Rzeszowskie Zeszyty Naukowe Prawo-Ekonomia, vol. 16, pp. 203-211.

BOŻYK, P 1999, 24 kraje Europy Środkowej i Wschodniej. Transformacja (24 countries of Central and Eastern Europe. Transformation), SGH, Warszawa.

CZAPLIŃSKI, P 2011, 'Funkcjonowanie przemysłu przetwórstwa rybnego w Polsce w okresie kryzysu gospodarczego' ('Functioning of the fish processing industry in the period of economic crisis'), Prace Komisji Geografii Przemysłu Polskiego Towarzystwa Geograficznego, no. 17, pp. 114-128

DOMAŃSKI, B 2003, 'Industrial change and foreign direct investment in the postsocialist economy: the case of Poland', European and Regional Studies, no. 10 (2), pp. 99-118.

DOMAŃSKI, B 2006, 'Polski przemysł na tle przemysłu Europy Środkowej i Wschodniej' ('Polish industry against that of Central and Eastern Europe'), Prace Komisji Geografii Przemysłu Polskiego Towarzystwa Geograficznego, no 8, pp. 27-36.

DOLOREUX, D & PARTO, S 2005, 'Regional innovation systems: Current discourse and unresolved issues', Technology in Society, vol.27, issue: 2, pp. 133-153

GIERAŃCZYK, W 2003, 'Wybrane aspekty konkurencyjności polskiego przemysłu w dobie globalnych wyzwań rozwoju' ('Selected aspects of competitiveness of Polish industry in the age of global development challenges'), Prace Komisji Geografii Przemysłu Polskiego Towarzystwa Geograficznego, no. 6, pp.77-86.

GIERAŃCZYK, W 2009, 'Przemysł zaawansowanej technologii a konkurencyjność przemysłowa krajów UE' ('High-tech industry and the industrial competitiveness of the EU states'), [w:] Zioło Z & Borowiec M (eds), Problematyka XXV Międzynarodowej Konferencji Naukowej nt. Procesy transformacji przemysłu i usług w regionalnych i krajowych układach przestrzennych, pp. 36-37.

GIERAŃCZYK, W 2010, 'Development of High Technologies as an Indicator of Modern Industry in the EU', Bulletin of Geography. Socio-economic Series, no. 14, pp. 23-35.

GIERAŃCZYK, W & RACHWAŁ, T 2012, 'Structural changes in the industry of Poland against the background of eastern European Union states', Quaestiones Geographicae, no. 31(2), pp. 83–93.

GOLEJEWSKA, A 2012, 'Innowacyjność a konkurencyjność regionalna krajów Grupy Wyszehradzkiej w latach 1999–2008' ('Innovation and regional competitiveness in the Visegrad Group, 1999–2008'). Prace Komisji Geografii Przemysłu Polskiego Towarzystwa Geograficznego, no. 19, pp. 93-115.

GOLEJEWSKA, A 2013, 'Competitiveness, Innovation and Regional Development. The Case of the Visegrad Group Countries', Gospodarka Narodowa, no. 7-8, pp. 87-112.

JAKÓBIK, W 1993, Restrukturyzacja przemysłu w okresie transformacji (The restructuring of industry during the transition period), Friedrich Ebert Stiftung, Warszawa.

KARPIŃSKA-MIZIELIŃSKA, W & SMUGA, T 1995, 'Proces przekształceń własnościowych w Polsce – próba oceny' ('The process of privatization in Poland - an attempt to assess'), Raporty Instytut Rozwoju i Studiów Strategicznych, no. 41, pp. 189-205.

KARPIŃSKI, A 2008, Przemiany strukturalne w procesie transformacji Polski 1989-2003-2025 (Structural changes in the Polish transformation process 1989-2003-2025, SGH, Warszawa.

KILAR, W 2008, 'Zatrudnienie w działalności badawczej i rozwojowej jako czynnik rozwoju gospodarki opartej o wiedzę' ('Employment in research and development as a factor influencing the growth of knowledge-based economy'), Przedsiębiorczość – Edukacja, no. 4, pp. 60-69.

KILAR, W 2010, 'Zmiany potencjału korporacji informatycznych w Unii Europejskiej w latach 2004–2008' ('Changes in the potential of IT corporations in the European Union: years 2004–2008'), Przedsiębiorczość-Edukacja, no. 6, pp. 49-66.

KOŁODKO, G 2000, From Shock to Therapy: The Political Economy of Postsocialist Transformation, Oxford University Press, Oxford and New York.

KORNAI, J 1997, Struggle and Hope: Essays on Stabilization and Reform in a Postsocialist Economy, Edward Elgar, Cheltenham.

KOŹMIŃSKI, AK 1998, Odrabianie zaległości. Zmiany w organizacji i zarządzania w byłym bloku socjalistycznym (Catching up. Organizational and management change in the ex-socialist block), WN PWN, Warszawa.

LIZAK, P 2009, 'Kształtowanie się przemysłu samochodów osobowych w krajach Europy Środkowej w latach 1997–2007' ('Development of the automotive industry in the Central European countries in years 1997–2007'). Prace Komisji Geografii Przemysłu Polskiego Towarzystwa Geograficznego, no. 14, pp. 50-56.

LÓPEZ-BAZO, E & VAYÁ, E & MORA, AJ & SURIÑACH, J 1999, 'Regional economic dynamics and convergence in the European Union', The Annals of Regional Science, vol. 33, issue: 3, pp. 343-370.

LUX, G 2010, 'Location differences of services and industry: A Central European dichotomy', Prace Komisji Geografii Przemysłu Polskiego Towarzystwa Geograficznego, no. 16, pp. 29-37.

ŁUKAWER, E 1994a, 'Transformacja systemowa w Polsce w oczach ekonomistów, cz. I' ('Systemic transformation in Poland in the eyes of economists. Part 1'), Gospodarka Narodowa, no. 1 (48), pp. 18-23.

ŁUKAWER, E 1994b, 'Transformacja systemowa w Polsce w oczach ekonomistów, cz. II' ('Systemic transformation in Poland in the eyes of economists. Part 2'), Gospodarka Narodowa, no. 2 (49), pp. 17-21.

MACIAS, J 2006, 'Structural Changes in Polish Industry', Ekonomika i Organizacja Przedsiębiorstwa, no. 7 (678), pp. 25-32.

MALISIEWICZ, E & ZIOŁO, Z 1994, 'Zarys procesów restrukturyzacji przemysłu w województwie rzeszowskim' ('The outline of the processes of industrial restructuring in the rzeszowskie voivodship), [in:] Zioło Z (ed), Zachowania przestrzenne przemysłu w zmieniających się warunkach gospodarowania, COMSN, Komisja Geografii Przemysłu PTG, Kraków-Warszawa, pp. 126-131.

MARSZAŁ, T 1993, 'Some remarks on the Polish textile and clothing industries – prospects and policy recommendations', Problems in Textile Geography, no. 7, pp. 33-50.

MIKOŁAJEWICZ, Z 1995, 'Procesy restrukturyzacji przemysłu w regionach' ('The processes of industrial restructuring in the regions'), Studia i monografie Uniwersytetu Opolskiego, nr 222, Opole.

MISZTAL, S 1993, 'Regionalne zróżnicowanie procesu prywatyzacji przemysłu w Polsce' ('Regional differentiation of the privatization process of the industry in Poland'), Przegląd Geograficzny, vol. LXV, no. 3-4, pp.255-277.

MISZTAL, S 2000, 'Regionalne efekty procesu prywatyzacji przemysłu w Polsce w latach 1989-1995' ('Regional effects of the privatization of the industry in the years 1989-1995'), Prace Komisji Geografii Przemysłu Polskiego Towarzystwa Geograficznego, no. 1, pp. 23-34.

MISZTAL, S 2003, 'Transformacja własnościowa działalności przemysłowej w Polsce według województw' (The ownership transformation of industrial activity in Poland by voivodship'), Prace Komisji Geografii Przemysłu Polskiego Towarzystwa Geograficznego, no. 5, pp. 9-30.

MROZIŃSKA, A 2013, 'Zmiany strukturalne w przemyśle przetwórczym według województw w latach 1999–2010' (The structural changes in the manufacturing by voivodeship in the years 1999–2010), Prace Komisji Geografii Przemysłu Polskiego Towarzystwa Geograficznego, no. 21, pp. 157-172.

OORT, FG & BOSMA, NS 2013, 'Agglomeration economies, inventors and entrepreneurs as engines of European regional economic development', The Annals of Regional Science, vol. 51, issue: 1, pp. 213 – 244.

PAKUŁA, L 1992, 'Postępy restrukturyzacji przemysłu w wybranych gałęziach przemysłu w okręgach Górnośląskim, Częstochowskim i Bielskim' (Advances in industrial restructuring in some industrial branches in the districts of Upper Silesia, Częstochowa and Bielsko', Folia Geographica, Series Geographica-Oeconomica, vol. XXIV, pp. 37-49.

PAKUŁA, L 2003, 'Tendencje restrukturyzacji przemysłu Górnośląskiego Okręgu Przemysłowego w dobie transformacji' ('Trends in industrial restructuring of Upper Silesian Industrial District in the era of transformation'), Prace Komisji Geografii Przemysłu Polskiego Towarzystwa Geograficznego, no. 6, pp. 59-66.

PARYSEK, JJ 1998, 'Efekty procesu transformacji społeczno-gospodarczej w Polsce. Bilans okresu 1989-1996' ('The effects of the socio-economic transformation process in Poland. The balance of the period 1989-1996'), [in:] Parysek, JJ & Rogacki H (eds), Przemiany społeczno-gospodarcze Polski lat dziewięćdziesiątych, Bogucki Wydawnictwo Naukowe, Poznań, pp. 25-45.

PASZKOWSKI, M 1996, Zmiany strukturalne przemysłu. Metody badania i tendencje światowe a transformacje w krajach Europy Środkowo-Wschodniej (Structural changes in the industry. Research methods and global trends and transformations in the countries of Central and Eastern Europe), Wyd. UJ, Kraków.

PEŁKA, B 1994, Restrukturyzacja przedsiębiorstwa przemysłowego, cz. I i II (The restructuring of industrial company. Part 1 & 2), Instytut Organizacji i Zarządzania w Przemyśle „Orgmasz", Warszawa.

PIRAS, G & POSTIGLIONE, P & AROCA, P 2012, 'Specialization, R&D and productivity growth: evidence from EU regions', The Annals of Regional Science, vol. 49, issue: 1, pp. 35 – 51.

RACHWAŁ, T 2002, 'Proces restrukturyzacji przedsiębiorstw przemysłowych Polski Południowo-Wschodniej (na wybranych przykładach)' ('The process of industrial enterprises restructuring in south-east Poland (based on selected examples)'), Prace Komisji Geografii Przemysłu Polskiego Towarzystwa Geograficznego, no. 4, pp. 79-88.

RACHWAŁ, T 2006a, 'Efekty restrukturyzacji wybranych przedsiębiorstw przemysłowych Polski Południowo-Wschodniej' (Effects of industrial enterprises restructuring in south-east Poland), Prace Komisji Geografii Przemysłu Polskiego Towarzystwa Geograficznego, no. 9, pp. 98-115.

RACHWAŁ, T 2006b, 'Restrukturyzacja technologiczna przedsiębiorstw przemysłowych Polski Południowo-Wschodniej jako czynnik podnoszenia ich konkurencyjności na rynku międzynarodowym' ('Technological restructuring of industrial enterprises in south-east Poland as a factor improving their competitiveness on the international market'), Prace Komisji Geografii Przemysłu Polskiego Towarzystwa Geograficznego, no. 8, pp. 192-203.

RACHWAŁ, T 2007, 'Zmiany powiązań przestrzennych przedsiębiorstw przemysłowych Polski Południowo-Wschodniej w latach transformacji systemu gospodarowania' ('Changes in spatial links of industrial enterprises of south-east Poland in the transformation of economic system'), [in:] Lach, J & Borowiec, M & Rachwał, T, Procesy transformacji społeczno-ekonomicznych i przyrodniczych struktur przestrzennych, Wydawnictwo Naukowe, Kraków, pp. 325-351.

RACHWAŁ, T 2008, 'Problematyka badawcza funkcjonowania przedsiębiorstw przemysłowych' ('Research problems concerning the operation of industrial enterprises'), Prace Komisji Geografii Przemysłu Polskiego Towarzystwa Geograficznego, no. 11, pp. 53-85.

RACHWAŁ, T 2009, 'Changes of Industry in the Countries of Central and Eastern Europe Under Conditions of Economic Transformation and European Integration', Geopolitical Studies, vol. 15, pp. 133-164.

RACHWAŁ, T 2010a, 'Problematyka badawcza zmian powiązań przestrzennych przedsiębiorstw przemysłowych' ('Research problems concerning the changes in spatial links of industrial enterprises'), Studia i Prace Uniwersytetu Ekonomicznego w Krakowie, no. 8, Kraków, pp.157-176.

RACHWAŁ, T 2010b, 'Struktura przestrzenna i działowa przemysłu Polski na tle Unii Europejskiej w dwudziestolecie rozpoczęcia procesów transformacji systemowej' (Spatial and division structure of Polish industry against the European Union in the twentieth anniversary of the start of the transformation processes'), Prace Komisji Geografii Przemysłu Polskiego Towarzystwa Geograficznego, no. 16, pp. 105-124.

RACHWAŁ, T 2011a, 'Transformations of the Employment Structure as an Expression of the Transformation of Polish Industry Against the Background of the European Union', Bulletin of Geography. Socio-economic Series, no. 15 / 2011, pp. 5-25.

RACHWAŁ, T 2011b, 'Wpływ kryzysu na zmiany produkcji przemysłowej w Polsce' ('The impact of crisis on changes in industrial production in Poland'), Prace Komisji Geografii Przemysłu Polskiego Towarzystwa Geograficznego, no. 17, pp. 99-113.

RACHWAŁ, T 2013, 'Rola przedsiębiorstw przemysłowych w rozwoju gospodarki opartej na wiedzy' (The role of industrial enterprises in the development of the knowledge-based economy'), Prace Komisji Geografii Przemysłu Polskiego Towarzystwa Geograficznego, no. 21, pp. 189-211.

RACHWAŁ, T & BOGUŚ, M 2012, 'The Competitiveness of Industrial Enterprises in European Union Countries' [in:] Krstić, B & Chodyński, A (eds.), Current problems of Competitiveness Improvement in National Economies and Enterprises, Faculty of Economics, University of Niš, Serbia, Niš, pp. 133-156

RACHWAŁ, T, WIEDERMANN, K & KILAR, W 2008a, 'Wydajność i koszty pracy jako czynniki konkurencyjności przemysłu regionów Polski w Unii Europejskiej w ujęciu regionalnym' ('Productivity and labour costs as competitiveness factors of the Polish regions in the European Union in a regional approach'), Rozprawy Naukowe Instytutu Geografii i Rozwoju Regionalnego Uniwersytetu Wrocławskiego, no. 3, pp. 79-89.

RACHWAŁ, T & WIEDERMANN, K & KILAR, W 2008b, 'Zmiany potencjału przemysłowego województw Polski wschodniej na tle regionów Unii Europejskiej' (Changes in the industrial potential of eastern Poland voivodships against the regions of the European Union'), [w:] Fedan R., Makieła Z. (red.), Przyrodniczo-ekonomiczny potencjał regionów na pograniczu polsko-ukraińskim, PWSZ w Jarosławiu, Stowarzyszenie Instytut Polsko-Ukraiński, Jarosław, pp. 287-306.

RACHWAŁ, T & WIEDERMANN, K & KILAR, W 2009, 'Rola przemysłu w gospodarce układów regionalnych Unii Europejskiej' ('The role of industry in the economies of the European Union regional systems'), Prace Komisji Geografii Przemysłu Polskiego Towarzystwa Geograficznego, no. 14, pp. 31-42.

ROCHNOWSKI, H 2001, 'Zmiany strukturalne w przemyśle Polski w procesie integracji z Unią Europejską' ('Structural changes in the Polish industry in the process of integration with the European Union'), [in:] Rajman J (ed), Polska – Europa. Gospodarka, przemysł, Wydawnictwo Naukowe AP, Kraków, pp. 87-108.

ROSATI, DK 1998, Polska droga do rynku ('Polish path to the market'), PWE, Warszawa.

Rydz, E & Jażewicz, I 2001, 'Przemiany strukturalne przemysłu na przykładzie małych miast Pomorza Środkowego' ('Structural changes in the industry on the example of the small towns of the Central Pomerania'), Prace Komisji Geografii Przemysłu Polskiego Towarzystwa Geograficznego, no. 3, pp. 71-86.

RYDZ, E & SZYMAŃSKA, W 2002, 'Funkcjonowanie zakładów przemysłu obuwniczego regionu słupskiego w zmieniających się warunkach gospodarowania' (The functioning of the footwear industry plants in the Słupsk region in changing economic conditions', Prace Komisji Geografii Przemysłu Polskiego Towarzystwa Geograficznego, no. 4, pp. 43-56.

SUDOŁ, S & KARASZEWSKI, W (eds.), 1996, Proces transformacji rynkowej przedsiębiorstw (w świetle badań empirycznych) (The process of market transformation of enterprises (in the light of empirical research)), Wyd. UMK, Toruń.

STRYJAKIEWICZ, T 1999, Adaptacja przestrzenna przemysłu w Polsce w warunkach transformacji (The spatial adaptation of industry in Poland in the conditions of a transformation). Wydawnictwo Naukowe UAM, Poznań.

ŚWIADEK, A 2006, 'Przestrzeń a innowacyjność przemysłu w polskich regionach' (Area and innovative industry in the Polish regions', Przegląd Organizacji, no. 12, pp. 18-21.

TKOCZ, M 2001, Restrukturyzacja przemysłu regionu tradycyjnego (The restructuring of industry of the traditional region, Wydawnictwo Uniwersytetu Śląskiego, Katowice.

TKOCZ, M 2006, 'Efekty restrukturyzacji górnictwa węgla kamiennego w Polsce' ('The effects of the coal mining restructuring in Poland'), Prace Komisji Geografii Przemysłu Polskiego Towarzystwa Geograficznego, no. 9, pp. 28-39.

VISHNEVSKY, V, ALEKSANDROV, I & POLOVYAN, A 2011, 'Scenarios of the old industrial regions' development: selecting the methodology', Environment, Development and Sustainability, vol. 13, issue: 1, pp. 65 – 78.

WIEDERMANN, K 2002, 'Restrukturyzacja i modernizacja hutnictwa żelaza GOP po 1989 r.' ('Restructuring and modernization of the steel industry of Upper Silesian Industrial District after 1989'), Prace Komisji Geografii Przemysłu Polskiego Towarzystwa Geograficznego, no. 4, pp. 115-128.

WÓJTOWICZ, M & RACHWAŁ, T 2014, 'Globalization and new centers of automotive manufacturing – the case of Brazil, Mexico, and Central Europe', Prace Komisji Geografii Przemysłu Polskiego Towarzystwa Geograficznego , no. 25 (in print).

ZIOŁO, Z 2009, 'Rola przemysłu w procesie kształtowania społeczeństwa informacyjnego' ('Role of industry in the formation of an information society'), Prace Komisji Geografii Przemysłu Polskiego Towarzystwa Geograficznego, no. 13, pp. 11-20.

14

Technological Market Conjuncture: Risk Assessment Commercialization of Intellectual Property

ALEKSANDRA KOSENKO, Ph.D.
ASSOCIATE PROFESSOR

PETRO PERERVA, Ph.D.
UNIVERSITY PROFESSOR

e-mail: a.kosenko@rambler.ru

SUMMARY

This paper deals with the determination of the risk assessment process in market conditions using the method of paired comparisons. The most important factors influencing the level of market appeal of intelligent technology are defined and stipulated. Recommendations are made for reducing the impact of risk factors in course of the commercialization of intellectual property.

Keywords: market conditions, risk, market technology, intellectual property, paired comparison

INTRODUCTION

Intellectual property has become one of the most important resources in the 21st century. Companies are increasingly becoming aware of the importance of intellectual property (IP) assets nowadays, as a means to expand their business, to raise capital and to provide financial gain (European IPR Helpdesk, 2012). Just like financial capital or commodities or labor, IP is more than an economic asset – it also forms the basis of a global market. Since 2010, the number and scale of patent and intellectual property transactions worldwide has increased a great deal. Deals such as the Nortel patent sale (US$ 4.5 billion), and Google's acquisition of Motorola Mobility for its patent portfolio (US$ 12.5 billion) have propelled the pure intellectual property market into the spotlight (EverEdgeIP, 2014). However, this market is not just for technology giants — given the right advice, small and medium enterprises can participate and profit as well. We frequently encounter the "Rembrandt in the attic" phenomenon, where local companies were previously unaware of hidden intellectual property related value on their balance sheets.

Commercialization is the process of bringing intellectual property (IP) to the market in order for it to be exploited in return of business profits and growth. Commercialization is the end goal of the innovation process — it is the stage at which the strongest innovations, having been carefully selected, assessed and managed, are converted into commercial value.

In the market of intellectual property there are three key models of commercialization: sale, license, and manufacture & distribution (Figure 1). Risks should also be counted for in any IP commercialization. Although the very nature of risks will depend on the type of commercialization and its arrangement, their preventive identification, assessment and management would give organizations a lower exposure to risks (Fact sheet, 2013).

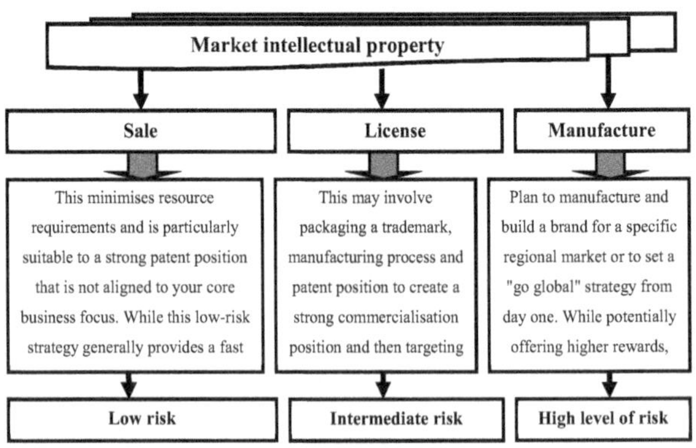

Figure 1 The risk level of market commercialization of intellectual property

Any entrepreneur should then make a start to identify and monitor the IP assets owned and used for their proper accounting, to assess risks, to overcome problems and to assess their commercial value in order to use them strategically and increase the company's revenues.

Recent studies show that a significant number of factors used in assessing the technological conditions of the market (demand, supply, price, quality, effect, etc.) are probabilistic in nature and ultimately lead to uncertainty and lack of validity of the calculated results.

In our opinion, the results of these kinds of indexes need to ensure an appropriate methodological evaluation of the results, the level of which is consistent with the risk assessment calculations based on the full group of disparate phenomena. The lower the level of risk assessment in market conditions, the greater the accuracy of the calculations of the commercial potential of intellectual property, and the better the transfer process will proceed without any problems.

Description and Method of Formation of the Factors of Risk

Quantifying the probability of risk is difficult; the results of the calculations are based on calculations of the frequency of display of certain phenomena, i.e. the presence of certain statistics. Statistical calculations should be considered more objective, since they are based on objective (actual) data. However, their use is difficult for several reasons:

- such data are not always available; in most cases they simply cannot be obtained;
- statistics do not account for sudden changes in market conditions;
- they do not include all elements of the formation of market conditions, as some of them are not quantifiable measurements.
- In such circumstances, the theory and practice of risk assessment recommends the use of expert (subjective, heuristic) methods, which are devoid of the above deficiencies. They are oriented to the average estimates of some experts about the level of opportunistic risk (Kucherenko 2005). We consider it appropriate to study the level of risk of market conditions consisting intellectual property using heuristic methods, including the method of paired comparisons. This is the method adapted by Gerasymchuk & Koschiy (2009) and Kobeleva & Pererva (2012) to market conditions, to evaluate the risk of market operation under limited statistics and te performance of a number of factors that are difficult to measure (Golubkov 2000; Machine 2003).

Method

To assess the risk of opportunistic functioning in the technology market and the electrical industry, according to recommendations in the literature (Gerasymchuk & Koschiy 2009; Kobeleva & Perera 2012), the authors carried out interviews with a group of experts (leading specialists of JSC "Ukrelectromash", JSC "Electric machine", JSC "Electric motor"), who were asked a specific set of factors that are media market risks (see Table 1).

Table 1

Factory risks in the Ukrainian market for electrical engineering technology

Code	Factors	Notes
F1	Deterioration nation-Ukrainian market	Activities of all kinds of markets are closely linked
F2	Disadvantageous legal support for market processes in Ukraine	Transparency and consistency of commercial law
F3	The emergence of shortages of electricity for industrial needs	No electricity in electrical engineering IP does not make sense
F4	The emergence of alternative intellectual technologies (reducing market size)	This is one of the integral risk factors
F5	Increasing the share of imports in the technological market of Ukraine	Imports replacing Ukrainian developers
F6	Increased political instability in Ukraine	Political risks directly affect the economy
F7	Decrease in the intellectual development of domestic production	Quality is an important situational factor
F8	Increased fiscal pressures on the state of the IP	There may be unintended consequences
F9	The complexities of software production using IP	Leads to a reduction of production
F10	Changing target consumers for imported technologies	Leads to a change in market structure in favor of imports
F11	Rising cost of developing Ukrainian real IP	Leads to increased prices and reduced sales
F12	Turmoil in the banking sector (difficulty getting loans)	Difficulties in producing and distributing
F13	Decrease in exports of Ukrainian intellectual technologies	Increased supply in the domestic market
F14	The absence or reduction of state support for innovation activities	Difficulties in innovation policy
F15	Worsening job market mechanisms for production and marketing of innovative products	Leads to a deterioration in market conditions
F16	Unfair trading partners	Leads to frustration in themarket

The experts were asked to identify the importance of risk factors in terms of their impact on the deterioration of the technological market (Gerasymchuk & Koschiy 2009; Kobeleva & Perera 2012). Procedure of the examination is based on the method of pairwise comparison factors. They are compared with each other in pairs, in which each subsequent assessment is not related to the previous one. These paired scores form the matrix of paired preferences, and special treatment provides numerical indices for priority setting objectives for a particular company.

The responses of the experts were processed, grouped and presented in a table of benefits (Table 2). Evaluation of experts was carried out using a table of criteria, the construction of which was performed by the following algorithm. When comparing the two risk factors expert at their intersection (the intersection of the column and rows) exhibited one of three predefined ratings (Kobeleva & Perera 2012; Nikitin 2011; Machine 2003):

➢ grade "1.0" if the factor specified in column had, in his opinion, a greater degree of risk (priority column);
➢ grade "0.0" if the factor specified in column had, in his opinion, a lower level of risk (priority tape);
➢ grade "0.5" if the factor specified in column had, in his opinion, the same level of risk (equivalent risk factors).

Responses from all 16 experts are listed in Table 2, which presents the final results of the first stage examination of the importance of risk factors. In forming Table 2 estimates put each expert disposed.

Analysis of Expert Assessments

Analysis of the results allows us to draw several important conclusions. First, Ukrainian developers of intelligent technologies do not care much about opportunities for financial assistance from the state to support their business. Factor F14 "The absence or reduction of state support for innovation" has been identified by experts as the least risky (Table 2). In our opinion, this is due to lack of such support from the government over the years and the practical adaptation of IP to the situation.

Experts explain the minimal attention to the risk of opportunistic factor F16 "unfair trading partners" by the presence of elements of chaos and lack of signs of a civilized market. The same explanation can be used for factor F15 "Worsening job market mechanisms for the production and marketing of innovative products" (rated 11th) and factor F8 "Strengthening the fiscal pressure on the state of IP" (rated 13th). The low ranking factor F12 "turmoil in the banking sector (difficulty getting loans)", in our opinion, can be explained by the passage of local IP over obstacles of the global financial crisis and the entry in this field specific immunity. Getting credit loans was a challenge for Ukrainian innovative enterprises at the best of times. High grade Ukrainian scientific developments in the domestic market that do not generate a critical state process reduce exports of these products (factor F 13). Ukrainian science in electrical engineering still has an ample supply of technological possibilities for innovation of production.

Table 2

Expert assessments of the risk factors of technological Ukrainian market conditions (market IP)

Call risk factor	Call risk factor																Total	Rank
	F1	F2	F3	F4	F5	F6	F7	F8	F9	F10	F11	F12	F13	F14	F15	F16		
F1	X	10.0	7.5	3.5	7.0	12.5	6.5	12.5	11.5	10.0	8.0	13.0	14.5	15.0	11.0	15.5	158.0	5
F2	6.0	X	3.5	5.0	7.5	10.5	4.0	11.5	9.5	7.0	9.5	11.5	12.0	14.0	11.5	14.5	137.5	6
F3	8.5	12.5	X	7.0	9.5	12.0	9.0	14.0	11.5	10.5	10.0	14.0	14.0	15.0	12.0	14.5	174.0	2
F4	12.5	11	9.0	X	10.5	15.0	9.5	15.0	13.0	12.5	13.0	14.5	15.0	16.0	14.5	15.5	196.5	1
F5	9.0	8.5	6.5	5.5	X	10.0	7.0	12.5	12.0	11.0	9.5	11.5	12.5	15.0	13.5	15.5	158.5	4
F6	3.5	5.5	4.0	1.0	6.0	X	3.5	9.5	8.0	7.5	5.5	8.5	10.0	13.5	8.5	14.0	113.5	10
F7	9.5	12.0	7.0	6.5	9.0	12.5	X	12.5	12.0	11.0	10.5	13.0	13.5	14.5	12.0	15.0	161.5	3
F8	3.5	4.5	2.0	1.0	3.5	6.5	3.5	X	5.5	2.5	6.5	7.5	8.0	12.5	6.0	13.5	89.5	13
F9	4.5	6.5	4.5	3.0	4.0	8.0	4.0	10.5	X	8.0	8.5	9.5	10.5	15.0	12.5	14.0	123.0	9
F10	6.0	9.0	5.5	3.5	5.0	8.5	5.0	13.5	8.0	X	7.5	10.0	10.5	15.5	8.0	14.5	132.0	8
F11	8.0	6.5	6.0	3.0	6.5	10.5	5.5	9.5	7.5	8.5	X	9.5	11.5	15.0	12.5	13.5	133.5	7
F12	3.0	4.5	2.0	1.5	4.5	7.5	3.0	8.5	6.5	6.0	6.5	X	8.0	14.5	7.0	13.0	96.0	12
F13	1.5	4.0	2.0	1.0	3.5	6.0	2.5	8.0	5.5	5.5	4.5	8.0	X	9.0	7.0	10.5	78.5	14
F14	1.0	2.0	1.0	0.0	1.0	2.5	1.5	0.5	1.0	3.5	1.0	1.5	6.0	X	1.5	6.5	30.5	16
F15	5.0	4.5	4.0	1.5	2.5	7.5	4.0	10.0	3.5	6.0	3.5	9.0	9.0	14.5	X	14.0	98.5	11
F16	0.5	1.5	1.5	0.5	0.5	2.0	1.0	2.5	2.0	1.5	2.5	3.0	5.5	9.5	2.0	X	36.0	15

Using data from Table 2 the 10 most important risk factors of technological Ukrainian market conditions were identified: F4, F3, F7, F5, F1, F 2, F 11, F 10, F9 and F6. However, the data in Table 2 can establish only rank risk factor conditions; they do not allow us to set the "weight" factor in the creation of one or another market conditions. The theory and practice of paired comparisons to simplify the calculations weighting factors in tabular form recommend swapping columns and rows in Table 2 (Belyaevsky 2007). As a result of these actions an enhanced opportunistic risk factor table can be obtained (Table 3).

Table 3

Improved table reviewing the most important factors of the technological risk opportunistic market

Call risk factor	Call risk factor									
	F1	F2	F3	F4	F5	F6	F7	F9	F10	F11
F1	X	6.0	8.5	12.5	9.0	3.5	9.5	4.5	6.0	8.0
F2	10.0	X	12.5	11.0	8.5	5.5	12.0	6.5	9.0	6.5
F3	7.5	3.5	X	9.0	6.5	4.0	7.0	4.5	5.5	6.0
F4	3.5	5.0	7.0	X	5.5	1.0	6.5	3.0	3.5	3.0
F5	7.0	7.5	9.5	10.5	X	6.0	9.0	4.0	5.0	6.5
F6	12.5	10.5	12.0	15.0	10.0	X	12.5	8.0	8.5	10.5
F7	6.5	4.0	9.0	9.5	7.0	3.5	X	4.0	5.0	5.5
F9	11.5	9.5	11.5	13.0	12.0	8.0	12.0	X	8.0	7.5
F10	10.0	7.0	10.5	12.5	11.0	7.5	11.0	8.0	X	8.5
F11	8.0	9.5	10.0	13.0	9.5	5.5	10.5	8.5	7.5	X

In order to establish the weight of the highest rated risk factors of the opportunistic technological market, we assume that the factor obeys the normal law of distribution (Kucherenko 2008; Obolentseva 2010), and thus the number of experts who consider a certain factor more risky, in their opinion, and give it a higher (or lower) risk factor should be taken into account. Based on this premise, it is possible, knowing the appropriate proportion of experts, to establish the relative importance (preference) Factor *i* to factor *j*.

Determination of the Most Significant Risk Factors

According to the enhanced opportunistic risk factor table (Table 3) we find the benefits of HIV symptoms (factor) *i* on criterion (factor) *j*. Thus, we look at the total points received by each factor in a pairwise comparison of the 16 experts. This means that the maximum score that could get the most important risk factor is 16 (one of the experts in this factor compared to the other would give an advantage to it). In this case, the proportion of cases benefits would be equal to unity (16 : 16) = 1, where there is full agreement of expert opinion as to the advantages of this opportunistic risk factor over another. The results of the calculations are summarized in Table. 4.

In a mathematical model that underlies the scale by the method of paired comparisons, it is assumed that the number of cases is subject to the normal distribution law and is described by the Laplace integral function $F(Q_{ij})$:

$$F(Q_{ij}) = \frac{1}{\sqrt{2\pi}} \int_{-\infty}^{Q_{ij}} e^{-\frac{Q_{ij}^2}{2}} dQ, \qquad (1)$$

where Qij is a random variable, which then determines the specific location of each trait and can be interpreted as a quantitative assessment of the relative advantages of variable (factor) *i* on criterion (factor) *j*; F(Qij) - the probability of favoring signs *i* and sign before *j*.

Table 4

Calculation of particle instances of expert preferences factor i and to factor j

Call risk factor	Call risk factor									
	F1	F2	F3	F4	F5	F6	F7	F9	F10	F11
F1	X	0.375	0.531	0.781	0.562	0.219	0.594	0.281	0.375	0.500
F2	0.625	X	0.781	0.687	0.531	0.344	0.75	0.405	0.562	0.405
F3	0.469	0.219	X	0.562	0.405	0.25	0.437	0.281	0.344	0.375
F4	0.219	0.312	0.437	X	0.344	0.062	0.405	0.187	0.219	0.187
F5	0.437	0.469	0.594	0.656	X	0.375	0.562	0.25	0.312	0.405
F6	0.781	0.656	0.75	0.937	0.625	X	0.781	0.500	0.531	0.656
F7	0.405	0.25	0.562	0.594	0.437	0.219	X	0.25	0.312	0.344
F9	0.719	0.594	0.719	0.812	0.75	0.500	0.75	X	0.500	0.469
F10	0.625	0.437	0.656	0.781	0.687	0.469	0.687	0.500	X	0.531
F11	0.500	0.594	0.625	0.812	0.594	0.344	0.656	0.531	0.469	X

In this case, the value of $F(Q_{ij})$ can be interpreted as the proportion of cases with a comparative advantage of one feature over another. Relative advantages and features to feature *j* can be determined from the tables of integral Laplace function (normal distribution functions normalized distribution). Table 5 allows you to find the value function of Laplace for the values of the argument, or, alternatively, by the values of the Laplace function you search for the value of the argument that will work in this case. This means that during this study we have to know the probability of occurrence (percentage of cases of preferences) we estimate the value of a random variable (numeric value of comparative advantage).

However, the feature table of the integral Laplace function is that it is built for argument values between 0 and Q_{ij}, and not for the range of values from $-\infty$ to Q_{ij}, as required by Equation (2). The table of values of the integral Laplace function can determine the value of Q_{ij} (relative advantage factor and to factor *j*), only in cases where the proportion of cases favoring factor and to factor *j* is greater than or equal to 0.5 ($F(Q_{ij}) \geq 0.5$). Positive values correspond to probabilities Q_{ij} $F(Q_{ij}) \geq 0.5$. Therefore, to find the probability of occurrence for negative values Q_{ij} when using this table based on the principle of symmetry ($Q_{ij} = -Q_{ij}$), take in the first table $F(Q_{ij})$ larger than 0.5, subtract the difference $[F(Q_{ij}) - 0.5]$, and then calculate the function in the table. The symmetrical number Q_{ij} has a negative sign and the same absolute value. Based on these provisions of the probability of occurrence for negative values Q_{ij} is based on the symmetry of the normal distribution (Feschur et al. 2009; Gerasimchuk & Koschiy 2009; Nikitin 2011):

$$F(-Q_{ij}) = 1 - F(Q_{ij}) \quad (2)$$

Using the table of Laplace integral function (Gerasymchuk & Koschiy 2009; Kobeleva & Perera 2012) and using Equation (2) will determine the numerical value of relative advantage. The calculation results are summarized in Table 5.

The next stage of calculation of weighting coefficients opportunistic risk factors is to convert the particular instances of the expert preferences factor and to factor *j* (Table 4) $F(Q_{ij})$ in the value of the argument Q_{ij} using Equation (3) and Table 5. The calculation results are given in Table 6, which is based on the asymmetric principle that is the accepted premise $Q_{ij} = -Q_{ij}$, and diagonally the table exhibited zero.

Table 5
Table (numeric) value of relative advantage, by using the integral function of the Laplace proportion of cases in Table 4

Probability of the benefits, $F(Q_{ij})$	The numerical value of the relative advantages, Q_{ij}	Probability of the benefits, $[1- F(Q_{ij})]$	The numerical value of the relative advantages, $-Q_{ij}$
0.500	0.00	0.500	0.00
0.531	0.08	0.469	-0.08
0.563	0.16	0.437	-0.16
0.594	0.24	0.405	-0.24
0.625	0.32	0.375	-0.32
0.656	0.41	0.344	-0.41
0.687	0.49	0.312	-0.49
0.719	0.58	0.281	-0.58
0.750	0.67	0.250	-0.67
0.781	0.78	0.219	-0.78
0.813	0.89	0.187	-0.89
0.875	1.15	0.125	-1.15
0.937	1.54	0.062	-1.54
0.9997	4.00	0.000	-4.00

Using the data of Table 6 is necessary to determine the significance of factors that affect the level of the situation of the Ukrainian market of intellectual property in the direction of deterioration. It has been proposed to solve this problem using selection criteria better option (Gerasymchuk & Koschiy 2009; Kobeleva & Perera 2012), which gives the most "weight" in the deterioration process as market factors, which will be the largest amount relative advantages provided by experts. The importance of other (already less important) factors is determined by a similar scenario.

Table 6
The value of the relative merits of factor i in front of factor j

Call risk factor	Call risk factor									
	F1	F2	F3	F4	F5	F6	F7	F9	F10	F11
F1	0	-0.32	0.08	0.78	0.16	-0.78	0.24	-0.58	-0.32	0.00
F2	0.32	0	0.78	0.49	0.08	-0.41	0.75	-0.24	0.16	-0.24
F3	-0.08	-0.78	0	0.16	-0.24	0.25	-0.16	-0.58	-0.41	-0.32
F4	-0.78	-0.49	-0.16	0	-0.41	-1.54	-0.24	-0.89	-0.78	-0.89
F5	-0.16	-0.08	0.24	0.41	0	-0.32	0.16	0.25	-0.49	-0.24
F6	0.78	0.41	0.75	1.54	0.32	0	0.78	0.00	0.08	0.41
F7	-0.24	0.25	0.16	0.24	-0.16	-0.78	0	0.25	-0.49	-0.41
F9	0.58	0.24	0.58	0.89	0.75	0.00	0.75	0	0.00	-0.08
F10	0.32	-0.16	0.41	0.78	0.49	-0.08	0.49	0.00	0	0.08
F11	0.00	0.24	0.32	0.89	0.24	-0.41	0.41	0.08	-0.08	0

The results of the corresponding calculations quantitative evaluation values of the factors in the deterioration of operating conditions of technological intellectual property market are presented in Table 7.

Table 7

Defining opportunistic risk factors of loss

Call risk factor	Call risk factor									
	F1	F2	F3	F4	F5	F6	F7	F9	F10	F11
F1	0	-0.32	0.08	0.78	0.16	-0.78	0.24	-0.58	-0.32	0.00
F2	0.32	0	0.78	0.49	0.08	-0.41	0.75	-0.24	0.16	-0.24
F3	-0.08	-0.78	0	0.16	-0.24	0.25	-0.16	-0.58	-0.41	-0.32
F4	-0.78	-0.49	-0.16	0	-0.41	-1.54	-0.24	-0.89	-0.78	-0.89
F5	-0.16	-0.08	0.24	0.41	0	-0.32	0.16	0.25	-0.49	-0.24
F6	0.78	0.41	0.75	1.54	0.32	0	0.78	0.00	0.08	0.41
F7	-0.24	0.25	0.16	0.24	-0.16	-0.78	0	0.25	-0.49	-0.41
F9	0.58	0.24	0.58	0.89	0.75	0.00	0.75	0	0.00	-0.08
F10	0.32	-0.16	0.41	0.78	0.49	-0.08	0.49	0.00	0	0.08
F11	0.00	0.24	0.32	0.89	0.24	-0.41	0.41	0.08	-0.08	0
$\sum F_{ij}$	0.74	-0.69	3.16	6.18	1.23	-4.07	3.18	-1.71	-2.33	-1.69
$\overline{F}_{ij} = \frac{\sum F_{ij}}{16}$	0.04	-0.04	0.19	0.38	0.07	-0.25	0.19	-0.10	-0.15	-0.10
$\overline{F}_{ij}^{mp} = \frac{\sum F_{ij}}{16} - (-0{,}25-1)$	1.29	1.21	1.44	1.63	1.32	1.0	1.44	1.15	1.10	1.15
$\sum \overline{F_{ij}^{mp}}$	12.73									
Нормування вагомості факторів кон'юнктурного ризику: $F_{ij}^{ваг} = \overline{F_{ij}^{mp}} \Big/ \sum \overline{F_{ij}^{mp}} = \overline{F_{ij}^{mp}} \Big/ 12{,}73$										
$F_i^{ваг}$	0.10	0.09	0.12	0.13	0.11	0.07	0.12	0.09	0.08	0.09

To calculate the weight of opportunistic risk factors in Table 7, the calculations of the arithmetic mean of the relative advantages was carried out, and then transformed to obtain only positive values and normalized (the sum of normalized values of weighting factors analyzed is equal to one).

The next action is a quantitative assessment of risk deterioration of the Ukrainian market of intellectual property generated by each of the above mentioned factors. The evaluation displayed was performed by the same expert group on a 10-point scale (10 points – the strongest impact factor on the deterioration of market conditions). Results of expert risk assessment by each factor are shown in Table 8.

Table 8

Expert assessment of the impact of situational factors on the deterioration of the conditions for the functioning of the Ukrainian market of intellectual property

Number of experts	Call risk factor									
	F1	F2	F3	F4	F5	F6	F7	F9	F10	F11
№1	4	5	5	6	5	4	6	3	6	5
№2	3	3	6	8	4	3	9	4	5	6
№3	5	4	8	5	6	5	6	3	7	7
№4	4	2	3	6	3	2	7	3	5	5
№5	3	5	4	9	5	5	9	4	6	6
№6	2	4	7	7	4	3	7	2	5	4
№7	1	2	5	5	7	4	5	5	8	8
№8	5	3	8	9	5	6	9	6	6	5
№9	4	5	3	8	4	4	8	4	6	8
№10	4	3	6	7	6	3	6	2	8	6
№11	3	4	4	9	4	2	8	3	9	4
№12	2	5	6	8	7	5	6	5	5	7
№13	5	6	8	6	5	3	8	3	7	5
№14	2	3	3	9	3	4	7	2	8	6
№15	3	5	5	7	6	5	7	5	5	8
№16	2	3	6	5	4	3	8	2	6	5
Total points	52	62	87	114	78	61	116	56	102	95
Mean score	3.25	3.87	5.43	7.12	4.87	3.81	7.25	3.50	6.37	5.93

Using data from Table 7 and 8 we have the opportunity to conduct a quantitative assessment of risk measures leading to a deterioration process of the market. For this purpose we use the following formula (Belyaevsky 2007):

$$O_{risk} = \sum_{i=1}^{i=n}(F_i^{risk} F_i^{imp}), \qquad (3)$$

where

Orisk - risk deterioration of the Ukrainian market of intellectual property;

F_i^{imp}- The weight of i factor opportunistic risk;

F_i^{risk}- The degree of opportunistic risk and expense, the i factor.

The corresponding calculations for determining the quantitative assessment of the risk of worsening market conditions are summarized in Table 9.

Table 9

Calculation of the quantitative evaluation of the risk of deterioration of the Ukrainian market of intellectual property

Code	What are the factors	F_i^{imp}	F_i^{risk}	$\Phi_i^{imp}\Phi_i^{risk}$
F1	Deterioration of Ukrainian market	0.10	3.25	0.325
F2	Disadvantages legal support market processes in Ukraine	0.09	3.87	0.348
F3	The emergence of shortages of electricity for industrial needs	0.12	5.43	0.652
F4	The emergence of alternative intellectual technologies (reducing market size)	0.13	7.12	0.926
F5	Increasing the share of imports in the technological market of Ukraine	0.11	4.87	0.536
F6	Increased political instability in Ukraine	0.07	3.81	0.267
F7	Decrease in the intellectual development of domestic production	0.12	7.25	0.870
F9	The complexities of software production using IP	0.09	3.50	0.315
F10	Changing your target consumers for imported technologies	0.08	6.37	0.510
F11	Rising cost of developing Ukrainian real IP	0.09	5.93	0.534
Total:		1.00		5.283

To evaluate the results obtained (Table 9) it necessary to make the criteria of interpretation of quantitative assessments of the risk of deterioration of the Ukrainian market of intellectual property. Based on the processing and completion of research proposals in this area (Belyaevsky 2007) appropriate recommendations were given, the use of which enables us to provide an economic interpretation of the quantitative results presented in Table 9. Suggestions in this regard are summarized in Table 10.

Table 10

Guidelines for assessing opportunistic risk

The value of an interval of Powers line		General description of the risk	Detailed description of the risk of worsening market conditions
beginning	end		
0	0.5	Missing risk	The market is under development. The level of competition is low. Technology dominates the preferences of consumers.
0.5	2.8	Minimal risk	The market is almost formed. A healthy level of competition. No specific threat of deterioration.
2.8	5.5	The risk increased	Market in the stage of commercial success. Threat of increased competition. Technology should be modernized or replaced by a more progressive approach.
5.5	7.5	Critical risk	Market in the early stages of decline. Threats of competition intensified. An urgent need to diversify the market and technological policy.
7.5	10.0	Unacceptable risk	The critical state of the market. The technology is not competitive. Need replacement technology or to change segment.

CONCLUSIONS

Estimation of the risk of opportunistic suggests that the domestic market of intellectual property in the field of electrical production is at high risk (5.283 points out of maximum 10) of deterioration in the conditions of its operation. The most important risk factors for conditions of the market are defined as follows: a decrease in the production of Ukrainian intellectual technologies and the emergence of alternative national scientific developments (reduction of market size).

REFERENCES

BELYAEVSKY, I.K. (Ed.)(2007). Statistics of market goods and services. Moscow: Finance and Statistics.

European IPR Helpdesk (2012). Fact sheet: IP due diligence: assessing value and risks of intangibles. Available at: http://www.iprhelpdesk.eu/sites/default/files/newsdocuments/IP_due_diligence_0.pdf

European IPR Helpdesk (2013). Fact sheet: Commercializing Intellectual Property: Joint Ventures, Available at: http://www.iprhelpdesk.eu/sites/default/files/newsdocuments/Commercialising_Intellectual_Property_Joint_Ventures_0.pdf

EverEdgeIP (2014). Transactions. Available at: http://everedgeip.com/transactions/

FESCHUR, R.V., BARVINSKYY, A.F. & KICHOR, V.P. (2009) Statistics. Lviv : "Intelligence-West".

GERASYMCHUK, Z.V. & KOSCHIY, O.V. (2009). Risk assessment of functioning domestic market for dairy products in Ukraine. Available at: http://194.44.242.244/portal/soc_gum/vcndtu/2009_38/7.htm

GOLUBKOV, E.P. (2000). Marketing research: theory, methodology and practice. Moscow: Fynpres, 2000.

KOBELEVA, T.O. & PERERVA, P.G. (2012). Determining the risk assessment of the situation of the domestic market asynchronous motors. Management and Marketing Innovation, 1, 79-88.

KUCHERENKO, V.R. (2005) Problems market research on markets for goods and services. Research publication. Odessa.

KUCHERENKO, V.R. (2008). Conditions of scientific and technical products / V.R.Kucherenko / / Investing in Ukrainian economy market conditions. - Odesca: Institute of Market Problems.

MACHINE, N.I. (2003). Economic risk and methods of measurement / N.I.Mashyna. - Kiev, 188 p.

NIKITIN, A.V. (2011). Marketing in Banks. Kiev: MBK.

OBOLENTSEVA, L.V. (2010) Opportunistic market research industry.

15

The Choice of the Public-Private Partnership Model to Address Social and Economic Development of the State in the Context of a Competitive Environment with Uncertainty and Risks

SERGEY MEKHOVICH, Ph.D.
PROFESSOR
e-mail: energotex_2004@mail.ru

ANASTASIIA KOLESNICHENKO
POST-GRADUATE STUDENT
e-mail: anasko86@inbox.ru

SUMMARY

This article discusses the growing importance of public-private partnership due to modern economic conditions and extensive privatization activity. The institute of public-private partnership provides mechanisms for redistribution of risk among the subjects of new market relations. This cooperation appeared as a result of the complex development process during the last two decades. Today it plays a significant role in problem solving concerning public infrastructure development.

Keywords: public-private partnership, the partnership model, partnership schemes, market relations, public-private partnership, risks.

INTRODUCTION

The privatization process has dramatically changed the structure of the national economy of Ukraine. As a result, a strong private sector has been created in the last 20 years. This has significantly affected both the internal and international economy. The private sector includes the largest machine-building, metallurgical, steel and chemical plants, fuel and energy complexes, transport and educational settings. Business owners have formed the new influential class. The functions of the state have been fundamentally changed. Constantly increasing tax burdens, unreasonable fiscal policy and illegal activity of representatives of the Prosecutor's office, investigative bodies, tax administrations and other state officials caused conflict between business and government. The budget deficit led to serious difficulty in industrial and social sphere. However, some representatives of small, medium and large businesses have achieved good results. They successfully participate in solving important national issues on mutually beneficial terms.

This cooperation is particularly important in case of discussing re-engineering issues based on innovation of the entire industrial sector. It goes without saying that it would be problematic to achieve strategic development objectives without constructive interaction and partnership of the private business and government institutions. If programs are focused only on the use of budgetary funds, they would not allow the authorities to perform large-scale projects aimed at improving the domestic manufacturing competitiveness.

PUBLIC-PRIVATE PARTNERSHIPS

The public-private partnership (PPP) is an internationally recognized cooperation which aims to solve such kinds of problems. Nowadays public-private partnerships (PPP) are growing in popularity all over the world. They allow the state government and municipal authorities to establish cooperation with the private sector in the matter of modernization and development of required infrastructure. Indeed, the Ukranian government is interested in expanding public-private cooperation. However, many countries still face difficulties in conducting negotiations, planning and formation of PPP. A good thing about countries with economies in transition is that they are trying to find the b ways and methods of overcoming their difficulties. Fortunately, the European Bank for Reconstruction and Development

(EBRD) is at the forefront of those who assist them in these issues.

The works of Bhavnani K. (2009), Cokins G. (2009), Zapatrina & Lebeda (2011), Pavlyuk K. (2010), Pyltyay (2011), Sharinger L. (2004), Tarash & Petrova (2012), Varnavsky V. (2011), Vilisov M. (2006), Cherevikov E. (2009) Wirick D. (2009), Zapatrina I. (2011) and other authors are devoted to development problems in different aspects of public-private partnerships. This form of relationship between the state and private sector is widely used in various activities of enterprises all over the world. Therefore, the importance of more profound study of this issue is constantly growing. The term "public private partnership" appeared in the early 1990s. It is associated with the British model of PPP. In 1992, the government of John Major announced the Private Finance Initiative (PFI) which represented a modernized State Property Management concept. The essence of the PFI is to provide the private sector with the opportunity to finance objects owned by the state (social-cultural and industrial infrastructure) according to public-private partnership agreements. This radical change in the UK state management system led to a significant transformation in the institutional environment as well as in the relationship between the state apparatus and private business.

Various PPP forms have become a typical feature of the modern mixed economy. They can be intensively used in different branches of production worldwide. The mixed economy combines the elements of market and team management. It tends to be an alternative form of management. In fact, a 100% market economy has never existed, although, England in the nineteenth century was close to such a kind of system. Nowadays in the USA the majority of decisions are made by the market; however, the role of government is not reduced. The government plays an important role in market conditions. The state authorities are responsible for decrees and regulations governing economic environment, health services, education, law enforcement, business and environmental pollution (Zudin A.Yu. 1999).

In modern understanding, partnership between the state and business is considered to be the crucial direction in the innovation of world economy development. It provides constructive relations between the state and business that are based on the set of advantages of the market and state regulatory mechanisms and management. The main task of the state is to ensure the public interest, not only to support business. The partnership between the state and business is important for solving social issues as well as for implementing socially-significant tasks and programs. The partnership is especially relevant in times of crisis, when the state becomes an organizer, regulator and customer of innovative transformations in accordance with economic and socio-political demands of the society.

Public-private partnership in the context of innovation environment should be focused on the formation of the necessary level of innovation activity. Besides, it has to ensure the balance of interests between participants of innovation and investment processes. The nature of these relations, methods and concrete forms can vary significantly depending on the level and peculiarities of national market development. Along with this, the state should never be free from the social features related to national interests. In its turn, business is always the source of the social wealth increment.

Numerous studies indicate the trend towards intensification of relations between the state and private business within modern economic globalization, when the money goes into the sphere of state property.

The institutional environment, which implies the partnership, tends to be one of the newest stages of partnership development. It appears in the period of liberalization and plays an important role in improving market structures and the economy in general. Unlike traditional relations, developing a partnership creates its base models of financing, ownership and management methods. The efficient use of traditionally consecutive principles of state governance is an essential factor in ensuring the effectiveness of innovation processes. In turn, private enterprise features quick response to market signals, the propensity for innovation, efficiency, and the ability to take risks.

As global practice shows, using the advantages of both forms of property is possible within various forms of public-private partnership. A rage of these forms makes it possible to keep the most important national objects in state ownership and devolve a part of the ownership rights on the private sector. In this case, the partnership of the state and business attracts additional capital (including foreign capital) to the public sector. Apart from that, the state reduces budget problems and shares the majority of the risks with the business sector. In turn, business gets the volume of work, certain state guarantees and support. The system combines the resources and potentials. This form is based on decreasing the direct state influence on economy, devolving functional competences on the private sector and improving the regulatory process. The state can be compared with an agency which realizes socially significant goods and services. The state can partly produce these goods by itself and at the same time attract the capacity and ability of the private sector. To put it briefly, business is invited to participate in state assets management in order to improve the quality of state projects implementation. "Public-private partnership is a specific, multidimensional form of interaction between the state and private sector in the economic sphere. Its basic feature is the balance of interests, rights and obligations of participants during its implementation." (Deryabina M. 2009, p. 122).

The Ukrainian energy market is a good example of PPP. It includes representatives of both the public and private sector. However, the relationship between participants of the energy market seems to be rather difficult today, especially if the issue concerns the balance of interests for different forms of ownership. Taking the characteristics of the energy system into consideration, the use of a contractual partnership model would be the most appropriate. Within the framework of the program of the energy market liberalization the conclusion of bilateral agreements is provided to all participants of the energy market in order to reduce uncertainty and risks. Over the last years constant work on establishing the conditions and rules is being conducted. This can help to reduce the risks since the first stage of the new energy market, particularly during the conclusion of bilateral agreements, for both state ownership and other participants of private property market.

Nowadays the most active partnership of state and business is carried out in branches of production infrastructure: power engineering, railway transport, ports, airports, main gas transportation, communal services and other branches associated with the support of the economy and society. Besides, much work related to redistribution of property rights between the state and private business in public services sector is being conducted. This branch is historically connected with the dominant role of the state in a range of key powers. The concept of risk sharing is an efficient mechanism which helps to solve conflicts between participants. According to this concept, certain types of risks should be taken by the party which is the most adapted for their objective assessment, control and management.

The organizational and legal basis of interaction between public partners and private partners as well as the main principles of state-private partnership in Ukraine are carried out according to the Law of Ukraine "On state private partnership" on a contractual basis. Public-private partnership in Ukraine is a system of relations between public and private partners. The resources of both partners are combined with an appropriate distribution of risks, liability and remuneration (claims) between them. This implies mutually beneficial long-term cooperation in the creation (restoration) of new facilities and/or modernization (reconstruction) of existing facilities requiring the attraction of investments, and use (operation) of objects. The law "On public-private partnership" in Ukraine provides for the implementation of projects only in the form of the contract, whereas some European countries have no such limitation. In most cases, a special structure is created in the form of a legal entity with the participation of the public and private partners. Sometimes financial institutions can also take part in the process. The agreements are concluded within this association. This allows the achievement of maximum transaction transparency. The law defines legal, economic and organizational principles of public-private partnership in Ukraine. Besides, it regulates the relations connected with the preparation, execution and termination of contracts concluded within public-private partnership. The law guarantees the observance of rights and legitimate interests of the participants (The Law of Ukraine "On Public-Private Partnership" 2010). At the legislative level, some aspects of regulating the use of PPP in practice are covered in laws (Law of Ukraine "On the lease of state and communal property" 1992; Law of Ukraine "On the financial leasing" 1997; Law of Ukraine "On the lease of earth" 1998) but there are still a number of unresolved problems in this area.

Projects implemented within the public-private partnership have a strategic character for development of the state economy as well as for separate regions.

The basic principles of public-private partnership include:

- ➢ Equality of public and private partners before the law;
- ➢ Prohibition of discrimination human rights of public and private partners;
- ➢ Coordination of interests of public and private partners for mutual benefit;
- ➢ Fair distribution of risks associated with the implementation of the agreements concluded within public-private partnership;
- ➢ The choice of private partner on a competitive basis, except as required by law.

Public-private partnership is widely used in mechanical engineering and in other spheres.

Implementation of public-private partnership in certain areas provides the execution of one or more of the following functions: designing, financing, construction, rehabilitation (reconstruction, modernization); exploitation, search, services, and other functions associated with the execution of the agreements concluded within public-private partnership.

Objects are subject to return to the public partner after the termination of the agreement concluded within public-private partnership. Ownership of the objects which were built, rebuilt, or reconstructed within a public-private partnership belongs to the public partner. The state guarantees compliance with the legislation of Ukraine requirements for activities of private partners associated with the implementation of the agreements concluded within public-private partnership, and protection of the rights and lawful interests of private partners.

If we consider the situation in Russia, then it is necessary to notice that at present intensive work is being conducted there on creation of a normative legal base for the development of a State Private Partnership with regards to the original national experience of Russia, world political and economic tendencies, possibility of borrowing foreign mechanisms, instruments and technologies and their adaptation in the Russian terms.

For decisions on many socially meaningful problems special-purpose programs are widely used in Russia. These are accepted to attribute to the forms of SPP on the grounds that initiative of statement of a problem for decision with a programmatic method can belong to not only any imperious organ (to public authority of the Russian Federation, subjects of the Russian Federation or organ of local self-government) but also to other participants – to physical and/or legal persons.

At present in Russia four basic forms of SPP are commonly distinguished:

- concession (long-term agreements that a private partner builds and carries out exploitation of an object, and the property of an object is in the hands of the state; for indemnification of the charges a private company gets payment from a population and/or state);
- projects financed by the Investment fund of Russia, which is used by the federal government as a channel of financing;
- special economic zones, which are territories where tax treatment is in force and other privileges for businesses operating in accordance with the Russian legislation;
- other forms (Yemelyanov Yu. S. 2012).

The practice of state-private partnerships is widely distributed in the European countries and this fact presents undoubted interest. Only for the period 2001-2009 they signed 750 SPP-projects for the sum of 100 billion pounds. In the United Kingdom alone there are 526 projects with a volume of 61 billion pounds. In countries EC specific gravity of investments on principles of SPP makes: railways - 46%, motorways - 35%, energy - 7%, airports - 6%. The largest project on a concession basis is the Eurotunnel (the general volume of investments is 15 billion dollars). For 20 years EC plans to attract approximately 400 billion Euros in trans-European transport, telecommunication networks and power infrastructure by means of SPP (U Di 2009).

A considerable role in the stimulation of development shallow firms in the United Kingdom belongs to the fiscal policy of the government. They refer establishment for the shallow firms of the lowered rate of tax behaves from corporations to the measures of general character. The record of income and expenses is conducted only de-facto, regardless of what period they behave to.

Programs for providing financial help:

- "Chart of grants",
- "Agencies of help to the enterprises of local value" that carry out sponsorship of shallow firms at regional level have enormous value in the development of small business in Great Britain
- "Chart of assistance in creation of enterprises" envisages financial help to unemployed people who intend to begin their own business. Special programs provide financial help to young people for the creation or expansion of their business, preparation of businessmen in the field of shallow business; help to municipal authorities on business of creation of new and development of existing shallow business in cities. Professional preparation of shallow businessmen is carried out by special councils of preparation of specialists.

The practice of grants to small and medium-sized businesses of risk capital will be realized in some countries (Belgium, France, the Netherlands and others). In particular, the governments of these countries guarantee indemnification of possible losses of venture funds.

The economy of a number of developed and lately developing countries widely applies the new special form of cooperation of the state and private business. This special form of partnership is designated usually by the term Public Private Partnership (PPP). This form is based on weakening of direct influence of the state in economy, delegation of functional powers to the private sector both simultaneous maintenance and strengthening of adjusting. The state is an agency for the realization of socially meaningful benefits and services. It can produce some parts of these benefits independently, and others by bringing in possibilities and capabilities of the private sector. Business is invited to join in the management of state assets for the improvement and quality realization of state projects.

Today direct state support of innovative activity in the form of SPP is one of the major instruments of development the sphere of research and development in the developed western countries. So, for example, in France in 2002 78% of the direct financing of R&D was through PPP projects as compared to 37% in 1998. The government of the Netherlands reserved 805 million Euros in the 2003-2010 period for financing SPP in strategically important spheres.

In the USA assistance in the development of small business is in the competence of a special state organization - the Administration in Matters of Small Business (AMB), created by the Congress of the USA in 1953. Its duty is to render a financial and consultative help to the shallow businessmen, to assist in the receipt of governmental orders and contracting with major concerns.

The typical experience of the USA is that the state actively takes under its guardianship the accumulated potential of fundamental science with the purpose of converting it into a market commodity and increasing on this basis the competitiveness of national economy (Abdulov A.N. 2005). This policy is complemented by such important elements as innovative strategy; this is the basis for commercialization of most technological novelties.

In accordance with the federal programs of support, small businesses get direct and assured loans. Another measure for the encouragement of private initiative is tax and depreciation deductions.

The federal authorities pay special attention to stimulation of development of innovative small businesses both by the selection of grants (subsidies) and by means of contracting for development of new products and technologies.

In Japan they practice the selection of subsidies and loans - direct credits (the Japanese bank of development offers them to small enterprises functioning in industries with the best prospects) and assured loans (due to introduction of tax deductions, commercial banks gladly offer credit to small business), also granting long-term (5-20 years) loans to the association of small enterprises from facilities.

Thus, given the experience of the world of PPP application, as well as features and patterns of development of the Ukranian market, it is possible to highlight the advantages and disadvantages of the practical use of partnerships between business entities that are presented in Fig. 1.

Factors that distinguish the types of partnerships include the volume of the competences of property, investment obligations of parties passed to the private partner, principles of division of risks between partners, to responsibility for realization of different types of works, including building, exploitation, management, etc.

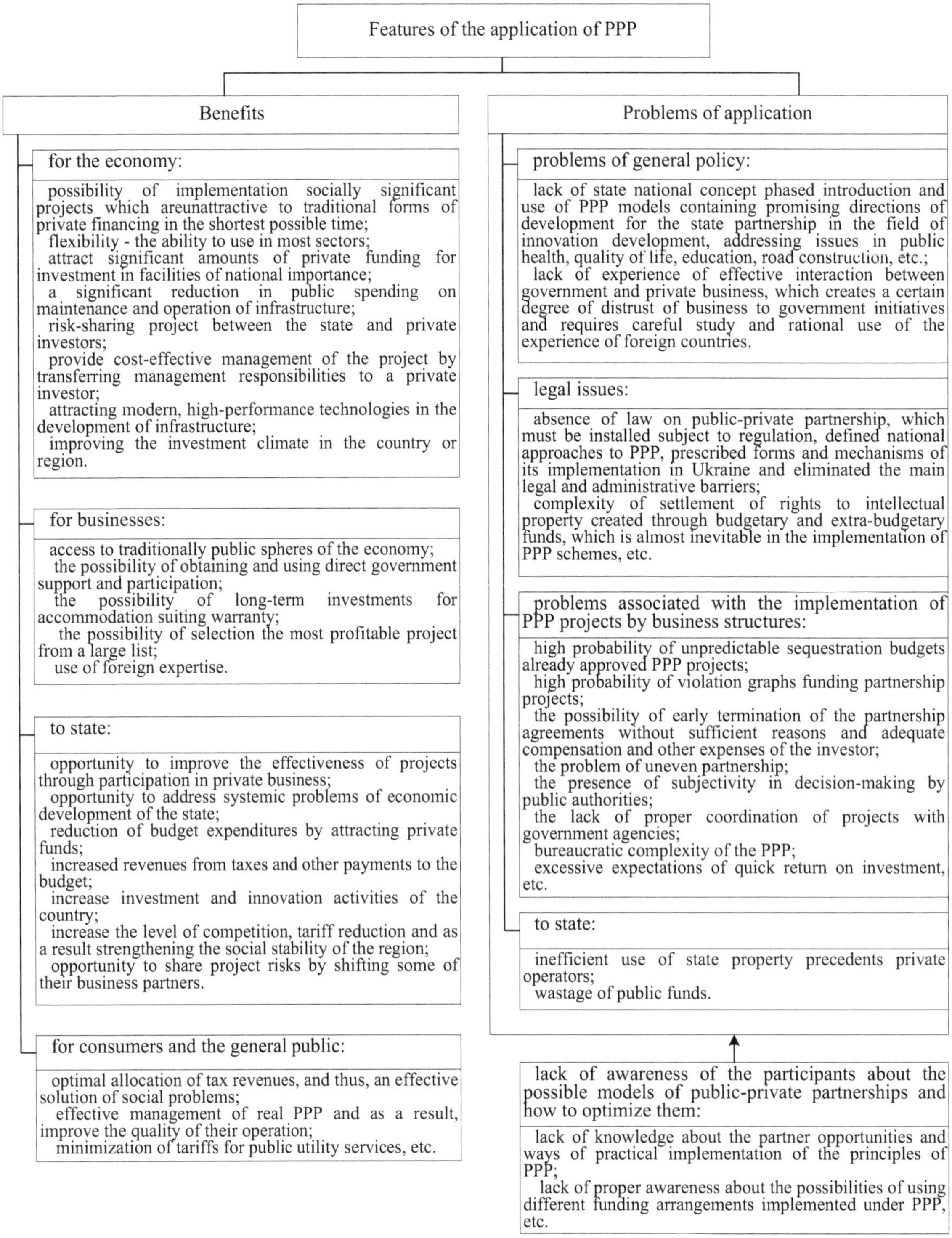

Figure 1 Analysis of the use of public-private partnerships

First chart of them is BOT (Build, Operate, and Transfer – building, exploitation/management, and transmission). This chart is used mainly in concessions. An infrastructural object is created due to a concessionaire that after completion of building takes the title exploitation of the erected object during a term sufficient for recoupment of the inlaid facilities. After expiration of ths term the object returns to the state. A concessionaire gets the competence of the use, but does not possess the object, whose owner is the state.

The second chart is BOOT (Build, Own, Operate, Transfer – building, possession, exploitation/management, transmission). In this case a private partner gets not only the competence of the use but also possesses an object during the term of agreement, after expiration of the agreement the object is passed to the public power.

Reverse BOOT also exists, where power finances and erects an infrastructural object, and then passes it in a confidence management to the private partner with a right for the priate partner to gradually buy back the property.

The chart of BTO (Build, Transfer, and Operate – building, transmission, exploitation/management) supposes the transmission of object to the public power at once after completion of building. After its reception by the state it is passed to the use of the private partner, but without the transmission of rights for possession.

During realization of chart of BOO (Build, Own, Operate – building, possession, exploitation/management) the created object is not passed to public ownership after expiration of the term of agreement, and remains at the disposal of the investor.

In the use of chart of BOMT (Build, Operate, Maintain, Transfer – building, exploitation/ management, service, transmission) the special focus is on responsibility of the private partner for maintenance and permanent repair of the infrastructural objects that it has erected.

DBOOT (Design, Build, Own, Operate, Transfer – planning, building, possession, exploitation/management, transmission). The feature of agreements of this type consists of the responsibility of the private partner not only for building infrastructural objects but also for their planning.

In case of agreements of the type DBFO (Design, Build, Finance, Operate – planning, building, financing, exploitation/management) besides the responsibility of the private partner for planning, there is a special provision that it is also responsible for financing the building of infrastructural objects (Deryabina M. 2009).

Global experience of the realization of partner projects testifies to flexibility in the choice of model of the partnership. The choice of one of these models is produced depending on in what spheres an agreement will be realized (Makhortov E.A. 2008).

CONCLUSIONS

1. The model of operator is characterized by the clear division of responsibility between a private partner and the state for the maintenance of supervisory functions after the state.
2. The model of co-operation is used wherein certain services are not clearly enough distinguished and certain, and that is why it is difficult to make them the separate objects of taxation and depreciation decrees. At that rate partnership will be realized through a joint project company of the state and private investor.
3. The model of concession operates in industries with a protracted term of realization of projects, and also in those cases when assignment of ownership rights from the state to a private partner is eliminated for political or legal reasons. For Ukraine it is attractive during realization of projects for re-engineering of machine-building enterprises having a strategic value.
4. A contractual model is used in the energy industry in which investments are first of all allotted to lowering current expenses. Thus the economy gained from the decline of current expenses quite often exceeds investment expenses. Application of the contractual model to the participants of the modern power market within the framework of its reformation is especially urgent.
5. A leasing model is most suitable for building public buildings.

REFERENCES

ABDULOV A.N., KULKIN A.M. (2005): The systems of state support of scientific and technical activity are in Russia and USA : Processes and basic stages of their forming. - M.: INION RAN, 2005.

CHEREVIKOV E.L. (2009): Publicly-private partnership as socio-economic institute. The Economic theory. No. 4, 2009. pp. 31-40.

BHAVNANI K. et al. (eds). (2009): On the Edges of Development: Cultural Interventions. N-Y, 2009. 238p.

COKINS G. (2009): Performance Management: Integrating Strategy Execution, Methodologies, Risk, and Analytics. Hoboken. N.j., 2009. 240p.

DERYABINA M. (2009): The Economic analysis: State-private partnership: theory and practice [Electronic resource]. Economic portal. M., April, 2009. Access Mode: http://institutiones.com/general/1079-gosudarstvenno-chastnoe-partnerstvo.html

MAKHORTOV E.A. (2008): State-private partnership as a form of relations of power and business is in Russia [Electronic resource]. Lobbing.ru, M., 2008. - Access Mode: http://lobbying.ru/index.php?article_id=2359&link_id=16

PAVLYUK K.V. (2010) Basic and role of sovereign-private partnership in social- economic development of the state [Electronic resource]. Scientific works KNTU. Economics. Vol. 17. 2010. Access Mode: http://www.kntu.kr.ua/doc/zb 17 ekon/stat 17/02.pdf.

PILTYAY O.V. MODERN (2011) conceptions and handlings to determination of sovereign-private partnership [Electronic resource]/ - Access Mode: http://www.ukrppp.com/images/stories/PPP Concept 2011.pdf.

SHARINGER L. (2004): The New model of investment partnership of the state and private sector. The World of changes. No 2, 2004. pp.13.

TARASH L.I., PETROVA I.P. (2012) State-private partnership in Ukraine [Electronic resource]. - Access Mode: http://www.rusnauka.com/36_PVMN_2012/Economics/10_123880.doc.htm

The Law of Ukraine "On Public-Private Partnership" (2010) № 2404-VI from 01.07.2010 with amendments

The Law of Ukraine "On the lease of state and communal property" (1992) № 2269 - XII from 10.04.1992.

The Law of Ukraine "On the financial leasing" (1997) from 16.12.1997 N 723/97 is SR.

The Law of Ukraine "On the lease of earth" (1998) from 06.10.1998 N 161 – XIV.

U DI (2009) China: motion to the state of innovative type (2009) [Electronic resource]. - Access Mode: www.chelt.ru/2009/7 - 09/udi 709.html Varnavsky V. (2011): State-private partnership: some questions of theory and practice. The World economy and international relations. No 9, 2011. pp. 41-50.

VILISOV M.V. (2006): State-private partnership: political and legal aspect. Power. No. 7, 2006. pp.4-6.

WIRICK D. (2009): Public-Sector Project Management: Meeting the Challenges and Achieving Results. Hoboken. N.j., 2009. 270p.

YEMELYANOV YU. S. (2012): State-private partnership in innovative development of economy of Russia. PhD dissertation, WOUNDS Institute of Economics, Moscow.

ZAPATRINA I.V., LEBEDA T. (2011): State-private partnership as a factor of economic growth and problems of its development in Ukraine [Electronic resource] Economist, No. 3, 2011. pp. 52-58. Access Mode: http://archive.nbuv.gov.ua/portal/soc gum/ekonomist/2011 3/16.pdf

ZUDIN A.YU. (1999): Oligarchy as political problem of the Russian post-communism. Social sciences and contemporaneity. No1, 1999. pp. 45-65.

16

The Role of Higher Education Institutions in the Entrepreneurship of Hungarian Students[1]

ANDREA S. GUBIK Ph.D.
ASSOCIATE PROFESSOR
e-mail: getgubik@uni-miskolc.hu

SUMMARY

Entrepreneurial activity is a decisive factor in the dynamics of job creation and economic growth. That is why it is crucial to identify the most important factors influencing the attitudes and the entrepreneurial intentions towards entrepreneurship and to determine the possible fields of intervention targeting the creation of as many new and viable enterprises as possible. Although education may play an important role in entrepreneurship, its direct impact has not yet been revealed. Education may be crucial in awaking of entrepreneurial thinking, in obtaining the basic knowledge about starting and running one's own business and in directly promoting enterprises. The Hungarian database of the GUESSS research project, with almost 6,000 respondents, helps us to evaluate the role of education on entrepreneurship. We compare the course, service and resource supply of Hungarian higher education institutions and the exploitation of them by Hungarian students, than we highlight the positive relationship between the efforts of colleges and universities and the entrepreneurial intentions and activities of students.

Keywords: entrepreneurship; role of higher institutions in entrepreneurship; entrepreneurial intentions

INTRODUCTION

Small and medium enterprises (SMEs) are of high importance to economic growth (Blanchflower 2000; Carree et al. 2002; Carree & Thurik, 2010), primarily through their favourable effects on knowledge spillover (Acs et al. 2005). They have a significant role in innovation, too (Papanek et al. 2009). Entrepreneurial activity reduces unemployment and stimulates entrepreneurial activity (Audretsch et al. 2001). The SME sector provided 85% of new jobs in the European Union between 2002 and 2010 (de Kok et al. 2011), while in Hungary its contribution to employment was 70% (HCSO 2011: 26). Among SMEs the role of the high-growth gazelles is of higher importance in the above mentioned fields (Békés & Muraközy 2012), in addition they are more responsive to innovation than SMEs who cannot reach such a fast growth (OECD 2002; Autio et al. 2007; Papanek 2010). Due to these characteristics, becoming an entrepreneur and motivating fast-growing enterprises are of high priority in national economic policy.

LITERATURE REVIEW

As promoting entrepreneurship is a core objective of many countries, measuring its actual level and developing models to understand its contributing factors are crucial. Several methodologies can be found in the literature. The Eurobarometer Survey on Entrepreneurship has been studying the development of entrepreneurship in EU Member States for over a decade in order to explain the setting up of businesses and business growth (EC 2012a).

The Global Entrepreneurship and Development Index (GEDI) of the Global Entrepreneurship Monitor (GEM) regards entrepreneurship as a multidimensional concept where both individual and environmental factors are important and the institutional setup determines the effectiveness of individual (Szerb et al. 2012).

The Social Cognitive Theory of Bandura (1977), the Entrepreneurial Event model of Shapero and Sokol (1982) and the Theory of Planned Behaviour of Ajzen (1991) try also to describe the above-mentioned multidimensional nature. The three models consider the value system, attitudes and impressions of the individual to be crucial, and they include the environment and the reaction of the society into the model and emphasize the interrelationship between them. In evaluating the role of environment, education plays a vital role, since here students' entrepreneurial intention can be influenced in a relatively easy, organised way.

Although education may play an important role in the growth aspiration of enterprises (Storey 1994), its direct effect on business start up is doubtful. It stimulates

[1] *The paper was prepared within the framework of OTKA Project No. K 109839*

entrepreneurial intention of students to be an entrepreneur (EC 2012b), but there in no consensus as far as the mechanism is concerned. Traditional educational methods (like lectures) develop entrepreneurial traits and attributes to a lesser degree (EC 2008), but still have a significant role on entrepreneurial intention (Gubik & Farkas 2014). Skills crucial to run a successful enterprise are more likely to be acquired in existing businesses (Szirmai & Csapó 2006), however, educational methods that seem to be more effective are very challenging for the institutions. They not only have high resource needs, but also both teachers and students must realise and appreciate their possibilities.

The aim of this paper is to identify the type of courses and services of a particular institution which really contribute to the students' intentions to set up a business of their own, and to determine how efficient these courses and services are in creating a business-friendly atmosphere that promotes entrepreneurship intentions.

METHODS

The paper uses the database of the international research project GUESSS (Global University Entrepreneurial Spirit Students' Survey). This project is coordinated by the Swiss Research Institute of Small Business and Entrepreneurship at the University of St. Gallen (KMU-HSG) and it investigates entrepreneurial intentions and activities of students, basically with four groups of questions, namely the willingness to start a venture traceable in the students' career plans, the influence of university/college environment, the entrepreneurial intention of students and the role of family businesses influencing this attitude.

The survey is conducted every second year. The first survey was conducted in 2003 with the participation of two countries. The last questionnaire was published in 2011, when 26 countries joined the project.[2] In the fifth survey in 2011, 93,265 students took part in the survey from 502 higher education institutions. In Hungary, 5,677 students filled in the electronic questionnaire (the average response rate was 8%, and only institutions where over 1,000 students studied were selected for the survey). Table 1 shows the distribution of Hungarian respondents by institution.

THE CONCEPT OF THE RESEARCH

The research concept of GUESSS relies on Ajzen's Theory of Planned Behaviour (1991). According to this theory, attitude, subjective norms and the degree of behavioural control together influence the individual's willingness to become an entrepreneur who can eventually manifest in actions. Figure 1 illustrates Ajzen's Theory of Planned Behaviour (TPB).

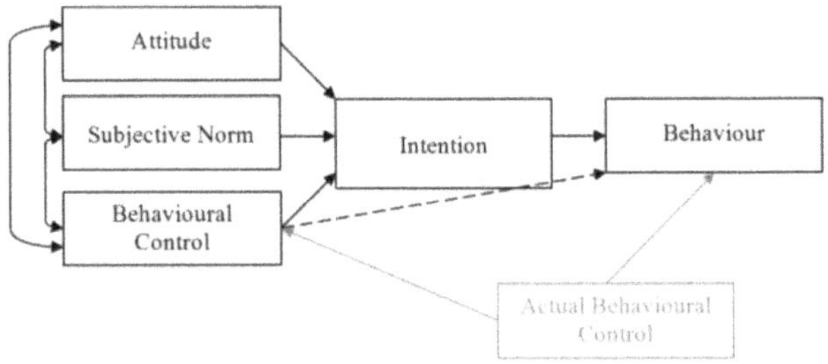

Source: Ajzen, 2006

Figure 1 Factors Shaping Entrepreneurial Intentions

One of the main ideas of Ajzen's Theory is the difference between intentions and behaviours. If there is a serious entrepreneurial intention, it does not necessarily mean that the entrepreneurial activity will be pursued and an enterprise will be set up. Intentions depend on the attitudes towards behaviour, subjective norms and the perceived behavioural control. Actual pursued activities cannot be expected without serious intentions. Objective factors such as available financial resources and opened-up opportunities (money, time, etc.) that are required for carrying out intentions also influence business activities. This factor is termed actual control in the revised model of Ajzen's Theory (Ajzen, 2006).

According to this model, there is a direct positive relationship between the entrepreneurial attitude and the willingness to start up a business. The more favourable a person's attitude toward entrepreneurship is, the stronger his intention to run an enterprise. A supportive social environment is also nourishing for entrepreneurship intentions. Thus, the more positively the individual's environment reacts to his entrepreneurial intention, the more likely he will show a willingness to start up his own business.

The third factor, the perceived control over events, has also a direct influence on the individual's intention to start up an enterprise, and can have a significant effect on the behaviour as well. The impact of the perceived behavioural control on intentions and actions is twofold. Firstly, the more an individual feels that he is in control of his surroundings, the more likely he is to be in favour of starting up his own venture. Secondly, self-efficacy also has a positive effect on entrepreneurial intention. The more the person feels that he has acquired the appropriate skills and knowledge to start up an enterprise, the more likely he is to think his own business can be launched (Ajzen 2002).

The factors influencing intention are interlinked as well. The twofold nature of the perceived behavioural control consisting of susceptibility to control and self-

[2] *For the details of the survey see Farkas & Gubik 2013, or the homepage of the survey: http://www.guesssurvey.org/.*

efficacy are also positively related. The latter can be interpreted as an individual who feels he has the required skills and experience and thinks that he is in control of the events.

Education seems to be able to support entrepreneurial intentions through subjective norm behavioural control. Subjective norms can be promoted by creating a supportive entrepreneurial environment in higher education institutions in general. Up-to-date information about how to start and run a business (e.g. courses, seminars) and direct practical entrepreneurial experience (e.g. mentoring, coaching, networking with entrepreneurs) can contribute to the increase of self-efficacy, which is the feeling of the individual that he/she has acquired the appropriate skills and knowledge to start up an enterprise. This positive feeling increases also the perception that the individual is in control of events (controllability).

Table 1

Participation data for Hungarian institutions in GUESSS 2011

Name of Institution	No. of students enrolled for 2009/2010	Distribution of enrolled students	No. of sent inquiries (link)*	No. of completed questionnaires	Distribution of completed questionnaires	Response rate
BME – Budapest University of Technology and Economics (Budapesti Műszaki és Gazdaságtudományi Egyetem)	23,219	8.0%	0	5	0.1%	
BCE – Corvinus University of Budapest (Budapesti Corvinus Egyetem)	17,422	6.0%	4,800	201	3.5%	4.2%
SZE – Széchenyi István University (Széchenyi István Egyetem)	10,786	3.7%	8,900	681	12.0%	7.7%
DE – University of Debrecen (Debreceni Tudományegyetem)	30,728	10.6%	n.a.	538	9.5%	
ME – University of Miskolc (Miskolci Egyetem)	13,940	4.8%	14,055	620	10.9%	4.4%
PTE – University of Pécs (Pécsi Tudományegyetem)	29,032	10.0%	8,400	757	13.3%	9.0%
SZTE – University of Szeged (Szegedi Tudományegyetem)	27,436	9.5%	n.a.	254	4.5%	
PE – University of Pannonia (Pannon Egyetem)	10,125	3.5%	0	1	0.0%	
KE – Kaposvár University (Kaposvári Egyetem)	3,244	1.1%	n.a.	38	0.7%	
NYME – University of West Hungary (Nyugat-magyarországi Egyetem)	14,261	4.9%	7,600	291	5.1%	3.8%
ELTE – Eötvös Lóránd University (Eötvös Lóránd Tudományegyetem)	30,767	10.6%	n.a.	175	3.1%	
SZIE – Szent István University (Szent István Egyetem)	10,786	3.7%	n.a.	166	2.9%	
BGF – Budapest Business School (Budapesti Gazdasági Főiskola)	17,911	6.2%	13,622	620	10.9%	4.6%
BMF – Óbuda University (Óbudai Egyetem)	11,438	4.0%	0	5	0.1%	
DF – College of Dunaújváros (Dunaújvárosi Főiskola)	4,312	1.5%	2,460	158	2.8%	6.4%
KRF – Károly Róbert College (Károly Róbert Főiskola)	11,530	4.0%	8,000	97	1.7%	1.2%
ÁVF – Budapest College of Management (Általános Vállalkozási Főiskola)	2,949	1.0%	n.a.	147	2.6%	
GDF – Dennis Gábor College (Gábor Dénes Főiskola)	2,720	0.9%	n.a.	182	3.2%	
EJF – Eötvös József College (Eötvös József Főiskola)	1,634	0.6%	1,350	65	1.1%	4.8%
BKF –University of Applied sciences Budapest (Budapesti Kommunikációs és Üzleti Főiskola)	2353	0.8%	0	1	0.0%	
KJF – Kodolányi János University of Applied Sciences (Kodolányi János Főiskola)	6,673	2.3%	n.a.	423	7.5%	
MÜTF – College for Modern Business Studies (Modern Üzleti Tudományok Főiskolája)	2,073	0.7%	1,200	145	2.6%	12.1%
SE – Semmelweis University, (Semmelweis Egyetem)	3,173	1.1%	330	65	1.1%	19.7%
Others		0.0%		42	0.7%	
Total	289,336	100.0%	70,717	5,677	100%	8.0% (average)

* Sent inquiry (link) – the number of students that received the internet link for filling in the GUESSS questionnaire. 0 means that the institution has not made the questionnaire available for its students either through its internal system or in any other form.

Source: own calculation according to the GUESSS 2011 database

Results

The higher education courses, services, infrastructure and resources offered to students differ from institution to institution. Differences in the students' exploitation of the offered courses can also be observed. This paper analyses the institutional differences related to perception of these offerings and investigates whether there is a link between the study profiles of the institutions surveyed and the extent of differences between them.

The first question series is related to the offered courses and seminars by the universities. The students were asked whether they were aware of what was on offer at their institution and whether they attended the offered courses. Figure 2 shows that the students studied the basics of management in the frame of 'Entrepreneurship in general'. Only a few students were aware of specialised courses ('Family firms', 'Innovation and idea generation' etc.*)*. The course 'Entrepreneurship in general' had the highest ratio of attendance (77.3%). This can be explained by the fact that this was a core and probably compulsory course in most fields of study.

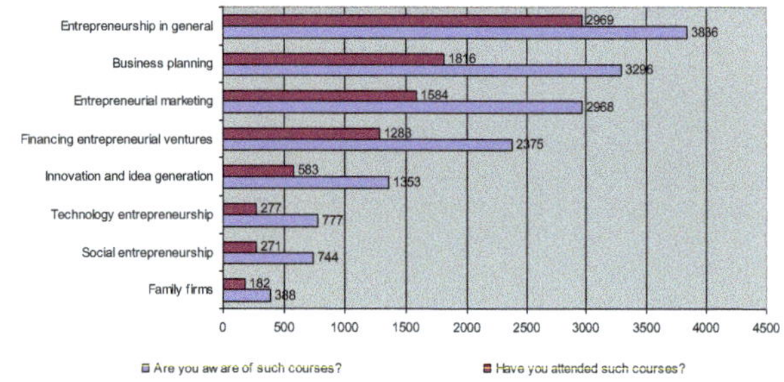

Own calculation, N=5677

Figure 2 Students' awareness of university offerings and their utilisation

The second question was about the networking and coaching offerings (services) and their utilisation. The 'Business plan contests/workshops' were the best-known offerings of networking and coaching. Just over 20 percent of respondents were aware of 'Contact platforms with potential investors' and even fewer of them knew about 'Workshops/networking with experienced entrepreneurs' or 'Contact points for entrepreneurial issues'. It is also noteworthy that the utilisation of these services was extremely low. Only 'Workshops/ Networking with experienced entrepreneurs' and 'Contact platforms with potential investors' (e.g. "business angels") amounted to 30%. Without the high exploitation of such services, these programs increase the entrepreneurial environment of the institution but have little direct effect on students' entrepreneurial intention.

The results related to networking and advisory services are shown in Figure 3.

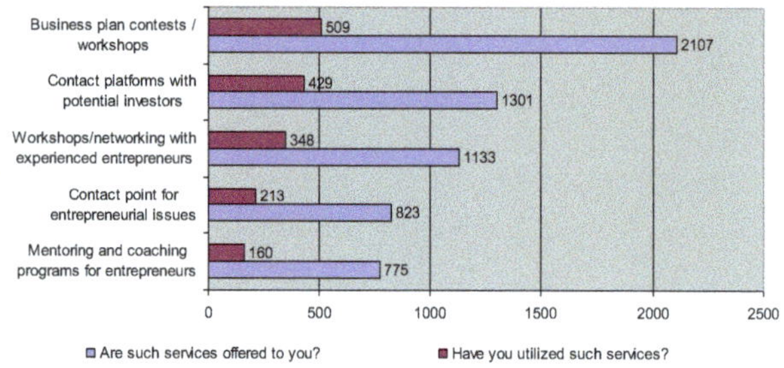

Own calculation, N=5677

Figure 3 Students' awareness of university's networking and coaching offerings and their utilisation

The third question dealt with the resources institutions offered to students. Figure 4 shows the provision of higher education resources which were available and utilised by founders/entrepreneurs. A high ratio of responding students reported the availability of the resources and a large number of them utilised the resources offered by their institution.

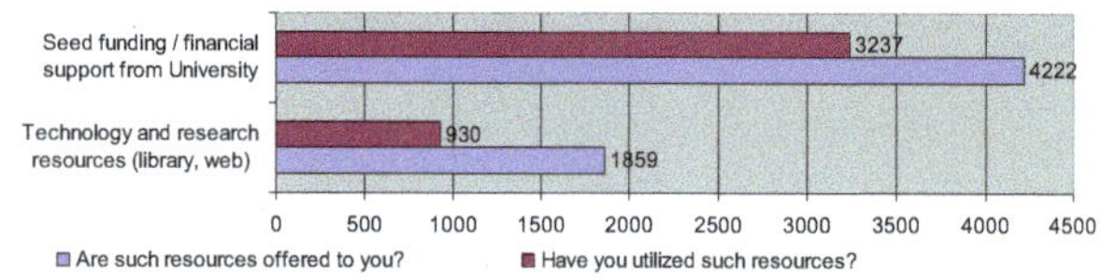

Own calculation, N=5677

Figure 4 Resources offered by higher education institutions and their utilisation

In order to compare the institutions' supply of courses, services, infrastructure and resources, and to find the relationship between this and entrepreneurial intention, three new variables were created: the three indexes show the number of offered courses and services (the variables have the values 0-8 in case of courses, 0-5 in case of services and 0-2 in case of resources). The utilisation of each service is expressed by the ratio of utilisation measured in percentages. Table 2 summarises the average availability and utilisation of the higher education courses, services and resources offered by universities in Hungary according to the students of our database.

The Hungarian higher education institutions have an average of 2.77 business courses (according to the students). The attended courses have an average of 1.58, which represents an average exploitation of 56.69 percent. The average value of networking and mentoring services is 1.08. The utilised services have a national average of 0.29 and the rate of exploitation is 26.12 percent. The provided resources have a national average of 1.07 percent, the exploited resources have an average of 0.73 percent and the rate of exploitation is 69.97 percent. This shows that students are passive as far as services' exploitation is concerned. Institutes should motivate students so that the exploitation of these services increases and their positive impact on intention can be experienced.

Table 2
Average number of courses and services provided by the higher education institutions

	N	Average	Standard deviation
Number of all lectures and seminars	5677	2.77	2.07
Number of all networking and coaching offerings	5677	1.08	1.37
Number of provided resources	5677	1.07	0.75
Number of attended lectures and seminars	5677	1.58	1.70
Number of utilised networking and coaching offerings	5677	0.29	0.74
Number of utilised resources	5677	0.73	0.71
Ratio of attended lectures and seminars	4508	56.69	38.50
Ratio of utilised networking and coaching offerings	2818	26.12	38.62
Ratio of utilised resources	4260	69.98	41.89

Own calculation

Relationship between Services of Higher Education Institutions and Entrepreneurial Intention

Entrepreneurial intention could be measured by the following item on the questionnaire: Please indicate if and how seriously you have been thinking about founding your own company. The possible answers were as follows: 0 Never; 1 Sketchily; 2 Repeatedly; 3 Relatively concrete; 4 I have made an explicit decision to found a company; 5 I have a concrete time plan when to make different steps for founding; 6 I have already started with the realisation; 7 I am already self-employed in my own founded firm; 8 I have already founded more than one company, and am active in at least one of them. Here we use the variation of the variable consisting of three categories: active founder (7-8), intentional founder (2-6), non-founder (0-1). Table 3 shows the average values of the previously generated indexes grouped by the entrepreneurial intention of the students.

Table 3
Courses and services provided by the higher education institutions by entrepreneurial intention of the students (average)

	Not founders	Intentional founders	Active founders	Average	Cramer V	Sig.
Number of all lectures and seminars	2.56	3.00	3.07	2.77	.090	.000
Number of all networking and coaching offerings	1.01	1.17	1.04	1.08	.050	.001
Number of provided resources	1.07	1.09	0.77	1.07	.059	.000
Number of attended lectures and seminars	1.37	1.80	2.08	1.58	.101	.000
Number of utilised networking and coaching offerings	0.24	0.35	0.27	0.29	.074	.000
Number of utilised resources	0.72	0.77	0.46	0.73	.057	.000
Ratio of attended lectures and seminars	53.33	59.54	69.80	56.69	.093	.001
Ratio of utilised networking and coaching offerings	22.81	29.31	29.11	26.12	.073	.066
Ratio of utilised resources	68.19	72.30	61.31	69.98	.044	.003

Own calculation, *p=0.000

The results clearly show that as for the courses and services, the active and intentional founders have a better knowledge about the opportunities provided by their institutions and in the same time they exploited the available services at a higher ratio than the non-founders. Every relationship is significant, but the correlation is stronger for exploitation than for having information about the possibilities.

The correlation between the exploitation of courses – services and the business start-up intentions remained if the field of study – business/economics, natural sciences (including engineering), social sciences (including humanities) – was a control variable.

The conclusion to be drawn is that higher education institutions' services play a significant role in students' entrepreneurial intention. Traditional methods (courses, seminars) and new ways (e.g. mentoring, coaching, networking with entrepreneurs) also significantly contribute to the entrepreneurial intention of students, but the effect of traditional methods seems to be higher.

Differences by Higher Education Institution

Significant differences can be observed in the above analysed fields from institution to institution. Figure 5 lists the 16 higher education institutions whose students returned at least 70 completed questionnaires. The vertical axis shows the number of seminars, services and resources.

Corvinus University of Budapest (3.95), the Budapest College of Management (3.94) and Károly Róbert College (3.72) lead the list in terms of the number of offered courses and seminars. The average number of attended courses is 1.58 in Hungary, which represents an average utilisation of 56.69 percent. There are also differences between the institutions in terms of utilisation of the offered courses and seminars. Students at the Dennis Gabor College (72.40 percent utilisation, 1.39 attended courses) and the College for Modern Business Studies (72.10 percent, 2.46 attended courses) were the most active. The highest number of networking and coaching services were offered by Corvinus University of Budapest (2.13), the University of Miskolc (1.43) and Széchenyi István University (1.37). The utilised networking and coaching offerings accounted for an average of 0.29 in Hungary, the average rate of utilisation amounted to 26.11 percent.

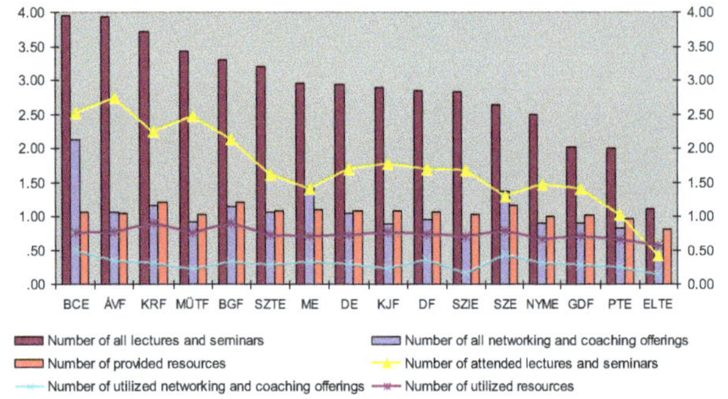

Own calculation

Figure 5 Types of services of higher education institutions and their utilisation

No significant differences could be detected in provided resources and their utilisation at the higher education institutions. This is partly due to the fact that only two response possibilities were offered in the questionnaire, so the new variable could only have three values. The national average in terms of provided resources is 1.07 while the average of utilisation is 0.73.

Differences by Fields of Study

All three groups of questions showed significant differences by field of study. Figure 6 shows the national average for the fields of study considering number of provided courses, services and resources. Figure 7 represents the average national utilisation by fields of study.

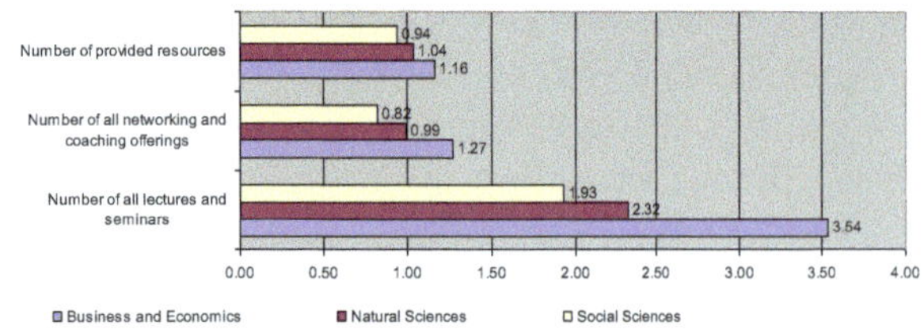

Own calculation, N=5677

Figure 6 The number of courses, services and resources of higher education institutions by fields of study

Students at the field of business/ economics have the widest choice of entrepreneurial lectures and seminars. The exploitation is also high, with an average of 2.34. They were either offered the highest number of networking and coaching services and resources or were the most aware of them. Students of the field business/ economics utilised the offered services at the highest ratio, as well. Students of the field social sciences utilised the least these services.

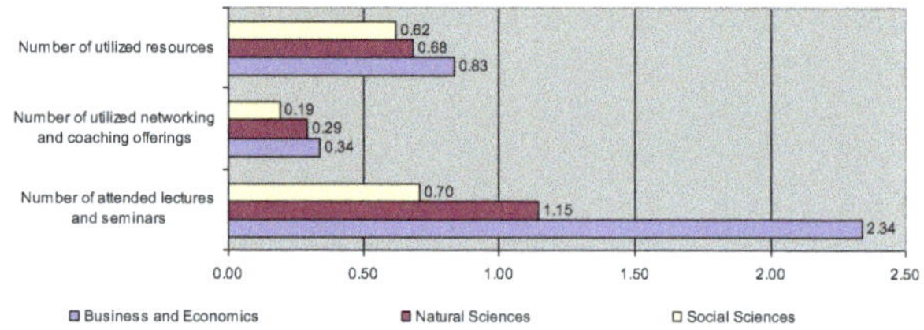

Own calculation, N=5677

Figure 7 Number of attended courses, utilised services and resources by fields of study

Figure 8 shows that the business/economics students had almost the same opportunities in terms of offered courses and available resources. According to the students' responses, the best performing institution offered only one course more than the worst performing one. There is only a slight difference in ranking of institutions between the current and the previous combined results. The best performing institution was the University of Szeged (4.28), followed by Corvinus University of Budapest (4.12), and the Budapest College of Management (4.00). The ranking of the institutions is slightly different if the utilisation of courses was taken into account. The Budapest College of Management (2.89) and Budapest Corvinus University (2.73) remained leaders, but the performance of the University of Szeged (2.24) was lower.

Significant differences can be observed in terms of offered services. The best service providers offered almost four times as many services to its students as the worst performing ones. The three best service providers were the University of Szeged (2.36), Corvinus University of Budapest (1.92) and Széchenyi István University (1.75), and the ratio of utilisation was also the highest in these three institutions. There is no notable difference between the institutions in providing resources considering the reasons described above.

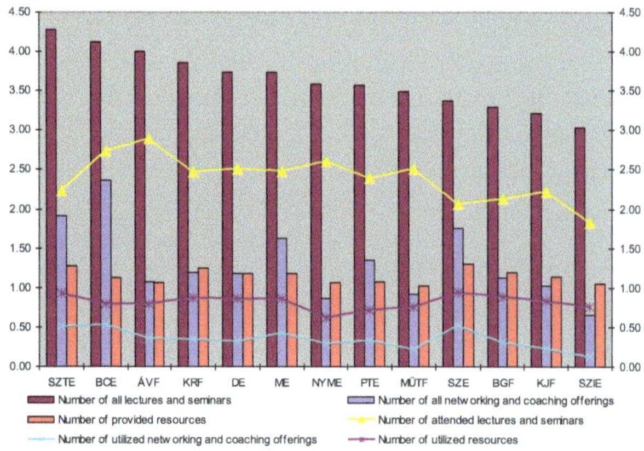

Own calculation

Figure 8 Provided services and their utilisation at the field of business/economics

Figure 9 shows the responses of natural science students. The University of Szeged (2.91), offered the highest number of courses followed by the College of Dunaújváros (2.66), and the University of West Hungary (2.55). Considering the rate of course attendance these three institutions are also leaders. It is clearly seen that the utilisation of offerings is lower in almost all institutions than in the field of business/ economics.

There are striking differences in terms of networking and coaching offerings. The difference between the highest and lowest service providing institutions is nearly twice as much.

The University of Miskolc (1.32) leads the chart. It is followed by Széchenyi István University (1.26) and the University of Debrecen (0.98). All in all, the utilisation is low and shows no significant differences between the institutions. Considering the provision of resources and their utilisation in the surveyed institutions, only a slight difference can be observed.

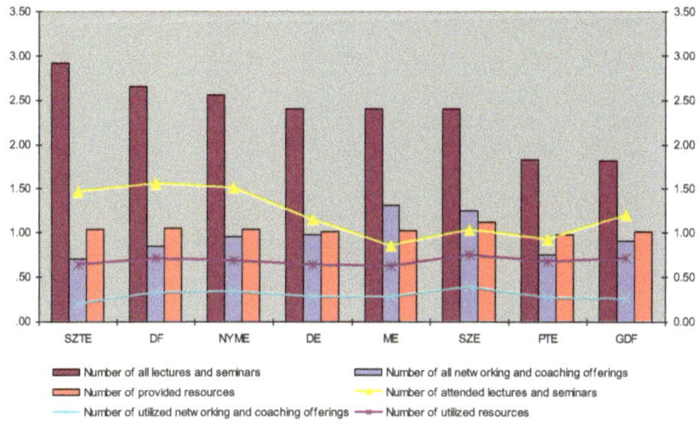

Own calculation

Figure 9 Services offered by higher education institutions of natural sciences and their utilisation

Figure 10 contains the responses of social science and humanities students. There are significant differences in terms of offered courses. The University of Miskolc (2.63) offered the highest number of courses, followed by Széchenyi István University (2.43), and Kodolányi János University of Applied Sciences (2.40). Considering the number of utilised lectures and seminars, the performance of the University of Miskolc (0.52) is less prominent. The students at Széchenyi István University (1.12) and Kodolányi János University of Applied Sciences (1.05) proved to be the most active.

In terms of provided services the University of Miskolc (1.34) is ranked the first again, followed by Szent István University (1.15) and the University of West Hungary (0.92). However, there are no significant differences between the institutions considering the offered resources.

The analyses by field of study show that ranking entire higher education institutions without taking their profile into consideration is impossible, mainly because this would pose the institutions offering programs only in business and economics in a more positive light. However, it can be stated that these institutions – due to their clear profile – offer better access to business/ economics services than the institutions with a wider training profile.

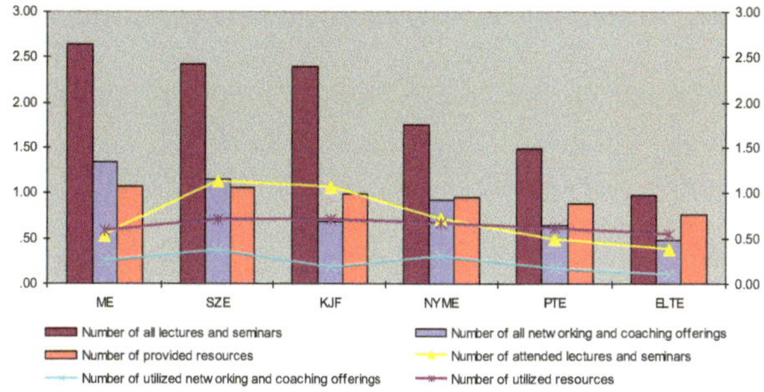

Own calculation

Figure 10 Services offered by higher education institutions of social sciences and their utilisation

At the same time the wide profile of institutions, namely the existence of business programs, helps also students in the fields of natural sciences and social sciences to meet the adequate number of courses and services. As was stated previously, such courses and services are essential in the evolution of entrepreneurial intentions.

SUMMARY

According to the model of the research (the Ajzen Theory of Planned Behaviour) entrepreneurial intention depends on the attitudes towards behaviour, subjective norms and the perceived behavioural control. Education seems to be able to support intentions through the second and third factors. Subjective norms can be promoted by creating a supportive entrepreneurial environment in institutions of higher education in general. Up-to-date information about how to start and run a business (e.g. courses, seminars) and direct practical entrepreneurial experience (e.g. mentoring, coaching, networking with entrepreneurs) can contribute to the increase of self-efficacy, which is the feeling of the individual that he/she has acquired the appropriate skills and knowledge to start up an enterprise. This positive feeling increases also the perception that he/she is in control of the events (controllability). This is why education may be crucial in awaking entrepreneurial intention, in obtaining basic knowledge about starting and running one's own business, and in directly promoting enterprises.

The higher education courses, services, infrastructure and resources offered to students differ from institution to institution. It is worth mentioning that these numbers show students' perception and not necessarily the real situation. If the communication of the institution toward students is insufficient, the rank of the institution can be weaker than it would be according to objective data.

Differences in the student exploitation of the number of offered courses and networking and coaching services can also be observed. Beside the increase in the availability of services, also an increase in the students' demand for them is needed. In those fields where this demand is extremely low and/or the increase of it is difficult, higher education institutions might want to consider using pressure – for example in form of compulsory subjects – to increase the exploitation.

Informative, opinion-shaping programs would be as important as the professional programs, since they contribute to the creation of an entrepreneurial environment. The social status of entrepreneurs is low and entrepreneurship as a career is less accepted in Hungary than would be desirable (EC 2007). This fact has a negative impact on business start-up. Here again, higher education institutions can play a leading role.

All three groups of questions (courses, resources, services) showed significant differences considering field of study. Students in the field of business/ economics were either offered the highest number of services and resources or were the most aware of them. Students of business/economics utilised the offered courses and services at the highest ratio, too. The entrepreneurial intention is the highest among them.

The analyses by field of study show that ranking entire higher education institutions without taking their profile into consideration is impossible, mainly because this would pose the institutions offering programs only in business and economics in a more positive light. It can be stated that these institutions – due to their clear profile – offer better access to business/ economics services than institutions with a wide training profile. At the same time students of social sciences and natural sciences in higher education institutions with wider profiles (that also have business programmes) have better access to such services, and therefore have advantages compared to institutions with only a social or natural science profile.

REFERENCES

ACS, Z.J, AUDRETSCH, D.B., BRAUNERHJELM, P., & CARLSSON, P. (2005). The Knowledge Spillover Theory of Entrepreneurship. Working Paper http://www.indiana.edu/~idsspea/papers/ISSN%2005-11.pdf (downloaded: 8th October 2013)

AJZEN, I. (1991). The Theory of Planned Behavior. Organizational Behavior and Human Decision Processes, 50(2), 179-211.

AJZEN, I. (2002). Perceived Behavioral Control, Self-Efficacy, Locus of Control, and the Theory of Planned Behavior Journal of Applied Social Psychology, 32(4), 665–683.

AJZEN, I. (2006). Constructing a Theory of Planned Behavior Questionnaire - Brief Description of the Theory of Planned Behavior http://people.umass.edu/aizen/pdf/tpb.measurement.pdf (downloaded: 8th October 2013)

AUDRETSCH, B.D, CARREE, M.A, & THURIK, A.R. (2001). Does entrepreneurship reduce unemployment? Tinbergen Institute Discussion Paper 074/3. http://repub.eur.nl/res/pub/6857/2001-0743.pdf (downloaded: 8th October 2013)

AUTIO, E., KRONLUND, M., & KOVALAINEN, A. (2007). High-Growth SME Support Initiatives in Nine Countries: Analysis, Categorization, and Recommendations. Helsinki: Edita Publishing Ltd.

Bandura, A. (1977). Social Learning Theory. Englewood Cliffs, New Jersey: Prentice-Hall

BÉKÉS, G., & MURAKÖZY, B. (2012). Magyar gazellák: gyors növekedésű vállalatok jellemzői és kialakulásuk elemzése Magyarországon (Hungarian gazelles: what makes a high-growth firm in Hungary?) Közgazdasági Szemle (Economic Review - monthly of the Hungarian Academy of Sciences), 2012, 59(3), 233-262.

BLANCHFLOWER, D.G. (2000). Self–employment in OECD Countries. National Bureau of Economic Research, Working Paper 7486.

CARREE, M., STEL, A., THURIK, A.R., & WENNEKERS, S. (2002). Economic Development and Business Ownership: an Analysis using Data of 23 OECD Countries in the Period 1976-1996. Small Business Economics, 19(3), 271-290.

CARREE, M.A. & THURIK, A.R. (2010). The Impact of Entrepreneurship on Economic Growth. Zoltan Acs and David Audretsch (eds.) International Handbook of Entrepreneurship Research, 2nd ed. New York: Springer pp. 557-594

DE KOK, J., VROONHOF, P., VERHOEVEN, W., TIMMERMANS, N., KWAAK, T., SNIJDERS, J., & WESTHOF, F. (2011). Do SMEs create more and better jobs? EIM Business & Policy Research. http://ec.europa.eu/enterprise/policies/sme/facts-figures-analysis/performance-review/files/supporting-documents/2012/do-smes-create-more-and-better-jobs_en.pdf (downloaded: 8th October 2013)

EC (2007). Entrepreneurship Survey of the EU (25 Member States), United States, Iceland and Norway. Analytical Report. Flash EB No 192 – Entrepreneurship European Commission, Directorate-General for Enterprise and Industry, Brussels.

EC (2008). Entrepreneurship in higher education, especially within non-business studies. Final Report of the Expert Group European Commission 2008 March http://ec.europa.eu/enterprise/policies/sme/files/support_measures/training_education/entr_highed_en.pdf) (downloaded: 8th October 2013)

EC (2012a). Entrepreneurship in the EU and Beyond. Flash Eurobarometer 354. European Commission, Directorate-General for Enterprise and Industry, Brussels.

EC (2012b). Effects and impact of entrepreneurship programmes in higher education. European Commission, Entrepreneurship Unit, Directorate-General for Enterprise and Industry, Brussels

FARKAS, S., & GUBIK, S.A. (2013). Az egyetemi-főiskolai hallgatók vállalkozói attitűdkutatásának módszertani sajátosságai (Methodological peculiarities of the research on students' entrepreneurial intentions). Statisztikai Szemle, 91(10), 993-1012.

GUBIK, S.A., & FARKAS, Sz. (2014). Enterpreneurial Activity of Hungarian Students. Management, Enterprise and Benchmarking (MEB) Conference, 30-31 May, 2014, Budapest

HCSO (2011). A kis- és középvállalkozások helyzete a régiókban (The situation of small and medium sized companies in the Hungarian regions). Központi Statisztikai Hivatal (Hungarian Central Statistical Office) September

OECD (2002). High-Growth SMEs and Employment http://www.oecd.org/dataoecd/18/28/2493092.pdf (downloaded: 8th October 2013)

PAPANEK, G. (2010). A gyorsan növekvő magyar kis- és középvállalatok a gazdaság motorjai (Rapidly growing small and medium-sized firms as the driving force behind the Hungarian economy) Közgazdasági Szemle (Economic Review - monthly of the Hungarian Academy of Sciences), 2010, 57(4), 354-370.

PAPANEK, G., ANDRÁSI, Z., BORSI, B., FARKAS, L., NÉMETHNÉ PÁL, K., & VISZT, E. (2009). A mikro-, kis és közepes vállalatok növekedésének feltételei (Growth conditions of the micro-, small and medium sized companies). GKI Gazdaságkutató Zrt.

SHAPERO, A., & SOKOL, L. (1982). The social dimensions of entrepreneurship. Kent, C.A., Sexton, D.L., & Vesper, K.H. (Eds.) Encyclopedia of entrepreneurship Prentice-Hall, Inc., New Jersey: Englewood Cliffs, pp. 72-90

STOREY, D.J. (1994): Understanding the Small Business Sector. London: Routledge

SZERB, L., AIDIS, R., & ÁCS, Z.J. (2012). The comparison of the Global Entrepreneurship Monitor and the Global Entrepreneurship and Development Index methodologies: The case of Hungary. Entrepreneurship in Hungary in the 2006-2010 time period: The role of individual and institutional variables. http://www.gemconsortium.org/assets/uploads/1337684852GEM_GEDI_Hungary_2006-2010_Report.pdf (downloaded: 8th October 2013)

SZIRMAI, P., & CSAPÓ, K. (2006). Gyakorlati vállalkozásoktatás - Diákvállalkozások támogatása a Budapesti Corvinus Egyetemen (Entrepreneurship education – promoting of students' enterprises at the University of Corvinus). Új pedagógiai szemle (New Pedagogical Review), 56(4), 72-83.

17

Conventional or Atypical: FDI in the Internationalisation Process of Polish Firms

PIOTR TRĄPCZYŃSKI
LECTURER
e-mail: piotr.trapczynski@ue.poznan.pl

SUMMARY

The principal aim of this study is to provide preliminary evidence on whether Polish firms behave according to the conventional theory of firm internationalisation. To fulfil this objective, an overarching research hypothesis that Polish firms follow gradual expansion patterns is formulated based on theoretical concepts and available data on Polish internationalisation. It is subsequently tested on a sample of 98 Polish outward investors. While the study confirms the gradual expansion patterns of Polish firms, in which exports and contract manufacturing mostly precede foreign direct investiment (FDI) projects in a given host country, there is also visible evidence for irregular internationalisation paths, in which FDI is the first entry mode into foreign markets. The vast majority of Polish outward investors still control a limited network of foreign subsidiaries. The paper is one of the few studies explicitly related to establishment chains of Polish firms, thus providing an empirical contribution to the debate on the internationalisation of emerging multinationals. The limited scope of Polish firms' internationalisation indicates an important need for a more widespread implementation of support policies.

INTRODUCTION

Outward foreign direct investment (OFDI) by firms originating from the region of Central and Eastern Europe (CEE), including Poland, has dramatically increased throughout the last decade. This trend raises the need for explanations related to numerous specific issues connected with this new category of multinationals, their international competitiveness, their motives for undertaking foreign expansion and the optimal operating modes, or the role of previous experience for the internationalisation process. While the region is obviously heterogeneous in terms of economic and institutional development, with several countries lagging behind on the path of economic transition, even relatively more advanced new EU members like Poland are still not unanimously regarded as advanced economies (see e.g. FTSE 2013). Indeed, indigenous firms suffer from competitive disadvantages due to the fact of being latecomers to the global economy and international business operations (Svetličič 2003).

This emergence of new corporations in the global economy, as demonstrated by both large greenfield investments and significant cross-border acquisition transactions – often carried out in developed countries by firms based in developing countries – has quite rightly attracted the attention not only of scholars, but also of policy makers and practitioners (Jormanainen & Koveshnikov 2012). It has strongly polarised international business academics in regards to its specific character. Hence, calls to revisit extant theoretical concepts have been formulated, while other scholars claim that the explanation of this phenomenon does not necessitate new dedicated theories. A position inbetween argues that the context of "infant" multinational enterprises (MNEs), which have only recently embarked on their international expansion paths, enables us to test and enrich extant theories (Obłój 2014).

Accordingly, the purpose of this paper is to investigate the role of FDI in the internationalisation of Polish firms in the light of existing theoretical concepts. It is theorised, based on conventional process models, that Polish firms would follow gradual expansion paths. This claim is explored based on primary data from a sample of Polish outward investors. The paper is organised as follows: first, theoretical models of conventional internationalisation paths, which explicitly embrace FDI, are briefly presented and discussed. Second, they are complemented by new theoretical perspectives based on the experience of emerging multinational firms. Third, the Polish context is introduced on the level of geographical and sectoral trends in Polish outward FDI, which is subsequently supplemented by a brief review of studies on the expansion paths of Polish firms. Fourth, the results of the present empirical research are presented and discussed with a focus on their implications.

LITERATURE REVIEW

FDI as a Stage in the Internationalisation Process – Theoretical Perspectives

While there have been a number of internationalisation process models based on the concept that firms start their foreign expansion with entry modes requiring the lowest commitment of resources and gradually increase this commitment (e.g. Cavusgil 1984; Reid 1981), these models have predominantly been focused on export entry modes. Researchers from the so-called Uppsala school considered internationalisation as a gradual, evolutionary and sequential process, which develops in an interaction between the creation of knowledge about international markets and operations on the one hand, and a rising commitment of resources on the other hand (Johanson & Vahlne 1990). The model has its origins in the behavioural theory of the firm, as internationalisation is regarded as a result of managerial decisions (Johanson & Vahlne 1977). The internationalisation mechanism comprises state aspects and change aspects. The former are the resource commitment to foreign markets and knowledge about foreign markets and operations. Change aspects relate to decisions about resource commitments and performance of extant business activities. Market knowledge and market commitment are supposed to affect decisions leading to further commitment and the way in which present operations are executed. On the other hand, commitment decisions and current activities influence the level of market knowledge and resource commitments (Johanson & Vahlne 2009).

Accordingly, Johanson and Vahlne propose that the internationalisation process occurs in a causal cycle of development of experiential knowledge, i.e. it can be developed through one's own experience. An important premise of the Uppsala model is namely the fact that the perception of foreign market opportunities and challenges is affected by experiential knowledge, which helps reduce uncertainty and thus constitutes a key driver of internationalisation. They also distinguish between general and market-specific knowledge, the former referring to overall management practices or customer characteristics, regardless of location, while the latter one being more strongly influenced by a country's culture, local business environment and individual customers. Eriksson et al. (1997) differentiate between two types of experiential knowledge: internationalisation knowledge, referring to a firm's capability and resources to engage in international operations, and market knowledge. The latter concept embraces foreign business knowledge and foreign institutional knowledge. The lack of general internationalisation knowledge may afflict foreign business and foreign institutional knowledge while, conversely, deficiencies in the latter two types of knowledge can act as inhibitors of further internationalisation (Eriksson et al. 2001).

Internationalisation patterns can be analysed from the viewpoint of two dimensions. First, the establishment chain refers to operating modes within a given host country. According to the establishment chain, firms pass from a stage of no regular export activities through stages of exports via agents, sales subsidiaries and manufacturing subsidiaries (Johanson & Wiedersheim-Paul 1975). The sequence of a firm's engagement in the foreign market is related to an increasing resource commitment and embeddedness in local market environments. Second, firms expand into foreign markets in accordance with the psychic distance chain, i.e. initially host countries with smaller differences in language, culture, political systems, etc. are selected. These are factors which might disturb the flow of information between the firm and the market. The notion of psychic distance is inherently related to that of the liability of foreignness, or the costs of doing business abroad which cause a competitive disadvantage for the foreign venture of the firm (Zaheer 1995).

The Uppsala model has been an influential approach in international business scholarship. However, it has also faced criticism in different aspects. First, empirical evidence demonstrates that the actually observed paths might often be irregular (e.g. Van de Ven 1992). The falling importance of country boundaries accelerated by information technology progress, as well as overall trade and capital flow liberalisation, increase the pace of international competition (Axinn & Matthyssens 2002; Fletcher 2001). Hence, the deterministic character of the stages model has been challenged by the emergence of such phenomena as leapfrogging of sequential internationalisation modes posited by the Uppsala model, or even the establishment of born global firms (Freeman & Cavusgil 1984). Further, the Uppsala model has been criticised for not considering all essential internationalisation modes (see e.g. Vissak 2010) or the fact that the concept of distance might not apply to all firms in the same manner, since factors such as the amount of the firm's prior experience may play a crucial role in distance perception (Langhoff 1997). In response to the said limitation, Johanson and Vahlne (2009) later admitted that their model holds more for smaller firms with more limited resources, or that experience acquired in other similar contexts may also moderate the propensity to expand abroad (Johanson & Johanson 2006).

Proponents of the Finnish perspective on the internationalisation process, Welch and Luostarinen (1988) do accommodate some of the aforementioned criticisms by acknowledging that foreign expansion does not necessarily have to be linear, since learning from other markets can accelerate the process or, conversely, unfavourable conditions may result in partial contraction decisions. They attempt to incorporate more explanatory variables in the mechanism of internationalisation, both accelerating or curbing the process, inter alia resource availability, knowledge development, communication networks, coping with risk and uncertainty, the desired level control over foreign markets in order to exploit one's own resources and implement firm strategy abroad, or the commitment of management to developing international strategy. Furthermore, internationalisation is considered to be affected by context-based factors, including government policies or activities of intermediaries. The authors also recognise that the rising number of international acquisitions allow firms to shorten the paths of foreign expansion. They also draw attention to the fact that even if a gradual expansion pattern is followed within one country market, this may not be the case in other markets, since internationalisation experience can be transferred between markets.

The aforementioned emergence of multinational firms from emerging markets and the related firm-level evidence has raised several questions as to the applicability of internationalisation models formulated in the context of advanced economies. Mathews (2006) argues for new multinationals from the Asia-Pacific region that they leapfrog the usual stages of foreign expansion in order to catch up in technological terms and reduce the competitiveness gap vis-à-vis international players. In his LLL model, he regards linkages with other players as a source for obtaining new resources necessary to be initially successful in foreign markets. Second, these linkages have to possess the potential to be leveraged by the newcomers in global competition. Finally, the learning dimensions imply that in order to sustain international competitiveness, latercomer firms have to internalise and spread new knowledge within the corporate network in order to improve the effectiveness of operations. In a similar vein, Luo and Tung (2007) argue in their "springboard" perspective that the latecomer advantage of emerging market firms can be overcome by aggressive acquistions of assets from developed MNEs in order to close the competitiveness gap. In other words, internationalisation occurs despite the lack of resources, traditionally seen as a foundation for successfully competing abroad (e.g. Hymer 1976). On the contrary, it is internationalisation which is used to improve the firms' international competitive position. In this pursuit of competitiveness, the said firms frequently also follow accelerated internationalisation paths, as compared to conventional theory predictions (Bonaglia et al. 2007). Child and Rodrigues (2005) also provide evidence for competitive enhancing by emerging multinationals from China who seek technological and brand assets abroad, although they began this process through passive internationalisation by becoming original equipment manufacturers.

Polish Outward FDI – a Macro- and Mesoeconomic Perspective

The scrutiny of macro- and mesoeconomic level data concerning Polish outward FDI allows us to formulate several general conclusions. First, Polish investments abroad have dynamically grown in the period 2002-2012, with a slowdown related to the financial crisis of 2008-2009 (see Table 1). Second, in terms of the geographic structure of outward FDI, Europe has consistently remained the major destination for Polish firms throughout the last decade, including both institutionally and economically more and less developed countries as compared to Poland. However, a peculiar observation can be made that the most important locations in terms of the total value of stocks include Luxembourg, Cyprus, the Netherlands and Switzerland. While the latter two host countries can arguably constitute locations of Polish subsidiaries engaging in business operations, it is rather doubtful that the two former nations host operational FDI on such a large scale, given particularly the size of their home markets. It can be argued whether typical motives described by conventional internationalisation motives explain these capital flows, since the tax profiles of these locations make them likely to become attractive destinations for capital-in-transit, which is directed to third countries (Zimny 2011). Thus, in order to remain coherent with the theoretical reasoning presented above, it is more legitimate to consider such countries as United Kingdom, Germany or Czech Republic as the recipients of actual operational FDI. Among non-European locations, North America occupies a significant place, while the role of Asia and other locations is still limited.

In terms of the sectoral structure of Polish outward FDI, a clear rise in the relevance of service investments can be witnessed (see Table 2). These include, inter alia, wholesale and retail trade and repairs, transportation and storage, accommodation and food services, information and communication, as well as financial and insurance activities. Among industry sectors, manufacturing has clearly prevailed, followed by construction and mining. On the whole, the structure of Polish OFDI increasingly resembles the structure of activity sectors typical of mature economies. However, the dominance of services among foreign affiliates may be to some extent explained by the fact that many of them engage in sales and marketing activities for their Polish parent firms and thus are registered under another type of activity.

Polish Outward FDI – Selected Empirical Studies

Empirical studies on Polish OFDI have been conducted using both macro- and micro-level data. On the whole, a geographic focus on neighbouring economies could be observed (Gorynia et al. 2012; Rosati & Wilinski 2003). Obłój and Wąsowska (2012) examined the connection between host-country resources and Polish outward investment to these locations. They found that market size and economic growth are the most influential variables, with a lesser role of labour costs. This finding remains coherent with other studies (Czaplewski & Wiśniewska 2007; Kępka 2011; Karpińska-Mizielińska & Smuga 2007). Moreover, Obłój and Wąsowska's (2012) findings suggest that although geographic distance was a relevant barrier to FDI, psychic distance was not found to be a statistically significant variable, since the bulk of investments have been focused on culturally proximate CEE countries. The same marginal impact could be stated for political risk specific to the region (Obłój & Wąsowska 2012). Jaworek (2008, 2013) found that market-seeking was a major motive for outward FDI, while other motives were found to be contingent on the level of economic development of the foreign market. A similar interrelationship could be found in the qualitative study of Gorynia et al. (2013). Likewise, while investment barriers in new and old EU member states pertained rather to saturated target markets and a high level of competitiveness, the major impediments in non-EU CEE countries were related to excessive bureaucracy, corruption and regulative instability (Jaworek 2008, 2013). Moreover, a relationship between the motives and modes of FDI was found, in that strategic asset-seeking FDI was carried out in the form of acquisitions, while efficiency-seeking investments rather took the form of greenfield investment (Gorynia et al. 2014).

In terms of internationalisation paths and the character of FDI as opposed to received theory, there have been few attempts at investigating Polish outward FDI from this perspective. Previous studies have suggested a gradual expansion pattern, whereby exports precede FDI in a gradual internationalisation pattern (Gołębiowski & Witek-Hajduk 2007; Śliwiński 2012). However, on the other hand Jarosiński (2013) identifies born global firms in Poland that follow accelerated internationalisation paths. While Polish firms have been argued to possess certain marketing, managerial and organisational skills which can be leveraged in foreign markets (Gorynia et al. 2014), they have also been found to be limited in their financial potential or foreign market knowledge (Karpińska-Mizielińska & Smuga 2007). Thus, it is proposed that Polish firms engaging in FDI will behave according to the prediction of the Uppsala model:

H: Polish outward foreign direct investors follow gradual internationalisation paths.

Table 1
Polish OFDI stocks in million PLN by geographical location (2002-2012)

Country	2002	2003	2004	2005	2006	2007	2008	2009	2010	2011	2012
Europe	4 112	6 237	8 498	18 482	39 300	48 809	65 674	78 162	121 045	156 325	165 964
Luxembourg	344	238	372	604	10 341	10 161	14 098	16 755	26 765	40 382	38 723
Cyprus	512	337	289	500	1 020	1 001	2 272	2 354	5 659	11 177	18 194
United Kingdom	157	240	302	925	3 175	2 792	3 410	3 717	16 600	18 649	17 975
Netherlands	1 048	1 128	1 581	1 537	3 667	3 158	6 618	6 572	9 345	10 278	13 182
Switzerland	382	415	1 459	6 386	8 335	12 547	16 322	19 168	9 053	8 500	12 860
Belgium	0	21	149	8	11	109	61	3 369	6 762	9 314	9 334
Czech Republic	167	322	293	2 326	2 758	4 155	4 195	4 333	7 160	8 384	8 079
Germany	109	856	1 174	952	1 219	2 012	2 480	3 044	6 190	7 122	7 993
Lithuania	90	137	140	224	2 203	2 808	3 119	3 517	6 456	8 419	7 671
Norway	-1	0	-12	45	140	1 165	1 602	3 124	3 833	4 859	5 160
Russian Federation	33	204	285	645	817	1 397	2 064	2 227	3 034	3 989	4 382
Africa	146	150	197	294	363	321	480	498	584	690	703
North America	302	270	247	458	557	613	1 247	1 267	6 008	7 519	6 408
Central America	40	45	42	107	102	146	1 290	1 655	289	228	515
South America	0	3	1	5	8	12	14	17	107	186	242
Asia	687	1 009	731	834	1 044	1 386	2 007	2 288	3 592	4 167	3 870
Oceania and Polar Regions			1	2	4	7	37	49	102	108	102
Total World	5 591	8 035	10 031	20 478	41 673	51 569	71 069	84 252	131 735	169 697	177 805

Source: own calculations based on data of the National Bank of Poland (2003-2013).

Table 2
Polish OFDI stocks in million PLN by sector of activity (2002-2012)

Economic activity of the direct investment enterprise	2002	2003	2004	2005	2006	2007	2008	2009	2010	2011	2012
Agriculture, Forestry and Fishing	1	9	4	-1	-5	-5	-6	-2	6	78	129
Mining and Quarrying	43	165	-2	29	136	50	126	359	1 900	3 027	3 242
Manufacturing	301	1 450	1 805	3 511	4 257	5 226	6 938	12 130	50 672	58 780	51 223
Electricity, Gas, Steam and Air Conditioning Supply	12	16	16	16	5	829	1 143	1 891	3 024	4 244	1 918
Water Supply; Sewerage, Waste Management and Remediation Activities									-125	-137	24
Construction	87	137	121	691	912	1 029	1 335	1 204	4 265	7 142	6 240
Total Services	4 446	4 434	5 100	5 902	8 213	8 878	43 549	49 772	65 468	90 550	114 715
Total	5 591	8 035	10 031	20 478	41 673	51 569	71 069	84 252	131 735	169 697	177 805

Source: own calculations based on data of the National Bank of Poland (2003-2013).

MATERIAL AND METHODS

Data Collection

Data were gathered from a sample of firms investing abroad and registered in Poland, regardless of their ultimate ownership. A proprietary database of 910 firms was created based on several data sources, including Amadeus, Kompass Poland, BPR Benchmark Poland and Deal Watch, as well as press articles and company reports. Between May and June 2013, an invitation to participate in the study with a link to a web-based survey was sent to top managers directly responsible for foreign operations or other managers with a request to forward it to the former. The survey contained a broader catalogue of questions, since it is designed for a larger project on Polish OFDI. Therefore, it contained a number of aspects not explicitly explored in this paper.

Due to frequent concerns about technical reliability, response rates or security of electronic surveys (Kim & Gray 2008), a professional IT services agency was entrusted with the preparation of the survey, its execution and repeated reminders. The automated survey management system was supported by a substantial number of personal contacts with the sample firms in order to identify appropriate respondents and persuade them to take part in the study. Moreover, additional interviews and secondary sources including annual reports were used to complete missing survey data. Therefore, a total sample of 98 complete surveys was obtained, which corresponds to a usable response rate of approximately 11%.

Sample Structure

The distribution of sample firm characteristics is by and large similar to that of the entire population in regards to industry classification and parent nationality (compare GUS 2012). Thus, the collected data allow for a detailed exploration of sectoral, geographic, modal and size structure of Polish OFDI. The studied sample was dominated by manufacturing industries (59% of firms), followed by services (39%). In terms of firm size, companies with over 500 employees constituted 48% of the sample. While in order to qualify for the study, the surveyed firms had to be registered in Poland, their ultimate owners might be located abroad. Therefore, firms with more than 10% of foreign capital constitute 46% of the sample. With regard to FDI forms employed, 57% of the firms had already had experience with wholly-owned greenfield subsidiaries, while 22% had established joint ventures abroad. Notably, 42% of the sample had undertaken foreign acquisitions, while a further 5% can be classified as brownfield investments (Meyer & Estrin, 2001). See Tables 3-6 for a summary of key descriptive statistics.

Table 3
Sectoral distribution of major FDI of each firm in the sample (N=98)

Sector	Total Manufacturing	Total services
Number of FDI	59	39
Percentage	60.0	40.0

Source: survey data.

Table 4
Firm size distribution of FDI in the sample (N=98)

Size (employment)	0-49	50-99	100-249	250-499	500-999	1000-1999	>1999
Number of firms	8	8	13	21	13	15	20
Percentage	8.0	8.0	13.0	21.0	13.0	15.0	21.0

Source: survey data.

Table 5
FDI modes in the sample (N=98)

FDI Mode	Greenfield	Acquisition	Joint venture	Others (incl. brownfield)
Number of firms	57	42	23	9
Percentage	58.0	43.0	23.0	9.0

Source: survey data

Table 6
Ownership structure of surveyed firms (N=98)

Foreign ownership level	0%	1-10%	11-24%	25-49%	50-74%	75-100%
Number of firms	28	24	21	9	16	0
Percentage	29.0	24.0	21.0	9.0	16.0	9.0

Source: survey data

RESULTS

The study reveals that the surveyed firms located their first FDI projects in Germany (18%), the Czech Republic (14%) and Romania (13%) (see Table 7). Accordingly, this reveals a clear concentration on geographically close markets. The same finding applies to the location of major FDI projects to date, whereby in some cases these were identical with the first investment (see Table 8). Firms undertook their largest FDI to date mostly in Germany (16%), Ukraine (15%), the Czech Republic (13%) and Romania (10%). In the context of Polish OFDI described in the preceding section, this also reflects the fact that respondents were requested to refer only to affiliates engaged in manufacturing and distribution, as opposed to special purpose vehicles and other elements of corporate financial structure, thus diminishing the notable role of such locations as Luxembourg, Switzerland or the Netherlands (Zimny 2011).

Table 7
Geographic distribution of the first FDI (N=98)

Country	Germany	Czech Republic	Romania	Ukraine	Russia	Lithuania	Other
Number of FDI	18	14	13	12	8	5	28
Percentage	20.0	15.0	14.0	13.0	9.0	5.0	43.0

Source: survey data.

Table 8
Geographic distribution of biggest FDI of each firm (N=98)

Country	Germany	Ukraine	Czech Republic	Romania	Russia	Slovakia	Other
Number of FDI	16	15	13	10	9	5	30
Percentage	18.0	16.0	14.0	11.0	10.0	5.0	45.0

Source: survey data.

This still limited geographical scope of foreign operations is further reflected by the fact that 70% of the firms have foreign subsidiaries in only up to 3 countries (see Table 9). Thus, sales and marketing activities are predominant (58% of the studies major affiliates of each firm, as opposed to 31% engaging also or instead in services, while 37% were active in production). This coincides with the declared motives of undertaking the biggest FDI project. On a scale from 1 (irrelevant) to 5 (highly relevant), most firms indicated market-seeking motives, such as further expansion abroad (3.77), access to a new market (3.71), or market share increase (3.53).

These were followed by the intention to realise scale effects (3.41) and access to distribution channels (3.23). However, contrary to the aforementioned experience of firms from some other, particularly Asian, emerging markets which sought to enhance their competitiveness by undertaking FDI, asset-seeking motives were on the whole found to be only marginal (1.98 for new human resources, 1.88 for new brands or 1.61 for new technology). This is additional evidence for a rather conventional development of Polish firms' international expansion.

Table 9
Total number of foreign affiliates per outward investor (N=98)

Foreign affiliates per firm	1-3	4-6	7-10	11-15	>15
Number of FDI	69	19	4	2	4
Percentage	70.0	19.0	4.0	2.0	4.0

Source: survey data.

Table 10
Internationalisation modes prior to first FDI (N=98)

Internationalisation mode	Export	Contract Manufacturing	Licensing	Franchising	Other	None
Number of FDI	53	12	1	0	0	37
Percentage	54.0	12.0	1.0	0.0	0.0	38.0

Source: survey data.

Table 11
Internationalisation modes prior to subsequent FDI projects (N=98)

Internationalisation mode	Export	Contract Manufacturing	Licensing	Franchising	Another FDI	Other	None
Number of FDI	42	7	2	1	5	0	17
Percentage	63,0	3,0	3,0	1,0	7,0	0,0	25,0

Source: survey data.

In regards to the establishment chain, Polish firms followed predominantly sequential paths (see Tables 10 & 11). In relation to both the first FDI, as well as to the subsequent ones (if applicable), exports were the most frequent mode of initial foreign market penetration (53% for the first FDI and 42% for subsequent ones), followed by contract manufacturing. Meanwhile, subsequent FDI projects were also followed by other investments in the same host country, revealing a more developed network of foreign affiliates. However, while these results do confirm the hypothesised gradual character of Polish firms' internationalisation, they nevertheless reveal that about 37% of first FDI projects and 17% of all subsequent ones occurred without any prior operations in the target market.

Discussion and Conclusion

The present study aims to make an explorative contribution to the current debate as to the unconventional character of FDI undertaken by firms from emerging markets. Descriptive statistics from a sample of outward investors from Poland indicate that their internationalisation patterns have mostly followed a gradual pattern, as predicted by conventional internationalisation motives. This statement refers to the fact that foreign markets were penetrated by a sequence of gradually rising resource commitments, as well as to the geographical patterns of Polish foreign affiliate locations, whereby geographically proximate locations clearly prevail. In the same vein, the said affiliates predominantly carried out sales and marketing activities and were driven by motives related to increasing global presence or accessing distribution channels.

However, there is also evidence that a not insignificant proportion of FDI projects in a given country were not preceded by any other form of presence. A possible explanation for this phenomenon would be that the penetration of other foreign markets with non-equity entry modes allowed firms to gather sufficient market knowledge on doing business in similar country contexts and thus facilitated the decision to commit substantial resources without any prior presence there. Another argument is related to the existence of the so-called home-country advantage related to the knowledge of operating in an institutionally and economically similar market, which facilitates operation in a foreign market even despite the lack of earlier experience.

This study is obviously burdened with several methodical limitations, one of them being the mere use of descriptive statistics. Further research requires econometric tests of interrelationships between variables affecting the internationalisation paths of Polish firms. Future studies on the expansion of firms from CEE countries should investigate the role of prior experience in countries with a similar institutional and economic development level as compared to the analysed host country, and on the sequence and pace of expansion to that market, an aspect which was indirectly signalled in the present study, but clearly deserves more attention. Another relevant research problem is the impact of resource-based variables which can affect the propensity of firms to follow shorter internationalisation paths.

Finally, the results also bear an implication for economic policy related to firm internationalisation in the form of both exports and FDI. The still limited geographic scope, as well as a careful approach to committing resources abroad, calls for dedicated support measures to increase the propensity of domestic firms to accept risks and leverage opportunities related to foreign operations. This refers not only to support measures directly related to financing or transaction insurance, but also the availability of specific data on foreign markets, opportunities in terms of business projects and potential partners abroad. At the same time, the results have consequences for the management of firm internationalisation. Accordingly, given limited managerial, financial and informational resources, particularly in case of younger firms, a gradual process of foreign expansion may be a more appropriate solution. However, substantial evidence for an immediate entry into a new market via FDI suggests that the transfer of experience from other foreign operations could encourage firms to allocate more significant resources more quickly to exploit new foreign opportunities which can be beneficial to parent firm competitiveness.

Acknowledgement

This project has been financed by the research grant of the Polish Science Centre based on decision No. DEC-2012/07/N/HS4/00283.

Dr. Piotr Trapczynski is supported by the Foundation for Polish Science (FNP).

REFERENCES

AXINN, C.N. & MATTHYSSENS, P. 2002. Limits of Internationalization Theories in an Unlimited World. International Marketing Review, 19(5), 436-449.

BONAGLIA, F., GOLDSTEIN, A. & MATHEWS, J.A. 2007. Accelerated Internationalization by Emerging Markets Multinationals: The Case of the White Goods Sector. Journal of World Business, 42, 369-383.

CAVUSGIL, ST, 1984, Organizational Characteristics Associated with Export Activity, Journal of Management Studies, 21(1), 3-22.

CHILD, J & RODIGUES, SB 2005, The Internationalization of Chinese Firms: A Case for Theoretical Extension?. Management and Organization Review, 1(3), 381-410.

CZAPLEWSKI, L. & WIŚNIEWSKA, E. 2007. Zamierzenia i motywy podejmowania bezpośrednich inwestycji zagranicznych przez polskie przedsiębiorstwa (Intentions and motives of foreign direct investment by Polish firms). In W. Karaszewski (Ed.), Bezpośrednie inwestycje zagraniczne w budowaniu potencjału konkurencyjności polskich przedsiębiorstw i regionów (Foreign direct investment in building the competitiveness potential of Polish firms and regions) (pp. 229-244). Toruń: Wydawnictwo Uniwersytetu Mikołaja Kopernika.

ERIKSSON, K, JOHANSON, J, MAJKGARD, A & SHARMA, DD 1997, Experiential Knowledge and Cost in the Internationalization Process. Journal of International Business Studies, 28(2), 1-25.

ERIKSSON, K, JOHANSON, J, MAJKGARD, A, & SHARMA, DD 2001, Time and Experience in the Internationalization Process. Zeitschrift für Betriebswirtschaft, 71(1), 21-43.

FLETCHER, R, 2001, A Holistic Approach to Internationalisation. International Business Review, 10 (1), 25-49.

FREEMAN, S & CAVUSGIL, TS 1984, Strategic Management - a Stakeholder Approach. Journal of International Marketing, 15(4), 1-40.

FTSE 2013, Country Classification in FTSE Global Benchmarks, FTSE Group, London, . Retrieved: March 2014: http://www.ftse.com/Indices/Country_Classification/index.jsp.

GOŁĘBIOWSKI, T & WITEK-HAJDUK, MK 2007, Formy internacjonalizacji polskich przedsiębiorstw (Internationalisation forms of Polish firms). Marketing i Rynek, 2/2007, 16-22.

GORYNIA, M, NOWAK, J & WOLNIAK, R 2012, Emerging Profiles of Polish Outward Foreign Direct Investment. Journal of East-West Business, 18(2), 132-156.

GORYNIA, M, NOWAK, J, TRĄPCZYŃSKI, P & WOLNIAK, R 2013, The Determinants of Location Choice in the Internationalization Process of Polish Companies: A Qualitative Study. Journal of Economics and Management, 14/13, 61-76.

GORYNIA, M, NOWAK, J, TRĄPCZYŃSKI, P & WOLNIAK, R 2014, Internationalization of Polish Firms via Foreign Direct Investment: A Multiple-Case Study Approach. In MA Marinov & ST Marinova (Eds.), Successes and Challenges of Emerging Economy Multinationals (184-216). Houndmills, New York: Palgrave Macmillan.

GUS 2013, Polskie inwestycje bepośrednie w 2011 roku (Polish Foreign Direct Investment in 2011), Departament Strategii i Analiz, Warszawa, 5-47.

HYMER, S 1976, The International Operations of National Firms: A Study of Direct Foreign Investment. Cambridge, Massachussets: MIT Press.

JAROSIŃSKI, M 2013, Procesy i modele internacjonalizacji polskich przedsiębiorstw (Processes and models of internationalisation of Polish firms). Warszawa: Oficyna Wydawnicza Szkoła Główna Handlowa w Warszawie.

JAWOREK, M 2008, Stymulanty i destymulanty podejmowania inwestycji bezpośrednich za granicą przez polskie przedsiębiorstwa (Stimulants and barriers of foreign direct investment by Polish firms). In W Karaszewski (Ed.), Bezpośrednie inwestycje zagraniczne polskich przedsiębiorstw (Foreign direct investment of Polish firms) (pp. 61-88). Toruń: Dom Organizatora.

JAWOREK, M 2013, Stymulanty i destymulanty aktywności inwestycyjnej polskich przedsiębiorstw za granicą (Stimulants and barriers of FDI activities by Polish firms). In W Karaszewski (Ed.), Aktywność inwestycyjna polskich przedsiębiorstw za granicą. Czynniki i skutki (Investment activities of Polish firms abroad. Determinants and consequences) (pp. 55-48). Warszawa: Polskie Wydawnictwo Ekonomiczne.

JOHANSON, J & WIEDERSHEIM-PAUL, F 1975, The Internationalization of the Firm – Four Swedish Cases. Journal of Management Studies, 12(3), 305-323.

JOHANSON, J & VAHLNE, JE 1977, The Internationalization Process of the Firm – A Model of Knowledge Development and Increasing Foreign Market Commitments. Journal of International Business Studies, 8(1), 23-32.

JOHANSON, J & VAHLNE, J.E 1990, The Mechanism of Internationalisation. International Marketing Review, 7(4), 11-24.

JOHANSON, J & VAHLNE, J.E 2009, The Uppsala Internationalization Process Model Revisited: From Liability of Foreignness to Liability of Outsidership. Journal of International Business Studies, 40, 1411-1431.

JOHANSON, M & VAHLNE, J.E 2006, Turbulence, discovery and foreign market entry: A longitudinal study of an entry into the Russian market. Management International Review, 46(2), 179-205.

JORMANAINEN, I, KOVESHNIKOV, A 2012, International Activities of Emerging Market Firms. A Critical Assessment of Research in Top International Management Journals. Management International Review, 52(5), 691-725.

KARPIŃSKA-MIZIELIŃSKA, W & SMUGA, T 2007, Determinanty bezpośrednich inwestycji polskich przedsiębiorstw na rynkach zagranicznych (Determinants of Polish outward FDI). Gospodarka Narodowa, 9, 31-53.

KĘPKA, H 2011, Struktura geograficzna polskich bezpośrednich inwestycji (Geographic structure of Polish outward FDI). In L. Pałys (Ed.) Polskie inwestycje za granicą (Polish outward FDI), Studia i Materiały Nr 92, Warszawa, 18-43.

KIM, Y & GRAY, S.J 2008, The Impact of Entry Mode Choice on Foreign Affiliate Performance: The Case of Foreign MNEs in South Korea. Management International Review, 48(2), 165-188.

LANGHOFF, T 1997, The Influence of Cultural Differences on Internationalisation Processes of Firms. An Introduction to a Semiotic and Intercultural Perspective. In I Björkman & M Forsgren (Eds.), The Nature of the International Firm (pp. 135-164). Handelshøjskolens Forlag.

LUO, Y, Tung, R 2007, International Expansion of Emerging Market Enterprises: A Springboard Perspective. Journal of International Business Studies, 38, 481-498.

MATHEWS, JA 2006, Dragon Multinationals: New Players in 21st Century Globalization. Asia Pacific Journal of Management, 23, 5-27.

MEYER, KE & Estrin, S 2001, Brownfield Entry into Emerging Markets. Journal of International Business Studies, 32(2), 575-584.

OBŁÓJ, K 2014, Firma międzynarodowa jako przedmiot badań (Multinational enterprise as a research subject). In K Obłój & A Wąsowska (Eds.) Zarządzanie międzynarodowe. Teoria i praktyka (International Management. Theory and Practice) (pp. 28-46). Warszawa: Polskie Wydawnictwo Ekonomiczne.

Obłój, K & Wąsowska, A 2012, Strategiczne wybory polskich firm – motywy i kierunki budowania powiązań zewnętrznych drogą kapitałowego umiędzynarodowienia działalności (Strategic choices of Polish firms - motives and directions of external linkage creation by FDI). In W Morawski (Ed.) Powiązania zewnętrzne. Modernizacja Polski (External linkages. Poland's modernisation) (pp. 102-120). Warszawa: Wolters Kluwer.

REID, SD 1981, Decision Maker and Export Entry and Expansion. Journal of International Business Studies, 12(2), 101-113.

ROSATI, DK & WILINSKI, W 2003, Outward Foreign Direct Investments from Poland. In M Svetličič & M Rojec (Eds.), Facilitating Transition by Internationalization: Outward Direct Investment from Central European Economies in Transition (pp. 175-204). Aldershot: Ashgate.

SVETLIČIČ, M 2003, Theoretical Context of Outward Foreign Direct Investment from Transition Economies. In M Svetličič & M Rojec (Eds.) Facilitating Transition by Internationalization: Outward Direct Investment from Central European Economies in Transition (pp. 3-16). Aldershot: Ashgate.

ŚLIWIŃSKI, R 2012, Zróżnicowanie przestrzenne i strategie internacjonalizacji polskich przedsiębiorstw (Geographic patterns and internationalisation strategies of Polish firms). Przegląd Organizacji, 4/2012, 15-19.

VAN de VEN, A 1992, Suggestions for Studying Strategy Process. A Research Note. Strategic Management Journal, 13(S1), 169-188.

VISSAK, T 2010, Nonlinear Internationalization: A Neglected Topic in International Business Research, The Past, Present and Future of International Business & Management, Advances in International Management, 23, 539-580.

WELCH, LS & LUOSTARINEN, R 1988, Internationalization: Evolution of a Concept. Journal of General Management, 14(2), 34-55.

ZAHEER, S 1995, Overcoming the Liability of Foreignness, Academy of Management Journal, 38(2), 341-363.

ZIMNY, Z 2011, Outward FDI from Poland and Its Policy Context, Columbia FDI Profiles, Vale Columbia Center on Sustainable International Investment.

18

Mises' Incomplete Theory of the Value of Money

KATARZYNA APPELT, Ph.D.
ASSISTANT PROFESSOR

POZNAŃ UNIVERSITY OF ECONOMICS
e-mail: katarzyna.appelt@ue.poznan.pl

SUMMARY

Ludwig von Mises introduced the concept of marginal utility into Austrian economics. He presented what he described as a complete theory of the value of money on the basis of the subjective theory of value and its peculiar doctrine of marginal utility. It is shown here that Mises' theory of value is unclear for at least three reasons. Mises states that his theory of money is based on Menger's theory of value, while in fact his theory refers to Jevons' rather than to Menger's. Secondly, the essence of Mises' theory contradicts his earlier assumption on the immeasurability of the use value of money. Thirdly, Mises' concept of continuity in the objective exchange value of money is not grounded in the subjective theory of value.

Keywords: theory of money value, subjective use value of money, objective exchange value of money, marginal utility, Menger, Jevons

INTRODUCTION

Ludwig von Mises belongs to the so-called Austrian school of economics. His scientific achievements are impressive and go beyond the accomplishments of that school. Although Mises dealt with the general theory of economics, the central focus of his interest was always *money*. Mises proved that resource allocations begin and end in the exchange of commodities – consequently all economic issues are related to the theory of money.

The Theory of Money and Credit (1912) is more than 100 years old, but it nonetheless contains theses that call into question the contemporary approach to money. Mises' theory of money value derives from that of Carl Menger, a founder of the Vienna school of economics. Although Mises' theory is rooted in Menger's, the author departs to a certain extent from its core. Mises introduced, among other things, the concept of the objective exchange value of money, and attributed to it a special significance in the process of money valuation. He showed that the subjective value of money is derived from the objective exchange value. 'While the utility of other goods depends on (…) conditions that do not belong to the category of economics at all but are partly of a technological and partly a psychological nature, the subjective value of money is conditioned by its objective exchange value, that is, by a characteristic that falls within the scope of economics' (Mises 1981, p. 118).

The primary goal of this article is to determine whether Mises remains a successor to the Mengerian subjective theory of value, or whether his theory of money value relies rather on Jevons' scientific rigor.

ON THE (IM)MEASURABILITY OF THE SUBJECTIVE VALUE OF MONEY

A central element in Mises' theory of money value (1912) is the concept of objective exchange value. Subjective valuation of money is based on the assumption that money has a certain objective exchange value, i.e. the possibility of obtaining a certain quantity of other economic goods in exchange for a given quantity of money. 'If we wish to estimate the significance that a given sum of money has (...) we can do this only on the assumption that money possesses a given objective exchange value' (Mises 1981, p. 119). 'Both the subjective use value of money and its subjective exchange value are derived from its objective exchange value' (Mises 1981, p. 118).

This approach to the value of money may be viewed in certain respects as inconsistent with Menger's subjective theory of value. Let us start from the beginning, however, namely by explaining the essence of the theory of commodity valuation and its reference to the medium of exchange.

In the second chapter of his book *Theory of Money and Credit* (1912) Mises argues that 'the notion of money as a measure of value is fallacious' (Mises 1981, p. 51). This conflicts with the fundamentals of Menger's theory of value. 'Every economic activity presupposes a comparison of values' (Mises 1981, p. 51). The process of valuing means ordering commodities according to their importance to each individual. Each person draws up a list of comparative values for a given point of time (Mises 1981, p. 52). The need for such a comparison is due to the circumstance that the process of valuation itself leads eventually to the exchange of commodities. Instead of stating that 'this commodity is worth so much' we can only say that 'the value of this commodity is greater than the value of that'. 'The subjective use value of a commodity is immeasurable. It is impracticable to ascribe a quantity (of values) to it' (Mises 1981, p. 58).

In *Theory of Money...* Mises refers to Carl Menger's contributions to the general theory of value. According to Menger, the notion of value belongs to the category of human judgment. A value is the importance we assign to a good because we are aware that the satisfaction of a need depends on command over the good in question[1]. The value that we attribute to a good derives from the importance of the need it satisfies[2]. It is the result of a *transfer* of the importance of the need onto the good that satisfies that need[3]. The magnitude of the value depends on the relative rank of the need satisfied by the good and on the quantity of good being available to a person[4]. The nature of value is subjective. It directs human economic choices, i.e. commodity exchange. Carl Menger showed that the origin of money as a medium of exchange refers to money as an economic good. Each exchange transaction is preceded by an act of valuation. When individuals exchange commodities, they reveal their individual value scales. If commodity *a* is exchanged for commodity *b* it is because the individuals involved assign opposite values to them. If commodity *a* is a loaf of bread, and commodity *b* is half a dozen eggs, then the first party to the transaction values the half-dozen eggs 'higher' than the loaf of bread, while the other values the loaf of bread higher than the half-dozen eggs. In other words, an individual will exchange a good or certain quantity of it as long as the goods acquired are more valuable than the goods given up. The exchange ratio is a result of their different importance to the individuals concerned.

Although Mises argued that the subjective estimates of individuals are the basis for the economic valuation of money, just as for other goods (Mises 1981, p. 117), he unexpectedly introduced into the theory of money value a concept of marginal utility, based on its objective exchange value. Mises assumed that a valuation of money is possible only on the assumption that money has a certain objective exchange value (Mises 1981, p. 130). 'Since there is no direct connection between money as such and any human want, an individual can obtain an idea of its utility and consequently of its value only by assuming a definite purchasing power' (Mises 1981, p. 130). As we can see, Mises does not apply universal rules governing the value of goods to the value of money. On the contrary, he states that the theory of money must take account of the fundamental difference between the principles that govern the value of money and those that govern the value of commodities. 'We need to undertake a different approach in the theoretical approach to the value of money and other commodities' (Mises 1981, p. 122). 'It is not the task of economics (...) to explain why corn is useful to man and valued by him. But it is the task of economics alone to explain the utility of money' (Mises 1981, p. 119). This line of argument leads Mises to conclusions that contradict earlier theses, firstly on the immeasurability of the subjective value of money, and secondly on the nature of value as a category of human judgement. In stating a link between the objective exchange value of money and subjective valuations of the medium of exchange, Mises introduced the concept of marginal utility as a measure of value. 'The subjective use value of money must be measured by the marginal utility of the goods for which the money can be exchanged' (Mises 1981, p. 130). All of this shows that Ludwig von Mises did indeed depart from the Mengerian concept of the process of valuation. This would appear to have had many far-reaching consequences.

[1] *(...) Es ist somit der Werth die Bedeutung, welche concrete Güter oder Güterquantitäten für uns dadurch erlangen, dass wer in der Befriedigung unserer Bedürfnisse von der Verfugung über dieselben abhängig zu sein bewusst sind (Menger 1871/2010, p. 78).*

[2] *Der Güterwerth ist in der Beziehung der Güter zu unseren Bedürfnissen begründet, nicht in den Gütern selbst (Menger 1871/2010, p. 85).*

[3] *Die Bedeutung, welche die Güter für uns haben, und welche wir Werth nennen, ist lediglich eine übertragene. Ursprünglich habe nur die Bedürfnisbefriedigungen für uns eine Bedeutung, (...), wir übertragen aber in logischer Consequenz diese Bedeutung auf jene Güter, von deren Verfügung wir in der Befriedigung dieser Bedürfnisse abhängig zu sein uns bewusst sind (Menger 1871/2010, p. 107).*

[4] *Die Grösse der Bedeutung, welche die verschiedenen concreten Bedürfnisbefriedigungen (die einzelnen Acte derselben, welche eben durch concrete Güter herbeigeführt werden können) für uns haben ist eine ungleiche und das Mass derselben liegt in dem Grade ihrer Wichtigkeit für die Aufrechterhaltung unseres Lebens und unserer Wohlfahrt. (...) Die Grösse der auf die Güter übertragenen Bedeutung unserer Bedürfnisbefriedigungen, das ist die Grösse des Werthes, ist somit gleichfalls eine verschiedene (...) (Menger 1871/2010, p. 107).*

Utility as a Measure of Money Value

In *Theory of Money and Credit* (1912) Mises argued that 'the revolution in economics since 1870 had not provided a satisfactory solution to the theory of value problem' (Mises 1981, p. 137). Although Menger, as Mises argues, had initiated a deeper understanding of the nature and value of money, nobody had yet succeeded in solving 'the fundamental problem of the value of money'.

Mises assumed that the essence of money's utility derives from its objective exchange value. If an individual values money, he needs to assume that it has some purchasing power. The value of money is derived from the objective factor, namely money's purchasing power. We need to search for, as Mises writes, 'objective determinants of its subjective value' (Mises 1981, p. 119). Any investigation of subjective value demands prior investigation of this objective exchange value. 'There is no subjective value of money without objective exchange value' (Mises 1981, p. 119). 'The theory of the value of money leads us back through subjective exchange value to objective exchange value' (Mises 1981, p. 122). How does Mises eventually trace the objective determinants of the subjective exchange value of money? Mises assumes that the objective exchange value of money contains a historically continuous component. 'The past value of money is taken over by the present and transformed by it (...)' (Mises 1981, p. 133). 'Once an exchange ratio between money and commodities has been established in the market, it continues to exercise an influence beyond the period during which it was maintained; it provides the basis for the further valuation of money' (Mises 1981, p. 130). The money prices of today are linked to those of yesterday, and with those of tomorrow and beyond. In other words, the past objective exchange value of money has a certain significance for its present and future valuation. When searching for the objective determinants of subjective values of money, we will eventually reach a point in time where the object derives its exchange value from a value other than money. At this stage of his analysis, Mises is undoubtedly turning towards the approach proposed by Friedrich von Wieser, who attributed a special social and economic significance to the *'objective innere Tauchwert des Geldes'* (Taylor 1958). Although Wieser, as Mises noted, did not manage to develop a complete theory of money, '(...) it was Wieser who, by revealing the historical element in the purchasing power of money, laid the foundation for the further development of the subjective theory of the value of money' (Mises 1981, p. 139).

Let us pause at this point to analyse the essence of Mises' theory of value. Mises himself claimed that he had managed to present a complete theory of the value of money on the basis of the subjective theory of value and its peculiar doctrine of marginal utility (Mises 1981, p. 136). By introducing the concept of utility into the theory of money value, i.e. by assuming that the starting point of money valuations is its objective exchange value, Mises aligned himself with the school that associated the term utility with value. He followed the concept of utility within the subjective theory of value introduced by Jevons and Walras. Jevons referred the economic question of a commodity's value to its utility. 'Value depends on the utility' – he wrote in *Theory of Political Economy* (1871). Utility is an abstract quality of a commodity which serves human purposes. It is, as Jevons put it, the intensity of the effect produced upon the consumer[5]. Utility must be considered as measured by, or even as actually identical with, the addition made to a person's happiness (Jevons 1931, p. 45). A similar understanding of utility can be found in earlier works, including those of J.S. Mill (1806–1873), J.B. Say (1767–1832) and E.B. de Condillac (1715–1780)[6]. Ludwig von Mises followed the approach to value understood as the benefit that a good provides – that is, as a property of the good. 'If we wish to estimate the significance that a given sum of money has, in view of the known dependence upon it of a certain satisfaction, we do this only on the assumption that money possesses a given objective exchange value' (Mises 1981, p. 119). Mises attributed to money, as a medium of exchange, the concept of utility.

It needs to be pointed out that the concept of utility as a measure of value seems inconsistent with Menger's theory of value. In the latter theory there is a significant difference between the notions of utility and value. The value of a good is related to its economic character (its relative scarcity) and the importance of the good in the process of satisfaction of a person's need. For Menger the concept of utility ends in the *commodity attribute.*

[5] *Utility may be treated as a quantity of two dimensions, one dimension consisting in the quantity of the commodity, and the other in the intensity of the effect produced upon the consumer (Jevons 1871/1931, p. 47).*

[6] *Mill (1848) argued that utility is an inherent property of a good which serves the satisfaction of human need (Zawadzki 1949). In Say's treatise (1814) utility is a quality of a good that makes it desirable for each person (Zawadzki 1949). Condillac (1776) demonstrated that value is based on utility, on the need that is satisfied by a commodity or on the benefit ("behoof") that a good provides (Zawadzki 1949).*

A good is useful if it satisfies human needs[7]. A non-economic good is useful, i.e. able to satisfy human needs, but does not have value. Utility is in fact a non-economic term. It does not refer to the theory of value, but belongs to the theory of good. Since we face scarcity, we rank goods according to their importance in the satisfaction of needs; that is to say, we attach *value* to the commodities exchanged in the marketplace. We exchange goods directly or indirectly, always giving up goods that are less valued than those accepted. Money as a medium of exchange follows these rules just like other goods.

As we can see, Mises employed a notion of utility not in Menger's but in Jevons' sense. By introducing the objective exchange value of money, Mises turned to marginal utility as a measure of value[8]. Mises assumed that, since money does not meet human needs (as other goods do), we cannot assign value to it as we do to other goods. 'When explaining the value of commodities, the economist can and must be content to take subjective use value for granted and leave investigation of its origins to the psychologist (...)' (Mises 1981, p. 118). It is immaterial whether or not the commodity also has exchange value, but for money to have use value, the existence of exchange value is essential.

DISCUSSION

As we have shown, money as a means of exchange was considered by Mises not to be subject to the rules of valuation introduced by Menger. In making this exception, Mises introduced at least three unsolvable problems.

Firstly, he did not explain how the subjective value of money is derived from its objective exchange value. Mises stated that the past objective value of money is linked to its present and future valuations. The subjective value of money is conditioned by its given objective exchange value. Both theses fail to explain the nature of the subjective exchange value of money. When searching for 'objective determinants of money's subjective value' we do not recognise any factor or process which results in the magnitude of its utility.

Secondly, by introducing into Austrian economics the concept of marginal utility, Mises was essentially following a blind alley. He assumed that the subjective use value of money is measured by the marginal utility of the goods for which the money can be exchanged. This contradicts his earlier statement on the immeasurability of the subjective exchange value of money. 'So long as the subjective value of money is accepted, this question of measurement cannot arise' (Mises 1981, p. 51). 'Acts of valuation are not susceptible to any kind of measurement' (Mises 1981, p. 52).

The process of measuring requires the use of an objective means of measurement, namely a unit 'fixed in time and space' – a tool which is constant and material; for example we measure lengths of fabric in metres or body weight in kilogrammes. In valuing goods we do not measure the value of goods by money – neither do we measure the value of money by goods. Value – as Menger was the first to note – belongs to the category of human judgment. It cannot be measured or quantified. It is of qualitative character. Neither Commodity *a* nor Commodity *b* is a measure of the value of the good exchanged. 'In a market, exchange will continue until it is no longer possible for the reciprocal surrender of commodities by any individuals to result in their each acquiring commodities that stand higher on their value scales than those surrendered' (Mises 1981, p. 53).

Thirdly, the concept of the marginal utility of money assumes the existence of price. According to Mises, it is subjective valuations that are the basis for money prices. So prices are on the one hand a result of the valuation process, and on the other its cause. Although the prices in question are not the same ones, the category of price cannot be explained in terms of itself. In this context, the historical element of continuity in the objective exchange value of money, employed by Mises as proof of the commodity origin of money, also becomes unclear. It appears to depict a functional dependency, which is a category of descriptive rather than causal character.

And last but not least, if we take Mises' view that 'the subjective use-value of money (...) is nothing but the anticipated use-value of things that are to be bought with it' (Mises 1981, p. 130), then we will inevitably accept the assumption of the *objective theory of value* on the *reciprocal surrender of equivalent goods.* Its primary implication is that exchange transactions are preceded by measurements of the quantity of value contained in each of the objects that are to be exchanged. And money as a medium of exchange is a measure of value (!).

[7] *Nützlichkeit ist die Tauglichkeit eines Dinges, der Befriedigung menschlicher Bedürfnisse zu dienen und demnach (und zwar die erkannte Nützlichkeit) eine allgemeine Vorraussetzung der Güterqualität. Auch nicht ökonomische Güter sind nützlich, indem dieselben zur Befriedigung unserer Bedürfnisse ebenso wohl tauglich sind, als die ökonomischen, und diese Tauglichkeit muss auch bei ihnen eine von den Menschen erkannte sein, sonst könnten sie überhaupt nicht die Güterqualität erlagen. Was aber nicht ökonomisches Gut von einem solchen unterscheidet, welches in dem den ökonomischen Charakter begründenden Quantitätenverhältnisse steht, das ist der Umstand, dass nicht von der Verfügung über concrete Quantitäten des erstern, wohl aber von einer solchen über concrete Quantitäten des letztern die Befriedigung menschlicher Bedürfnisse abhängig ist, und somit die ersteren wohl Nützlichkeit, nur die letzteren aber neben ihrer Nützlichkeit auch jene Bedeutung für uns haben, die wir Werth nennen (Menger 1871/2010, p. 84).*

[8] *'Money utility is the possibility of obtaining a certain quantity of other economic goods in exchange for a given quantity of money. (...) money has no utility other than that arising from the possibility of obtaining other goods in exchange for it' (Mises 1912/1981, p. 118).*

In his later book *Human Action: A Treatise on Economics* (1949) Ludwig von Mises basically sustains the theses introduced in *Theory of Money and Credit* (1912). However, the theory of the value of money was presented there slightly differently[9].

The numerous references to *the quantity theory of money* appearing in Chapter XVII, titled *Indirect Exchange,* indicate that as far as money theory is concerned, the 1949 work may be regarded as a supplementation of the analysis first put forward by Mises in 1912. Mises argued, referring among others to the ideas of Menger, that 'the theory of money was and is always the theory of indirect exchange and of the media of exchange' (Mises 1949, p. 395). From that assumption he derived two important premises. First, money as a medium of exchange is an economic good – it is rare and there is a demand for it. Second, the subject matter of the theory of indirect exchange is the study of exchange ratios between the medium of exchange on the one hand and goods and services on the other hand.

In *Human Action* ... (1949) Mises used the so-called praxeological method, which, in Mises' words, 'traces all phenomena back to actions of the individuals' (Mises 1949, p. 403). He argued that when analysing monetary phenomena we need to take as a point of departure the value judgments of the people concerned. The method applied by Mises led him to two important conclusions. First, '(...) the appraisement of money is to be explained in the same way as the appraisement of all other goods: by the demand on the part of those who are eager to acquire a definite quantity of it' (Mises 1949, p. 400). Second, '(...) it would still be faulty to explain the purchasing power – the price – of the monetary unit on the basis of its services' (Mises 1949, p. 396). (...) It is always demand that influences the price structure, not the objective value in use (Mises 1949, p. 397). Having in mind Mises' theory from 1912, one can see that these statements contradict the theses presented there. In spite of this, Mises does not revise his theory. Instead, he returns to his *regression theorem,* arguing that 'the demand for a medium of exchange (...) depends on its value in exchange' (Mises 1949, p. 405).

REFERENCES

CALDWELL, B., ed. (1990): Carl Menger and his Legacy in Economics. Annual supplement to Vol. 22, History of Political Economy., London: Duke University Press.

CONDILLAC, E. B. (1776): Handel i rząd w ich stosunku wzajemnym. Le Commerce et le gouvernement, considérés relativement l'un a l'autre. In: Zawadzki W. (1949). Wartość i cena, Wypisy z dzieł autorów polskich i obcych, Warszawa, Łódź: Wydawnictwo Kazimierza Rutskiego.

JEVONS, W.S. (1931) [1871]: Theory of Political Economy. London: Macmillan.

MENGER, C. (2010) [1871]: Grundsätze der Volkswirtschafslehre. Reprint. Vienna: Wilhelm Braumüller, Nabu Press.

MENGER, C. (1950) [1871]: Principles of Economics (J. Dingwall, B.F. Hoselitz, trans.). Illinois: The Free Press, Glencoe.

MENGER, C. (2012) [1892]: On the Origins of Money (C.A. Foley, trans.). Auburn, AL, USA: Mises Institute.

MILL, J.S. (1848): Zasady ekonomii politycznej z niektórym zastosowaniem do filozofii społecznej. The Principles of Political Economy with Some of their Applications to Social Philosophy. In: Zawadzki W. (1949). Wartość i cena, Wypisy z dzieł autorów polskich i obcych, Warsawa, Łódź: Wydawnictwo Kazimierza Rutskiego.

von MISES, L. (1981) [1912]: The Theory of Money and Credit (H.E. Batson, trans.). Indianapolis, IN, USA: Liberty Fund.

von MISES, L. (2012) [1912]: Teoria pieniądza i kredytu (K. Śledziński, trans.). Warsaw: Fijjor Publishing.

von MISES, L. (1980) [1940]: Nationalökonomie: Theorie des Handelns und Wirtschaftens. Munich: Philosophia.

von MISES, L. (1949): Human Action: A Treatise on Economics. London: William Hodge.

von MISES, L. (2007) [1949]: Ludzkie działanie, Traktat o ekonomii (W. Falkowski, trans.). Warsaw: Instytut Ludwiga von Misesa.

SAY, J.B. (1803): Traktat o ekonomii politycznej. Traité d'économie politique ou simple exposition de la manière dont se forment, se distribuent et se composent les richesses. In: Zawadzki W. (1949). Wartość i cena, Wypisy z dzieł autorów polskich i obcych, Warsaw – Łódź: Wydawnictwo Kazimierza Rutskiego.

TAYLOR, E. (1958): Historia ekonomiki. History of Economics. Poznań: Państwowe Wydawnictwo Naukowe.

von WIESER, F. (1889): Der natürliche Wert. Vienna: Alfred Hölder.

[9] *A great part of the theory of the value of money in Human Action: A Treatise on Economics (1949) was first presented by L. von Mises in Nationalökonomie: Theorie des Handelns und Wirtschaftens (1940).*

Changing Trends in ICT Use - A Generation Y Analysis

LÁSZLÓ BERÉNYI, Ph.D.
ASSOCIATE PROFESSOR

UNIVERSITY OF MISKOLC
e-mail: szvblaci@uni-miskolc.hu

SUMMARY

The development in recent years of Information and Communication Technology (ICT) tools and equipment is notable. The question arises whether user behaviour follows technical progress. Statistics prove that the spread of the Internet in Hungary, especially the Mobile Internet, follows the EU trend. At the same time, the changes in equipment use are less spectacular. The paper analyses the data of a survey conducted among the business students of the University of Miskolc in 2012 and in 2015 related to the order of preference for some ICT tools. Empirical results confirm that changes in the utilisation of ICT tools are much slower than the appearance of new tools and solutions in the market; due to the increasing popularity of smartphones, the possibility of utilising them both in higher education and at work should be considered.

Keywords: ICT tools, preference analysis, digital competence

INTRODUCTION

Research activities in field of Information and Communication Technology (ICT) possibilities may serve several purposes. Expanding trade flow or establishing new software developments are obvious scopes, but also social aspects of the utilisation have an increasing importance. Consideration of user skills and intention to use ICT tools must have a similar priority in order to achieve evolution.

Nowadays ICT tools extend throughout our work and lives, including news reading, keeping in contact with relatives or friends, job searching, placing orders, etc. Computers or even mobile phones are essential during the mentioned activities. Higher education, among other sectors, is interwoven with ICT solutions: e-administration, e-learning systems and materials, video conferences and emails are common. However, the availability of the technology by itself is not enough for achieving a breakthrough. It is necessary to develop ICT systems, the learning content supply and the personal level of knowledge and competences in a coordinated manner.

Generational theory (Coupland 1991; Strauss & Howe 1991) offers a professional background for explaining typical ICT user profiles and behavioural patterns. Attitudes to information technology (IT) and ICT significantly determine differences between the characteristics of the latest generations. This is especially true in case of the related labour market research (see Szlávicz & Szretykó 2013; Törőcsik 2015). Studies dealing with Generations X, Y, Z and Alpha designate different years of birth of the persons belonging to each group. This is due to the local characteristics of social and economic structures. A major issue is that Hungarian diffusion of personal computers was delayed compared to Western Europe or the USA. In Hungary, people born between 1982 and 1995 are classified as Generation Y (Pais 2013).

The aim of the present study is to analyse some aspects of the changes of ICT usage among higher education students belonging to the late representatives of the Generation Y. Changes in the preferred data storage tools and computer type are representative indicators of the topic.

The paper summarises the general trend and the results of a pilot survey including the business students of the University of Miskolc.

USE OF ICT TOOLS

General Trends in Household Use

Regular reports of the Hungarian Central Statistical Office (KSH) in the field prove a clear improvement in computer usage among households (KSH 2016). 76% of the population were effective (active) computer users in 2015, i.e. they used a computer at least once in a three-month period. While the indicator is lower than the EU average (83%), a continuous increase can be observed in comparison with the previous years. 56.8% of the households had a desktop computer in 2009 and this ratio had barely changed to 2013 (58.3%). Nevertheless, the share of portable computers has been growing steadily; the ratio has changed from 21% to 41.6% in the period.

Using ICT tools is usually associated with using the Internet. The growing number of households with Internet access is a positive tendency. Hungary lags behind the EU average, but the headway is visible (Figure 1).

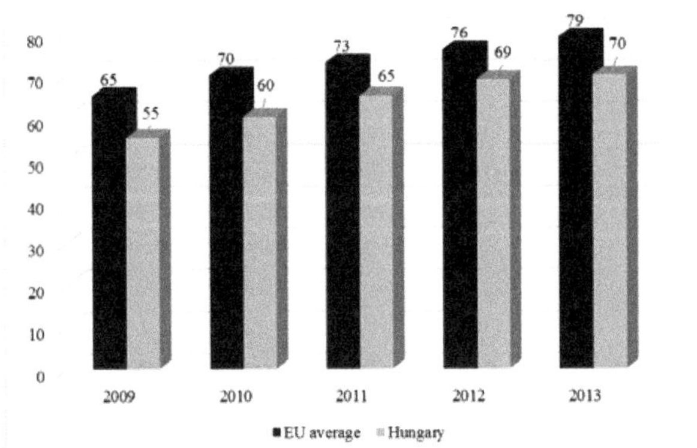

Source: KSH, 2016

Figure 1. Household internet access in Hungary and the EU (data in %)

The KSH report on telecommunications, Internet and TV services (KSH 2016) pointed out that there were 8.7 million Internet subscriptions in Hungary in the 3rd quarter of 2015, which is 35.9% higher than in the same period of 2013. Wired internet bandwidth has begun to grow dynamically; 75% were over 2 Mbit/s, 49% over 10 Mbit/s and 14% over 100 Mbit/s in 2016. The ratio of the latter category exactly doubled from the same period of the previous year. Development of data traffic on wired Internet is remarkable. The traffic was about 383 thousand Terabytes, which means a 34% increase over one year. Expansion has accelerated, which is proved by the fact that the value of the indicator was 39 thousand Terabytes in 2014 fourth quarter and 14.4 thousand Terabytes in 2010 fourth quarter based on data from KSH (2015).

Furthermore, Internet subscriptions included 5.9 million Mobile Internet subscriptions. The growing popularity of mobile use is also reflected in the fact that four-fifths of conversations were carried out using mobile phones.

Sending and receiving e-mails were the most popular computer activities in 2015. 93% of the 16 to 74-year old population within the group of effective Internet users reported using e-mail. There was an increasing ratio of users who made Internet phone calls (from 37.2% in 2013 to 54.7% in 2015) as well as participation in social networks (from 77.8% in 2013 to 83.4% in 2015). Browsing Wikipedia also became more popular (changing from 40.4% in 2013 to 59.8% in 2015).

General Trends in Company Use

Sasvári (2012a, 2012b) analyses the use of ICT tools on the corporate level. According to his results based on an international survey, the level of utilisation is diverse, especially with regard to company size. Small- and medium-sized companies were lagging in using information systems (Sasvári & Wolf 2014). Of course, this does not entail the total neglect of IT services and ICT tools, but the depth and scope of utilisation is fairly questionable. More than four-fifths of the corporations in the sample (Sasvári, 2012b) have a web page in 2010 and they used Internet for advertising products and services. 60% of micro- and small companies have had a product or service advertised on the Internet. Moreover, e-banking was taken advantage of by 80% of micro and 85% of small companies.

KSH (2014, 2016) results confirm Sasvári's findings. 91% of the companies used the Internet in 2013, and 27% of them had broadband Mobile Internet access. However, there are areas for improvement, including:

- low utilisation of cloud computing: only 26.2% of large companies (over 250 employees) took advantage of any cloud-based services (the national average ratio is 11.6%),
- corporate web pages focused on product and service information; on-line ordering was available in every fourth to fifth case, however every third company managed its purchasing also this way,
- an enterprise resource planning system was installed by 70.5% of large companies but by only 37% of medium-sized (50-249 employees) and 12.1% of small firms (less than 50 employees) (KSH 2016).

Statistics clearly confirm that the small companies utilise ICT at a lower level than large ones. In my opinion, the reason for this is not mainly the availability of the tools or even the financial possibilities. A large company can define a number of repeatable processes, which are manageable by IT systems, while a smaller company more rarely encounters with equally repetitive challenges. In these cases, individual treatment of the problem with marginal support of ICT can be more appropriate in several ways, including the costs. However, this means that personal IT competencies have fundamental importance in solving the problems.

RESEARCH SAMPLE AND METHOD

Research Goals and Limitations

Relevant literature and related statistics verify a dynamic expansion of ICT tools. Technological development may lead to changing user behaviour, as well as there being also an opposite effect. I believe that the investigation of changes in preferences related to ICT tools can contribute to establishing more effective development action. I started a survey in 2012 in order to explore the ICT competencies and attitudes of higher education students. The results allow us to designate new ways of educational methodology in practice, while the information is also valuable for the labour market.

Empirical results in this paper highlight the data storage tools and types of computer preferred by the respondents. Results in this paper are based on the business students of the University of Miskolc. Although the sample is not representative and generalisation of the statements is not available, its findings can be utilised.

Research Sample Characteristics

The data collection periods of the present analysis were in 2012 (n=437) and in 2015 (n=294). Some data of the sample are summarised in Table 1.

Table 1
Research sample data

	2012	2015
Female	62.5%	53.4%
Male	37.5%	46.6%
Full-time student	66.1%	85.0%
Part-time student	33.9%	15.0%
Weekday time spent with computer (average)	4.79 hours	4.81 hours
Weekend time spent with computer (average)	4.01 hours	5.03 hours

Source: own edition

The time spent with computer activities per day was quite much in each year (Table 2). Checking the data by gender, in case of male respondents there are higher values but the differences are statistically not significant. Average weekday time spent with computer activities was higher in the group of part-time students but the weekend time was higher in the group of full-time student (some ANOVA results show (*) significant differences).

Table 2
Time spent with computer work by sub-samples

		Weekday (hours)	ANOVA F	ANOVA Sig.	Weekend (hours)	ANOVA F	ANOVA Sig.
2012	Female	4.85	.286	.593	3.81	3.949	.048*
	Male	4.64			4.31		
2015	Female	4.74	.120	.729	4.76	2.032	.155
	Male	4.88			5.34		
2012	Full-time	3.91	47.857	.000*	4.49	33.986	.000*
	Part-time	6.50			3.05		
2015	Full-time	4.52	11.541	.001*	5.17	2.643	.105
	Part-time	6.45			4.27		

Source: own edition

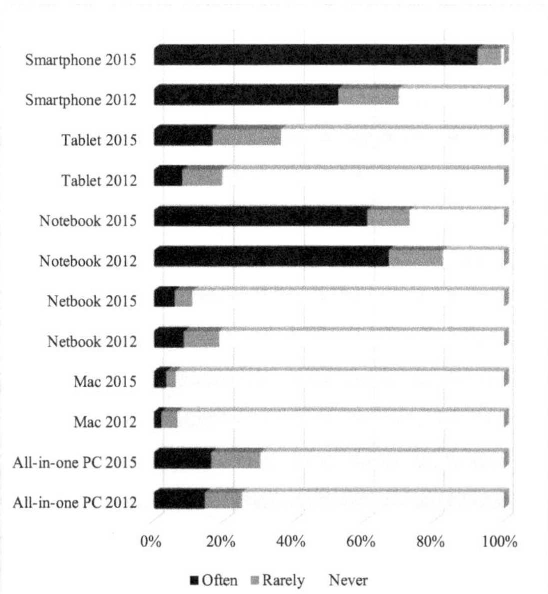

Figure 2. Frequency of ICT tools (%)

Figure 2 compares the use of some tools in the two periods. Beside the overall state of users' preferences there are some notable results:

- netbooks have not had a significant share and their popularity is fading,
- notebooks are preferred but the ratio of both frequent and occasional users decreased slightly,
- popularity of tablets has increased, but prevalence was only 16.6% in 2015,
- use of smartphones show dominant progress; the smartphone has become the ultimate tool of access to ICT.

METHODS

The online survey was prepared for preference analysis. The respondents were asked to mark the more preferred item pairwise. In case of data storage tools the items (for 6 comparisons) are as follows:

- memory card,
- external HDD,
- USB flach memory
- on-line (cloud) data storage.

Items related to the computer type (for 10 comparisons) are as follows:

- tablet
- netbook
- notebook
- smartphone
- desktop PC

Kendall (1970) proved the mathematical basis of pairwise comparison and introduced indicators for evaluating the quality of the preference orders. Kindler and Papp (1978) collected some applications for describing the preference orders on interval scale, including the Guilford transformation. One step of the Analytic Hierarchy Process (AHP) by Saaty (1980) offers a solution presenting the preference orders on a ratio scale, which allows the direct comparison of the results between various sub-samples. The results in this paper include:

- preference frequencies of the items, preference orders and ratio of weights,
- calculating the personal level of consistency (K) in the order of the factors ($0 \leq K \leq 1$, where 0 is the complete absence of consistency and 1 is the complete consistency; the latter means that the respondent has a clear list of preferences),
- group level consensus by Kendall's coefficient of concordance for pairwise comparison (ν) (Kendall, 1970), including the cases $K \geq 0.75$.

The maximum level of Kendall's coefficient of concordance is 1, while the minimum is not fixed, it depends on the number of cases (m): $\nu_{even} = -1/(m-1)$ and $\nu_{odd} = -1/m$ (Kindler & Papp, 1978:49). In order to ensure the comparison, I calculate a corrected coefficient of consensus as:

$$\nu_{corr.\ i} = 100 * \frac{\nu_i - \nu_{min}}{1 - \nu_{min}} \qquad (1)$$

The calculation of the significance (u) test is based on occurrences and possible sum of values below the main diagonal in the aggregated preference matrix, i.e. the number of non-preferred incidences. The details of the procedure can be found in Kindler and Papp (1978:187). In case of high u values ($u>1.65$) the result is statistically significant.

A step of the AHP method by Saaty (1980) determines the weights of items based on the eigenvector assigned to the highest real eigenvalue of a pairwise comparison result matrix. These weights are comparable between sub-samples after normalisation. Rapcsák (2007) shows that there is only one non-zero eigenvalue if the matrix is prepared as in (2).

$$\begin{bmatrix} 1 & \frac{w_1}{w_2} & \dots & \frac{w_1}{w_n} \\ \frac{w_2}{w_1} & 1 & \dots & \dots \\ \dots & \dots & 1 & \dots \\ \frac{w_n}{w_1} & \dots & \dots & 1 \end{bmatrix} \qquad (2)$$

RESULTS

Preference Order

The preferred data storage methods were USB flash memory and on-line solutions (cloud storage) the less one in 2012. The order is similar in 2015, but the ratio of the marking show a changing structure. The relevancy of memory cards decreased; and the popularity of on-line data storage expanded (Figure 3). Notebook computers were the preferred computer type considered by the respondents in both years. Netbooks and desktop PCs became less popular, and tablets and smartphone were appreciated, although the increase in the share of tablets was not really noticeable (Figure 4).

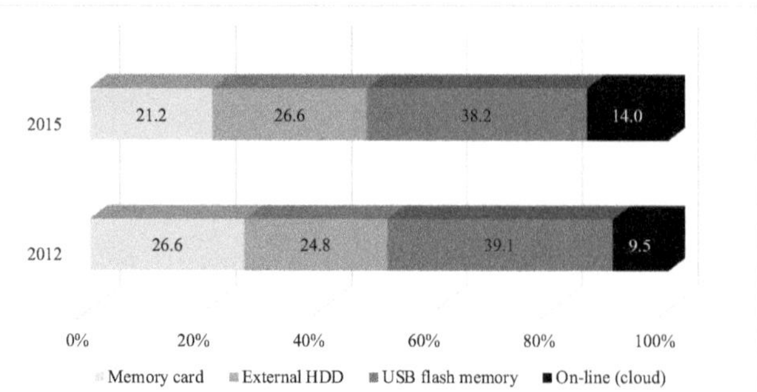

Source: own edition

Figure 3. Preferences about data storage tools (data in %)

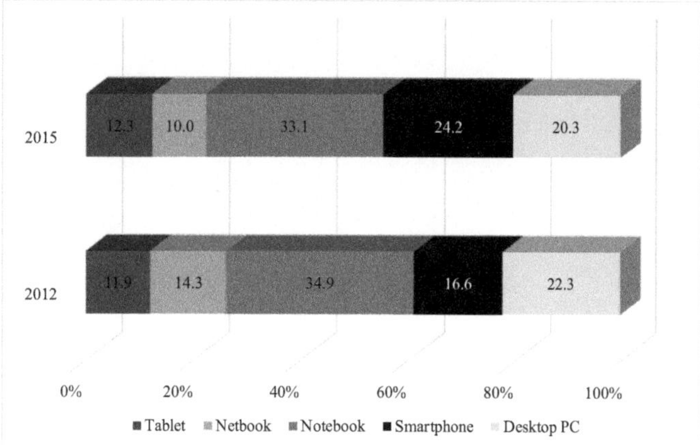

Source: own edition

Figure 4. Preferences about useful computer types (data in %)

Table 3
Results of preference order calculations

Data storage		Type of computer	
2012	**2015**	**2012**	**2015**
1. USB flash memory (53.9) 2. Memory card (21.1) 3. External HDD (18.9) 4. On-line (cloud) (6.0)	1. USB flash memory (52.3) 2. External HDD (22.5) 3. Memory card (15.4) 4. On-line (cloud) (9.7)	1. Notebook (68.0) 2. Desktop PC (13.3) 3. Smartphone (7.9) 4. Netbook (5.5) 5. Tablet (5.3)	1. Notebook (54.1) 2. Smartphone (20.7) 3. Desktop PC 14.0) 4. Tablet (6.4) 5. Netbook (4.8)

Source: own edition

The preference orders and ratio of weights (presented on a 0-100 scale) are summarised in Table 3.

Level of Consistency and Consensus

Reliability of a preference order can be questionable. The personal level of consistency allows us to evaluate whether a respondent has a clear preference order. 91.9% of the respondents in 2012 and 94.9% in 2015 had a clear preference order (K=1) about the data storage tools.

The list of useful computer type included more items that allows more category levels in calculating consistency (K), but also in this case the ratio of respondents with a clear preference order (K=1) was high. The survey results were 82.6% in 2012 and 79.9% in 2015. Moreover, the ratio of cases K>0.75 was 91.1% in 2012 and 91.5% in 2015.

It is interesting to check whether the gender or full-time/part-time status could have a group forming effect on the consistency. The Chi-square test of cross tabulation does not show any significant effect. Both grouping factors have a significant effect in case of the useful computer type. Responses of female respondents and full-time students show lower levels of consistency.

The group level of consensus is determined for cases K>0.75. Tables 4 and 5 summarise the results of some sub-samples (n shows the number of responses in the sub-sample). Each result is significant.

Table 4
Group level consensus on data storage tools

Data storage		n	v	v_{corr} (%)	d_f	u
Total sample	2012	402	.294	29.57	6.045	34.531
	2015	279	.208	21.11	6.065	23.350
Female	2012	253	.303	30.53	6.072	27.229
	2015	148	.233	23.85	6.124	17.368
Male	2012	149	.297	30.20	6.123	20.044
	2015	131	.195	20.11	6.140	14.563
Full-time	2012	266	.282	28.45	6.068	26.916
	2015	238	.208	21.11	6.076	21.321
Part-time	2012	136	.319	32.38	6.135	19.804
	2015	41	.221	23.97	6.469	7.704

Source: own edition

Table 5
Group level consensus on the preferred type of computers

Type of computer		n	v	v_{corr}	d_f	u
Total sample	2012	398	.291	29.28	10.076	44.026
	2015	269	.305	30.77	10.11	36.454
Female	2012	239	.273	27.62	10.127	32.102
	2015	143	.320	32.46	10.214	26.279
Male	2012	159	.341	34.48	10.192	28.927
	2015	126	.312	31.71	10.243	24.082
Full-time	2012	259	.285	28.73	10.117	34.343
	2015	127	.316	32.18	10.241	24.407
Part-time	2012	139	.309	31.36	10.220	25.337
	2015	142	.311	31.61	10.215	25.768

Source: own edition

DISCUSSION

Comparing the General Trends and Survey Results

IT and ICT appears in both personal and corporate everyday activities. Technological novelties are difficult to follow; physical product life nowadays is perceptibly longer than the new product versions on the market. Statistics show a huge and dynamic evolution of ICT tools and possibilities in the 2010s, including changes in user behaviour. The availability of Internet access has become general and its utilisation is now essential in personal and business contacts. However, the level of utilisation is diverse. Although the business administration of large companies widely depends on ICT, smaller ones enjoy fewer of the achievable benefits. Utilisation if often limited to presenting general and product information to customer; however, e-solutions in purchasing are appreciated.

Extension of data traffic, especially the mobile data traffic, is remarkable. This represents new horizons in information exchange because it eliminates the barriers of immobility. The recent mobile phones are ready to substitute for a desktop PC or notebook is many functions.

Generational theory draws up that Generation Y was born in the age of computers, Generation Z was born with the Internet, and Generation Alpha members are born into a permanent on-line era. The last group includes small children who are currently of less interest in terms of the aims of the presente paper, which focusses on higher education or the labour market. However, their attitudes to ICT may move forward the methodological developments for other generations. An Alpha child uses services and databases by touch screens without any knowledge of the technology or design behind it. These children perceive ICT as natural and obvious. I believe that service design shall give similarly simple utilisation possibilities for older generations as well, i.e. the user's attention must not devoured by the operation of the ICT tool, including the hardware or the service framework, rather the focus must be kept on the content of the service.

The empirical results of my survey are in harmony with the general trends. "Smartphoning" spread remarkably between 2012 and 2015. The fact that 89.1% of the respondents considered themselves as regular users in 2015 can be regarded as a ground-breaking result, especially considering that the ratio was 52.4% in 2012. The share of tablets is below my expectations. However, the ratio of both regular and occasional users doubled during the period, while the ratio of non-users decreased from 80.5% to 63.9%. Notebooks were the most popular both in 2012 and in 2015, even though the ratio of regular users decreased from 66.5% to 60.5%.

The survey asked about the time spent with computer activities (see Table 1). The average value of 4 to 5 hours per day is quite much. The survey shows an increase, but there is a significant change between the years only in case of weekend usage. Checking the results by sub-samples, on weekdays the part-time students spend more time in front of the computer but it is still the opposite on weekends.

Evaluation of Changing Preferences

The core element of the analysis was the calculation of preference orders related to data storage tools and useful type of computers. USB flash memory still remained the preferred data storage tool in 2015. The popularity of on-line data storage has increased greatly but its weight lags behind USB flash memory even in 2015 (9.7% versus 52.3%).

The preferred computer type was the notebook in both years. There is no change in the weight of desktop PCs, but its rank in the preference order dropped on the list. Usefulness of smartphones shows a notable step forward (the weight moved from 7.9 to 20.7).

There is a surprisingly high ratio of respondents who have a clear preference order in either year or topic analysed. Despite this, the coefficient of concordance shows a quite low group level of consensus. In the case of data storage tools, the consensus decreased from 2012 to 2015. This may be assign that the current technology-generated change in preferences is not finalised yet, and that adaptation takes place more slowly than the development of the technical background. This phenomenon is observed in each sub-sample of the research.

Conclusions

There are two main conclusions based on the survey:

- changes in utilisation of ICT tools are much slower than the appearance of new tools and solutions,
- the smartphone keeps its place as the key element of the actual utilisation.

Considering the limitations of data collection, further investigation is required that includes both the expansion of the research sample and deploying quantitative analysis for understanding personal motivations.

Karcsics (2007) detected three main development strategies based on the maturity of employee competencies:

- catching up (entry-level),
- compliance with current competitive situation,
- providing skills to ensure long-term competitive advantage.

I believe that nowadays entry-level tasks can be limited to the content and usage of specific corporate systems in case of the students belonging to Generation Y. On the one hand ICT background is granted and achievable, on the other hand the changes of related attitudes has begun. There is a need for improving compliance with the current competitive situation in order to achieve a harmonic development between education and labour market expectations. The focus must be on teaching how to exploit the ICT possibilities during problem solving. Case studies, homework assignments and targeted projects can foster the progress.

In addition, diffusion of smartphones is a warning sign to higher education institutions. Smartphones may give the way to reach the students and to arouse their interest in course materials and other relevant information. General and targeted information flow is channelled: Facebook, Twitter and mobile-conforming webpages are important but not enough. The content of education must be adapted in the interest of two main challenges:

- it allows the effective utilisation of the ICT tools held by the students,
- it motivates the ICT users to identify with the learning objectives.

REFERENCES

COUPLAND, D. (1991). Generation X: Tales from an Accelerated Culture. New York: St. Martin's Press.

KARCSICS, É. (2007). A versenyképes munkavállaló kompetenciái az Európai Unióban és Magyarországon. (Competences of Competitive Employees in the European Union and in Hungary). Európai Tükör, 12(3), 128-140.

KENDALL, M. G. (1970). Rank correlation methods. London: Griffin.

KINDLER, J. & PAPP, O. (1978). Komplex rendszerek vizsgálata: Összemérési módszerek. (Investigating Complex Systems: Comparison Methods). Budapest: Műszaki Könyvkiadó.

KSH (2014). Infokommunikációs (IKT-) eszközök és használatuk a háztartási, a vállalati (üzleti) és a közigazgatási szektorban, 2013. (Information and Communication (ICT) tools and their use in household, corporate (business) and the public sector, 2013). Retrieved: September 2015: http://www.ksh.hu/docs/hun/xftp/idoszaki/ikt/ikt13.pdf.

KSH (2015). Távközlés, internet, 2014. IV. negyedév. (Telecommunications, Internet, 4th quarter 2014). Statisztikai Tükör, 2015/21, 1-3.

KSH (2016). Távközlés, internet, televíziószolgáltatás, 2016. III. negyedév. (Telecommunications, Internet, TV services, 3rd quarter 2016). Statisztikai Tükör, 9. December 2016, 1-6.

PAIS, E. R. (2013). Alapvetések a Z generáció tudománykommunikációjához. (Foundations for the science communication of Generation Z). Project report. Pécs: University of Pécs.

RAPCSÁK, T. (2007). Többszempontú döntési problémák. (Multi-attribute decision problems). Budapest: Budapesti Corvinus Egyetem.

SAATY, T. L. (1980). The Analytic Hierarchy Process. New York: McGraw Hill.

SASVÁRI, P. L. (2012a). Az információs rendszerek kisvállalati alkalmazásának vizsgálata, magyar- és horvátországi összehasonlító elemzés. (The penetration of information systems in small and medium-sized enterprises in Croatia and Hungary: A comparative study). Vezetéstudomány, 43 (Special Issue), 56-65.

SASVÁRI, P. L. (2012b). The Impact of Information Technology on Business Productivity: Revealing the Link between Company Size Categories and the Proliferation of Business Information Systems in Hungary. Saarbrücken: LAP Lambert Academic Publishing.

SASVÁRI, P., & WOLF, R. (2014). Austria and Hungary: Different stages of readiness to create added value by using business information systems. PRO PUBLICO BONO – Public Administration, 3, 169-178.

STRAUSS, W., & HOWE, N. (1991). Generations: The History of America's Future, 1584 to 2069. New York: William Morrow.

SZLÁVICZ, Á. & SZRETYKÓ, G. (2013). Az Y generáció munkával kapcsolatos elvárásai és a cégek EEMrendszereinek új kihívásai. (New work expectations of Generation Y and new chalenges for corporate EEM systems). Tér–Gazdaság–Ember, 1(1), 69-84.

TÖRŐCSIK, M. (ed.) (2015). A Z generáció magatartása és kommunikációja. (Behaviour and communication of Generation Z). Pécs: University of Pécs.

Mergers and Acquisitions: Their Role in the Process of Diversification of an Enterprise

IRENEUSZ JANIUK, Ph.D.
ASSISTANT PROFESSOR

BIALYSTOK UNIVERSITY OF TECHNOLOGY
e-mail: irekj@interia.eu

SUMMARY

This article aims to present the possibilities of using mergers and acquisitions (M&As) in diversification. Its theoretical part contains definitions of diversification and a review of literature on M&As in enterprise growth. Next, it analyzes the M&A market in Poland compared to the markets of Central and Southeast Europe. It presents diversification in the light of the main theories of firm growth and contains a review of the research on the subject of diversification as a growth concept of companies. The empirical section presents case study analyses of six Polish companies regarding the ways in which the firms pursue diversification. The research shows that the dairy companies engage in product diversification, while the meat firms implement industrial diversification. The companies examined in the course of research exemplify the phenomena connected with the use of M&As in diversification.

Keywords: Mergers and Acquisitions, Diversification, Competitive Advantage, Strategy Processes

INTRODUCTION

The subject of mergers and acquisitions (M&As) has been discussed in the literature for many years and from various perspectives, both theoretical and empirical. Many scholars (Manne 1965; Walking & Long 1984; Allgood & Farrell 2000; Brigham & Houston 2001; Domadaron 2002; Gaugham 2002; Krug & Aguilera 2005; Arthaud-Day et al. 2006; Frąckowiak 2009) emphasize the role of M&A deals in enterprise expansion. They make it possible to access new organizational resources and markets, and frequently lead to diversification.

The issues concerning diversification are primarily connected with the growth concept of an enterprise (Ansoff 1957). Diversification is also analyzed on the grounds of the theory of firm growth as well as on the basis of the resource-based theory of a firm: Penrose (1959), Wernerfelt (1984) or Geroski (1999). Firm growth through diversification received attention also from Marris (1963, 1964) and Coad (2007). Other scholars such as Douma (1991), Grant et al. (1988), Montgomery (1982), Porter (1987) or Rumelt (1982) analyze the reasons for and methods of diversification and show that the greatest success is achieved by those firms that adopt the strategy of related diversification. This view is confirmed by the latest research (Jarosiński 2002, 2004; Romanowska 2004; Ferris et al. 2010). However, the theoretical studies that have been conducted so far leave a research gap. They do not go deep enough into the role of mergers and acquisitions in the methods of diversification. There is insufficient research regarding the use of mergers and acquisitions in the process of firm growth as well as the market-product character of diversification.

The objective of this article is to present the possibilities of using mergers and acquisitions in the strategy of diversification. The first part of the paper contains a survey of the literature. Firstly, the main definitions of the term 'diversification' are presented. Next, the article discusses M&A related issues and analyzes the M&A market in Poland, as opposed to the markets of Central and Southeast Europe. On the basis of the literature on the aforementioned subject, diversification is described in the light of the main theories of firm growth. Furthermore, the paper presents a review of the most important studies on diversification. It also cites research results concerning the use of M&As in two key branches of the Polish economy, namely, the dairy and meat industries. What is more, it identifies the top transactions that took place on the analyzed markets.

In the available studies concerning the use of M&As in diversification, the issue of the relation between them is only one element of given research, if it is at all discussed. Therefore, there is a need to conduct deeper analysis of this subject.

The second part of the paper presents the research methodology. It describes the methods adopted to carry out the study and carefully explains why given firms were selected for the purpose of the research. In order to illustrate the role of M&A deals in diversification, the case study method was employed. It was used to perform an in-depth analysis of two firms operating in the dairy industry *(SM Mlekpol* and *SM Mlekovita)* and four firms from the meat industry *(GK Animex, GK Sokołów SA, PKM Duda SA GK,* and *GK Farmutil HS SA)*. The aforementioned companies exemplify the phenomena connected with the use of M&As in diversification.

The analyses made it possible to identify the biggest firms first in the dairy industry and then in the meat industry. The model perspective presents the deals that were closed and the profiles of activity of the firms acquired by the companies from the discussed industries.

The third part of the article presents the results of the research as well as the author's final remarks. The results of research on diversification presented here are consistent with the world trends described in the literature. They also confirm the findings of previous studies on diversification. The dominant form of diversification is external development with particular emphasis on acquisition.

The novelty of the paper lies in the fact that it describes the market-product character of diversification. The analyses of the dairy firms present possibilities of growth achieved through product diversification, while the studies concerning the meat firms point out the opportunities brought on by industrial diversification. The research conclusions and final remarks may trigger discussion about the methods of diversification of companies as the deliberations presented in this article confirm the assumption that there is a need for further and more detailed research on these matters.

LITERATURE REVIEW

Globalization forces firms to cope with a growing number of competitors. Organizations of all sizes must combine effectiveness and competitiveness with being sensitive to the needs of their local customers. Such a situation poses new challenges to managers and necessitates dynamic adaptation. Contemporary firms are in the center of revolutionary transformations. The literature on management lists ten so-called megatrends in the changing environment of a firm. They are the following: strong growth impulses and recession processes, liberalization of economies, accelerated internationalization and globalization, increasing competition, technological advancement, shorter life cycle of products, new IT processes (virtual revolution), demographic changes, new values in the society and increasing awareness of the significance of ecology (Romanowska, 2001).

The megatrends enumerated above exert a strong influence on the economic system as well as on the concepts and methods of management. We can also observe continuous increases in the specialization, size and market value of contemporary firms. There is also a tendency to limit the scope of vertical integration and to create "slim" or even virtual firms. These changes increase the role of M&As as a method of enterprise expansion.

When analyzing the causes of M&As, Gaughan (2010: 18) directs his attention to liberalization of barriers to trade, expansion of capital markets and markets of the financial sector and development of new technologies, as well as increasing global competition. With the use of M&As firms gain access to new organizational resources and markets. They also introduce the strategy of diversification by means of investing in new sources of competitive advantage.

The literature on this subject defines diversification as a strategy involving setting up new, additional activity. This is the point of view on diversification expressed by Miller & Dess (1996: 42). Rue & Holland (1986: 124-125) emphasize that we can talk about diversification only when a company enters areas that differ considerably from its current activity. Similarly, for Mintzberg & Quinn (1992: 79), diversification signifies starting to operate on a different economic path. Another scholar (Romanowska, 2009: 67) perceives diversification as an expansion of the range of products and services beyond the borders of one sector.

As can be seen, all aforementioned authors associate diversification with the beginning of a new activity, one different than activities currently conducted, or with entering new markets with new products. Moreover, it leads to the creation of new quality in the market-product combination of an enterprise. According to Rajzer (2001: 63), notwithstanding its diversity, the process of diversification may be based on internal financing or on acquisitions and mergers with other firms.

M&A Deals and Enterprise Growth

The intensification of changes taking place in the market creates the need for increasing the potential of an enterprise. Further growth may be achieved in a variety of ways, depending on the possibilities of particular companies. They frequently do not possess enough strategic potential to be able to fully take advantage of the ongoing transformations. *The Economist* (2009) presents an opinion that the process of concentration as well as the growth of large firms is caused by their increasing awareness of the risk connected with sub-suppliers. Unreliable suppliers may indeed frequently affect the production cycle in large concerns in a negative way. So as not to lose their established brands and reputation, big firms must focus on their core competences. Instead of subcontracting particular areas of their operation, the enterprises take control over subsequent links of the chain of value. Through the use of M&As, they incorporate firms considered to be crucial in their growth concept. Actions involving the purchase of an entire firm or its part become alternatives to internal growth.

Frąckowiak (2009: 26-27) defines mergers as "consolidations or combining of enterprises, whereas acquisitions refer to the purchase of stocks or shares". A merger takes place when at least two autonomous firms are combined. This is a mutual agreement as a result of which a new business unit is created. Mergers can take two possible forms. The first one involves the combining of companies of similar sizes. Their economic powers are relatively equal. The firms are liquidated in order to create a new enterprise. The characteristic feature of such a merger is the fact that each firm loses its independence and ceases to be a legal entity. A new company is founded on the existing potentials. In this respect, we should understand a merger as a *consolidation* of enterprises.

In the literature the issue of mergers and acquisitions is analyzed from various angles. For instance, Manne (1965) discusses M&A deals by looking at them from the perspective of taking control over the assets of the acquired company. The author claims that what motivates an acquisition is the price of stocks, which is lower than that which would be possible if a given company was better managed.

However, other scholars (Walking & Long 1984; Allgood & Farrell 2000; Krug & Aguilera 2005; Arthaud-Day et al. 2006) turn their attention to hostile takeovers. They stress that such deals are a way of disciplining managers. When a takeover deal is closed, current management is usually replaced with new management that can use a firm's potential in the right way. The risk of being replaced is a very strong motivator for managers.

In the literature, the subject of M&As is also discussed from the perspective of multiplying owner benefit and achieving the synergy effect (Hamrol & Tarczyński 2002). Synergy means *combined work*, which in the context of M&As refers to the benefits brought by combining the operations in two or more business units. The synergy is connected with the fact that firms joined by capital or integrated in terms of organization can generate greater value than a business entity which functions on its own (Hamrol & Tarczyński 2002: 132).

In this context Brigham & Houston (2001) and Domadaron (2002) analyze factors that affect the creation of synergy. The researchers find that synergy can be achieved though: operational activity (an increase of sales revenues), financial activity (lower transaction costs, reducing the cost of capital, tax benefits), diversified effectiveness of operations conducted by the merging firms and the increase of market power.

When discussing M&A-related issues it is also worth quoting Wernerfelt (1984: 175). The scholar is of the opinion that M&As provide an opportunity to trade resources that would be unmarketable in a different situation, and also offer a chance to buy or sell resources in *bundles*. This signifies that in a given *bundle* one can sell or buy a combination of technological capabilities and business contacts. The author stresses, however, that the imperfection of these transactions stems from a relatively small number of buyers and sellers as well as from the diversity of firms. As a consequence, a given firm has different value for different buyers. It is crucial for the acquiring company that the *bundles of resources* make it possible to achieve synergy between resources that a firm already possesses and those that are bought.

As has already been mentioned, M&As are one of the ways of developing a firm. They are an alternative for growth based on the internal method involving the use of a firm's own resources and skills or traditionally understood capital investment. Moreover, M&As are processes which are of great interest for modern companies. They exert an enormous influence on the competitiveness and growth of not only firms but also entire sectors, or even economy.

In the course of discussion about M&As it should be noted that these transactions carry great risk and generate additional costs. What is more, M&As are connected with the change of organization culture, management or laying off some of the employees. Therefore, they are transactions that cause a number of various effects in firms and their environment. The motives for M&As notwithstanding, these deals frequently do not lead to the expected increase of the values of the companies. Thus, they are difficult and complicated processes. It ought to be emphasized that in many cases M&As end in failure and a definite identification of the factors determining their success is not simple.

In the literature on the subject matter of this paper scholars such as Sudarsanam (1998: 234-245) analyze the consequences of M&As and carry out an extensive survey of the world research. A common feature of these studies is the conclusion that M&As frequently fail, which means that the value of a given business drops in comparison to its value before the transaction. For instance, the findings of research conducted by the consulting company Coopers & Lybrand (1993) concern the experience gained during takeovers of British firms. On the basis of this research, Sudarsanam points out the causes of the failures or successes of the transactions. The most common factors contributing to failure include: the attitude of the managers of the company that is taken over and cultural differences (85%), lack of plans concerning integration (80%), lack of knowledge about the industry or about the target company (45%), bad management of the company that was taken over (45%), lack of experience in the area of acquisitions (30%). On the other hand, the factors contributing to the success of a merger or acquisition enumerated by Sudarsanam include: the creation of detailed integration plans and the pace of their implementation (76%), a clear objective of the takeover (76%), a cultural match between both companies (59%), good cooperation with the management of the company that was taken over (47%), knowledge about the taken-over company and its industry (41%).

A similar viewpoint on the factors conditioning the M&A processes is proposed by Korpus (2014). The author is of the opinion that successful combining of firms which contributes to the increase of their value does not take place very often. Moreover, Korpus notes that a great number of successful transactions largely depend on the skills and attitudes of the managers that conduct them. When analyzing the factors influencing M&As, the scholar emphasizes the importance of *due diligence*. According to her, *due diligence* serves to investigate the target, identify its potential problematic areas in the entire transaction as well as sufficiently prepare for integration. Therefore, *due diligence* minimizes the risk carried by M&As and is one of the factors determining their success.

Due diligence, also called *investment audit,* is an investigation of the current condition of a given firm, the aim of which is to identify its strengths and weaknesses as well as to point out potential opportunities and dangers. Such an examination involves every aspect of the potential transaction and its result has a significant influence on the decision to take over a firm and on its price. Generally, *due diligence* concerns commercial, financial, legal, environmental and technical aspects. Particular elements of the investigation ought to identify the main risks carried by the basic activity of the target company as well as the opportunities the transaction may create. More information on the subject of *due diligence* can be found in Gąsior (2005: 177–187) or Bernhardt (1994).

The discussion presented so far shows that M&A deals involve purchasing the entire company or a part of it. Their essential element is the expectation that the combined companies are going to be worth more than the sum of their individual values would be if they functioned independently. Synergy refers to the benefits which can be obtained only when firms become one and which lead to the increase of the value added. However, it should be emphasized that M&As are difficult and complicated processes and in numerous cases they result in failure.

The M&A Market in Poland Compared to the Markets of Central and Southeast Europe

The report *Poland compared to Central Europe – 2010 Edition* concludes that in the period from January 1to December 31 2009 firms in Poland closed 556 M&A transactions worth over €8.5 bn. The data concerning transaction values includes the value of operations disclosed, which make up about 72% of the total. The combined value of all the M&A deals in Poland closed in this period amounted to €12 bn. Among the 556 transactions, 36 involved restructuring within corporate groups and their value amounted to €1,827 m (KPMG & DEALWATCH, 2010). In comparison, in 2008 Poland recorded a total of 548 transactions worth almost €8.54bn.

When comparing the Polish M&A market in 2009 and 2008, we should notice that it was stable. The number of transactions rose by less than 1.5%. Moreover, the market comes out well when contrasted with the regional data. In 2009 in Central Europe 1,663 M&A transactions were concluded. Their total value (as the sum of transactions whose value was disclosed) amounted to almost €25 bn. The combined value of all the transactions was €43 bn. The data demonstrates that Poland's share in the M&A market made up about a third of all deals closed in Central Europe (KPMG & DEALWATCH, 2010).

When analysing the M&A market it is also worth quoting research results included in another report called *Central and Southeast Europe - M&A Barometer 2012.* The study was conducted by Ernst & Young in 11 countries: Bulgaria, Croatia, the Czech Republic, Greece, Hungary, Poland, Romania, Serbia, Slovakia, Slovenia and Turkey. The study revealed that only in five countries did the M&A market grow in 2012. These countries were the Czech Republic, Greece, Poland, Slovakia and Turkey. In the entire region the value of the transactions decreased by 17.6%. What is more, the findings show that in 2012 in Central and Southeast Europe 1,108 deals were closed and their value totalled $41.8 bn. In 2012 the highest number of transactions (297) was recorded in Turkey. As for the volume of closed deals, the second position belonged to Poland (276 transactions), while the third to the Czech Republic (155 transactions). As for the value of the deals, however, in 2012 Poland was in the third position with deals worth $8.02 bn. The first position belonged to Turkey, the second one to the Czech Republic. In 2012 in Poland, in comparison to 2011 ($22bn), the value of transactions decreased (EYGM, 2013).

The aforementioned research shows that in the whole region the highest number of M&As took place in the industrial, services, mining and energy sectors. Transactions of the highest value were carried out in the banking, food, and mining and energy sectors. Most of the transactions involved strategic investors. In Poland they made up 90% of the total. 59% of all the deals concerned firms operating in Poland, 30% were M&A deals involving foreign investors, while the remaining 11% were conducted by Polish firms operating abroad. The most active foreign investors in Poland were the USA, Germany and the UK.

When analysing the M&A market it is also worth quoting research results included in another report called *M&A Barometer H1 2014. Central and Southeast Europe* (2014). The report states that the total value of M&A deals in Central and Southeast Europe in the first half of 2014 amounted to US$18.5 bn. This is a rise by over a third compared with the same period in 2013. Turkey was the country that held the first position in terms of the value of transactions. It was followed by the Czech Republic and Poland. Turkey was the top country in terms of the volume of closed deals as well (153 transactions). The second position belonged to Poland (112 deals), while the third to the Czech Republic (111 deals). What is more, the report states that 629 transactions were completed in the first half of 2014 in the entire Central and Southeast Europe area (11 countries). The value of the transactions in the respective period was $18.5 bn. This is a 35.9% increase compared to the first half of 2013. Moreover, the research found that in the whole region the major target of transactions was IT companies (16%). Further targets of takeovers were manufacturing companies and service firms, which made up 13% and 10% of the deals, respectively. Other sectors in the region in which acquisitions took place were energy and mining (7%), pharmaceutical industry (7%) and real estate (7%). In Poland a majority of the M&As (63%) were closed by strategic investors, whereas financial investors completed 37% of all the transactions. The main sector of economy undergoing ownership transformations was IT (EYGM, 2014).

The analyses presented above allow one to conclude that, despite the changes in the number and value of the transactions, Poland is still an attractive country in terms of mergers and acquisitions. Over 50% of all the deals closed in Central and Southeast Europe were domestic. This signifies that both the buyer and the target company originated from the same country. In Poland, 32% of investors were foreign investors from countries such as Germany, the USA, Sweden, France and Greece. In 17% of the transactions Polish companies took over foreign firms. For instance, in June 2014 *PKN Orlen* acquired the Canadian mining company *Birchill Exploration* for over $200 m. This was the largest transaction in the oil industry. It is also worth remembering that at the end of 2013 PKN Orlen from Płock acquired *TriOil*, a Canadian company listed on the Toronto stock exchange. At the same time *Grupa Azoty* purchased the exploration rights for deposits of phosphate rock in Senegal for about $29 m. Further Polish mergers were carried out by the company *PZU*. They included the acquisition of *Link4* as well as insurance companies in Lithuania and Latvia for about €350 m. The examples of transactions mentioned above demonstrate that Polish companies are becoming more active in the international M&A market.

Diversification in the Light of the Theories of Firm Growth

In the theory of strategic management the classic model of the strategy of growth of an organization was designed in the 1950s by Ansoff (1957). Primary growth strategies based on this model involve investing in product and market development. Investing in product development entails modification of existing products and introducing product innovations, but most importantly, investing in new products. Investing in market development, in turn, involves competing in geographically new markets, which leads to internationalization. According to Ansoff (1957) the next step in the process of growth of a firm is diversification, which consists in abandoning not only the current technologies of product manufacturing but also the current market structure. According to Ansoff, diversification involves relocation of resources possessed by an enterprise to actions significantly different from those that the firm carried out in the past. He also emphasizes that diversification requires involvement in industries, technologies and markets that are new for the company, with products that are also new. Therefore, diversification is an undertaking leading to growth in new fields.

In the literature the issues connected with firm growth are explained in the *theory of the growth of the firm* developed by Penrose (1959). The central issue constituting the core of the theory is the optimal growth rate of a firm as well as the determinants and limits to growth. When analyzing the mechanisms of firm growth, Penrose stresses the role of resources. On the grounds of the theory of the growth of the firm, the author treats a company as a collection of physical and human resources. The scholar claims that a firm's directions of expansion are determined by its physical resources, skills and experience of the managers as well as by its unused resources. Thus, Penrose develops the *resource-based theory of the firm*. The author also believes that a firm is not only products and markets, but also particular internal resources which are indivisible, specialized and unique for a given company. She also emphasizes the role of possessing resources and, in particular, the importance of the services which these resources may provide. According to Penrose, a firm's success is determined not only by such resources as labor or capital, but also by the quantity and quality of the services which these resources introduce into the manufacturing processes. Penrose identifies the following fundamental strategies in the process of firm growth: internal expansion, diversification, expansion through mergers and acquisitions, and innovations.

Also the work of Wernerfelt (1984: 172-173) is in agreement with the resource-based theory of the firm. In his view, a company's resources can be both tangible and intangible. Examples of such resources include the brand, accumulated knowledge, technology, qualified personnel, business contacts, buildings and machinery, effective procedures, and capital. According to Wernerfelt, all the elements connected with a company which can be perceived as its strengths or weaknesses can be called resources.

Geroski (1999: 16-30), in turn, believes that when a firm is created it possesses some particular ability or knowledge that it develops later in a unique way. This signifies that on the basis of its current knowledge, a firm learns how to develop new skills and expand its knowledge. Similarly to Penrose, Geroski perceives a firm through its resources and emphasizes that internal resources are an individual matter and firms can possess stocks of underused resources that push them to grow. As for diversification, Geroski analyzes the organizational capabilities of a company. The scholar believes that the choice of the right diversification strategy is connected with the issue of core competences, and claims that diversification should be based on an understanding what a given firm is able to do to acquire particular skills.

Diversification is also of interest to Coad (2007: 34-35), who makes reference to the managerial growth model developed by Marris (1963, 1964). From the perspective of the aforementioned model, Coad assumes that firms grow only due to diversification. Above a certain level of growth, further diversification generates lower profit. This is confirmed by observations of the events taking place on the stock market. According to Coad, the reactions to diversification announcements as well as subsequent analyses of the profits of diversified firms show that diversification tends to exert a negative influence on a firm's financial performance. Conversely, diversified firms that decide to refocus their activities improve their financial results.

Diversification entails launching new activity, different from that or those currently conducted, or entering new markets with new products. However, before a decision to diversify is made, a company should thoroughly analyze its capabilities. According to Penrose (1959: 136), it ought to take into consideration if further growth is possible in the current field of operations. What should also be thought over is whether the resources and skills of a firm are sufficient to allow it to keep its position in its field and enter new areas at the same time, as well as whether the new fields are profitable and can be conquered. Penrose believes that the diversification strategy of a company should focus on the most effective use of the resources that are already possessed. The author stresses that growth by diversification is the most effective if the new activities are related to the existing resources.

In the professional literature the issues concerning the decisions to diversify are frequently connected with M&As. At this point it is again worth mentioning the words of Wernerfelt (1984: 175, 179) who points out that potential buyers tend to limit their search for firms they would like to take over to those that fulfill some simple criteria. The scholar's opinion is that in the process of managing the buyer's resource portfolio, the candidates for product or resource diversification must be evaluated both in terms of the short-term effects as well as in terms of their long-term capabilities for further expansion.

The discussion presented so far leads to the conclusion that diversification may be an attractive form of development for many firms that have reached considerable maturity. Moreover, it leads to the creation of new quality in the market-product combination of an enterprise, because it goes beyond the current processes in the chain of value added. Diversification may be connected with the processes currently taking place in a company or be conducted in fields completely new to a given firm.

When we look into growth from the perspective of products, it can be seen that companies expand their range of goods and services as well as cover new market segments. In this aspect, product development entails broadening their product portfolio. In a situation when investment in a product is done in a firm's current sector, we speak about product diversification. Therefore, *product diversification* means expanding the range of products by adding goods coming from new market segments of the current sector of operations.

Product development leads to the expansion of the range of products offered by a given company. In a situation when investing in product development involves products from outside a firm's current sector, with time we can speak of *industrial diversification*. This means entering new areas of operations understood as new sectors of the economy. In this case a sector is defined as a group of companies producing goods or services of similar purpose and using the same supply sources. Therefore, the market character of growth entails investment in products from new sectors or industries and signifies *industrial diversification*. In this sense, diversification is understood as broadening the product development strategy.

Diversification – a Survey of Selected Research

In the literature on the subject matter of this article the issues connected with diversification are viewed from various perspectives, both in the theoretical and the empirical sense. As it has already been mentioned,, they particularly concern issues related to mergers and acquisitions and the possibilities to find more beneficial conditions of operation. For instance the researchers from the field of strategic management – Ferris et al. (2010) point out growth opportunities brought on by industrial diversification and stress that it is a strategy which lets a firm use its resources effectively and achieve synergy. Wiersema & Bowen (2008) in turn, turn their attention to the process of globalization of markets and industries. The scholars also mention opportunities of diversification in the international sense.

The professional literature contains an entire branch of research on the connection between the methods of diversification and company performance. Studies carried out by Rumelt (1982) found that the firms which develop through related (industrial) diversification perform better than specialized companies (not diversified) and than those which developed through conglomerate (unrelated) diversification. However, another study (Montgomery, 1982) proved that the differences in the performance of firms that diversified their operations in different ways were a result of the type of sector structure rather than of a given type of diversification. Similarly, Grant et al. (1988) found that related diversification does not ensure better performance than unrelated (conglomerate) diversification.

Nevertheless, research conducted at the beginning of the 21st century confirms the previously widely-held opinion that initial increase in the level of diversification causes fast growth in company performance, but at the same time a too high level of diversification leads to a drop in performance (Palich et al. 2000; Gary 2005; Miller 2006). The research cited above demonstrates that for every company there exists an optimal level of diversification, and after crossing this limit a firm's profitability begins to fall.

Investigation of the relationship between the level of diversification and the economic performance of a company has been conducted in Poland as well, for example by a group of scientists from the University of Lodz (Bohdanowicz et al. 2010). Their research dealt with the subject of the strategies of public companies. The analyses demonstrated that the higher the level of diversification of a company's activities, the higher its return on assets.

In the context of the effectiveness of the diversification strategy it is worth mentioning the research conducted by a team led by Romanowska (2011). The scholars analyzed for instance the influence of the level and character of diversification on the economic performance of corporate groups. Their studies regarded three categories of enterprises: specialized groups, groups with a dominant share in one sector, and diversified groups. The findings revealed very weak dependence between the degree of diversification and financial performance measured e.g. with ROE and ROA. The comparison of economic performance of the groups that adopted the strategies of related and unrelated diversification found no relation between the type of diversification and the amount of revenues generated by the examined corporate groups.

From the perspective of designing a growth strategy for a firm, however, the earlier studies of the team of Romanowska (2004) are of crucial importance. The research *Strategic Behaviours of Polish Enterprises in Global Sectors* investigated various aspects and areas of strategic behaviors of Polish firms. In the context of directions of company development, the scholars present different strategies following the model created by Ansoff. They point out that the opportunities arising from industrial diversification allow a firm to achieve synergy.

As for the methods of implementing the strategy of diversification, it is worth quoting the research conducted by Jarosiński (2002). His study examined the reasons and motives behind the Polish entrepreneurs' decisions to venture into the strategy of diversification, the methods of carrying out the process as well as the level and type of diversification. The conclusions of Jarosiński's study demonstrate that the main motive for undertaking diversification by the analyzed companies was the need for growth, while the dominant reason was the risk of losing their traditional markets. The most common way of pursuing the strategy of diversification was internal development. The dominant methods of diversification included purchasing shares in other companies, which should be understood as acquisitions usually leading to related diversification. The analyses also show that the examined enterprises were fully diversified at the time of the research.

Another study carried out by Jarosiński(2004) confirms the interest of Polish entrepreneurs in related diversification. The research investigated the changes in the level of product and industrial diversification of companies from the following five sectors: household appliances, paints and varnishes, brewing, chemical fertilizers and shipbuilding. The examination of these changes in the years 1990-2002 concluded that in the group of diversified companies the percentage of those that adopted the strategy of related diversification and those that chose unrelated diversification declined. Moreover, the research demonstrated that firms diversify their operations in a mixed way only marginally. Jarosiński also concludes that among the total of diversified companies in the analyzed period the dominant form of diversification was related (industrial) diversification.

In the context of ways of diversification, as has already been mentioned, a firm can become involved in both internal and external growth. Porter (1987) and Douma (1991), however, showed that companies tend to choose external development, with particular emphasis on acquisition. What is more, Porter concluded that as many as 74% of acquisitions in unrelated sectors ended in failure. Similarly, Douma found that 81% of entries into unrelated sectors failed, while in the case of entries into related sectors the failure rate was only 41%. The latest studies demonstrate that the greatest success is achieved by those companies that adopt the strategy of related diversification.

The issues connected with adopting the strategy of diversification also appear in the research on capital and organizational concentration of companies (Janiuk 2011, 2014). This type of study shows that, in their growth concepts, the companies pursue diversification through involvement in M&As.

The research on the subject of concentration of the dairy industry in Poland (Janiuk 2014) identified the largest dairy companies: *SM Mlekpol – Grajewo* and *SM Mlekovita – Wysokie Mazowieckie.* These firms diversify through takeovers of smaller businesses with a similar profile. The top deals on the dairy market are presented in Figure 1.

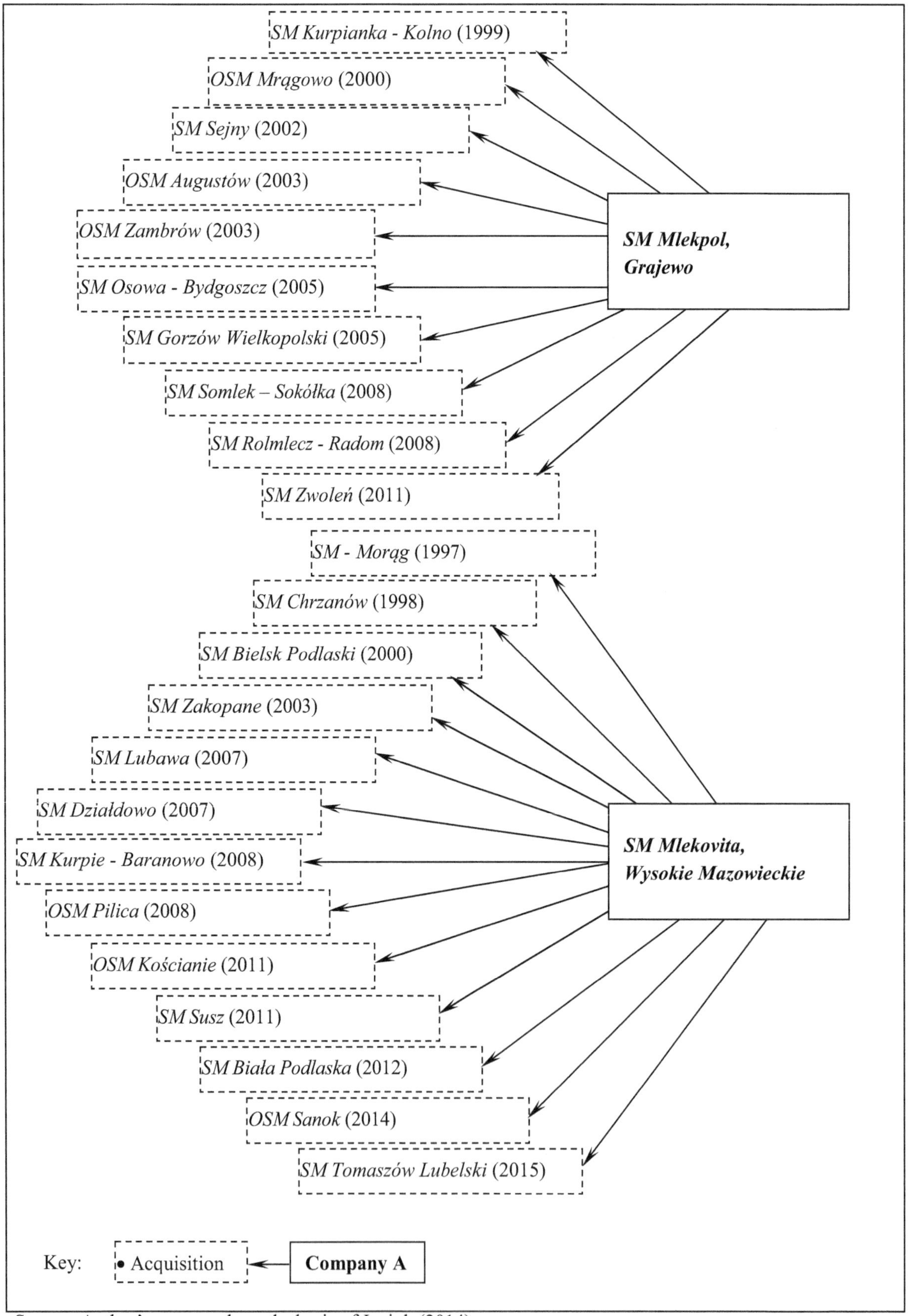

Source: Author's own work on the basis of Janiuk (2014)

Figure 1. Top transactions on the dairy market in Poland

Moreover, the research dealing with the meat industry in Poland (Janiuk 2011) shows that firms strive to diversify. The study also found that the companies incorporate M&As in their growth concepts. The top deals on the meat market are presented in Figure 2.

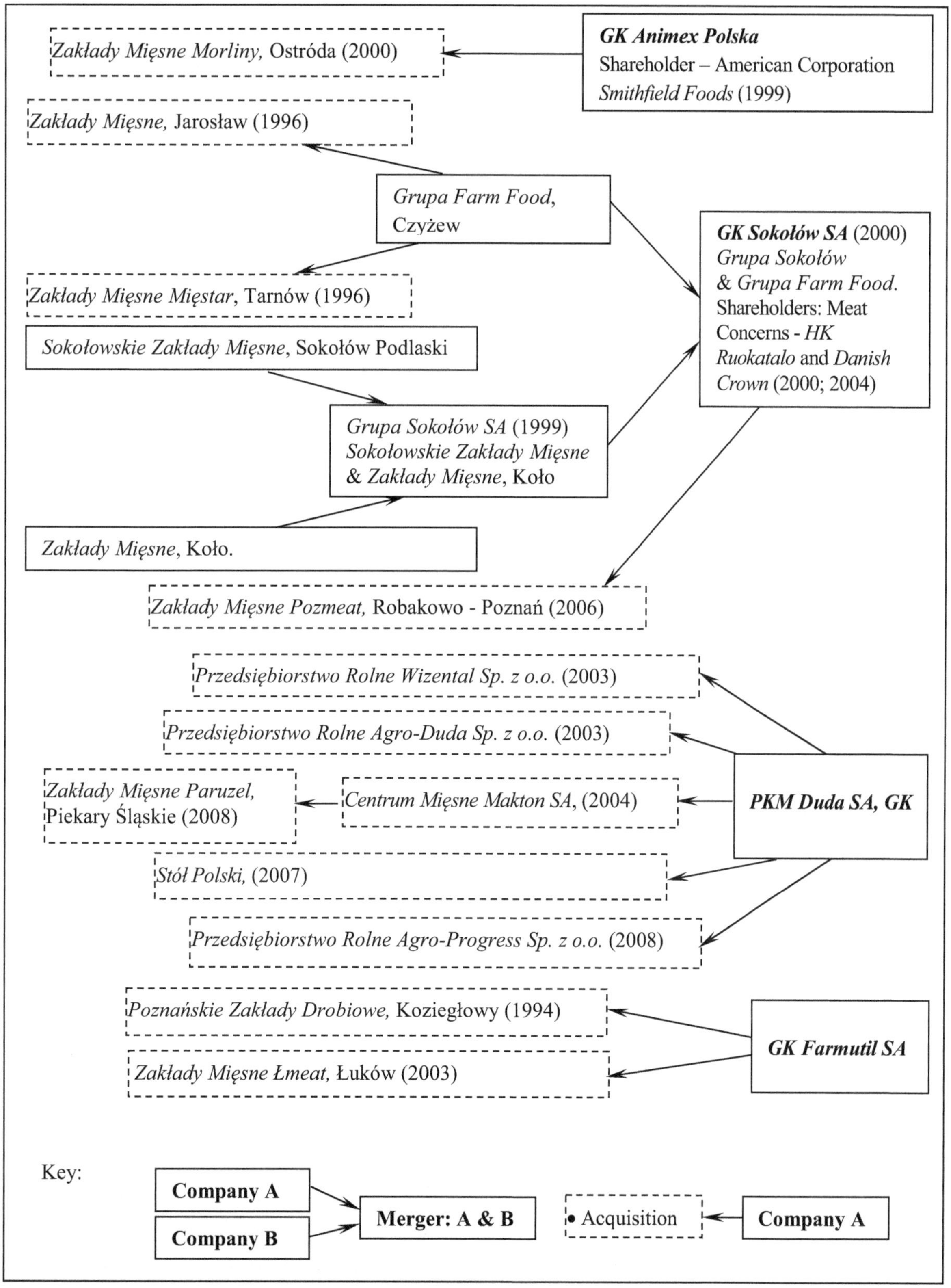

Source: Author's own work on the basis of Janiuk (2011)

Figure 2. Top transactions on the meat market in Poland

Research Gap

Research shows that in their pursuit of diversification, companies use mergers and acquisitions. However, the theoretical analysis conducted in this article reveals a research gap. The insufficiency of research regards the use of M&As in enterprise growth as well as the market and product character of diversification. In the available studies, which regard M&As and diversification, the issue of the relation between them is only one of the elements of the research, if it is discussed at all. Therefore, there is need to conduct a deeper analysis of the subject of the role of M&As in the methods of diversification of enterprises. Such research would make it possible to provide the answer to the following questions:

- What is the role of M&A deals in the diversification of enterprises?
- In what way do M&A deals enable a company to take control over subsequent elements of the economic path?
- How do M&A deals make it possible for companies to enter fields related in terms of technology, market or organization?

The answers to the questions posed above will make it possible to identify the opportunities which stem from the use of mergers and acquisitions in the strategy of industrial diversification of an enterprise.

METHODOLOGY

The study uses the data gathered in the course of previously conducted analyses regarding capital and organizational concentration of companies in the two key industries of the Polish economy, namely the dairy industry (Janiuk 2014) and the meat industry (Janiuk 2011). Next, unobtrusive research was carried out. The method adopted was content analysis involving the examination of recorded texts such as books, magazines or website information (Babbie, 2008).

On the basis of previous analyses and the information from websites an in-depth analysis of the largest M&As in the dairy and the meat industry was performed. The previously carried out quantitative analyses served as a basis for the identification of the enterprises which most frequently make M&A deals parts of their growth concepts.

The next step of the study concerned the analysis of opportunities to use M&As in the strategy of diversification. The analysis of the enterprises took the form of case studies. In line with the Grounded Theory, a case study is a research tool enabling the researcher to fully understand phenomena observed in a real-life context (Babbie, 2008).

The case studies investigated the most active entities on the M&A market in the dairy industry (2 firms) and the meat industry (4 firms). The cases studied in the dairy industry are *SM Mlekpol* and *SM Mlekovita*, whereas in the meat industry the analyzed firms are *GK Animex, GK Sokołów SA, GK Farmutil HS SA* and *PKM Duda SA GK.* The use of case studies as a research method allowed for formulating extensive conclusions concerning the methods of diversification. In order to investigate the role of M&A transactions in the growth concepts of companies, analyses of each of the six cases was performed. The aforementioned companies exemplify the phenomena connected with the use of M&As in diversification.

The firms chosen for the study are the most active entities in their industries in terms of engagement in M&As. Therefore, considering the highly uncertain chance of success of M&A deals, which was pointed out in the theoretical part of the article, it can be generally assumed that in the cases of the firms selected for the study the transactions positively affect their growth process. The companies mentioned above have for years been actively participating in the consolidation process of their industries. Preliminary observations allow one to conclude that the analyzed firms pursue the strategy of diversification. They gradually increase their sales revenues as well as their market share (Janiuk 2011: 94; 2014: 39). However, in terms of the market-product character of diversification, dairy firms differ from meat companies. Therefore, the selected business entities are worth attention with regard to the way they use M&As to diversify their activities.

In accordance with the growth model created by Ansoff, the research presented in this paper follows its assumptions regarding the market-product character of diversification. Growth of the product character is understood as the broadening of the range of products by adding goods coming from new market segments but targeted for the current sector of operations – this means *product diversification*. Growth of the market character, on the other hand, is understood as the widening of the product portfolio, which involves entering new fields of operation perceived as new sectors of the economy – this means *industrial diversification* (related).

In-depth analyses made it possible to identify the biggest firms first in the dairy and then in the meat industry and present them in a comprehensive way. The model presents the deals that were closed and the profiles of activity of the firms acquired by the companies from the discussed industries. As a result, it was possible to formulate detailed conclusions on the subject of the role of M&As in the process of diversification of companies. Comprehensive presentation of the research results leads to the answers to the research questions posed above.

RESEARCH RESULTS AND CONCLUSIONS

The analysis of the dairy industry demonstrates that *SM Mlekpol* and *SM Mlekovita* are enterprises which diversify their activities in the process of slow concentration of their industry. They are domestic capital companies which in the process of their growth take over smaller entities operating on the market. The takeovers they performed involved firms with a similar profile of activities and led to the widening of the firms' range of products. In the context of diversification the acquisitions allow the companies to expand their product portfolio by goods coming from new segments of the dairy market. The target entities operate in the same sector of economy (dairy processing). This signifies that, by investing in product development and increasing the variety of their products, *SM Mlekpol* and *SM Mlekovita* are involved in product diversification. Product diversification of dairy companies as well as the profiles of activities of the taken over firms are presented in Table 1.

Table 1
Product diversification of dairy companies and the profiles of activities of the acquired firms

Acquiring company Enterprise functions	Acquired company	Profile of activities after the acquisition
SM Mlekpol, Grajewo Purchase of raw milk; Milk processing plants: Manufacture of dairy products; Distribution and sales of dairy products;	*SM Kurpianka - Kolno* (1999)	Production: ripening and smoking cheeses, cheese spreads. Sales of dairy products.
	OSM Mrągowo (2000)	Production: fermented products, kefir, milk drinks, whey powder, hard cheeses. Sales of dairy products.
	SM Sejny (2002)	Production: ripening cheeses, spiced cheeses
	OSM Augustów (2003)	Sales of dairy products.
	OSM Zambrów (2003)	Production: UHT milk, quarks, whey powder, powdered milk. Sales of dairy products.
	SM Osowa - Bydgoszcz (2005)	Production: milk and flavoured milk, quark Sales of dairy products.
	SM Gorzów Wielkopolski (2005)	Production: powdered milk. Wholesale outlet of dairy products.
	SM Somlek - Sokółka (2008)	Production: yoghurts, fermented milk. Sales of dairy products.
	SM Rolmlecz - Radom (2008)	Production: UHT milk, UHT cream, butter, quark, cream cheese, bio-yoghurts, full and skimmed milk, powdered milk Sales of dairy products.
	SM Zwoleń (2011)	Production: powdered milk.
SM Mlekovita, ***Wysokie Mazowieckie*** Purchase of raw milk; Milk processing plants: manufacture of dairy products; Distribution and sales of dairy products;	*SM - Morąg* (1997)	Production: ripening cheeses. Wholesale outlet of dairy products.
	SM - Chrzanów (1998)	Production: ripening cheeses. Distribution Center. Sales network of dairy products.
	SM Bielsk Podlaski (2000)	Production: ripening cheeses. Wholesale outlet, Distribution Center, Sales network
	SM Zakopane (2003)	Production: mozarella cheese, smoked ewe's milk cheese (oscypek). Sales of dairy products.
	SM Lubawa (2007)	Production: cottage cheeses, quark. Cheese Packing Plant. Sales network of dairy products.
	SM Działdowo (2007)	Production: hard cheeses, butter. Wholesale outlet, Distribution Center. Sales network of dairy products.
	SM Kurpie – Baranowo (2008)	Production: Cheddar cheese, butter. Sales of dairy products.
	OSM Pilica (2008)	Production: cheeses, whey. Sales of dairy products.
	OSM Kościanie (2011)	Production: flavoured cheeses, cream. Wholesale outlet, Distribution Center. Sales network of dairy products.
	SM Susz (2011)	Production: cheeses, whey. Sales of dairy products.
	SM Biała Podlaska (2012)	Production: cheeses, whey. Sales network of dairy products.
	OSM Sanok (2014)	Production: cheeses, whey. Wholesale outlet of dairy products.
	SM Tomaszów Lubelski (2015)	Production: cheeses, whey. Wholesale outlet, Distribution Center. Sales network of dairy products.

Source: author's own work on the basis of the conducted research.

The subsequent stage of the research regards firms operating in the meat industry. The investigation concluded that the largest meat companies are *GK Animex, GK Sokołów SA, GK Farmutil SA* and *PKM Duda SA GK.* When we look into the methods of diversification of the studied firms, what should draw our attention are the specific conditions in which the companies were set up.

GK Animex is a link of a foreign international corporation, *Smithfield Foods.* In Poland *Animex* has developed on the basis of the assets of state companies. In the processes of privatization and abolishment of monopolies in Polish economy, the firm went througha series of ownership transformations. It acquired stocks and shares in domestic fodder manufacturers, meat processing companies and meat product manufacturers. The target companies are specialized firms operating in the agricultural and food industry. In the case of *Animex*, restructuring involves for example incorporating independent businesses. The acquisitions tend to involve former partners and competitors on the meat market. One of the key transactions in line with this tendency was the acquisition of *Zakład Mięsny Morliny* in Ostróda. Apart from the development of *Animex's* production potential, the deal entailed gaining another well-known brand on the market.

GK Sokołów SA is also a company with a share of foreign capital. It was set up as the result of a merger between *Grupa Sokołów SA* and *Grupa Farm Food* (2000). The analysis reveals that the origins of these companies lie in the processes of ownership transformations of former state-owned manufacturing plants as well as with earlier M&As in the industry. *Grupa Sokołów SA* was created as a result of a merger between *Zakłady Mięsne SA* and *Zakłady Mięsne* in Koło (1999), whereas the genesis of the development of *Grupa Farm Food* involves the acquisitions of *Zakłady Mięsne Jarosław* in Jarosław (1996) and *Zakłady Mięsne Mięstar* in Tarnów (1996).

PKM Duda and *Farmutil,* on the other hand, are firms based on domestic capital. They have established their positions in the agricultural and food industry predominantly by exploiting the transformations of private companies. On the basis of their principal area of operation, the companies enter new fields with which they are related technologically, organizationally or in terms of market. In the process of natural investment of their financial surplus, they gradually expand their industrial and market scope of operations. They are aware of the opportunities arising from consolidation of the industry; therefore, they purchase shares or stocks of business entities functioning in the areas creating a chance of further growth. They pursue investment in technological development.

The studies of the cases of the meat companies allow one to conclude that diversification of their activities is based on M&As involving entities that are for example their suppliers, partners or competitors. The investigated companies take over firms operating in the broadly-defined agricultural and food industry by performing partial or full buyouts. They undertake forward or backward vertical diversification. These processes are called backward vertical diversification and forward vertical diversification, respectively. When the companies enter new areas of operation they also assume control over comparable phases of the creation of value on other economic paths. These types of activities are characteristic of industrial diversification. Industrial diversification of meat companies as well as the profiles of activities of the taken over firms are presented in Table 2.

Table 2

Industrial diversification of meat companies and the profiles of activities of the acquired firms

Acquiring company Enterprise functions	Acquired company	Profile of activities after the acquisition
GK Animex Polska: Agricultural production: Production and processing of fodder, livestock farms. Meat processing: animal slaughter and meat processing. Operations on the market of pork, beef and poultry. Manufacturing of meat products. Manufacturing and sales of down and feathers. Distribution and sales.	*Zakłady Mięsne Morliny,* Ostróda (2000)	Production department: pork and beef processing.
GK Sokołów SA: Production of raw materials: agricultural and livestock farms; Meat processing: animal slaughter and meat processing. Operations on the market of pork. Manufacturing of meat products. Distribution and sales.	*Zakład Mięsny Pozmeat,* Robakowo - Poznań (2006)	Production department: pork processing.
PKM Duda SA:	*Wizental Sp. z o.o.* (2003)	Livestock farming: trade in livestock.
	Agro-Duda Sp. z o.o. (2003).	Livestock farming: trade in livestock.

Agricultural production: production and processing of fodder, livestock farming; Meat processing: purchase of cattle and pigs for slaughter, slaughtering, processing and distribution of meat, purchase and processing of game. Operations on the market of pork, beef and game. Manufacturing of meat products. Distribution and sales.	*Centrum Mięsne Makton* (2004)	Production department: meat processing. Wholesale outlet. Meat distribution center.
	Stół Polski (2007)	Network of sales of meat and meat products.
	Agro Progress Sp z. o.o. (2008)	Livestock farming: trade in livestock.
	Zakłady Mięsne Paruzel, Piekary Śląskie (2008)	Meat processing and cold cuts production.
ZRP Farmutil SA: Agricultural production: processing of fodder, farming of pigs, poultry and cattle. Meat processing: purchase of livestock, slaughter and meat processing. Operations on the market of pork, beef and poultry. Manufacturing of meat products. Distribution and sales.	*Zakłady Drobiarskie*, Koziegłowy (1994)	Production department: poultry processing.
	Zakłady Mięsne Łmeat, Łuków (2003)	Production department: pork and beef processing. Wholesale outlet. Network of sales of meat products.

Source: author's own work on the basis of the conducted research.

The research demonstrates that when the examined firms undertook and carried out diversification, in various respects they behaved in a way similar to that described in the literature. Although the motives and ways of diversification were formulated in a slightly different way, they still fully correspond to those cited in the references. The dominant form of diversification of the aforementioned companies is external development with particular emphasis on acquisition. The results of the case studies described above made it possible to formulate particular conclusions that lead to the answers to the research questions posed above.

The analyses of the dairy firms found that *SM Mlekpol* and *SM Mlekovita* perform takeovers of firms with profiles of activities similar to theirs, which leads to product diversification. The acquired companies are local competitors specialized in production for particular segments of the dairy market. The acquisitions create chances of benefitting from the incorporated assets and divided competences. In the process of research it was discovered that the transactions enable the companies to quickly strengthen their positions on the market. The observed acquisitions ought to be understood as incorporations as a result of which new branches or plants are created and function within the structures of the buyer. From this point of view, diversification concerns these entities which possess complementary resources in the product or market areas. These complementary resources and competences strengthen the core activity of the buyer. Such a form of product diversification contributes to the modernization of the production potential, optimization of the use of particular links of the chain of value and limits industrial risk. As a result, the number of unnecessary production factors is reduced, while product specialization of given businesses increases. Product diversification enables a firm to reduce costs as well as expand its product portfolio and distribution network. This empowers companies to become leaders in the dairy industry. It may be assumed that in the process of their future growth *SM Mlekpol* and *SM Mlekovita* are going to establish their positions with regard to their core activity and go beyond the borders of dairy industry later on. As a consequence, further investment in related areas of operation is going to lead them to industrial diversification.

Also the case studies of the meat companies presented above demonstrate that they have been using the strategy of diversification for years. However, in their case, it is industrial, not product diversification. *GK Animex, GK Sokołów SA, GK Zakład Rolniczo-Przemysłowy Farmutil HS SA,* as well as *Polski Koncern Mięsny Duda SA GK* are involved in mergers and acquisitions. When diversifying their activities, the companies take over businesses functioning in areas treated as crucial for their further growth. They pursue investment in technological development. Moreover, they purchase shares or stocks of firms that are their suppliers, partners or competitors. They adopt the strategy of industrial diversification by means of entering new areas of operation related to their core activity. The examined companies display interest in both backward and forward industrial diversification. In their growth concepts they create entities joined by capital connections. On the basis of their principal area of operation, they take control over new areas with which they are related technologically, organizationally or in terms of market. The M&As contribute to functional improvements and to changes in the involvement in the market. The firms' strategic decisions lead to the achievement of synergy as well. Their functioning in related fields makes it possible for them to expand their areas of operation to cover new elements of the economic path – this means industrial diversification.

Diversification is a strategy which determines investment priorities on given markets and points out directions of expansion. It decides to what extent a company is going to focus on particular areas of its operations. What is also noteworthy in this context is that in both the dairy and the meat industry the process of production concentration is of key importance. This creates the need to increase the scale of investment directed at modernizing the processing potential and at the construction of new production plants. Managers are aware that in such conditions success cannot be achieved solely by means of internal growth. Therefore, the role of M&A deals as means of enterprise expansion is growing. Through the use of these transactions firms gain access to new organizational resources and to new markets. As a result, initially small corporate groups emerge and gradually increase their revenues. This brings on a steady intensification of consolidation processes in the sectors as well as technological concentration of production.

The basic limitation of this research is its lack of representativeness. The case studies presented above exemplify the phenomena regarding the use of diversification. The findings presented here can be of use only to entities possessing sufficient organizational potential to allow them to diversify their activities. In addition, the results may serve managers in the process of making decisions about the directions and methods of diversification.

The analyses also carry implications for further research, which can examine the optimum level of diversification and its types or investigate the relation between diversification and the economic condition of companies.

Final Remarks

The discussion presented above confirms that advancing globalization involves sectors of the economy, industrial markets, enterprises and competition. The fact that foreign firms are gradually entering the Polish market intensifies internationalization of the economy. In order to adapt to the changing conditions, enterprises must become actively involved in the changes. The pressure generated by globalization and increasing competition forces them to adjust to the new conditions. A characteristic feature of such adjustment is the act of setting ambitious goals. The completion of the tasks stemming from these goals leads to fast growth and sometimes also to expansion. It is expressed in the willingness to catch up with the best or assume the position of a leader.

M&As can be observed in various sectors of the economy. The motives behind these ways of combining of enterprises are diverse. They stem from the evolution of the environment, diversification of activity or the resources possessed by a given company. The interest in M&A transactions is also triggered by the need to accelerate growth and strengthen market positions. As a result, firms gain the possibility to complement their resources and competences. The transfer of knowledge and technology makes it possible to achieve synergy, economies of scale and to expand the scope of operations. However, M&As frequently fail. Only in a few cases do they lead to cost reduction and an increase of market share. The most common mistake made during M&As is insufficient analysis of such important aspects as risk, price and integration. The discussion presented so far in this paper indicates that *due diligence* minimizes the risk carried by the M&A transactions. It is treated as a factor determining their success.

Diversification entails launching new activity, different from that currently conducted, or entering new markets with new products. The study demonstrates that in their pursuit of diversification companies get involved in M&As. From the perspective of diversification it is crucial that the transactions ensure synergy between the resources that a firm already possesses and those to be purchased.

The results of research on diversification presented in this article are consistent with the world trends described in the literature. They also confirm the findings of Polish studies on diversification reviewed earlier in this paper. The dominant form of diversification in the cases of companies described here is external development with particular emphasis on acquisition. The investigated transactions make it possible for the companies to enter fields related in terms of technology, market or organization. As a consequence, the firms develop and strengthen their enterprise functions. Their brands become recognizable and their industrial and market scope of activity grows. This strengthens their competitive position on the market and helps them reduce the risk carried by cooperation with suppliers.

References

ALLGOOD S., & FARRELL K.A. (2000): The effect of CEO tenure on the relation between firm performance and turnover. The Journal of Financial Research, 23(3): 373-390. http://dx.doi.org/10.1111/j.1475-6803.2000.tb00748.x

ANSOFF, H.I. (1957): Strategies for Diversification. Harvard Business Review, 35(5): 113-124.

ARTHAUD-DAY M.L., CERTO S.T., DALTON C.M., & DALTON D.R. (2006): A changing of the guard: Executive and director turnover following corporate financial restatement. Academy of Management Journal, 49(6): 1119-1136. http://dx.doi.org/10.5465/amj.2006.23478165

BABBIE E. (2008): Podstawy badań społecznych (The Basics of Social Research), Warsaw: Wydawnictwo Naukowe PWN.

BERNHARDT, R.G. (1994): The Acquisition Process: A Program for Success. In: Miller, B.J. (Ed.): Mergers and Acquisitions. New York: John Wiley & Sons: 3-18.

BOHDANOWICZ L., JEŻAK J. & MATYJAS Z. (2010): Strategie rozwoju polskich spółek publicznych a ich wyniki finansowe – dylematy metodyczne w ramach przeprowadzonych badań (Growth Strategies of Polish Public Companies and Their Financial Results - Methodological Dilemmas of the Research) In: Studia i Prace Kolegium Zarządzania i Finansów. Zeszyt Naukowy Nr 99: 79-89. Warsaw: SGH.

BRIGHAM, E.F. & HOUSTON, J.F. (2001): Fundamentals of Financial Management, Orlando: Harcourt College Publisher.

COAD, A. (2007): Firm Growth: A Survey. Papers on Economics and Evolution, #0703: 34-35. ftp://papers.econ.mpg.de/evo/discussionpapers/2007-03.pdf Accessed 14 May 2015.

COOPERS & LYBRAND. (1993): Making a Success of Acquisitions. London: Coopers and Lybrand.

DOMADARON, A. (2002): Investment Valuation: Tools and Techniques for Determining the Value of Any Asset, New York: John Wiley & Sons.

DOUMA S. (1991): Success and failure in new ventures. Long Range Planning, 24(2): 54-60. http://dx.doi.org/10.1016/0024-6301(91)90079-4

EYGM Limited. (2014): M&A Barometer H1 2014 - Central and Southeast Europe, www.ey.com. Accessed 14 May 2015.

EYGM Limited. (2013): M&A Barometer H1 2012 - Central and Southeast Europe, www.ey.com. Accessed 14 May 2015.

FERRIS S.P., SEN, N., & THU, N.T.A. (2010): Firm value and the diversification choice: international evidence from global and industrial diversification. Applied Economics Letters, 17(11): 1027-1031. http://dx.doi.org/10.1080/00036840902817433

FRĄCKOWIAK W. (Ed.) (2009): Fuzje i przejęcia (Mergers and Acquisitions), Warsaw: PWE.

GARY M. (2005): Implementation strategy and performance outcomes in related diversification. Strategic Management Journal, 26(7): 643-664. http://dx.doi.org/10.1002/smj.468

GAUGHAN, P.A. (2010): Mergers, acquisitions, and corporate restructurings, Fifth Edition, New York: John Wiley & Sons. http://dx.doi.org/10.1002/9781118269077

GĄSIOR, A. (2005): Due diligence jako istotna analiza przy wyborze kandydata do nabycia (Due Diligence as an Important Analysis when Choosing a Target Company). In: Janasz, W. (Ed.).: Innowacje, ryzyko, zarządzanie wiedzą, strategie przedsiębiorstw (Innovation, Risk, Knowledge Management, Strategies of Firms): 177-187. Szczecin: Wydawnictwo Naukowe Uniwersytetu Szczecińskiego.

GEROSKI, P. A. (1999): The Growth of Firms in Theory and in Practice, Discussion Paper No. 2092:16-30. Centre for Economic Policy Research, London. http://math.unife.it/economia/ls.applicata-politica/insegnamenti/economia-e-politica-industriale-avanzato/materiale-didattico/materiali-prof.ssa-labory-a.a.-2010-2011/geroski%20growth%20of%20firms%201999%20cepr.pdf Accessed 14 May 2015.

GRANT R.M., JAMMINE A.P. & THOMAS H. (1988): Diversity, diversification and profitability among British manufacturing companies, 1972-1984. Academy of Management Journal, 31(4): 771-801. http://dx.doi.org/10.2307/256338

HAMROL, M., & TARCZYŃSKI, J. (2002): Wpływ fuzji i przejęć na wartość rynkową przedsiębiorstw w Polsce (The Influence of Mergers and Acquisitions on Market Value of Companies in Poland). In J. Duraj (Ed.), Przedsiębiorstwa na rynku kapitałowym (Enterprises on the Capital Market): 132. Łódź: Wydawnictwo Uniwersytetu Łódzkiego.

JANIUK I. (2014): Manufacture of Dairy Products in Poland as an Example of a Fragmented Industry. Slovak Scientific Journal – Management: Science and Education ~ m:se. 3(1): 38-39.

JANIUK, I. (2011): Grupy kapitałowe w procesie koncentracji przetwórstwa mięsnego w Polsce. (Corporate Groups in the Process of Consolidation of the Meat Processing Industry in Poland). Organizacja i Kierowanie, 2(145): 93-97.

JAROSIŃSKI M. (2002): Dywersyfikacja branżowa przedsiębiorstw handlu zagranicznego w Polsce w okresie transformacji (Businesses Diversification of the Polish Foreign Trade Enterprises in the Period of Transformation). Organizacja i Kierowanie, 3(109): 69-73.

JAROSIŃSKI M. (2004): Dywersyfikacja produktowa i branżowa (Product and Industrial Diversification), In: Romanowska M. (Ed.) Strategiczna transformacja polskich przedsiębiorstw (Strategic Transformation of Polish Companies): 229-232. Warsaw: Warsaw School of Economics.

KORPUS, J. (Ed.). (2014): Fuzje i przejęcia: kluczowe czynniki sukcesu i przyczyny niepowodzeń transakcji (Mergers and Acquisitions: Determinants of Success and Causes of Failures). Warsaw: Wydawnictwa Profesjonalne PWN.

KPMG & DEALWATCH, (2010): Rynek fuzji i przejęć. Polska na tle Europy Środkowej. Edycja 2010. (The Market of Mergers and Acquisitions. Poland Compared to Central Europe. 2010 Edition), https://www.kpmg.com. Accessed 14 May 2015.

KRUG J.A., AGUILERA R.V. (2005): Top management team turnover in mergers & acquisitions, Advances in Mergers and Acquisitions, Vol. 4: 121-149. http://dx.doi.org/10.1016/s1479-361x(04)04005-0

MANNE H.G. (1965): Mergers and the market for corporate control, Journal of Political Economy, 73(2): 110-120. http://dx.doi.org/10.1086/259000

MARRIS, R. (1964): The Economic Theory of 'Managerial' Capitalism. Macmillan: London. http://dx.doi.org/10.1007/978-1-349-81732-0

MARRIS, R. (1963): A model of the 'managerial' enterprise. The Quarterly Journal of Economics, 77(2): 185-209. http://dx.doi.org/10.2307/1884399

MILLER D.J. (2006): Technological diversity, related diversification, and firm performance. Strategic Management Journal, 27(7): 601-619. http://dx.doi.org/10.1002/smj.533

MILLER, A. & DESS, G.G. (1996): Strategic Management, New York: McGraw-Hill Inc.

MINTZBERG, H. & QUINN, J.B. (1992): The Strategy Process - Concepts and Contexts, Toronto: Prentice-Hall Inc.

MONTGOMERY, C.A. (1982): The measurement of firm diversification: Some new empirical evidence. Academy of Management Journal, 25(2): 299-307. http://dx.doi.org/10.2307/255992

PALICH, L.E., CARDINAL, L.B., & MILLER, C.C. (2000): Curvilinearity in the diversification – performance linkage: an examination of over three decades of research. Strategic Management Journal, 21(2): 155-174. http://dx.doi.org/10.1002/(sici)1097-0266(200002)21:2<155::aid-smj82>3.0.co;2-2

PENROSE, E. (1959): The Theory of the Growth of the Firm. Oxford: Basil Blackwell and New York: Wiley.

PORTER, M.E. (1987): From competitive advantage to corporate strategy. Harvard Business Review, May/June, 1987: 43-59.

RAJZER, M. (2001): Strategie dywersyfikacji przedsiębiorstw (Strategies of Diversification of Enterprises), Warsaw: PWE.

ROMANOWSKA, M. (Ed.) (2011): Grupy kapitałowe w Polsce. Strategie i struktury (Corporate Groups in Poland. Strategies and Structures), Warsaw: PWE.

ROMANOWSKA, M. (2009): Planowanie strategiczne w przedsiębiorstwie (Strategic Planning in an Enterprise), Warsaw: PWE.

ROMANOWSKA, M. (Ed.) (2004): Strategiczna transformacja polskich przedsiębiorstw (Strategic Transformation of Polish Enterprises). Warsaw: Warsaw School of Economics.

ROMANOWSKA, M. (Ed.) (2001): Podstawy organizacji i zarządzania (The Fundamentals of Organization and Management), Warsaw: Wydawnictwo Difin.

RUE, L.W. & HOLLAND, P.G. (1986): Strategic Management - Concepts and Experiences, New York: McGraw-Hill Inc.

RUMELT, R.P. (1982): Diversification strategy and profitability. Strategic Management Journal, 3(4): 359-369. http://dx.doi.org/10.1002/smj.4250030407

SUDARSANAM, S. (1998): Fuzje i przejęcia (Mergers and Acquisitions). Warsaw: WIG-PRESS.

THE ECONOMIST. (2009): Big is back. August 27: 9.

WALKING, R.A. & LONG, M.S. (1984): Agency theory, managerial welfare, and takeover bid resistance. Rand Journal of Economics, 15(1): 54-68.

WERNERFELT, B. (1984): A resource-based view of the firm. Strategic Management Journal, 5(2): 171-180. http://dx.doi.org/10.1002/smj.4250050207

WIERSEMA M.F. & BOWEN H.P. (2008): Corporate diversification: the impact of foreign competition, industry globalization, and product diversification. Strategic Management Journal, 29(2): 115-132. http://dx.doi.org/10.1002/smj.653

Tax Evasion or Tax Optimization: Is there any Narrow Path between the Two?

MIKLÓS FELLEGI, Ph.D.
ASSOCIATE PROFESSOR
e-mail: pzfemi@uni-miskolc.hu

SUMMARY

There are three disadvantages of the taxation system in Hungary: the explicit and implicit taxes on work income, its transparency and the long-term predictability of tax regulation, and the extent of tax evasion. Minimizing tax evasion has always been a significant task in defending a country's budget-based income. Besides the loss of revenue, tax-avoidance also deforms the effects of the tax system's redistribution, simply because it causes an unintended redistribution between those who pay and those who avoid taxes. Discovering the causes and repairing the tax morals are only possible after a thorough 'diagnosis'. In the present phase of the research, the different forms of tax evasion are dealt with.

Keywords: tax evasion, tax wedge, competitiveness, tax regulation, tax reform, tax morals

INTRODUCTION

In Hungary, regulations about not letting the moral risks grow could be one – if not the only – solution for breaking out of the long-existing (economic) stagflation. The Department of Economics of the University of Miskolc (DE-MU), in collaboration with the National Tax and Duty Office (NTDO), aims at researching the possible causes and forms of tax evasion, ways of repairing the tax morals, and the formation of the present opinions on the NTDO as an organization. This article summarizes the present state of the research.

Minimizing tax evasion has always been a significant task in defending the budget-based income of a nation. Colloquially, the two concepts mentioned above in the title – tax evasion and tax optimization – are often used interchangeably. Tax evasion clearly means an illegal activity, while tax optimization functions within legal frameworks. Based on an example of an enterprise, hiding and not providing tax declaration of the actually acquired income is tax evasion (or simply tax avoidance[1]). However, presenting the same income as capital income (instead of work-income) can be considered tax-optimization[2] (Scharle et al., 2010).

OPTIMUM TAXATION

Based on tax theories and empirical results, there are three disadvantages of the taxation system in Hungary: the explicit and implicit taxes on work income (especially the different social allowances), the transparency and long-term predictability of tax regulation and the extent of tax avoidance. Merely reconstructing the present tax system is not enough for economic growth, but tax reform can strengthen the positive effects achieved in other areas. The financial crisis puts a burden on such reform ideas, but on the other side it forces/encourages the reconstruction of Hungarian economic regulations (Elek & Scharle, 2008).

Taxes Imposed on Work

Comparison reports by international organizations state that the taxes imposed on work in Hungary are too high, despite the significant lowering of the income tax rate (Scharle et al., 2010). This is in fact also the most dominant barrier to economic growth. As a result of tax regulations, the proportion of work taxes (within the GDP) dropped; however, from the global investment

[1] *In present study, considering that the two concepts (tax avoidance as part of tax evasion) are the same from a budgetary deficit point of view, they will be used interchangeably.*

[2] *This is particularly emphasized in tax systems where the two types of income fall under different taxation methods (i.e. capital income has a lower tax proportion than work income).*

point of view, it remained high in comparison to the regional competitors. The explanation for this ambivalence is that in the last few years (as a result of the global crisis), the European countries also lowered the taxes on work in order to keep up a normal level of purchasing and consumption. The core process is well-presented by the tax wedge: the 55% tax wedge in the years before 2010, due to the 16% flat-rate personal income tax, dropped to 49% by 2013. Despite this 6 % drop, our position has not changed due to strong tax competition. Figure 1 & 2 gives an indication of the situation described above.

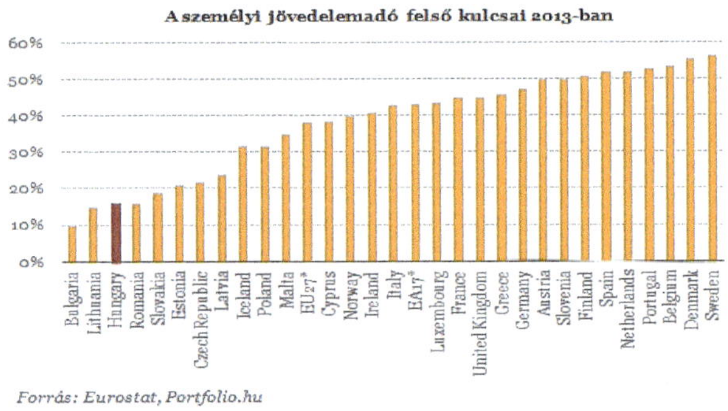

Source: Eurostat, Portfolio.hu

Figure 1. The upper tax bracket of the personal income tax in 2013

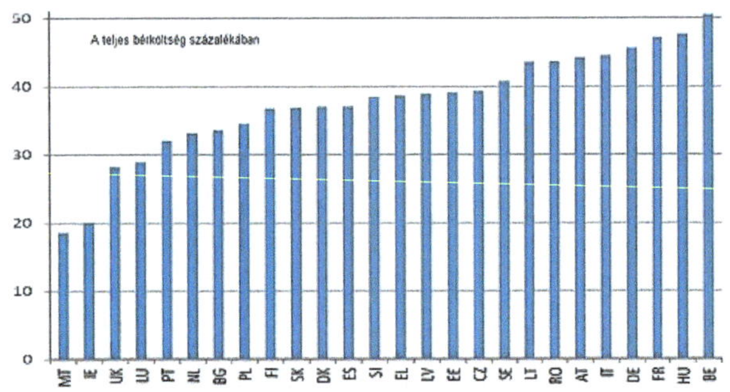

Source: Eurostat, Portfolio.hu

Figure 2. Taxes imposed on work in proportion to the full income in %, 2013

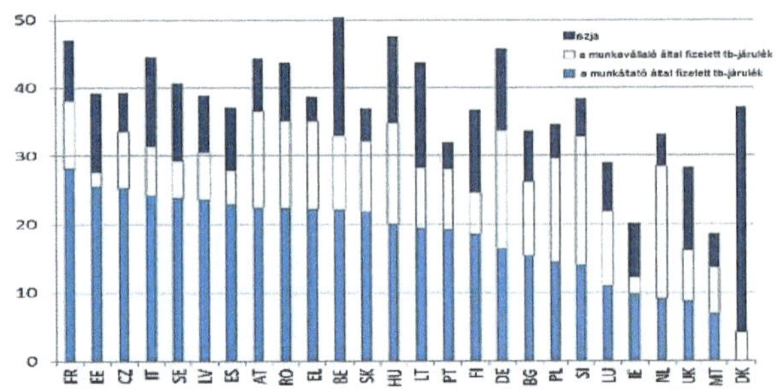

Source: Eurostat, Portfolio.hu

Figure 3. Percentage indication of taxes imposed on work (dark blue: personal income tax, white: the social insurance paid by the employee, light blue: social insurance paid by the employer)

[3] *The research of this essential problem is not part of the present study.*

Among the EU countries, Hungary occupies the second place after Belgium in the tax wedge proportion list. This position was also typical in the last decade. Therefore, as lowering the tax rate does not seem to help in the country's competitiveness, further lowering proposals should be considered carefully. Figure 3 indicates in which areas potential lowering can occur.

In Hungary, the general tax level per income, in the form of personal income tax and social insurances paid by the employer and employee is higher than the EU average. Consequently, it is a question of political values, economic rationality and fiscal force, by which figure (employer or employee), in which area (tax or contribution), and to what extent taxes imposed on work can be lowered. Obviously, further research is required on which tax types should be enhanced and which investments from the budget should be cut down on in order to counterbalance this process.[3]

Tax Regulation

Besides the rate of taxes, the lack of the tax system's transparency and predictability poses the largest threat to the country's competitiveness and judgement about its business environment quality. The administrative burdens connected with taxation and the effect of the different legal regulations on the economic figures also belong to this dilemma.

The main characteristic of the Hungarian tax system is its complexity and ever-changing nature (Kátay, 2009). According to theoretical models and empirical research, the unpredictability of the tax system reduces the volume of investment. In general, uncertainty lowers the future value of the income of enterprises. Great uncertainty, nevertheless, postpones the decision about irreversible investments. The most significant source of uncertainty is the (lack of) authenticity of the economic-political steps. The investor should consider in advance whether a given reform is durable enough or not. In case of an economic-political step with questionable authenticity, the waiting time is prolonged, and obviously, investments are postponed. A general feature in decision-making observed in ex-socialist countries is that the stability and predictability of the incentives is far more important than the mere proportion of the incentives (Bélyácz, 2009).

Besides their real function, legal regulations and their changes always have an unintended negative effect on society. The cost of tax administration is an example of this. The main question is: what costs do the tax imposition; its collection and its verification carry in themselves? On the one hand, they usually emerge in the public sphere in the form of direct costs of the tax-collection and verification institutions. On the other hand, they emerge in households and enterprises. In these last two cases, the most notable loss of costs (which can be neglected on a social level) is the costs of the actual payment of taxes and the cost of fines (Deloitte, 2009). From a social point of view, further costs on a national level are also significant to mention. One part of them is the costs of investment and education connected to obeying the tax regulations; another part is the costs of registration and the continuous declaration. These emerging costs are not necessarily correlated with the income generated by the present type of tax; they rather show a connection to the frequently changing, complex and often ambiguous legal regulations[4] (Barr, 2004).

The sustainability of a tax reform largely depends on the reactions of the entrepreneurs. If an economic-political step is not credible and thus the enterprises do not respond, without the intended prosperity (as a self-fulfilling prophecy), the government is forced to withdraw the reform ideas. Another typical example of the effect of taxes is when the various tax- and subsidy elements change the behaviour of the economic figures. For instance, when the tax imposed on work keeps the employee from activities on the labour market; when the enhancement of the work costs lowers the labour demand of enterprises; when the interest tax influences savings; or when the corporate tax cuts down on the investments of enterprises. These examples are of essential value and influence – although to various extents – the income and expenditures of public finance (Brys, 2010). For now, it is sufficient to be able to recognize the phenomenon; later in the article it will be differentially examined.

Tax Avoidance

In the present phase of the research the different forms of tax avoidance are dealt with. Discovering the causes and repairing the tax morals are only possible after a thorough 'diagnosis'. Besides the loss of revenue, tax avoidance also deforms the effects of the tax system's redistribution, simply because it causes an unintended redistribution between those who pay and those who avoid taxes. It also affects the economy, because nowadays in several industrial branches the avoidance of taxes is leading pricing practices and creating employee expectations. Therefore, those who do pay taxes have to face a vast competitive disadvantage, while tax-avoiding enterprises gain an unrightfully high level of competitive advantage. A further negative consequence is that the tax avoiding possibilities (without the tax avoidance) in fact lead investments towards less profitable activities. Nevertheless, if the tax system makes other economic activities impossible, then from a social welfare point of view tax evasion and the continuation of the present activity could be seen as advantageous. The tools of legal inspection cannot always catch up with the tax avoiding techniques, so these inspections often reach individuals who do fulfil their taxation responsibilities. As a consequence, the moral tension is growing in taxing processes, which turns even the regularly taxing individual towards tax avoidance (Fortin et al., 2007).

Based on recent estimations of the OECD about the shadow economy, tax avoidance can be seen as a general characteristic in Hungary. The extent of the problem is indicated in Figure 4, showing that the untaxed incomes are equal to 23% of the GDP. The tax effect of this is 2 trillion HUF.

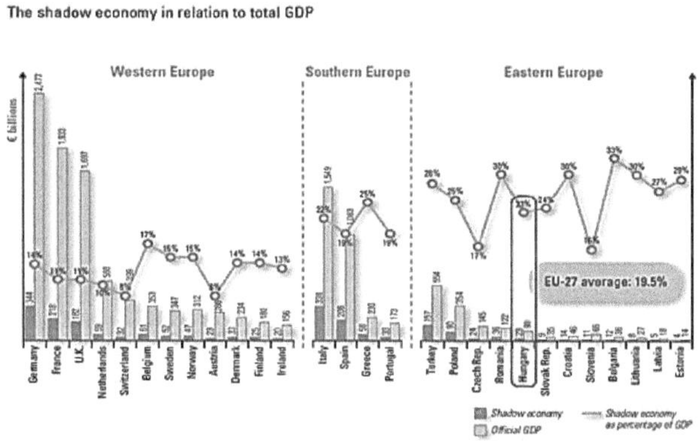

Source: Eurostat, Portfolio.hu

Figure 4. The shadow economy in relation to total GDP 2012

In view of the Hungarian budgetary data, it becomes evident that if by the reparation of the tax morals, structural reform of the tax system and broadening the rate of tax-payers, the role of the grey economy could be lowered to the EU-average of 19.5%, then it would mean a 1 trillion HUF budgetary income growth for the country.[5]

Possible Causes

In studies about the grey- and black economy and corruption, research question about the causes of tax-avoidance often rises. Obviously, various answers can be found among countries with different taxation cultures.[6] According to the standard economic view, tax avoidance depends on the rate and inspection of taxes. Inspection, however, has two essential aspects: the risk of being caught red-handed and the rate of the fine (Slemrod & Yitzhaki, 2002).

The inspection of the Tax Authority can only be successful if it has adequate remedies against tax-avoidance. This statement from the economic figures' point of view is as follows: tax avoidance depends on its relative yield; in other words, what is the degree of 'savings' by fraud in proportion to tax paying? A risk-neutral tax payer will be lawful if the degree of tax is lower than that of the expected fine.[7]

[4] *In case of certain environmental product prices, the costs can be in proportion to the budget income, generalized by the tax type.*
[5] *Such an amount would obviously in itself compensate for the budgetary deficit.*
[6] *This could be a particularly interesting comparative analysis, using cross-cultural elements, which would provide useful information for governments and international companies.*
[7] *The expected value of the fine is the probability of being revealed multiplied by the combination of the fine and the taxation responsibility.*

An effective counter-act to tax evasion is the enhancement of fines and inspection procedures.

According to applied models, the risk of being unveiled and the degree of the fine is always in inverse ratio to tax avoidance. The degree of the tax, however, does not show correlations with tax avoidance; tax rates can positively or negatively affect tax avoidance, depending on the calculation method of the fine and the speculations about being revealed (Ali et al., 2001). The tendency to pay tax in reality cannot be explained only by the risk of being caught red-handed or by the rate of the fine; as opposed to the forecasts of standard models, more people pay taxes than expected. However, models that take social correlations into consideration make a more accurate estimation. According to these models, social influence can have three resources:

- The need for conformity, following rules, and belonging to groups
- The possibility of learning from others
- The need for justice

Therefore, the following aspects may also influence a tax paying tendency: information about others' tax paying customs, information about tax evasion methods, a well-balanced distribution of tax burden, the quality of governmental policy and the customer-friendly functioning of the tax office (Fortin et al., 2007).

Existing Consequences

The economic split of Hungary is a well-known fact. Numerous studies have dealt with the comparison of the western and eastern regions (e.g. Fazekas et al., 2013). There is no homogeneity on a regional level, but the phenomenon exists, fuelling social and economic problems. Considering it from a tax evasion point of view, there is also a well-defined line between the western and eastern regions; however, having a closer look at the more homogenous micro-regions, interesting patterns can be seen. In Figure 5, the income division of the small regions can be observed. The lighter shades indicate lower average incomes.

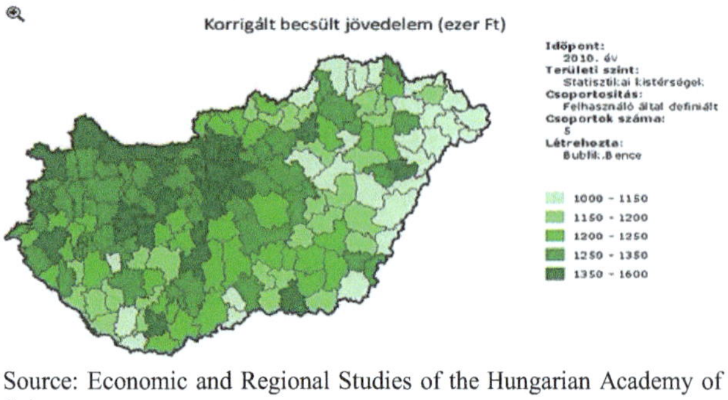

Source: Economic and Regional Studies of the Hungarian Academy of Sciences

Figure 5. Corrected estimated income (in thousand HUF), 2010

North-East Hungary and the Northern Great Plain, along with the southern part of the Great Plain and southern Transdanubian regions, belong to the lower income line. Contrarily, Central Hungary and the northern Transdanubian regions show higher income rates. This not so surprising result for economic experts and laymen alike is worth further analysis, using Figure 6. On this map of the hidden economy, Hungary is also divided into small regions, where the darker areas indicate the presence of hidden or shadow economy.

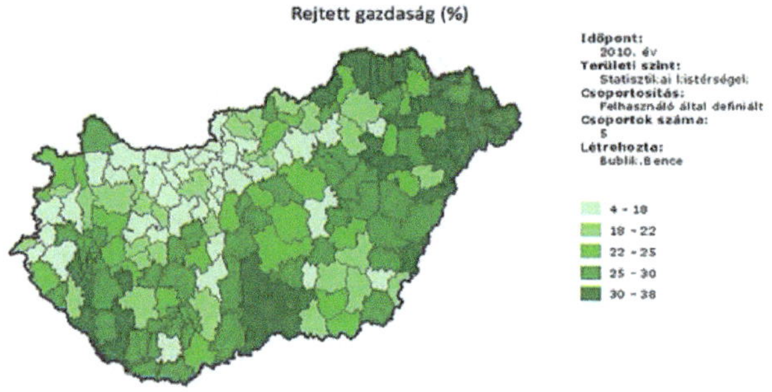

Source: Economic and Regional Studies of the Hungarian Academy of Sciences

Figure 6. The division of shadow economy by micro regions

This map of Hungary seems to be the reflection of that depicted in Figure 5. Tax avoidance as a response to tax rates thus not only varies among countries or country groups. According to the chart it has become obvious that within a country (belonging to a certain tax culture) the regions can also simultaneously show different tax morals. Discovering the causes of this phenomenon can greatly contribute to the explanation of tax avoidance and the definition of the parameters for enhancing tax morals, which could form the aim of the next phase of the study.

THE MOST FREQUENT ECONOMIC CRIMES

The two most important categories of economic crimes involve budgetary fraud (including tax evasion) and bankruptcy crime in windup processes. Figure 7 gives an indication of the criminal procedures[8] initiated by the NTDO's Criminal Directory department in the first quarter of 2013.

In total 2756 criminal procedures were initiated for 37.82 billion HUF; blue: budgetary fraud (tax fraud); green: violating copyrights; red: bankruptcy crime (e.g. windup processes); purple: other.

The economic crimes[9] known up to this point can be broken into 37.4% budgetary fraud, 27.54% violation of copyrights, and 9.4% bankruptcy crime. In all, 77.84% of the 37.82 billion HUF deficit (i.e. 29.44 billion HUF) was caused by crimes belonging to budgetary fraud.

[8] *In case of bankruptcy crime it is usually not the NTDO who starts the prosecution, but rather the enterprise itself who initiates the windup.*

[9] *In 2012, the financial detectives of the NTDO discovered various economic crimes with a total value of 121 billion HUF. The budgetary fraud (mainly tax fraud) committed at the expense of the Hungarian state was worth 94.86 billion HUF.*

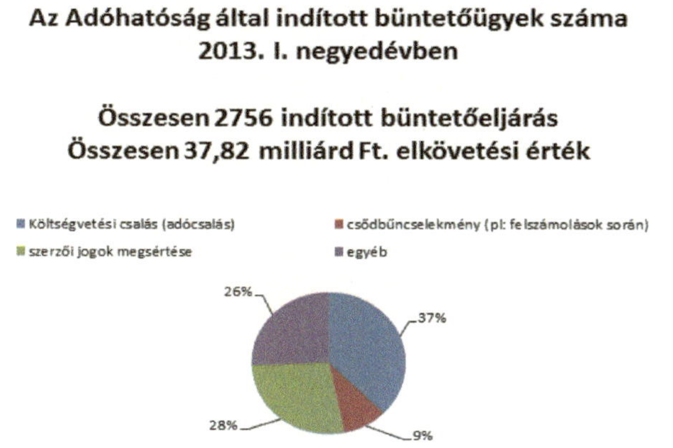

Source: NTDO Criminal Directory

Figure 7. Criminal procedures initiated by the NTDO (1st quarter of 2013)

Budgetary fraud is the most frequent crime in inspection reports. Along with this, the perpetrator is also sued for the falsification of private documents, as the tax declaration is in fact a private document. The most important cause of prosecution within budgetary fraud is connected to the VAT; however, other types of misuse with social insurance and other social allowances cannot be neglected. In windup procedures, the most important cause is indicated as bankruptcy. Figure 8 depicts windup procedures in the last few years.

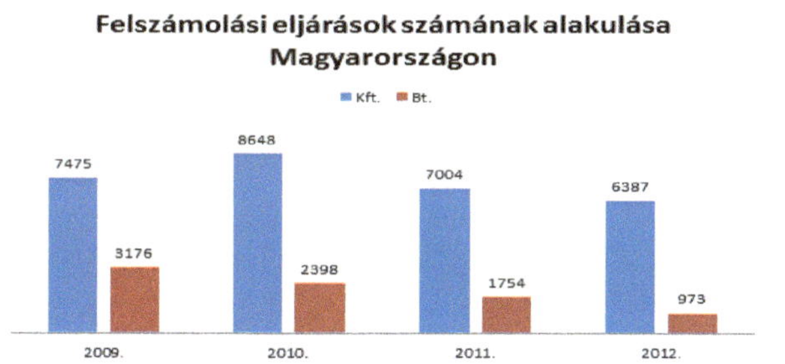

Source: NTDO Criminal Directory

Figure 8. Windup procedures in the years 2009-2012. Blue – limited corporations; red – partnerships

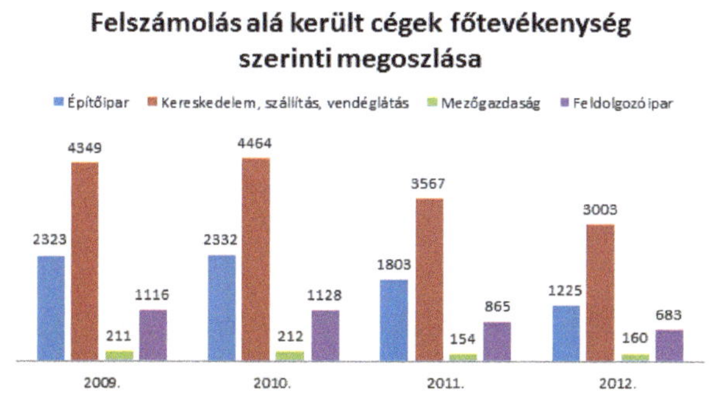

Source: NTDO Criminal Directory

Figure 9. Distribution of main activities of companies undergoing windup procedures, 2009-2012. Light blue – construction; red – trading, hospitality; green – agriculture; purple – processing industry.

As a result of the financial crisis, the tendency for number of companies winding up to continue growing has been disrupted, and, although the numbers are still high, nowadays a reduction can be observed. When researching this tendency of this economic structure, dividing windups into the main activities of these enterprises can be revealing. The results are indicated in Figure 9.

This division according to industrial branches may contribute to the efforts taken to reach the goals of present study.

SUMMARY

In the last period, the fight against tax avoidance has been moving through an essential process, as a result of which a better tax system is about to evolve in Hungary, living up to international standards. It is the foremost task of the NTDO to synchronize, unite and develop the efforts against tax avoidance. Due to professional cooperation, the discovery of tax evasion and other economic crimes is year by year more efficient, contributing to the 'whitening' of the economy. However, it would be an illusion to say that tax avoidance can be completely eradicated. There will always be individuals/enterprises who try to represent income gained from tax fraud as legally obtained. Therefore, emphasis should be put on prevention, based on a tax system and inspection structure that is able to resist tax avoiding intentions. Its realization should occur on an international level as economic crimes know no national bounds. Cooperation with international organizations and living up to the international conventions and protocols are a keystone for effective prevention. Immediately adopting the international practise is especially significant, since tax avoiders have good knowledge of the regulations of different countries. They tend to establish their enterprise in a country where the measures still prove to be weak against their tax-evasive methods. Although the focus of present study lies somewhere else, this could be an interesting research topic.

A tax reform can be considered successful if it enhances economic performance, lowers the administrative burdens around taxation and tax avoidance itself, and if the government's value corresponds with the social justice, as also defined in the tax laws (Sivák, 2012). Namely, the market figures react sensitively to taxation changes. Consequently, the demand and supply of the labour force, the investments, savings and the consumption may also change. In case of unexpected reactions of the economic figures,[10] substantially less or more income from taxes can appear in the revenue. These consequences should not only be the priority of economic politicians who aim at enhancing the competitiveness of the country and keeping up the budgetary balance, but also that of the Hungarian society.

[10] *This predictability can be transformed into a highly accurate prognosis with the help of targeted efficiency examinations.*

REFERENCES

ALI, M. M., CECIL H. W., KNOBLETT J. A. (2001). The effects of tax rates and enforcement policies on taxpayer compliance: a study of self-employed taxpayers. Atlantic Economic Journal 29(2).

BARR, N. (2004). The Economics of the Welfare State (4th ed.). Oxford University Press and Stanford University Press.

BÉLYÁCZ, I. (2009). Befektetési döntések megalapozása (Founding investment decisions). Aula.

BRYS, B. (2010). Making fundamental tax reform happen. In: Making Reform Happen – Lessons from OECD Countries (p. 101-128). Paris: OECD.

Deloitte (2009). Áttekintő vizsgálat az államigazgatási szabályozásból fakadó vállalkozói adminisztratív terhek teljes köréről, illetve egyes fókuszterületekkel kapcsolatosan részletes felmérések elkészítése (Overview research about the entreprenural administration taxes -based on government regulations- and detailed tests about the various focus areas).

ELEK, P., & SCHARLE, Á. (2008). Optimális adózáselméletek és az empirikus mérés lehetőségei (Optimal taxation theories and the possibilities of empirical research), Pénzügyi Szemle 53(3).

FAZEKAS, K., BENCZÚR, P., TELEGDY, Á. (2013). The Hungarian Labour Market 2013. Centre for Economic and Regional Studies, Hungarian Ac ademy of Sciences & National Employment Non-profit Public Company Ltd.

FORTIN, B., LACROIX, G., VILLEVAL, M. C. (2007). Tax evasion and social interactions. Journal of Public Economics, 91.

KÁTAY, G. (2009). Az alacsony aktivitás és foglalkoztatottság okai és következményei Magyarországon (The causes and consequences of low activity and employment in Hungary). MNB tanulmányok, 79.

SCHARLE, Á., BENCZÚR, P., KÁTAY, G., VÁRADI, B. (2010). Hogyan növelhető az adórendszer hatékonysága? (How can the tax system's effectiveness be enhanced?). Közpénzügyi füzetek, 26.

SIVÁK, J., VIGVÁRI, A. (2012). Rendhagyó bevezetés közpénzügyek tanulmányozásába (Irregular introduction to the research of public finances). Complex.

SLEMROD, J., & YITZHAKI, S. (2002). Tax Avoidance, Evasion, and Administration. In: Handbook of Public Economics (3rd ed.).

22

Integrated Approach to Managing Sustainability

LÁSZLÓ BERÉNYI, Ph.D.
ASSOCIATE PROFESSOR
e-mail: szvblaci@uni-miskolc.hu

SUMMARY

Achieving a higher level of sustainable development needs both individual and corporate efforts. An effective solution needs an integrated approach that allows the consideration of environmental and social values in addition to the economic interest. Additional management tools may be useful but sustaining them needs often untenable efforts from the organisations.

This paper draws up a framework for how to integrate the values of sustainable development into the corporate activities by using competence management.

Keywords: competence management; sustainable development; environmental management

INTRODUCTION

It is the responsibility of environmental management to coordinate corporate activities to meet a higher level of sustainable development. There are many application problems, even though the tool set of environmental management is well established. New methods may lead to resistance on the personal and corporate level as well. Development actions shall consider the existing management system instead of forcing additional elements upon the organisation.

Competence management exceeds the disciplines of pedagogy: it is general in corporate human resource management and development. Dedicated competence management is a novelty for most companies but the approach is implicitly represented. Human resource management shall explore, acquire and keep competent staff. The aim of developing organisational competences is to achieve a higher level of coherence between abilities, capabilities and corporate strategy.

The key competences of lifelong learning defined by the EU are general. For greater consistency of organisational development actions (including increasing environmental and social sensitivity) this basis should be used.

INDIVIDUAL AND ORGANISATIONAL COMPETENCES

Spencer and Spencer (1993) define competency as an underlying characteristic of an individual that is causally related to criterion-referenced effective and/or superior performance in a job or situation. Competence can be generally defined as knowledge and ability for performing certain tasks or roles.

Interpretation and categorization of the topic is not uniform. The content of the definitions depends on the purpose of the researchers. It is also problematic that while some languages have one word, others have more for the expression. The English language distinguishes between competence and competency but consensus on the content is missing. For example Boak (1991) regards them as synonymous. Others (e.g. Burgoyne 1988) use competence related to workcontent and competency related to possessing the necessary abilities. Competency can be interpreted as a behavioural expectation as well. Woodruffe (1991) proposes to separate competency (as a person-oriented expression) and competence areas. The approach of Lóth (2007) is useful for isolating the requirements and the performance. This approach defines competence as the capacity to perform job functions and competency as the actual performance.

This paper does not focus on the comprehensive interpretation of competences and competencies. Based on the European Reference Framework (2007) the word 'competence' is consequently used where it is suitable for analyzing the integration possibilities of sustainable development.

The competence management is broadly defined.The wording of Laakso-Mannien and Viitala (2007:27) says that it is the "activity that aims to safeguard and strengthen a company's operating capability and competitiveness by means of its knowledge base. Competence management nurtures and develops a company's competencies on all levels" and in order to achieve it includes direction, definition, evaluation, planning and development.

Competence management is generally built into the human resource managementprocesses. Kiss Tóthné (2012) highlights that competences have an influence on every field of human resource management. Expectations of the organisation are formulated as competence requirements which give selection criteria of staff. Establishing a comprehensive competence management system enables the companies to match their human resources with the human resource needs. The scope and content of competences depend on the tasks and the corporate culture.

There are various typologies ofcompetences. In an organisational view Szabó (2008) summarizes in her PhD Dissertation four categories of competences based on the practice-oriented approach of the European Union:

- Basic competences: general and frequent ones that are used in various areas of the life. These give the basis for developing other competences.
- Keycompetences: general elements of each profession. It is categorized by an EU framework and can be defined as important competences from a specified aspect.
- Generic competences: general and independent support elements of successful work, e.g. decision-making skills, innovative approach, problemorientation.
- Functional competences: special skills and abilities in connection with a specified job.

It is useful and critical to consider the norms of the European Union that focuses on key competences. This categorization is not the particularization of key competences mentioned by Szabó (2008). The individual competences can be classified based on the two approaches parallel.

The eight key competences of the EU (European Reference Framework, 2007) are necessary in order to realize the objectives of lifelong learning:

- Communication in the mother tongue: ability to express and interpret concepts, thoughts, opinions etc. in both oral and written way.
- Communication in foreign languages: it has a similar role to communication in mother tongue but it allows the understanding between various cultures and countries.
- Mathematical competence and basic competences in science and technology: basic mathematical and scientific knowledge and thinking is necessary to solve problems in everyday situations, and to understand the happenings around us.
- Digital competence: digital communication has a broad role in the organisation and in our whole life, including the access to learning materials as well.
- Learning to learn: it is related to learning processes by establishing the ability to carry on and organise learning in one's own way.
- Social and civic competences: social competence refers to personal, civic competence to interpersonal and intercultural situations and problem solving.
- Sense of initiative and entrepreneurship is the ability to turn ideas into action: it involves creativity, innovation and risktaking, as well as the ability to plan and manage projects to achieve objectives.
- Cultural awareness and expression: it covers appreciation of the importance of the creative expression of ideas, experiences and emotions in a range of media (music, performing arts, literature and the visual arts).

Competence and performance measurement are inputs for organisational development. Personal and organisational competences should be harmonized to increase the business competitiveness. Knowledge, readiness, and preparedness of people as workers has a significant effect on corporate performance. Elementary, secondary and higher education systems shouldprovide knowledge that prepares students for success at work but most of the requirements come from the employer. Some elements of knowledge, ability and skills are to be learned only in the organisation. (Berényi 2012)

Awuah (2001) interprets organisational competence as the sum of personal and organisational abilities, knowledge and capacities. Of course organisational competence and competency are more than the simple sum of personal competences; synergic effects can be expected.

In a simplified approach an organisation should focus on the organisational competences to increase its competitiveness. Based on the individual knowledge and competence necessary corporate tasksarecollecting knowledge, selection of employees, seeking for motivation points, supporting the flow of knowledge by coordination tools (meetings, teamwork, etc.), building up databases and knowledge bases.

Barriers of Sustainable Development

The way and content of contributions to sustainable development has been the subject of research in the last 30 years. The principle and fundamental aim of sustainable development is known but there is no consensus on how to achieve these objectives. The economic pillar of sustainable development means the source of solving environmental and social problems but it often gives an escape point for people, companies and governments. Actions are postponed by claiming the lack of necessary resources.

"The Business of business is business". This statement of Friedman (1970) refers to the main responsibility of companies being to increase their profit. Efforts towards environmental protection and social actions decrease the profit so the company steals from the owners. But integrating environmental and social problems in the corporate strategy can be a source of future profitmaking in long term. Friedman points out that an organisation does not have a conscience, only the people. Integrating environmental sensitivity can be interpreted as a game: companies try to recognize and/or build up the consumers' sensitivity, the important decision-making criteria and establish an optimal strategy. This strategy should consider sustainability but the lack of information and economic interests may lead to 'satisfactory decision-making'. The real environmental and social impacts of the decision are impossible to predict, i.e. that the deficiencies of the decision-making may derogate the achievement of sustainable development.

Sustainability is obvious in ecological systems: usage of the natural resources does not exceed the rate of their regeneration. However, the diversity of goals in a social system makes interpretation difficult. Education experts (such as Bábosik 2004) state that education and as a result behaviour cannot be independent of the accepted values. This leads to an evaluation problem: judgment of the behaviour will depend on the actual values of the those judging. Sustainable development is a global challenge with different interpretations and successfactors.

In summary the main barriers to achieving a higher level of sustainable development are the following:

- The presence of several social values makes the interpretation of sustainable development difficult;
- Profitorientation and conflicts between individual and corporate interestshinder effective activities;
- Information asymmetries make planning and evaluation difficult.

It can be concluded that the general barriers of sustainable development limit the functionality of corporate initiatives (e.g. environmental management systems or corporate social responsibility) as well. Achieving sustainable development is not possible by forcing environmental/social programs or systems upon people; there is a need for a comprehensive approach that integrates environmental consciousness with the daily operation. Local (corporate) values of sustainability must be formulated horizontally, woven into the values and the management system.

Competences and competencies seem to be the most effective tool for integrating sustainability.

The Role of Organisations in Achieving Sustainable Development

Individual (personal) needs and wants relegate the environmental pollution and prevention of the pollution to the background. A significant part of pollution can be attached to production but this is derived from the consumer demand. Companies and other organisations have special roles related to pollution prevention and to the general development of sustainability. The reason for this is that people during their work activities subordinate themselves to the organizational rules. It should be expected that the effect of an organisation on the individuals is usually more dominant than the other way around. It is possible to integrate the values of sustainable development into the regulation of operation so that the environmentally conscious behaviour of people can be influenced even beyond the work.

There are structural and cultural challenges to solve in order to establish sustainability. Szegedi (2001) analyses them as barriers. Structural factors are the following:

- Division of labour: staff members see through sub-problems, both responsibility and capacity for action are limited. Everybody should know and understand their own role to enhance the effectiveness.
- Separation of decision-making competence: decision makers and executives are not the same people. Information asymmetry or retained information lowers the effectiveness of decisions.
- Traditional command hierarchy: resistance to commands can be expected when it is a formal command. Spill over of this problem leads to collective irresponsibility. Involvement of the staff may increase the acceptance of the corporate will.

Cultural factors are the following:

- Strict behavioural expectations: new members usually try to learn the dominant norms. These norms may lead to different behaviour than the person's own behaviour patterns. The workplace has the possibility to integrate environmental consciousness into the norms.
- Cohesive communities: rivalry between formal/informal groups may lead to hostility. The result is frozen coordination and communication that slow down decision-making as well. The inverse of this culture is a problem-oriented one that supports the new initiatives.

- Unclear priorities: it is impossible to consider each viewpoint in decision-making. Priorities shall be established but there is the risk that economic interest will override the values of sustainable development.
- Retained information practice: it is a bad practice that the management tries to hidedamaging information. A missing information base lowers the effectiveness of decisions and if the secrets are revealed, the trust in management will crash.

There are fundamental problems to be solved in order to integrate the values of sustainability into the organisational strategy and operation:

- The content of the values,
- The process of integration.

Defining the content of values of sustainable development is a difficult challenge because of economic and cultural barriers and diversity. Global problems are common but the local representation may significantly differ by nation and geographical area. Establishing values and managing the related processes is much easier to implement.

Environmental Competences

Varga (2009) has a useful approach to the description of environmental competences. Because of the difficulty of direct specification he interprets key competences the European Reference Framework (2007).

Using the mother language both in written and oral form is necessary to be able to understand and communicate information. Recognizing both the frames and details of the problems is only the first step on the way of becoming sustainable. Collecting background information, working out action plans and discussing them with others needs the adequate knowledge of the mother language. The fact that environmental and social problems have a global nature requires the knowledge of foreign languages. Digital competence is important for implementing data analysis and searching for information as well as for electronic communication.

Factual knowledge (mathematics, natural sciences, technology) should be applied to development actions. An environmental or social program shall consider each future effect of the activities in order to achieve desired objectives.

Living in a sustainable way is a challenge for most people and organisations. New concepts, tools and solutions should be learned and accepted. The learning process is lifelong but often in non-school form. Workplaces can enforce atypical forms of behaviour but the goal is changing attitudes. It also assumes that people shall re-learn how to learn.

Social, civic and entrepreneurship competences cover two pillars of sustainable development. Furthermore, the existence of these competencies may enhance the acceptance of the development actions.

Of course other requirements can be formed like accuracy, reliability, saving money, helpfulness, etc. that may include environmental or social expectations. The system of competence requirements needs to be harmonized with the corporate strategy and the expectations of the stakeholders. The focus and content of sustainability depend on the scope of activities. However, there are competence dictionaries, related research reports and industry best practices that can be addressed in building up an organisation's own solution.

It is the responsibility of the management to form the competences and to evaluate the competencies. Environmental and social values can be summarized in an ethical codex, but its usability may be limited if it is only "shop window decoration" (Szegedi 2012). Operating procedures and human resource management processes can indicate the topic. A general mistake is to force separated expectations in connection with sustainability from other expectations. This leads to neglectingthe interest of sustainability in case of any economic problem. In addition sustaining the related management activities requires unreasonable efforts. Management must think about how to contribute to sustainability with each task and formulate the appropriatecompetences.

Process of Integration

The source of the competences is the environment, primarily the customers. Management needs to explore the external expectations and translate them into internal requirements. Strategic and operational plans shall consider the requirements to achieve satisfaction while realizing business profit. The Quality Management Process model (Figure 1) summarizes the critical elements of management focus.

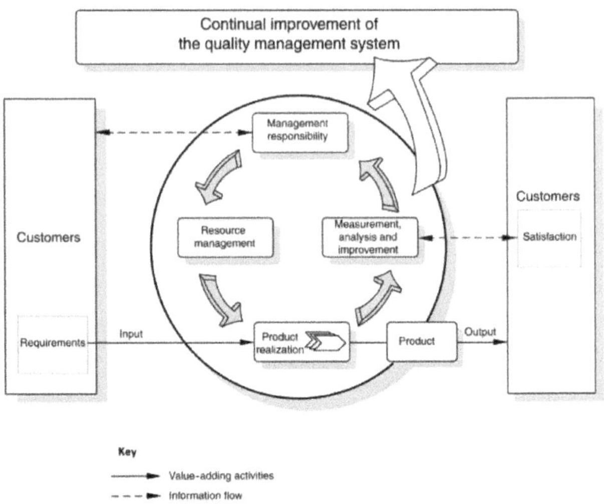

Figure 1. Model of a Process-based Quality Management System (ISO 9001)

The model of ISO 9001 describes how to satisfy customers. If this can be achieved, the organisation could identify the relevant competence requirement and could manage the individual and organisational competences. Figure 2 summarizes the main steps of this process and its extension to the supply side.

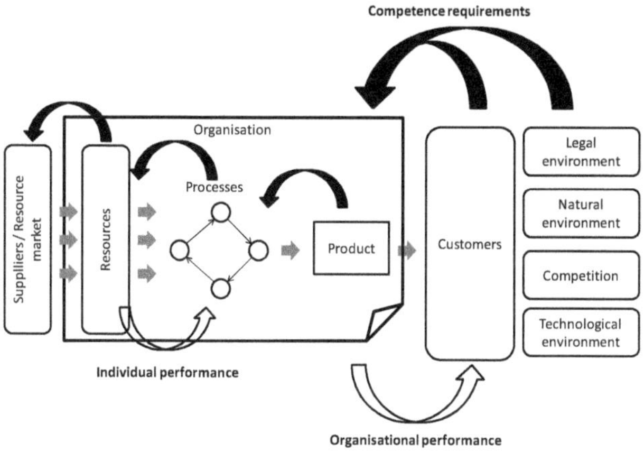

Figure 2. Competence requirements and performance in the organisation

The responsibility of the management is to identify the external expectations and barriers, including the customer requirements, legal possibilities, natural and technological possibilities and the position of competitors. The expectations are the source of the product-requirement and the organisational competences which may manifest as corporate image.

Product requirements appoint directly the main characteristics of the production processes. Requirements of other processes and resources (including the competence of the staff) can be deduced jointly from the product requirements and the corporate image.

Satisfaction of customers mainly depends on the performance of the product but in the long term corporate image influences the organisational performance. Social acceptance is important because society gives the future customers. Product performance (quality) depends on several factors. Beyond the subjective judgement of the customer,the quality of raw materials or machines and conformity of procedures can be noted (Szintay 2005). Product requirements designate the competence requirements of processes and resources (including human resources) and the performance of the resources finally determinesthe performance of the organisation.

This process gives a framework for integrating the values of sustainability with effective content and allows the controlling of success.

The limits gobeyond a single organisation. In the resource market an organization is a customer with specified expectations. By integrating the values of sustainable development into the supplies the whole supply chain can work and develop its activities based on shared values and the interpretation of sustainable development. These values are horizontal values, so the same content can be adapted for various activities.

EVALUATION OF ENVIRONMENTAL CONSCIOUSNESS

Environmental and social competence requirements need to be integrated into other requirements but it the management is recommended to pay attention to evaluating the effectiveness of the efforts. This allows an increase in the environmental performance.

Based on the idea that environment and environmental problems go beyond the individual or organisation, evaluation needs a comprehensive approach. The model in Figure 3 fulfils the requirements.

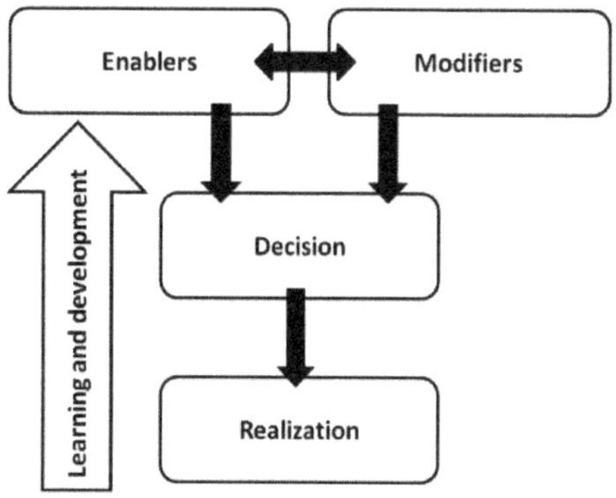

Figure 3. Comprehensive model of environmental consciousness (based on Berényi 2009)

The core of the model is based on the process of decision making because decision is a critical point of each action, including both everyday shopping and work activity.

- People have specified objectives and a specified level of knowledge. They have conceptions about good and bad, handsome, useful and ugly. These opinions and the actual knowledge may be difficult to change, so these shall be handled as enablers.
- There are situational circumstances. When alone, with friends or with family our behaviour may be different. Sometimes these circumstances motivate people to decide inconsistently. This is another conflict between financial possibilities and desires.
- Decision making means choosing between the known possibilities. Realisation is the accomplishment and evaluation of the selected solution.
- Learning is based on the evaluation. New experiences will confirm or overwrite the factors covered as enablers in my model. Even in similar situations the decision may be different.

The evaluation progress based on this model allows the management to work out and develop the sustainability content of competences.

CONCLUSION

Achieving sustainable development is a serious challenge. There are many methods and tools available for individuals and organisations for evaluating and developing their operations but several barriers should be considered. Engel (2000) emphasizes that wide dissemination is important and easy tools shall be established in order to achieve it. In my opinion breakthrough can be expected if the values of sustainability are integrated into the organisational strategy, structure and culture. Forcing environmental departments or corporate social responsibility programs on companies will fail because of the commitment of maintenance.

Nowadays competence management is very popular both in the business world and EU regulation so it is inevitable. Actual studies generate useful databases and competence dictionaries which are widely available. Competences include both professional and behavioural expectations which can give a frame to integrating values of sustainability.

Through a harmonized management system of competencies it is possible to make them a part of the culture, establishing the appropriate behaviour and performance without any additional tools. This way effectiveness and acceptance can be enhanced.

REFERENCES

AWUAH, G.B. (2001). A firm's competence development through its network of exchange relationship. Journal of Business and Industrial Marketing, Vol. 16 No. 7, 574-599.

BÁBOSIK I. (2004).Neveléselmélet (Educational Theory). Budapest: Osiris Kiadó.

BERÉNYI, L. (2009).Környezetmenedzsment (Environmental Management). Miskolc: Miskolci Egyetem Gazdaságtudományi Kar.

BERÉNYI, L. (2012). Developing Environmental Competence.Regional formation and Development Studies, Vol. 8 Nr. 3, 15-24.

BOAK, G. (1991). Developing Managerial Competences: The Management Learning Contract Approach. London: Pitman.

BURGOYNE, J. (1998). Competency Based Approaches to Management Development. Lancaster: Centre for the Study of Management Learning.

ENGEL, H.W. (2000). Ökotérképezés (Eco-mapping). Budapest: Követ-Inem Hungária

FRIEDMAN, M. (1970): The Social Responsibility of Business is to increase its profits. The New York Times Magazine, September 13.

ISO 9001:2008: Quality Management Systems – Requirements

KEY COMPETENCES FOR LIFELONG LEARNING - European Reference Framework (2007).European Communities, 2007.

KISS TÓTHNÉ, A. (2012). Competence-based Operation in Human Processes of Companies. TMP, Vol. 8., Nr. 1., 96-100.

LAAKSO-MANNIEN, R. & VIITALA, R. (2007).Competence Management and Human Resource Development. Helsinki: HAAGA-HELIA University of Applied Sciences

LÓTH, L. (2007). Adalékok a hazai kompetenciafelfogáshoz (Contributions to the Hungarian perception of competence). In: Bábosik I. (ed.). Pedagógia és személyiségfejlesztés (Education and personal development). Budapest: Okker Kiadó

SPENCER, L.M. & SPENCER, S.M. (1993). Competence at work: Models for Superior Performance. New York: John Wiley& Sons

SZABÓ, SZ. (2008). A vezetői kompetencia-fejlesztés tapasztalatai és lehetőségei egyes rendvédelmi szervek hivatásos állománya körében (Experience and Professional Strength among Law Enforcement Agencies with the Capability of Driving Competence Development). PhD dissertation: Zrínyi Miklós Nemzetvédelmi Egyetem.

SZEGEDI, K (2001). Vállalati etika (Corporate Ethics). Miskolc: Bíbor Kiadó

SZEGEDI, K (2012). Hazai nagyvállalati etikai kódexek tartalmi elemzése.(Content Analysis of Corporate Codes of Ethics of Large Hungarian Corporations).Vezetéstudomány, Vol. 43 Nr. Special Issue, 47-55.

SZINTAY, I. (2005). Minőségmenedzsment I. Elmélet (Quality Management I. Theory). Miskolc: Bíbor Kiadó

VARGA, A. (2009). Környezeti kompetenciák fejlesztése tanítási gyakorlatban (Developing Environmental Competencies in Education Practice). OFI, Budapest, Retrieved:http://www.ofi.hu/tudastar/hidak-tantargyak-kozott/kornyezeti-kompetenciak

WOODRUFFE, C. (1991). Competent by any another name.Personnel Management, Vol. 23 No. 9, 30-33.

23

Main Changes in European Tax Policies between 2007 and 2011

SÁNDOR BOZSIK, Ph.D.
ASSOCIATE PROFESSOR
e-mail: pzbozsi@uni-miskolc.hu

SUMMARY

The paper is devoted to studying the tax policy changes of the European Union countries in the period of economic crisis. The main aim of the paper is to categorise the main types of tax policy responses to the economic challenges and the major influencing factors determining these responses. The main findings are the followings: the crisis intensified the tax competition among the countries. The countries with relatively low indebtedness and deficits tried to decrease the tax rates (especially the income tax rates) to reinstate their international competitiveness. Countries with high indebtedness and/or deficits could not follow this route without cutbacks in spending and finding new source of revenues. And finally there were countries that did not enter the field of tax competition.
Keywords: tax policy; European Union; economic crisis

INTRODUCTION

Near the end of the first decade of the 21th century clear tax policy tendencies can be detected in the European Union countries. The free movement of production factors (capital, enterprises and labour force) led to specific tax competition, which was more intensive in the recently joined, less developed countries. The core reason for tax competition is to decrease the tax burden of production factors (i.e. the marginal rates of corporate and personal income taxes) in order to encourage the direct capital investments and economic growth. (Noregaard-Kahn, 2013) The decreasing revenues were financed from loans or from increasing other types of taxes – especially indirect taxes.

The economic crisis in 2008 meant a break in this process. The heavily indebted counties could not continue decreasing the direct tax rate; the increasing budget deficit caused by the consolidation of the bank system and by the crisis generally forced the policymakers to find new source of finance. But a tax increase can threat the chance of economic recovery and may lead to an vicious circle. The tax increase further deteriorates the competitiveness, investments fall, and the recession decreases the budget revenues, which provokes further tax increases. If the government cuts the expenses, the same would happen. The fall in demand caused by the public spending cut can freeze the economy, while poorer public services may lead to social tensions and/or weaker competitiveness.

In this paper I study the tax policies applied by the European Union countries in order to categorise the main types of response to the challenges of economic crisis and to detect the main influencing factors determining the response. The study examines the relationship among GDP growth, tax burden, and foreign direct investment, creating clusters by gross public debt/GDP, export/GDP, public deficit/GDP and balance of current accounts/GDP. The data for the examinations are obtained from the Eurostat databases.

TAX POLICY TENDENCIES BEFORE THE CRISIS

Taxation has almost the same age as the mankind. As Benjamin Franklin said, “In this world nothing can be said to be certain, except death and taxes.” (cited in Adókalauz, 2009). Taxation is an integrated part of fiscal policy and the taxation is different in the particular countries. The main reasons for this phenomenon are the following (Taxation trends, 2013):

1. The ratio of public spending to the GDP differs significantly in each country. Where the public spending is more significant, the rate of taxation should be bigger.
2. For historical reasons we can observe meaningful differences in the rate of direct and indirect taxes. Direct taxes are levied on incomes and wealth, while indirect taxes are those in regard to the consumption of products and services.

3. The direct taxes may employ progressive or flat tax rates. The flat tax regimes use the same rate independently of the tax base size. The progressive tax rates are higher if the tax base is greater.
4. The tax system can use special taxes levied on particular sectors or products. Furthermore, the tax systems can differ from each other in point of employed tax allowances and tax exemptions. The complexity of tax rules, the frequency of tax declarations and payments, and the various approaches of double taxation also differ country to country.

This paper examines how the taxation has changed in answer to the crisis in the European Union countries, and what the effect of tax policy was on economic growth and public budget deficit, according to the available Eurostat data. In the analysis I examine only the first two aspects, as the database enables only this.

Although the tax systems differ, several common global tax policy tendencies were observed before the economic crisis broken out in 2007 (Norregard & Khan, 2007). The main features were the following:

1. Widespread use of Value Added Tax (VAT) – VAT was introduced by France in 1957, then it became the first harmonised and official tax of the European Union. Since then the VAT has been introduced in several countries outside the EU. Currently only 11 countries among the world's 160 countries have no VAT. The most meaningful exemption is the USA (Ebrill et al. 2001).
2. Globalisation and within this the freedom of capital movement strengthened the tax competition among countries. It meant that the capital began to move to the countries with lower corporate tax rates from the countries with higher ones. An efficient defence against tax havens has not been built up, so the capital-hungry countries were forced to decrease the corporate tax rate and the rates of other taxes on company profits. At the same time several countries began to use flat personal tax regimes. The flat taxes are extremely popular in the Eastern European region, where all of the countries except Poland introduced it by 2011. (Keen et al. 2006). However in 2011 one of the early introducers – Slovakia – turned back to a progressive personal tax.
3. Similar process can be traced in case of other types of labour taxes. The creation of new jobs became more and more important, and the multinational companies play a crucial role here. The cost of labour has got major significance in the settlement decision, which can be influenced by the fiscal policy if it lowers the tax burden of employment or increases tax allowances.
4. The tax competition decreased the share of direct taxes in the state budgets. Since the redistribution role of the state did not decrease, the share of indirect taxes to GDP increased before the crisis.
5. Globalisation strengthened the demand for tax harmonisation – especially in case of indirect taxes. Harmonisation – except for tax rates – has occurred in the case of VAT and excise taxes, but the harmonisation of direct taxes came up against difficulties. Tax harmonisation is not only the feature of the European Union. The same process can be observed in the case of the Central American Customs Union, too. (Ter-Minassian, 1997)
6. Double tax avoidance agreements are widespread; in the frame of this the taxation of capital income (interest and dividend) decreased or was eliminated.
7. From the 1980s the demand to support sustainable growth has appeared in taxation. During the 1990s several environmental taxes have been introduced. In line with this the consumption of fossil energy (natural gas, crude oil) was also more heavily taxed. The increasing concern about global warming and the insufficient fossil energy reserves forced policymakers to moderate energy consumption with tax policy measurements.
8. The weight of property tax increased especially in the taxation of local governments (Ter-Minassian, 1997).
9. Finally the economic cycles plays an important role in the tax policy. In the economic recovery period tax incomes increased, which stimulated the economic policy to decrease the tax rates. This tax rate moderation strengthened the economic boom and had a pro-cyclical effect. The short-term political popularity undermined long-term responsible thinking, so the tax moderation threatened the stability of pension and health systems where the birth rate was low (Tax reforms…, 2012).

In my research I examined Features 2, 3 and 4 in the European Union countries.

THE HYPOTHESES OF RESEARCH AND THE INPUT FACTORS

This paper examines which countries try to get a competitive advantage by tax moderation, and what the major influencing factors are to enter a tax competition. Secondly, I examine whether entering the tax competition leads to greater economic growth or not.

The data used come from the website of Eurostat and the analysed period was the 11-year period between 2002 and 2011. The chosen period is split by the crisis, since I tested with time series analysis if the deductions are prevalent in the different phases of economic cycles. The research covers the 27 member states of the European

Union. Croatia was excluded from the analysis, because during the examined period it was not yet a member of the EU.

The hypotheses of research were the following:

1. The smaller the GDP per capita, the greater the country's stimulation to enter the tax competition. If the economic development is low, generally the amount of tax revenues is also low compared to the GDP, so the foreign investment to the country can be increased by the lower taxation.
2. The relatively high economic growth rate enables the decrease of tax rates, since the tax base increase can compensate the effect of lowering rates. So the higher the GDP growth rate, the more the stimulation to enter the tax competition increases.
3. A high export ratio and a high foreign investment ratio also strengthen the stimulus for tax competition. Since economic growth is heavily determined by international competitiveness, economic openness makes the tax competition stronger.
4. There may be two factors which constrain the ability to enter a tax competition. Firstly the size of the public deficit, secondly the size of gross public debt. A European country will not take the risk to be in an excessive deficit procedure in long run, since this leads to the suspense of transfers and paying fines. That is why a higher level of public debt or deficit decreases the opportunity to take part in a tax competition.

Research Methodology

The test of the above hypotheses has been done by the following way:

The data required to test my hypotheses were downloaded from the website of Eurostat. The database gov_a_tax_ag provided detailed information about the tax revenue types compared to GDP. The main tax rates can also be downloaded, similarly the functional distribution of governmental spending compared to GDP.

After downloading the taxation figures, the public deficit/GDP, gross public debt/GDP, GDP per capita, GDP growth rate, FDI stock, export, and the GDP nominated in euro were also downloaded. To compare the country data, foreign investment and the export data were divided by the GDP.

The description of my input variables, the testable hypotheses and the abbreviation of input variables are shown in Table 1.

Table 1
Characteristics of input variables

Abbreviation	Description	Name of Eurostat database	Testable hypotheses
country	full name of the particular country		
abb	short name of the particular country		
def	deficit/GDP	gov_dd_edpt1	The larger the GDP, the smaller the tax rate decrease.
deb	gros debt/GDP	gov_dd_edpt1	The larger the gross debt, the smaller the tax rate decrease.
gdp	GDP per capita in euro	prc_ppp_ind	The larger the GDP per capita, the higher the tax burden and the smaller the tax rate decrease.
gro	GDP growth rate	nama_gdp_k	The higher the economic growth rate, the bigger the tax rate decrease.
fdi	Foreign direct investment to GDP	bop_fdi_main	The higher the ratio of FDI stock to GDP, the larger the tax rate decrease.
exp	annual export to GDP ratio	bop_exp_main	The higher the ratio of exports to GDP, the larger the tax rate decrease.

Source: Eurostat database, own

The arithmetical average of input variables was calculated between 2002 and 2011 for all of the 27 member states.

Creating Clusters by the Input Variables

The countries were classified into four clusters by the input variables. I employed clusters, since I supposed that the countries in the same cluster have got the same motivation for tax competition. In economic policy several factors should be considered, and therefore the hypotheses cannot be examined as a function of only one variable. The result of cluster analysis gave distinct and interpretable country groups.

The cluster analysis was done by SPSS. After several trials the hierarchical cluster analysis gave the best interpretable solution, where I created the clusters by the Ward method using Euclidean distance. The Ward method strives to minimise the in-group variance and to maximise the variance among groups. Since my variables were quantitative variables, the Euclidean distance had relevance. Table 2 shows the main characteristics of the clusters.

Table 2
Clusters of the input variables

Countries of the cluster	Name of cluster	Number of countries	Geographical and cultural features
Germany, United Kingdom, Finland, Belgium, Denmark, Sweden, Austria, Ireland, the Netherlands, Spain, Italy, France	Developed	12	The most developed old member states belong to here. Geographically it covers the western half of the Union.
Czech Republic, Portugal, Malta, Greece, Slovenia, Cyprus	Average	6	Except for two former socialist countries these are Southern European countries. Their development is around the average of the EU with moderate economic growth potential.
Poland, Bulgaria, Rumania, Estonia, Lithuania, Latvia, Slovakia, Hungary	Less developed	8	Most of the the former socialist countries belong to this group. This cluster covers the Eastern half of the Union.
Luxembourg	Very developed	1	In point of input variables Luxembourg was too far from the other clusters to place in any group. There were indeed cluster types which split the EU into Luxemburg and the rest of the Union.

Source: Eurostat, own computation

I calculated the arithmetical average of input variables in case of each cluster. The results are shown in Table 3.

Table 3
Average of input variables in each cluster

Factors	def	deb	gdp	gro	fdi	exp
Developed	-0.27	57.98	26,391.67	2.47	46.36	59.76
Average	-3.84	57.47	18,451.85	3.26	40.34	62.39
Less developed	-2.49	29.98	11,005.56	5.69	40.17	61.89
Very developed	2.43	7.23	55,900.00	4.13	134.01	436.38
Average	-1.60	47.70	21,161.3	3.70	46.40	74.90

Source: Eurostat, own calculation

From the data it looks as if the convergence of the European Union country groups has increased in this period. The less developed country group showed the highest economic growth, while the developed country group has the lowest figure. The average deficit and the average growth rate of the developed group was the lowest between 2002 and 2011. However, their GDP per capita and foreign direct investment stock was the highest. The developed countries have large internal markets, which is why the share of exports is a moderate percentage of their GDP compared to the other country groups.

The averagely developed group has the highest state debt and deficit, but their openness was the highest. While the less developed group showed the same openness pattern as the average group, their average GDP growth rate was higher and their deficit lower than the average group.

Luxembourg has got a special situation. This is the smallest member country, but economically this is the most developed. Luxembourg is a very open economy with a disciplined fiscal policy and relatively high growth rate.

A one-factor variance analysis was carried out to test the significance of these variables as cluster-building factors. I excluded Luxembourg from the analysis and treated it as an outlier. The results are given in Table 4.

Table 4
Relevance of clusters

Factors	def	deb	gdp	gro	fdi	exp
Variance among clusters	2.2	171.2	93,540,886.6	1.9	8.3	0.0
Total variance	6.8	673.9	183,491,353.4	3.1	813.7	0.1
Ratio	31.8%	25.4%	51.0%	61.2%	1.0%	1.1%

Source: Eurostat, own calculations

The explanation power of the clusters is strongest for development indicators (GDP level, and growth). The explanation power is moderate in the case of indebtedness indicators (deficit and gross debt) and insignificant for openness (foreign direct investment and export to GDP ratio). So the clusters are suitable for testing Hypotheses 1, 2 and 4 – which consider the linkage between economic growth, economic development, indebtedness and tax competition, but the relationship between economic openness and tax competition cannot be tested by using these clusters.

The Statement of Analysis

In the analysis the relationship between the tax income/GDP ratio and the clusters was examined in order to focus on the tax rates for the following reasons:

1. In point of tax competition the pure tax rates have no significance. If a country uses a high tax rate, but employs several allowances and tax relief, the real tax burden in terms of enterprises and households can be favourable. This statement is especially true in the case of personal and corporate taxes, where the tax base and the methods of tax deduction may differ widely.
2. If the black economy plays a significant role, the high taxes are only paid by a few honest taxpayers, and the tax rate cannot be a perfect figure to measure the real tax burden for the whole economy.

Let us look first at the overall tax burden. The collected tax revenues in European Union declined moderately during the period. This declining trend was not interrupted by the crisis. Figure 1 shows that the less developed EU countries have got smaller tax burdens than the more developed ones.

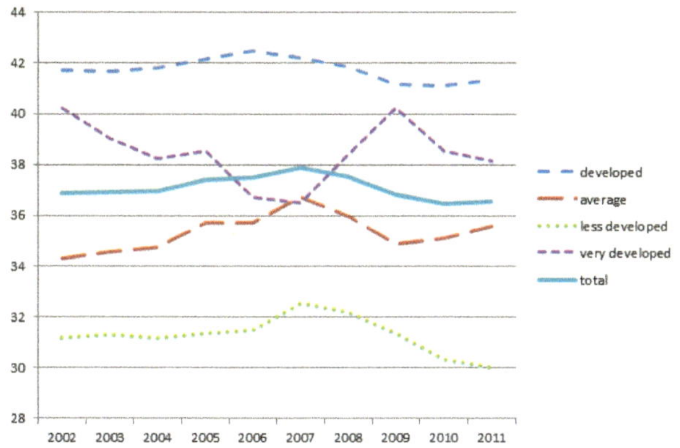

Source: Eurostat, own calculations

Figure 1. The average tax income/GDP rate of country clusters between 2002 and 2011

The lower income level and the smaller gross debt of the less developed countries encouraged them to decrease their average tax burden in this period. It is interesting that the major tax decrease happened after the eruption of the crisis. Because their indebtedness was much lower than the average, they could stimulate their economy by offering lower tax rates to investors. In the average group the tax burden increased. This also fits the hypothesis of my research, since the indebtedness and the deficits were highest here. Here the reinstatement of financial equilibrium was the top priority target, and they were unable to enter the tax competition.

If we focus on the importance of the various tax types we can derive a deeper conclusion regarding the tax competition. The international competition is worsened first of all by taxes on capital and income, while the role of consumption taxes is not so vital. The consumption taxes have no importance for the exporting sectors – only the domestic prices will be higher and therefore the domestic demand may be lower, which affects the profit of enterprises producing for the domestic market. But taxes on profit and employment decrease directly the profit of all enterprises. In the case of consumption taxes there are no big differences among the clusters, as you can see in Figure 2.

Note how the consumption tax burden varied over time and how close their GDP shares were to each other. The rules of consumption taxes are harmonised in the EU except for the rates. Although there are some minor differences by the country groups, the differences are much lower than for the average tax burden (see Figure 1).

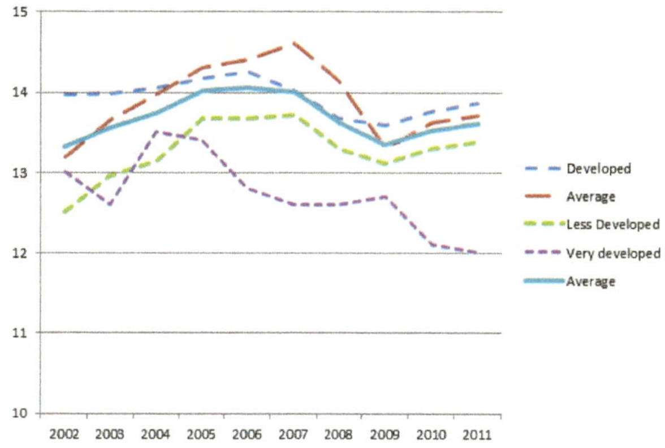

Source: Eurostat

Figure 2. Consumption taxes/GDP ratio in the clusters between 2002 and 2011

The indirect tax burden increased in all three country groups after the eruption of crisis (not in Luxembourg, however). It seems, that majority of the countries tried to compensate for the lacking tax revenues by increasing the taxation of consumption. By the way, this policy helps to balance the current account (by taxing imports) and indirectly to encourage savings and debt repayment.

If we look at the variance of indirect tax burden, only approximately 10% of the variance can be explained by the clusters (excluding Luxembourg); 90% of variance come from the clusters inside. So we can state that the level of indirect taxes does not depend on the indebtedness or economic growth indicators in the EU.

In point of tax competition, direct taxes have more relevance, since the final target of tax reduction is to improve the competitiveness of manufacturing. Within the category of direct taxes, corporate tax is of more importance than taxes on employment. Now significant differences can be observed among the country clusters. Let us look at first the changes in corporate tax income (Figure 3).

Source: Eurostat

Figure 3. Corporate tax income/GDP in the company clusters between 2002 and 2011

After the crisis the corporate tax income decreased in each country cluster. However, this decrease is better explained by the smaller tax base (fall in company profit) than the decrease in tax rates. But as a sign of tax competition the decrease was bigger in the less developed segment than for the other country groups, with the exception of Luxembourg. Here the corporate tax rates were also reduced.

If we study the variances, the explanatory power of clusters increased from 40% (2002) to 71% (2011). This means that the country clusters harmonise their corporate tax strategies, while the difference among the clusters increased. However, there was a moderate decrease in total variance (from 1.45 to 1.38).

Even larger differences can be observed for the taxes on employment. Taxes on employment include social contribution fees, personal income tax, and other taxes paid by employer or employee. Figure 4 shows the change in taxes on employment.

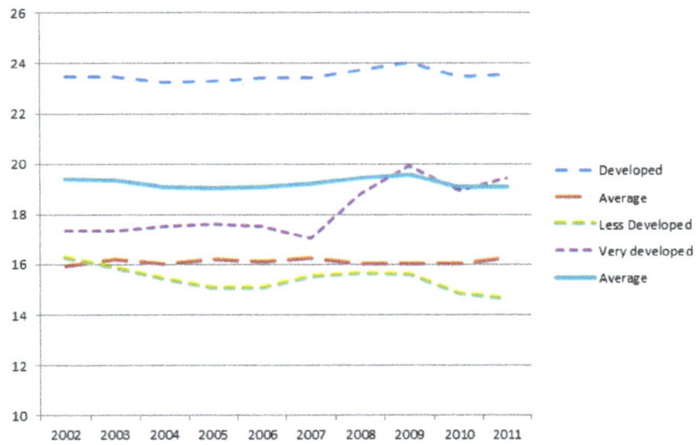

Data source: Eurostat

Figure 4. Taxes on employment/GDP ratio in the country clusters between 2002 and 2011

It is obvious that the developed countries have the largest burden on employment. These countries have got generous health and pension system whose financing requires sources. To finance the social contribution, the share of these taxes remained the same in the average and the developed cluster. But the less developed country cluster the tax burden decreased, regardless of whether we look at the pre- or post-crisis period.

One-factor variance analysis underlines the significant differences among the group. Here the variance among clusters rose from 81% to 89% (excluding Luxembourg) for total variance. In the less developed segment the lowering of taxes on employment seemed to be a common strategy to manage the post-crisis economy.

These clusters were not appropriate to test the linkage between tax competition and economic openness, because there was no significant difference in openness among the clusters. That is why I try to directly examine the relationship to draw the relationship in scatterplot. I plotted several charts for direct taxes, the change in direct taxes and the two indicators of economic openness (export to GDP, FDI to GDP). But the plots appeared ramdomly and did not indicate a relationship. The other examinations carried out in this way brought the same result. So I cannot justify Hypothesis 3. The failure max be caused by the fact that governments stimulate the settlement of multinational companies rather by giving targeted subsidiaries and tax allowances and by granting overall low tax environment. In addition, a favourable tax environment is only one factor which the companies consider when choosing a location: there are other more vital factors (security of investment, accountability of economic environment, skill and competence of labour force) which affect the decision.

CONCLUSIONS

From the analysis I have found that the tendency towards tax competition is the strongest in the less developed country cluster. These countries decreased the taxes on employment and corporate income rather than indirect taxes. This tendency was valid not only before, but also after the crisis. But after the crisis the stimulus for tax competition increased in the less developed country cluster.

The economic growth of the less developed cluster was significantly better than that of the other country clusters, but the level of public debt to GDP was lower. These two factors make it possible to enter the tax competition.

REFERENCES

Adókalauz (2009) Miniszterelnöki Hivatal 2009/június

NORREGAARD J. &- KHAN T. S. (2007): Tax Policy: Recent Trends and Coming Challenges IMF Working Paper 2007/274

EBRILL L. – KEEN M. – BODIN J – SUMMERS V. (2001): The modern VAT IMF ISBN: 1-58906-026-1

TER-MINASSIAN T. ed., (1997): Fiscal Federalism in Theory and Practice. Washington D.C.: International Monetary Fund Keen M. – Kim Y. – Varsano R. (2006): The "flat taxes": Principles and Evidence. IMF Working Paper /218

European Commission (2012): Tax Reforms in EU Member States. Taxation Papers 2012/34

Eurostat (2013): Taxation Trends in the European Union Luxembourg: Publications Office of the European Union

Eurostat database http://epp.eurostat.ec.europa.eu/portal/page/portal/eurostat/home/

24

Output and Staff Number in Hungarian Manufacturing before, during and after the Crisis

ÁDÁM BERECZK
PH.D. STUDENT
e-mail: bereczk.adam@uni-miskolc.hu

SUMMARY

The paper describes outcomes of recent research about connection between output and staff number related to specific sectors of manufacturing in Hungary. The method was to examine the existence of a linear relationship between the variables with cross correlation and regression modelling. The examined period includes the nadir of the crisis and the first years of recovery. In the textile and food industries co-movement of time series show a strong correlation between output and staff number. There is a strong positive correlation in the case of the automotive industry, but no linear relationship can be proved between the variables in the chemical industry.
Keywords: manufacturing; sector; staff number; output

INTRODUCTION, GOAL OF THE RESEARCH

The human resource or labour force, as one of the basic factors of production, is one of the main resources of corporate activity. Many factors affect the staff number employed in the sectors and the changes in that number. The three most significant factors are: increase in productivity caused by technological development, changes in sector output and changes in staff costs. Zimmermann presented the results of a study conducted on the data of 16 German manufacturing enterprises, the most important conclusion of which is that an increase in demand increases the demand for labour as well (Zimmerman 1991). Based on German data, Zimmermann found no correlation between the changes in labour costs and the sector labour demand. Based on their observations concerning the entire manufacturing of 28 developing countries, Mehta & Mohanty (1993) found that an increase in sector output increases the sector labour demand.

Based on the above research findings, I focus on the observation of output and number changes as the main research goal. In addition I pay attention to discovering the possible effects of labour costs on the staff number. To characterise the sectors I also observed other factors (ratio of export revenue, changes in gross added value, R&D intensity). Four sectors were included in the analysis: the manufacture of textiles, textile products, leather and leather products; the manufacture of food products, beverages and tobacco; the manufacture of transport equipment; and the manufacture of chemicals, chemical products and man-made fibres.

The following perspectives were dominant with regards to the choice: the availability and comparability of data concerning the sector, the role of the sector in employment and its conjunctural features. In the course of the analysis I avoid the use of the expressions labour demand or employment in order to separate the analysis this way from special labour economy questions (my analysis investigated the number of staff). For similar reasons I will not deal with the topics of job creation and job destruction, or adaptation costs. Based on Surányi (2002), the adaptation costs in Hungary are asymmetric, but low. This could serve as reason for I do not investigate this question here.

METHODOLOGY OF THE RESEARCH

I used the sector data of eleven years (2001-2011) for the analysis. Most of the data comes from the company tax databases of the National Tax and Customs Administration of Hungary (hereinafter: NTCA). Data concerning labour costs was obtained from the databases of the Hungarian Central Statistical Office. The NTCA gathers the data in the course of yearly mandatory data provision from Hungarian enterprises. The obligation concerns every enterprise operating in Hungary having double-entry bookkeeping. The Office produces sector-level data by summarising the company data, so the database represents the significant majority of Hungarian enterprises. The output is indicated on nominal values, so I calculated the output values based on 2001 prices. I used sector producer price indexes to define real values.

I first tested the correlation between the time series with cross-correlation calculations and then with regression alignment where a significant linear connection occurred. I decreased the possible significant autocorrelation distortion by using chain ratios. I consider the labour homogenous.

THEORETICAL BACKGROUND

Several empirical research results have been published worldwide that analyse the effect of different independent variables on labour demand or to some category close to staff numbers. Table 1 contains a brief review of frequently examined variables and the outcomes. Based on their research conducted on the processing industries of 28 developing countries, Mehta & Mohanty (1993) state that technological development has a tendency to decrease the staff number. Zimmermann (1991) came to the same conclusion observing German manufacturing sectors, finding that increase in demand for the product of an enterprise and the increase of output increase the demand for labour. Examination of the effects of technological development is included in both influential works, and their results also match; that is, technological development has a tendency to decrease the staff number. Falk & Koebel (2002) pointed out that the increase in output also increases the demand for heterogenic labour force. Considering labour costs, Zimmermann (1991) found that it had no defining role in the 1980s in German manufacturing. Instead he found changes in product market demand – that can be related to the changes in output – and technological development to have effective force. International studies concerning the wage flexibility of labour demand usually have found the labour market of the United States to be more flexible than the markets of the Euro zone. This is in connection with the industrial traditions and the greater power of European trade unions. The literature about Hungary mentions that in the end of the 1990s wages were not a significant part of company policies. At that time the most important challenges were the capital market and the labour market limitations. As a result of (basically beneficial) increases in the minimum wages that started in the beginning of the 2000s which were realised in several steps changes in wages again had a serious impact of staff number in certain sectors (e.g. in the textile industry). (Concerning miminum wages it could be interesting for foreign readers that Hungary has more than one minimum wages, depending on the educational level of the employee, which is quite unusual.)

Some studies have been published about the new European Union member states in this topic with regards to the change of regime. The most influential works abroad are, among others, Singer (1996) on the Czech Republic; Basu et al. (2000) on Poland, Hungary, the Czech Republic, Slovakia and Russia; and Brown & Earle (2005) on Hungary, Romania, Russia and Ukraine. These works present the effects of the structural changes accompanying the regime change on sector employment.

Important results in Hungary were published by Kőrösi (1997, 2000, 2002), Köllő (1998), and Kertesi & Köllő (2002), among others. Kőrösi states that capital costs do not significantly affect the labour demand Kőrösi (2000). The most important conclusion of Kőrösi (2002) is that changes in productivity do not affect directly the labour demand in a significant way (but greatly affect its production flexibility and to a smaller extent its wage flexibility, too). Among the international results concerning productivity Davis et al. (1998) and later Nordhaus (2005) found when observing manufacturing in the USA that an increase in productivity positively affects the sector, while Mahmood (2008) did not find a connection between the two variables when observing the SMEs of Australian manufacturing. Mann (2011) came to the conclusion that the increase in productivity decreases sector employment rates from his simulations based on sector life curves. The results of Falk & Koebel (2002) showed that sector capital increase enhances the heterogenic nature of labour demand. Yun (2008) came to the conclusion based on research on Swedish manufacturing that the effects of the intensity of R&D and commercial openness are dependent on the skill requirements characteristic of the sector.

In summary, it can be stated that many factors can affect the staff number employed in the sectors. The research results relevant here are unanimous that among the factors affecting the number of the workers (labour demand), the effect of the changes in output is obvious. Observed for a long enough time, the staff number in the sector (labour demand) changes in the same direction as the change in output in the sectors of manufacturing.

A similarly obvious relationship can be seen between technological development and changes in the staff number in the sector. This study does not examine this latest correlation. A negative direction relationship is usually considered to be found between labour costs and changes in the staff number, but the known research results did not prove it in the case of the manufacturing of Germany (Zimmermann 1991). Based on the above, my research involving four sectors of the Hungarian manufacturing primarily analyses the past correlation between the output and the staff number. In addition I try to predict the sectors in which possible future wage changes (e.g., further raising the minimum wage) could cause a significant change.

Table 1

Source	Sample	Independent variable	Dependent variable	Connection	Remarks
Mehta and Mohanty 1993	28 emerging countries manufacturing	change in technology	labour demand	negative	
		output		positive	
		input substitution		neutral	
William Nordhaus 2005	USA manufacturing	productivity growth	employment	positive	
OECD 2007	OECD members	offshoring	labour demand	no connection or slightly positive	
Muhammad Mahmood 2008	Australia manufacturing SMEs	labour productivity	employment	no connection	
Martin Falk and Bertrand M. Koebel 2002	Germany manufacturing	output	demand for heterogenous labour	positive	
		capital growth		positive	
Lihong Yun 2008	Sweden manufacturing	R&D intensity	demand for labour	positive and negative	positive in „high skilled sectors", negative in „low-skilled sectors"
Stefan Mann 2011	based on simulation model	productivity	employment	negative	consecutively by industry life cycle
K. F. Zimmermann 1991	Germany 16 manufacturing sectors	technological advance	employment	negative	in some cases
		demand for products		positive	in every case
		labor costs		not significant determinant	
Davis et al. 1998	USA manufacturing	capital intensity	net employment growth	negative	less capital intensive creates more jobs
		energy intensity		negative	depends on energy prices
		total factor productivity growth		positive	

Source: collected by the author

Research Results

Manufacture of Textiles, Textile Products, Leather and Leather Products

Sector Characteristics

Before the change of regime this sector was considered to be one of the greatest employers in the Hungarian economy. As the result of continuous transformation, nowadays contract work for European factories has become a characteristic business solution. In the course of the process European textile manufacturing ended up with a competitive disadvantage compared to its Asian rivals, so the market prospect of Hungarian production based on contract work also deteriorated.

The staff number in the sector decreased to less than half during the examined period. The ratio of textile production decreased to about 30% within the sector and the production of other textile products became dominant. (In 2011 the division of employees was: 30% textile production, 44% clothing production, 26% leather, leather products, footwear production. Within textile production: 16% weaving textile threads, 6% textile weaving, 5% textile preparation, 73% production of other textile products.) In 2011 the ratio of export revenue was 72%, higher than the manufacturing average (61%). The labour costs to total costs ratio was 23%. This is significantly higher than the manufacturing average (9%). The average wages are low, 58% of the average characteristic of manufacturing. Labour intensive production is specific in the sector, connected to low wages. Technological development is relatively slow in this sector.

Output, Staff Number and Work Productivity

The staff number in the sector decreased by 55% (43,852 employees) between 2001 and 2011. The output decreased by 22% calculated at 2001 prices (to 290.2 billion HUF). The increase in producer price was 9.6% during the 11 years examined. Work productivity increased significantly (from 3.86 M HUF/employee to 6.62 M HUF/employee), due to the decrease in staff number exceeding the decrease in output.

The correlation between the time series is strong (0.74). (To decrease autocorrelation I measured the strength of the correlation with chain ratios, which basically gives lower correlation values than if it had been calculated from the original data). It can be clearly seen in Fig. 1 that by 2009 the output had decreased to 60% of the 2001 value, while the staff number also decreased by 50%. As the effects of the crisis passed, the output significantly grew from 2009 to 2011, while the staff number stagnated.

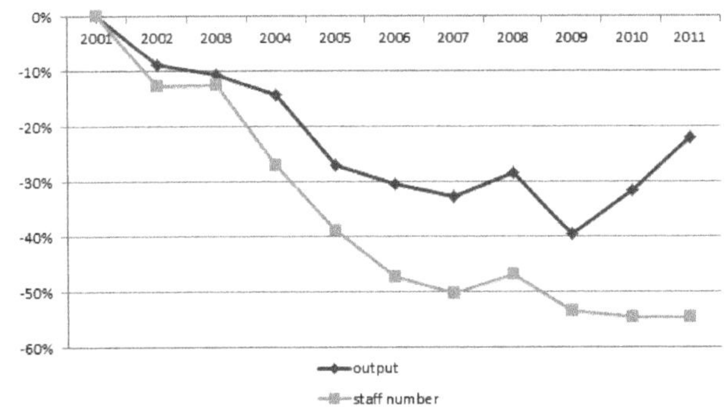

Source: calculations of the author based on NTCA database

Figure 1. Output and stuff number base ratios in the textile industry

Conclusion

The increasing work productivity is the consequence of the general market problems, the decrease of output. Raising minimum wages can have an effect, decreasing the staff number, because wages are relatively low and the labour costs to total costs ratio is high. The increase in output experienced since 2009 is not accompanied by an increase in the staff number (although its tendency to decrease has stopped), which is positive from a work productivity perspective, and negative from the perspective of sector employment goals.

Manufacture of Food Products, Beverages and Tobacco

Sector Characteristics

We can find two well separated groups of enterprises in the sector: enterprises adapted for mass production and enterprises producing goods by traditional methods. The food industry is a sector with slow technological development. The labour costs to total costs ratio is around 9%, which corresponds with the average value in the manufacturing. Average wages decreased to 80% of the manufacturing average by 2011. The ratio of export revenue is low (28%).

Output, Staff Number and Work Productivity

The staff number decreased by 25% from 2001 until 2011 (to 91,033 employees), meanwhile the output became lower by 18% calculated at 2001 prices. The cumulative producer price index is 51% in the full period; calculated on nominal value the output showed growth. Work productivity changed from 17 billion HUF/ employee to 19 M HUF/employee.

The correlation between the change in output and in staff number is moderately strong (0.59). It is a weaker strength than the correlation measured in the textile industry, but since the measured value concerns chain ratios, linear correlation can be qualified as strong. Similar to the textile industry, the two examined variables are characterised by decreasing tendencies until 2009, after which output started to grow (Fig. 2), and the decrease in the staff number stopped.

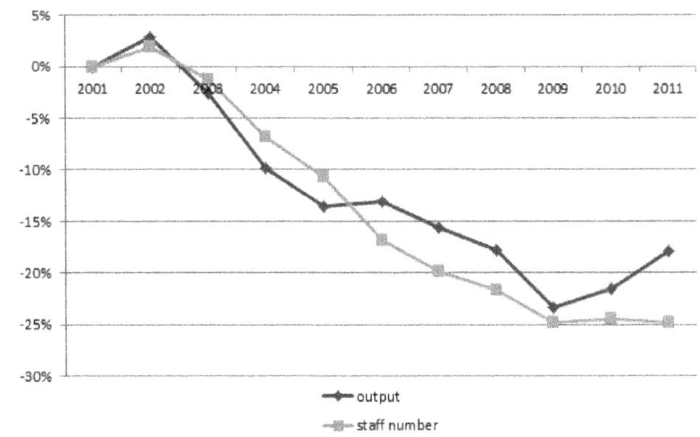

Source: calculations of the author based on NTCA data-base

Figure 2. Output and staff number base ratios in the food industry

Conclusions

Both output and the staff number significantly decreased before the crisis. The results indicate that the decrease of output had a role in the decrease in the staff number. When the industry was starting to overcome the crisis, the decrease in the staff number stopped, but enterprises did not replace the labour dismissed earlier, despite their increased production. This process is beneficial from the perspective of work productivity, but is very harmful from the perspective of employment. In the case of an increase in labour costs or a raise in the minimum wages, it is nearly certain that the staff number will decrease in this sector.

Manufacture of Vehicles

Sector Characteristics

In the sector the importance of suppliers is steadily growing, both in the value chain and in employment. In the past years several significant green field investments and factory expansions were realised in Hungary. Labour costs to total costs ratio make up 13% of all expenditures (the overall manufacturing ratio is 9%). The average wage is 18% higher than the manufacturing average (in 2011). The sector produces 92% of goods for export. Vehicle production gives 43% of the R&D costs of all manufacturing. The gross added value grew by 151% in

11 years. The technological development pace of the sector is rapid.

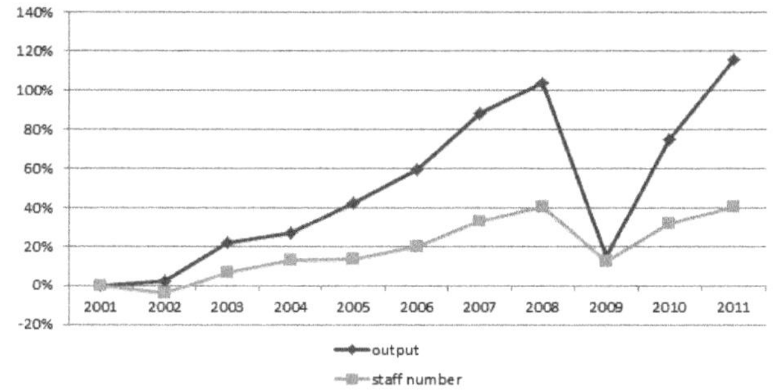

Source: calculations of the author based on NTCA data-base

Figure 3. Output and staff number base ratios in the automotive industry

Output, Staff Number, Work Productivity

The 2011 output of the sector is 116% higher than the 2001 level. (3,568 billion HUF on real value). The cumulative producer's price index is only 10% considering the 10 years, so nominal value data did not decrease significantly due to the method of deflation. The staff number is 40% higher than it was in 2001 (54,858 employees). Work productivity is exceptionally high, moreover, it grew by 55% within 10 years (to 65 M HUF/employee). The correlation between output and the changes in the staff number is very strong (0.93). Based on this we can assume that the increase in productivity is primarily due to the increase in output. In Fig. 3 it can be clearly seen that the output decreased back to almost the 2003 level in 2009, and the staff number decreased to the 2004 level due to the crisis. The sudden great depression was followed by fast growth from 2009, so by 2011 output exceeded and the staff number again reached its 2008 level.

Conclusions

There is a strong correlation between the time series of sector output and staff number. A very significant increase occurred in both series of data, considering the full period. The ratio of output increase is almost three times the ratio of the increase in the staff number, which results in the beneficial situation that besides expanding the sector employment a significant increase of productivity also occurred. During the period the average wages were relatively high and growing.

Manufacture of Chemicals, Chemical Products and Man-made Fibres

Sector Characteristics

The petrochemical industry and pharmaceutical industry are two great fields of the Hungarian chemical industry. The sector is classified as a sector with rapid technological development. The labour costs to total costs ratio in 2011 was the same as the 9% ratio that is usual in the manufacturing. Wages exceed the average manufacturing value by 39%. The ratio of export revenue is below average (55M HUF/employee). The chemical industry accounts for one quarter of the total R&D costs of manufacturing.

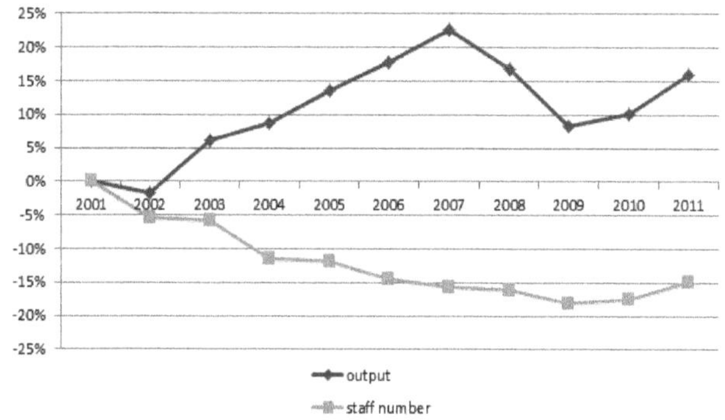

Source: calculations of the author based on NTCA database

Figure 4. Output and staff number base ratios in the chemical industry

Output, Staff Number and Work Productivity

During the examined 11 years output increased by 16% (to 901 billion HUF). Without the correction with the 104% cumulated producer price index the nominal output shows a 137% increase. The staff number decreased by 15% during the period (to 27,623 employees), and work productivity increased by 37.5%. We can observe an increase in real value output until 2007, while the number of workers decreases (Fig. 4). From 2007 the output also starts to decrease, and from 2009 both time series show an increase. The cross correlation value calculated for the full period is 0.26, which does not assume a real linear connection.

Conclusions

Compared to the previously examined sectors the changes that occurred in the chemical industry have a unique picture. This is the only sector where there is no actual connection between output and the changes in the staff number in the beginning of the period, and from 2009 the data change rise in parallel. The rate of technological development is fast, and we see that the staff number decreased, despite the significant increase in output before 2007. If we assume that the statements of Zimmermann (1991) and Mehta & Mohanty (1993) concerning technological development are true for Hungarian manufacturing, then we can state that the tendency of technological development to decrease the staff number is strong, and the tendency of the increase in output to increase the number of the workers is accidental.

SUMMARY

The study presents the results of the research done on the correlations between sector output and the staff number concerning four sectors of the Hungarian manufacturing. In addition I examined the possible effects of labour costs on the staff number. The data come from a period between 2001 and 2011, and I calculated the output on year 2001 values. In the textile industry, decreasing output and staff number is characteristic. Tests concerning the co-movement of time series show a strong correlation between output and the changes in staff number. In the food industry the staff number also decreased together with the decrease in output. The cross-correlation between the two variables is strong, although weaker than in the textile industry. In both the textile industry and the food industry we can see that the decrease in output before the crisis strongly correlated with the decrease in the staff number. Unfortunately, the correlation gets weaker during the period of overcoming the crisis: although the increase in production stopped the further decrease in the staff number, it did not increase the staff number. The forced increase of wages can have a tendency to decrease the staff number in both sectors of industry. Vehicle production is a high productivity sector with fast technological development. Output increased very significantly, even on real value, followed by a smaller but still significant rate of increase in the staff number. Changes in the two factors are strongly connected; the correlation between them is strong, as was expected. Results measured in the period of the crisis present new proof for the well-known dependency of the sector on economic trends. An increase in output and decrease in the staff number can be found in the chemical industry, though no clear correlation can be proved between the changes of the two characteristics. Accepting the unanimous statements of researchers on the topic, my results can be interpreted to mean that, the effects of technological development on decreases in the staff number is strong, and the tendency of an increase in production to increase the staff number is relatively weak in the sector. Summarizing the results we could come to the conclusion that in regards to sector policies, we have to be careful when making predictions or implement measures with a common assumption about manufacturing. There are significant differences among sectors according to the effect of growth on new labour generated. In the textile and food industry demonstrative correlation were measured (in a period of decreasing output), but in the chemical industry it is not proved to be true. In the automotive industry the correlation is strong. One of the reasons that chemical industry has specific features can be traced back to a unique profession structure. Investigating this question could be the topic of a different research. However that kind of project would demand special knowledge about labour skills and profession structure with regard to Hungarian labour market. My intention in contrast is to develop the research by involve input prices, primarily the effects of the cost of labour.

REFERENCES

BASU, S. & ESTRIN, S. & SVEJNAR, J. (2000). Employment and wages in enterprises under communism and in transition: evidence from Central Europe and Russia. William Davidson Institute Working Paper 440.
http://deepblue.lib.umich.edu/bitstream/2027.42/39824/3/wp440.pdf

BROWN, D. & EARLE, J. (2005). Does privatization hurt workers? – Lessons in comprehensive manufacturing firm panel data in Hungary, Romania, Russia and Ukraine. BWP, 10, MTA KTI, Budapest.

DAVIS, S. J., HALTIWANGER, J. & SCHUCH, S. (1998). Job creation and destruction. Cambridge, MA: MIT Press.

FALK, M. & KOEBEL, B. M. (2002). Outsourcing, imports and labour demand. The ScandiNTCAian Journal of Economics, Volume 104, No. 4.

KERTESI, G. & KÖLLŐ, J. (2002). Labour demand with heterogeneous labour inputs after the transition in Hungary, 1992–99–and the potential consequences of the increase of minimum wage in 2001 and 2002. BWP, 5., MTA KTI, Budapest.
http://konyvtar.mutf.hu/kozos/Temaportal/K%C3%A9t%20v%C3%A1ls%C3%A1g%20k%C3%B6z%C3%B6tt%20-%20Ecostat.pdf

KÖLLŐ, J. (1998). Employment and wage setting in three stages of Hungary's labour market transition. In: Enterprise Restructuring and Unemployment in Models of Transition. EDI Development Studies, The World Bank–EDI, pp 57–108.

KŐRÖSI, G. (1997). Labour demand during transition in Hungary. William Davidson Institute Working Paper, Issue 116., pp 19
http://deepblue.lib.umich.edu/bitstream/2027.42/39506/3/wp116.pdf

KŐRÖSI, G. (2000). Labour demand of corporations. BWP, 3., MTA KTI, Budapest, pp 68.

KŐRÖSI, G. (2002). Labour demand and efficiency in Hungary. BWPLM, Issue 3, Budapest.

MAHMOOD, M. (2008). Labour productivity and employment in Australian manufacturing SMEs. International Entrepreneurship and Management Journal, Volume 4, Issue 1, pp 51-62.

MANN, S. (2011). Sectors matter! Exploring Mesoeconomics. Ettenhausen: Springer.

MEHTA, R. & MOHANTY, S. K. (1993). Demand for labour in manufacturing sector: a decomposition analysis for developing countries. Indian Journal of Industrial Relations, Volume 29, No. 2.

NORDHAUS, W. (2005). The sources of the productivity rebound and the manufacturing employment puzzle. http://www.nber.org/papers/w11354

SINGER, M. (1996). Dynamic labor demand estimation, stability of coefficients. Case of Czech Republic. CERGE-EI https://iweb.cerge-ei.cz/pdf/wp/Wp99.pdf

YUN, L. (2008). Technical progress and labour demand in swedish manufacturing firms. Journal of industry, Competition and Trade from Theory to Policy, Volume 8, Issue 2, pp 147-167.

ZIMMERMANN, K. F. (1991). The employment consequences of technological advance, demand and labor costs in 16 German industries. Empirical Economics, Volume 16, Issue 2, pp 253-266.

Appendices

Appendix A: Textile industry

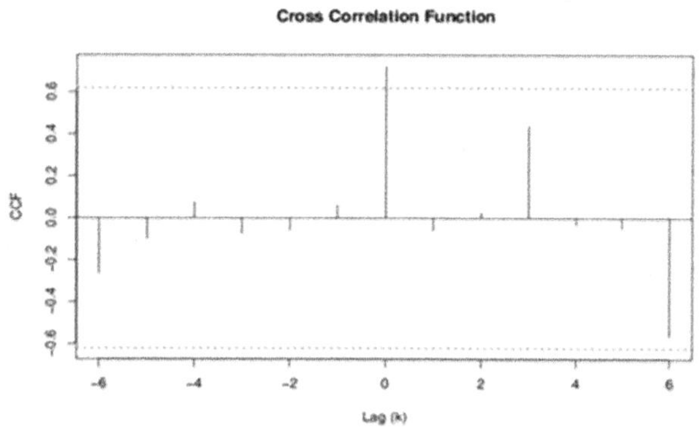

Appendix B: Food industry

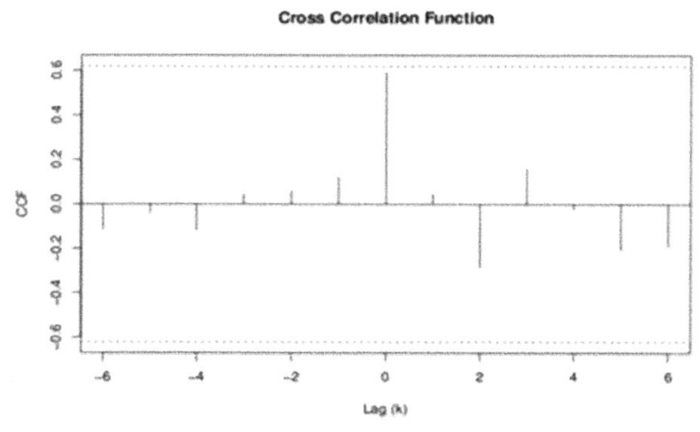

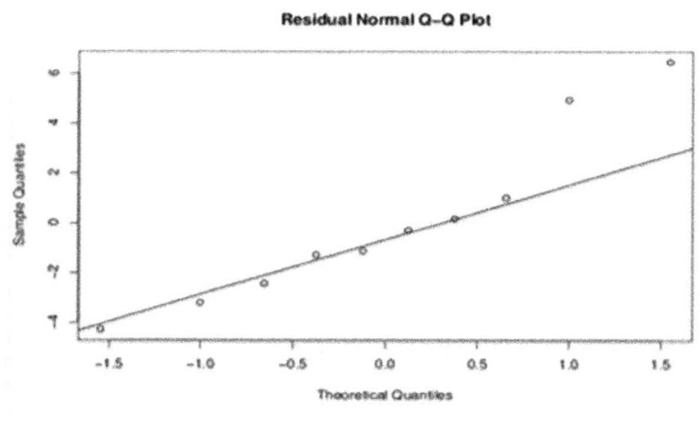

Appendix C: Automotive industry

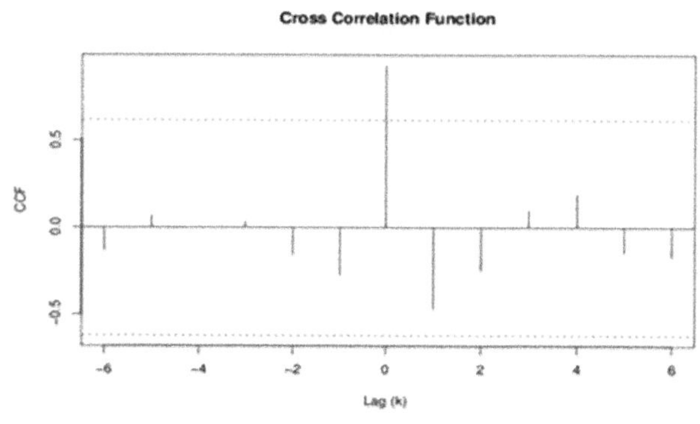

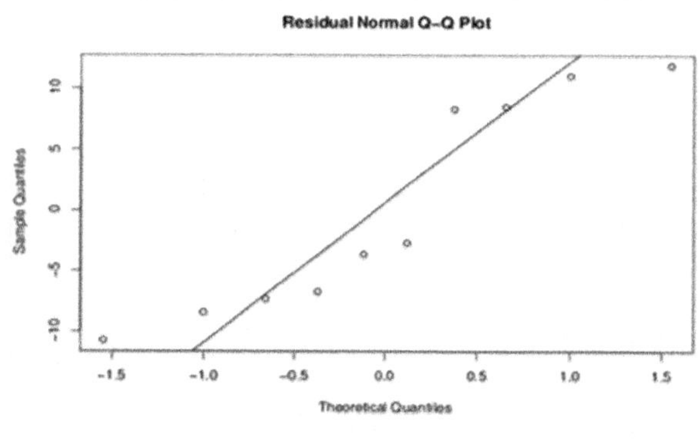

Permissions

All chapters in this book were first published in TMP, by University of Miskolc; hereby published with permission under the Creative Commons Attribution License or equivalent. Every chapter published in this book has been scrutinized by our experts. Their significance has been extensively debated. The topics covered herein carry significant findings which will fuel the growth of the discipline. They may even be implemented as practical applications or may be referred to as a beginning point for another development.

The contributors of this book come from diverse backgrounds, making this book a truly international effort. This book will bring forth new frontiers with its revolutionizing research information and detailed analysis of the nascent developments around the world.

We would like to thank all the contributing authors for lending their expertise to make the book truly unique. They have played a crucial role in the development of this book. Without their invaluable contributions this book wouldn't have been possible. They have made vital efforts to compile up to date information on the varied aspects of this subject to make this book a valuable addition to the collection of many professionals and students.

This book was conceptualized with the vision of imparting up-to-date information and advanced data in this field. To ensure the same, a matchless editorial board was set up. Every individual on the board went through rigorous rounds of assessment to prove their worth. After which they invested a large part of their time researching and compiling the most relevant data for our readers.

The editorial board has been involved in producing this book since its inception. They have spent rigorous hours researching and exploring the diverse topics which have resulted in the successful publishing of this book. They have passed on their knowledge of decades through this book. To expedite this challenging task, the publisher supported the team at every step. A small team of assistant editors was also appointed to further simplify the editing procedure and attain best results for the readers.

Apart from the editorial board, the designing team has also invested a significant amount of their time in understanding the subject and creating the most relevant covers. They scrutinized every image to scout for the most suitable representation of the subject and create an appropriate cover for the book.

The publishing team has been an ardent support to the editorial, designing and production team. Their endless efforts to recruit the best for this project, has resulted in the accomplishment of this book. They are a veteran in the field of academics and their pool of knowledge is as vast as their experience in printing. Their expertise and guidance has proved useful at every step. Their uncompromising quality standards have made this book an exceptional effort. Their encouragement from time to time has been an inspiration for everyone.

The publisher and the editorial board hope that this book will prove to be a valuable piece of knowledge for researchers, students, practitioners and scholars across the globe.

List of Contributors

Zoltán Bartha, Andrea S. Gubik

Gyula Fülöp, Bettina Hódi Hernádi

Jaroslaw Godyn

Holyevácz Csaba

Aleksandra Kosenko

Roman Poberezhnyi

Volodymyr V. Sysoiev

Iuliia Fadieieva

Piotr Gabrielczak, Tomasz Serwach

Aleksandra Gaweł, Dr Hab

Mária Illés

Ágnes Kádár Horváth

Wioletta Kilar, Tomasz Rachwał

Aleksandra Kosenko, Petro Pererva

Sergey Mekhovich, Anastasiia Kolesnichenko

Andrea S. Gubik

Piotr Trąpczyński

Katarzyna Appelt

László Berényi

Ireneusz Janiuk

Miklós Fellegi

Sándor Bozsik

Ádám Bereczk

Index